The Destruction of
Yugoslavia

The Destruction of Yugoslavia

Yugoslavia

Tracking the Break-up 1980–92

BRANKA MAGAŠ

VERSO

London · New York

First published by Verso 1993
© Verso 1993
All rights reserved

Verso
UK: 6 Meard Street, London W1V 3HR
USA: 29 West 35th Street, New York, NY 10001–2291

Verso is the imprint of New Left Books

ISBN 0–86091–376–7
ISBN 0–86091–593–X (pbk)

British Library Cataloguing in Publication Data
A catalogue record for this book is available from the British Library

Library of Congress Cataloging-in-Publication Data
A catalogue record for this book is available from the Library of Congress

Typeset by Type Study, Scarborough
Printed in Great Britain by Biddles Ltd, Guildford and Kings Lynn

*This book is dedicated
to the cities of
Vukovar and Sarajevo*

Contents

Introduction

The year 1992, scheduled to be a milestone on the road to European unity, has seen Sarajevo and other Bosnian cities slowly bombarded to pieces and their inhabitants starved before the television eyes of the world. It has seen two million Bosnian Moslems threatened with Europe's first genocide since World War Two, most already driven from their homes by massacre, rape and terror, thrown into concentration camps or made refugees within their own country or outside it. All this has occurred with the full knowledge of the outside world, which is also quite aware of the identity of the perpetrator, who has been perfecting these procedures for over a year now in occupied Croatia, including in zones formally under UN jurisdiction. The year has seen Bosnia's legal, multinational government holed up in Sarajevo, treated as a mere 'warring party', and pressed to surrender by Western governments eager for peace at any price. Short-sighted and cynical, divided among themselves, determined to avoid intervention, and seeking an eventual accommodation with the military strongman of the Balkans, these governments have settled for 'humanitarian' palliatives that amount to little more than a prolonging of the victims' agony. The same governments protested loudly about 'ethnic cleansing' only when the reality was exposed by their media, months after they first learned about it. At the same time, they maintained an embargo on the arms which alone would enable the Bosnian government to repel the aggression, reassert its authority over the whole territory of Bosnia-Herzegovina, and create conditions for the expelled population to return.

The year 1992 has also, it must be said, seen a Western Left largely silent before, if not actively complicit with, these crimes: a Left content to parrot the disinformation so artfully disseminated by their foreign offices; too indolent or ignorant to distinguish between fact and propaganda; and quite ready to accept the easier, essentially racist, interpretation, facilitated by centuries of world domination, that Balkan – or all Eastern – peoples (frequently referred to as 'tribes', rarely as real nations) are somehow genetically programmed for violence and thus equally to blame for the cataclysm. There can be no excuse this time that 'we didn't know!'; for everyone knows what is happening. The search is thus on for reasons to justify inaction. For example, nostalgia for the Yugoslavia created by the Partisans – a Yugoslavia finally buried in June 1991 when a so-called People's Army outside legitimate political control attacked Slovenia, a nation-state of the Partisan-created federation. Or, a repugnance at nationalism that makes no distinction between mobilization behind an expansionary chauvinist project and mobilization in defence of national sovereignty – even national existence – under military assault. Or, resentment of Germany, ignobly fostered by weaker post-imperial powers like Britain and France for their own petty purposes, and yet more ignobly echoed on the social-democratic and even Marxist Left. Or, the fetishization of supranational states in the East by the very people who fear them like poison in the West. Above all, perhaps, cynical indifference to the *democratic* rights of other peoples, which can be airily traded away for this or that minor tactical or pragmatic consideration borrowed from the repertoire of their own governments: 'Why couldn't they have waited?'; 'It was all the fault of the Germans, pressing for recognition'; 'Bosnia-Herzegovina was never viable as an independent state'; 'Ethnic cleansing is dreadful, but they all do it you know'; 'Once the lid came off . . . old ethnic passions . . . goes back to World War Two . . . goes back centuries . . . warring factions . . . competing nationalisms . . .' – the obscurantist litany is unending.

There is, however, another voice with which the Left can respond to events such as those that have been unfolding in the former Yugoslavia. It did not, after all, get things quite so wrong in the former Soviet Union, when for the most part – despite clinging to hopes that Gorbachev would succeed in negotiating some new common arrangement – it responded to the August Coup (in whose success, incidentally, Belgrade had invested great hopes) with the fundamental recognition that unity enforced by brute military might was a far worse option than break-up. That, above all, is the message of this book. Written over the ten years leading up to Yugoslavia's bloody demise, most of it is – was – guided by the belief that an understanding of the forces tearing the federation apart might help keep it together. The last part, however, beginning with the 'Requiem' I wrote when that hope had been comprehensively dashed, is inspired by a new and different commitment: to the future viability of the legitimate successor states of the former Yugoslavia – a future that offers the best, indeed the only, hope of a democratic development for all the peoples of what was once a far-from-artificial state, born of a genuine revolution, a country that was not fated to disintegrate but which has nevertheless been destroyed.

Tito's death in 1980 marked a point of no return for Yugoslavia. Although the occasion witnessed an authentic outpouring of Yugoslav patriotism, the country had in fact already entered a period of dramatic and potentially disintegrative change. Yugoslavia stood at a crossroads. One path led towards democratization, the other towards repression. Which path would be taken? The forces favouring the second soon showed their hand: first in 1981 in Kosovo, where force was used against student-led demonstrations; and then in 1984 in Belgrade, where intellectuals were put on trial for taking part in unofficial debating societies. Subsequent events proved, however, that the decentralization upon which the country had embarked in the more optimistic 1960s – embodied in the 1974 constitution – in fact precluded the federal party and state organs from acting as effective instruments for conservative reaction, spearheaded as it then was by active and retired army and police chiefs. Though that decentralization – a devolution of powers to the republics and provinces – was not accompanied by any significant loosening of the ruling party's monopoly of political initiative, it did allow a greater public airing of differences between the constituent states, hence also of alternative views within those states. If Yugoslavia was to be united on a neo-conservative platform, it would have to be recentralized first.

The neo-conservative project changed radically with the capture of power in Serbia by Great Serb nationalists. In the mid 1980s, Belgrade became the headquarters simultaneously of a new Yugoslav unitarism and of a 'Serb national renewal'. The history of Yugoslavia appeared now to be running backwards: the more the Serb nationalists embraced the cause of 'Yugoslavia', the more anti-federal that Yugoslavia of theirs became – and, inevitably, the greater was the resistance to it in other parts of the country. National coexistence would henceforth be threatened not only by power struggles within the institutions of the federal state, but also by the readiness of the new Serbian régime headed by Slobodan Milošević to use extra-legal means – mass mobilization on an ethnic basis – to destroy the 1974 constitution. The aim was not merely to return to the pre-1974 situation, but to revise completely the postwar settlement based on the principle of national equality. Belgrade sought nothing less than the destruction of the federal arrangement – in the name of a 'strong federation'! By proclaiming its right to speak not only for Serbia but for all Serbs in Yugoslavia, by seeking to redefine internal borders as purely administrative, and by erasing the autonomy of the provinces, the Belgrade régime negated the very foundations of the second, federal, Yugoslavia. Milošević thus emerged as the spokesman not simply of a conservative backlash, but for the cause of counter-revolution in the Yugoslav lands. What is more, this counter-revolution was armed and ready, if defied, to resort to war. Serbia's annexation of Kosovo and Vojvodina was the first instance in postwar Europe of alteration (obliteration) of recognized political borders by force. By the end of the 1980s –

before multi-party elections ever took place – it had become clear that, unless Milošević was stopped, Yugoslavia was doomed either to become a Greater Serbia or to fall apart.

Yugoslavia thus did not die a natural death: it was destroyed for the cause of a Greater Serbia. With the Army on his side, Milošević felt confident of victory. What Serbia had failed to gain in two Balkan Wars and two World Wars suddenly looked to be within reach. The whole nation was seemingly united behind the counter-revolutionary project – which had been formulated, indeed, by its most eminent intellectuals. It would be difficult to overestimate the role this self-confidence played in bringing about Yugoslavia's disintegration. The armed counter-revolution rejected all compromise solutions that might have kept the country together. The resistance was inevitably led (once Kosovo had been crushed, and Vojvodina and Montenegro swallowed up) by Slovenia and Croatia, whence came a first strategic counteroffensive in the shape of multi-party elections. These two republics, flanked by Macedonia and Bosnia-Herzegovina, then offered Serbia a confederal compromise: the transformation of Yugoslavia into an association of sovereign states. The offer was rejected out of hand. The Great Serb bloc stood firm, believing that the Army would deliver whatever it wished. Slovenia was allowed to go, after a brief military incursion in June 1991, by mutual consent; but not Croatia or Bosnia-Herzegovina, which would be squeezed to re-linquish as much of their territories as the Army could hold. As the war – which began in earnest in August 1991 – progressed, the contours of the projected, racially homogeneous, Greater Serbia became increasingly visible.

What the Great Serb bloc underestimated, however, was the readiness of Yugoslavia's constituent nations to defend themselves. In dismissing the possibility of people's war, the Serbian-dominated Army made its biggest mistake. Neither in Slovenia, nor in Croatia, nor in Bosnia-Herzegovina, did aggression result in the anticipated capitulation, despite the defenders' lack of arms. In Croatia, Serbia's great military advantage led to the occupation of one third of the republic's territory, but failed nevertheless to achieve Belgrade's minimal strategic goals – the establishment of a physical link between the disparate parts of the so-called Serb Krajina; the capture of a coastline commensurate with Serbia's ambition to become an Adriatic power. Each defeat suffered by the Serbian armies, however, served only to increase their destructive determination. The very fact that Croatia survived and received international recognition ensured that the onslaught on Bosnia-Herzegovina, when it came, would be that much more bloody and devastating. Whereas in Croatia the war gradually built up from local Serb 'uprisings' in the summer of 1990 to a full-scale war in the summer of 1991, Serbia's aggression against Bosnia-Herzegovina took the form of a blitzkrieg. In Croatia, 'ethnic cleansing' was to produce some 300,000 refugees in the course of a year; in Bosnia, the victims of the same policy perpetrated on a larger scale numbered almost two million within six months. A US Senate report estimated that during this period as many as 35,000 people were killed in Bosnia as a result of 'ethnic cleansing' alone. In Croatia, Serbia fought the war ostensibly to defend a Serb minority threatened by a 'fascist régime'. No such pretext was possible in the case of Bosnia-Herzegovina, where Serbs formed not a minority but one of three formally recognized constitutive nations. The Bosnian elections of October 1990 produced an Assembly in which Serbs were represented in numbers reflecting their weight within the population as a whole. A government was subsequently formed with appropriate Serb representation. Despite this, the war against Bosnia-Herzegovina was from the start waged with only one aim: the complete destruction of the republic. It was here that the Great Serbian project revealed the full extent of its criminal nature.

Preparations for the assault on Bosnia-Herzegovina followed a pattern set in Croatia. A Serb Democratic Party was once again set up – the SDS – which immediately proceeded (that is, prior to the elections of November 1990) to declare itself the sole representative of Bosnian Serbs, viewed as part of a seamless Serb nation. A Serb National Assembly and Serb National Council were established in Banjaluka in October 1990, as sovereign legislative and executive bodies wholly independent of Sarajevo. From October 1990 to December 1991, the SDS was busy consolidating this structure (including its police and armed forces) and demarcating new internal borders in Bosnia-Herzegovina. Six so-called Serb Autonomous Regions (SAOs) were thereby established: Bosanska Krajina, Northern Bosnia, Northeastern Bosnia, Romanija, Herzegovina and Old Herzegovina. These were then declared parts of a 'Serb Republic of Bosnia-Herzegovina', later renamed simply the 'Serb Republic'. Many non-Serb areas found themselves included in this self-proclaimed mono-ethnic state. The first aim of Serbian military operations in Bosnia-Herzegovina was subsequently to be the establishment of corridors between the different SAOs, cleared of all non-Serb population.

As the political arm of Serbia's impending aggression against Bosnia-Herzegovina, the SDS acted throughout the crucial year of 1991 to block all moves by the Bosnian government to save the republic. The elections had produced a coalition government and state presidency made up of representatives of the three main parties – the SDS, the Moslem-based Party of Democratic Action (SDA), and the Croatian Democratic Union (HDZ). Between them they controlled 86 per cent of National Assembly seats (72, 86 and 44 respectively, out of a total of 240). Thanks to the obstructionist policy of the SDS, the new administration found itself unable to take any strategic decisions regarding the republic's future. The National Assembly was divided *de facto* between two blocs of uneven size. The majority bloc, composed of deputies belonging to the SDA, the HDZ and most of the smaller parties, wished Bosnia-Herzegovina to become a sovereign state within Yugoslavia, or failing that an independent state. The minority, made up of the SDS and its satellite parties, wanted the republic either to join Serbia *en bloc* (with some 'federal' facade) or to be broken up. Again, no compromise was possible: thus, in February 1991, the SDS turned down a proposal by the SDA (supported by the HDZ) that a joint declaration be adopted giving the Bosnian legislature precedence over the 'federal' one, now controlled by Serbia.

As in other republics, the departing Communist administration had introduced constitutional amendments designed to enhance the integrity and sovereignty of Bosnia-Herzegovina. In October 1991, the Bosnian Assembly adopted a draft Memorandum confirming these changes. Though falling short of a declaration of independence, the Memorandum affirmed the inviolability of the republic's borders, while expressing support for a Yugoslavia made up of sovereign states. The SDS deputies walked out before the vote was taken. Their leader Radovan Karadžić warned not only that Bosnian sovereignty could not be achieved without Serb consent (which in any case would not be forthcoming), but also that insistence on sovereignty was leading the republic 'into a hell in which the Moslems will perhaps perish'.

For the Bosnian leaders, however, defining the republic's status was an urgent political matter, given that the EC-sponsored conference on Yugoslavia was about to begin. It was also important to keep Bosnia-Herzegovina out of the war already raging in Croatia. Adoption of the Memorandum provided the occasion to declare Bosnian neutrality in this war – although, in reality, the Army had from the start been using the territory under SDS control as a base for its offensive in Croatia. Strive as the Assembly might to distance itself from the war, however, Bosnian integrity was increasingly called into question. The National Assembly's affirmation of sovereignty was immediately followed by the SDS's proclamation of a separate Serb state – the so-called Serb Republic of Bosnia-Herzegovina. This was followed by the establishment by local HDZ leaders of two so-called Croat Communities, one in the north (Community of the Sava Valley) and one in the south (Herceg-Bosna). Although these lacked the formal state structures characteristic of the enclaves set up by the SDS, the intention behind them was unmistakable: the Sarajevo government would be recognized only 'as long as it retains its independence from the former or any future Yugoslavia'. The Bosnian HDZ leadership itself (supported by most Bosnian Croats and nearly all Croatian parties) denounced these moves towards an effective division of

Bosnia-Herzegovina. But they were, in reality, simply a sign that war was now seen as inevitable. Whether the establishment of these Croat 'communities' – in regions adjacent to the areas of greatest military activity in Croatia itself – was merely an act of self-defence, or whether it was done with Zagreb's encouragement, is hard to tell. What is certain is that they sat firmly athwart the two prongs of Serbia's planned military onslaught – the projected corridor to occupied central Croatia in the north, and the sweep towards the Adriatic Sea in the south – which threatened to cut off central Bosnia from the outside world.

Whereas Serbia never hid its territorial ambitions towards Bosnia-Herzegovina, Croatia's position was more ambiguous. It certainly did not initiate the war in the neighbouring republic. But it could hardly disregard the latter's considerable Croat population, or Bosnia's strategic import-ance for its own destiny, in circumstances in which it was itself still the victim of Serbian aggression, a fate that Bosnia would soon share. In any case, Croatia's president, Franjo Tudjman, had made clear quite early on that he believed neither in the likely survival of Bosnia-Herzegovina, nor in its historic legitimacy, in the event of Yugoslavia's disintegration into national states. The logical solution, he claimed, was to partition the republic between Croatia and Serbia. This, however, infringed the very principle of inviolability of Yugoslavia's internal borders upon which Croatia rested its own case for the return of its occupied territories! Unlike its Serbian counterpart, moreover, the Croatian régime was hampered by the fact that the idea of dividing Bosnia-Herzegovina remained deeply unpopular in Croatia. In trying to square this circle, Croat officials followed the SDS in proposing 'cantonization' of Bosnia-Herzegovina along ethnic lines. The SDS had justified the creation of the six SAOs on the grounds that, in a centrally run republic, Serbs would become an oppressed minority. Under Zagreb's influence, parts of the Bosnian HDZ now accepted the same logic. The EC, to its eternal discredit, also encouraged this 'ethnically based' programme – in whose name it has subsequently sought to qualify the Bosnian government's legitimacy.

Originally, six cantons were envisaged – two predominantly Serb, two Moslem and two Croat – but the number was soon reduced in the minds of their advocates to three. The intermingling of nationalities within Bosnia-Herzegovina, however, makes the whole notion of cantonization on ethnic lines dangerous nonsense. According to the 1981 census, out of 109 municipalities in Bosnia-Herzegovina, 35 had a Moslem absolute majority, 32 a Serb absolute majority and 14 a Croat absolute majority (in several of these, it should be noted, the Serb or Moslem predominance was a matter of a few percentage points). A further 15 municipalities had a relative Moslem majority, 5 a relative Serb majority and 7 a relative Croat majority. Since the combined population of these latter 27 municipalities in which no nationality could claim an absolute majority was about 1.7 million, it was clear that in order to create cantons with absolute national majorities, a great proportion of Bosnia-Herzegovina's inhabitants would have to be uprooted and resettled. Cantonization, in other words, involved not just civil war, but destruction of the very identity of the Bosnian state, created as it was on the basis of coexistence between the three nationalities. This is why cantonization was rejected by all Bosnian Moslems, by a majority of Bosnian Croats, by probably most Serbs in Bosnia's major cities, and by an unknown number of Serbs in areas under SDS control. Zagreb's acceptance of the principle of cantonization was thus a divisive act that could only gravely imperil the defence of Bosnia-Herzegovina. Although Croatia repeatedly denied all territorial ambitions towards its neighbours, recognized Bosnia-Herzegovina within its borders, took in half a million Bosnian refugees, helped with humanitarian relief, and provided the essential military supply route and rear base for Bosnia's armed resistance, its support for cantonization of the republic rendered it in this respect an objective accomplice of the régime in Belgrade.

Running against the clock, the Bosnian government was forced to stop appeasing Belgrade and the SDS. On 20 December 1991, with EC recognition of Croatia and Slovenia pending, it too asked that the republic be recognized as an independent state. The SDS leaders declared this decision null and void, warned again that 'one nation will disappear if the idea of Bosnian independence is not abandoned', and announced that, in the event of independence being granted, the 'Serb Republic' would become 'part of the federal state of Yugoslavia'. Following the recognition of Croatia and Slovenia on 15 January 1992, the EC arbitration commission invited the Bosnian government to hold a referendum on the issue of independence, as a condition of recognition. On 25 January the SDA and HDZ deputies, supported by most of the smaller opposition parties, approved the holding of such a referendum under international supervision. The question submitted to the electorate on the weekend of 1 March was: 'Are you in favour of a sovereign and independent Bosnia-Herzegovina, a state of equal citizens and nations of Moslems, Serbs, Croats, and others who live in it?' Almost two thirds of the population voted in favour. The Serbian Army struck the day after Bosnia-Herzegovina was recognized as an independent state.

In view of the attitude of the Serb Democratic Party – for which the majority of Bosnian Serbs had voted a year earlier, and which could thus claim to speak on their behalf – was it right for the Bosnian government to seek independence? The fact is that the republic had no other choice. The alternative of joining a Greater Serbia was not simply unpalatable to the majority of its population: it entailed the disappearance of Bosnia as a state. What is more, the SDS certainly had no mandate for waging war against Bosnia in order to prevent its independence. Indeed, whatever legitimacy the SDS may have possessed at the beginning of this whole process, its participation in the terrible crimes committed against the people of Bosnia-Herzegovina has since disqualified it from speaking for any part of it.

The Bosnian state was totally unprepared for war. The weapons of its Territorial Defence forces had been confiscated by the Army prior to the elections. Its government had, in addition, been persuaded by the EC and the United States to receive huge quantities of military personnel and armour leaving Slovenia and Croatia. (Although Zagreb had repeatedly requested of the EC mediators that heavy armour and tanks located in garrisons in Croatia be left there under international control, the West had insisted that they be allowed to depart for Bosnia-Herzegovina.) In preparing for independence, the Bosnian government clearly hoped for (and must indeed have been promised) international protection against aggression. Once war began, however, the EC countries and the United States accepted no responsibility for the country's defence. The arms embargo which had given Belgrade's forces such an advantage in Croatia was maintained to still more catastrophic effect in Bosnia, directly contributing to the human and material devastation visited upon the republic by the Serbian blitzkrieg. Bosnia-Herzegovina duly became a member of the United Nations, but its legitimate – and multi-national – government was now increasingly treated as a mere 'warring faction'. Western rhetoric here accurately reflected Western policy, for although Bosnia-Herzegovina had fulfilled the conditions set by the EC for international recognition, the West now bowed to Serbian pressure by making that recognition dependent upon Sarajevo's acceptance of cantonization.

The schizophrenic split between high principle and shabby pragmatism characteristic of Western policy towards Croatia – leading to a settlement apparently designed to reward aggression and condemn refugees to indefinite exile – was to attain quite morbid proportions in relation to the far greater tragedy of Bosnia-Herzegovina. The West did indeed condemn Serbia as the chief culprit of the war, imposing economic sanctions on the self-proclaimed 'Federal Republic of Yugoslavia' (made up of Serbia and Montenegro); yet it has done nothing to enforce their observance. It duly denounced the Serbian policy of ethnic cleansing, the shelling of cities, the creation of concentration camps; yet the perpetrators of these crimes were regularly welcomed in European capitals and treated as legitimate participants in the 'peace process'. The West has decried Serbia's and Croatia's annexationist ambitions, and yet continues to press ahead with cantonization. It pays lip service to the integrity of the Bosnian state, and yet, by maintaining the arms embargo, denies it the means to defend that integrity. By allowing Serbia to destroy much of Bosnia-Herzegovina, and by failing to distinguish between victim and assailant, the West has become an active participant in Serbia's aggression.

What the West – including most of the Left – has always refused to do is acknowledge the singular character of Milošević's régime: a racially based, proto-fascist formation that can survive only by creating new sources of war and conflict. It is waging the war in Bosnia-Herzegovina not just for territories, but for territories devoid of population: the primary target of Serbia's blitzkrieg has not been objects of military significance, but rather the population itself. That is why the war has taken the form of mass terror. The aggression, moreover, is being conducted not just against the people, but against their whole historical presence in the area, embodied in the architecture of cities and villages, in churches and graveyards, in archives and academic institutions, in museums and galleries. The scorched-earth policy practised by Serbia in Bosnia-Herzegovina aims to create a tabula rasa, to establish a new zero point in the history of this part of Europe. The genocide being conducted today against the Moslem population of Bosnia-Herzegovina, and the destruction of a unique society based on the centuries-long coexistence of different nations and religions, amount to a crime against humanity. How could this be allowed to happen in peacetime Europe?

Yet Bosnia lives on. Despite the cataclysm that has engulfed it, Bosnia-Herzegovina has not surrendered. Its multinational government manages somehow to function. Sarajevo, under daily bombardment, continues to resist. The Bosnian defence forces, embracing Moslems, Croats and Serbs, are being slowly and painfully assembled. Short of weapons and logistical support, they have in many places resorted to forms of guerrilla struggle reminiscent of the Partisan war. The Serbian military momentum has been checked; any thought of an easy or quick victory is receding. The Serbian corridor south of the River Sava remains unsafe; the liberated areas in central Bosnia are being extended; the siege of Goražde in the east has been broken; in western Herzegovina the lifeline to the outside world remains secure. The coming winter will impose a heavy toll, but it will not spare the aggressor either. The occupied areas that go under the name of the 'Serb Republic' are in turmoil. The war is gradually turning around, even though the decisive battle – the lifting of Sarajevo's blockade – is still to come. Bosnia needs outside help, of that there can be no doubt; yet its strength lies in a resolute determination to survive.

Bosnia-Herzegovina does not even need to win the war outright; its mere survival indicates that the Great Serb project has no future, entailing inevitable repercussions in Serbia itself. One can expect, however, that the Belgrade régime, frustrated but not thoroughly defeated in Bosnia-Herzegovina, will be tempted to open up another theatre of war, most obviously in Kosovo, which would become one more victim of military aggression and 'ethnic cleansing'. Macedonia, for opportunistic reasons denied international recognition, is likewise well aware that, in the event of a war in Kosovo, it risks being attacked. Such an extension of hostilities into Kosovo and Macedonia would inevitably draw in neighbouring states. Thus, the more comprehensive the defeat for Serbian expansion in the present war, the greater is the chance of avoiding its successors.

In 1980, I decided to research the history of Yugoslavia's formation, in order to prepare for the changes to be anticipated after Tito's death. However, study of Yugoslavia's birth in 1918, its speedy decline, and its rebirth in 1945, soon came to merge with examination and assessment of events that seemed to be heading irresistibly towards a final disintegration, not only of the system of 'socialist self-management' but of the country itself. Although the two dimensions of the crisis formed part of the same process, so cannot be separated in physical time, the present book does register the gradual shift from a preoccupation with the fate of 'socialism' in Yugoslavia to a concern with the fate of the country as such.

There was some hope in the early 1980s that the system might be saved through reform: that, under the pressure of an increasingly combative working class, an alliance of progressive forces could be forged, including reform-minded members of the League of Communists and democratic elements from among the intelligentsia and enterprise management. This would have been the 'organic' way out, shedding the layers of Stalinist inheritance and corrupt bureaucratic rule in favour of political pluralism and economic reconstruction. It was clear from the outset that such an undertaking could succeed only as an all-Yugoslav effort, building on initiatives in each of the republics and provinces to produce a new vision of the country's future. (There remained in the mind's eye, after all, the achievement of the Communist-led all-Yugoslav national and social revolution, still only one generation away.) This was a scenario which, *mutatis mutandis*, the Left – whether conceiving it as social revolution, political revolution or reformist evolution – at this time embraced not only for Yugoslavia, but also for the other countries of Eastern Europe. If it were to succeed anywhere, it would surely do so in Yugoslavia. But, of course, Yugoslavia was not isolated from events elsewhere. The political leadership necessary for the Yugoslav working class to assert itself as the primary agent of a positive social transformation could have emerged only as part of a wider continental shift to the left. Such a shift, after all, was occurring in the late 1960s and early 1970s. By the 1980s, however, the continent was moving steadily to the right. The suppression and disintegration of the Solidarity movement in Poland – a movement initially supported by millions of workers – was to change the parameters of

Yugoslav politics as well: the working class ceased to be perceived as a force able to deliver the final blow to a moribund system. The era of struggle for parliamentary democracy had arrived. Political vocabularies changed to suit local circumstances: in the Yugoslav west, 'comrades' became 'citizens'; in the east, *narodna volja* replaced 'working-class interests'.

Weakened by a dramatic fall in living standards and by escalating unemployment, unprepared for the loss of self-confidence of the system that had produced it, and confused by a growing realization that the party which still ruled the country in its name had abandoned it, the all-Yugoslav working class was taking only its first steps towards political independence when the crisis of the country's entire superstructure became terminal. Belgrade-based counter-revolution now imposed a different agenda. Political struggle became necessarily focused on the defence of basic national and democratic rights. In Kosovo, miners spearheaded a general strike in defence of the province's autonomy, while in Serbia workers were being mobilized behind chauvinist banners for a final assault on that autonomy. A Yugoslav Communist Party unable to defend the miners, and a Federal state unable to defend Kosovo, could not but break up.

In a multinational state like Yugoslavia, democracy – whatever its class basis – was inextricably bound up with a commitment to, and institutional safeguards for, equality between the constituent nations. An all-Yugoslav movement for democratic reform could have been built only within such parameters. Serbia, however – for the second time – turned out to be the weak link. In the country's vital hour, Serbia failed Yugoslavia and thus sealed its fate.

It can be argued that, as a state, Yugoslavia contained too many contradictions – above all in the field of economic development – to survive. The capitalist class emerging in the area at the beginning of the twentieth century favoured Yugoslavia for economic reasons: the creation of a large and protected market. Yet the unequal economic development of the individual nations made a common economic policy a matter of constant political contestation. Concentration of economic power at the Yugoslav centre always led to concentration of political power as well, which in practice meant Serbian domination. Decentralization, on the other hand, not only provoked Serbian resistance but also fed centrifugal tendencies in the country as a whole. In a sense, therefore, one might argue that Yugoslavia came into existence too soon: that is, before the area's economic growth could provide the preconditions for its viability and stability. On the other hand, the very fact that Yugoslavia did come into existence, not once but twice, suggests that there has always been a need for some sort of economic and political cooperation throughout the area.

One thing is certain, however. If and when this need again finds expression, it will not take the form of a common state, for Yugoslavia's historic time has run out. Nevertheless, unlike the war that has accompanied it, the break-up of Yugoslavia need not be seen as a tragedy. Once the Great Serb project has been defeated, allowing peace to return to the lands that once formed Yugoslavia, this need will seek and find its own channels and forms.

It is customary for an author to thank all those who have helped her work. Here I am confronted with a problem. My writings over the years have, after all, been the result of a collective effort by friends and co-thinkers from all the different constituent members of the former Yugoslav federation. I cannot thank them all individually. Some appear directly in these pages, others I can only hope will recognize their own contributions in what I have written. It is by reading their views, by talking to and arguing with them, that I have been able to form my own thoughts and conclusions – for which, of course, they bear no final responsibility. Here I wish to single out those friends in Serbia and Montenegro – some of whom I have never met! – who have dared to stand up to an overwhelming tide and who have actively opposed the war despite the physical danger to themselves. Special thanks and gratitude must also go to the Albanian workers and people, who at one point had to wage such a lonely battle for essential human dignity: they taught me the true value of political commitment and made me aware that there was more to Yugoslavia than its name. I would like also to salute here all those young women and men in Croatia and Bosnia-Herzegovina who, fighting against such daunting odds, have not hesitated to risk their lives in the defence of freedom and in the cause of democracy. Their time is still to come. I also wish to thank the members of the former Yugoslav community here in Great Britain, who have helped me overcome the sense of despair I have often felt when seeing the mindless destruction of a beautiful country in the name of a reactionary phantasm. To those journalists and cameramen, too, who have penetrated the fog of mystification and brought to public attention the horrific truth of the Great Serb terror, I can only offer my deep appreciation. My thanks go also to Ernest Mandel and Mike Davis, who gave me important early encouragement; to the British Council, which funded my first research trip to Yugoslavia; and to the Hamburger Institut für Sozialforschung, which granted me a two-year research scholarship to write a book that has, I hope, not changed too much or been completed too late! Finally, I should like to express my gratitude to all those, throughout the world, who have rallied in a myriad of individual ways to the flag of human solidarity and compassion, against and despite the indifference of their governments.

It is they, above all, who have helped me retain my belief in inter-nationalism.

This book has been constructed out of my writing on Yugoslavia over the past twelve years, and represents some two-thirds of what I have written. It would have been possible to recast this book as a single account written from today's vantage-point. But it seems to me that the rawer, more 'documentary' approach adopted here conveys more clearly to the reader that Yugoslavia's disintegration and the present war were predictable well in advance of their actual occurrence, as well as demonstrating the different options that were available at different moments, and how the Yugoslavs themselves saw these evolving. Linking introductions have been provided in order to produce a coherent narrative of the years leading to the country's break-up. Texts are printed in chronological order, except for the first two sections, which cover the same period; here the Kosovo issue has been separated out and considered first. This is because the destruction of Yugoslavia started in Kosovo in 1981, and also because the long text on 'Kosovo between Yugoslavia and Albania' gives a concise historical introduction to the two Yugoslavias (the interwar monarchy and postwar federation). I am only too aware that the book contains imbalances; one important gap – Croatia's internal politics since the 1990 elections – will be filled in my next book, which will be on Croatia.

Texts have been shortened to avoid repetition, and minor errors corrected; otherwise they have been reprinted as originally written, including judgments or predictions that have turned out to be mistaken. Most of the earlier texts were originally published under the pseudonym 'Michele Lee', adopted in order to avoid problems when visiting Yugo-slavia. A small proportion of the book comprises material translated rather than written by myself. The last text was co-authored by Quintin Hoare. For the sake of consistency, the standard international (Slav) spelling 'Kosovo' has been retained throughout the book, even though I now normally use the Albanian spelling 'Kosova', which should certainly be recognized as the new international standard, given this former Yugoslav province's declaration of independence.

The Introduction; the sectional introductions; Part Two, chapter 6; Part Four, chapters 4 and 7b; and Part Five, chapters 2, 3 and 4b are all published here for the first time. Other texts appeared in *Labour Focus on Eastern Europe* (Part One, chapters 1 and 3; Part Two, chapters 2, 3a, 3b, 4, 5 and 7; Part Three, chapters 1, 2a, 2b, 3; Part Four, chapters 1, 2, 7a and 8); in *New Left Review* (Part One, chapter 2; Part Two, chapter 3c; Part Three, chapter 2c); in the *New Statesman* (Part Two, chapter 1; Part Five, chapter 9); in the *London Review of Books* (Part Five, chapters 1 and 8); in *Marxism Today* (Part Five, chapter 7); in *Capital and Class* (Part

Five, chapter 5); in *RUSI*, journal of the Royal United Services Institute (Part Five, chapter 6); in *International Viewpoint* (Part Four, chapters 3, 5 and 6; Part Five, chapter 4a).

Lastly, an invaluable source for me of dailies and weeklies from all parts of the former Yugoslavia has been Ramadan Newsagents, of Queensway, London W.2. I wish to thank Mr Anwar Aziz and his colleagues for all their kindness and help over more than a decade.

September 1992

PART ONE

The Kosovo Watershed and its Aftermath (1981–87)

Introduction

In April 1981, when the Socialist Autonomous Province of Kosovo was placed under martial law following several days of mass demonstrations by the local Albanian population, it was clear that the country as a whole had reached a watershed. This was the first time since the Second World War that a member of the Yugoslav Federation had been treated in this way, and the first time (at least as far I knew) that police had used firearms against demonstrators, most of whom were in their teens. According even to official reports, there were twelve dead and around 150 wounded, while unofficial estimates were much higher. The novelty of this military–police intervention was quite shocking. I expected some form of public protest, at least from the intellectuals associated with the banned journal *Praxis*, whom we in the West had grown accustomed to treat as the voice of Yugoslavia's conscience. But their silence was deafening. I recall a deep sense of shame, indeed a sense of a collective Slav guilt towards this most impoverished non-Slav part of Yugoslavia's population. My own assessment of the meaning and implications of the Kosovo events, however, was hampered at the time by my virtually complete ignorance of Albanian history, forcing me to spend much of the following eighteen months researching the Albanian question in Yugoslavia. 'Kosovo between Yugoslavia and Albania', published in *New Left Review* in 1983, was the outcome.

Kosovo posed the question of whether post-Tito Yugoslavia would democratize or slide towards authoritarianism. Hence my concern with the reaction – or lack of it – of the country's Left opposition. My growing doubts about the prospects for democratic advance were temporarily stayed by the demand, put forward by students in October 1981, for release of imprisoned Albanian demonstrators. A survey of six months of harsh repression in Kosovo following the initial demonstrations, moreover, showed open differences emerging among Yugoslav leaders about the draconian measures used. At the same time, Albanian workers were already coming to be seen as politically unreliable: the entry of Territorial

Army units into factories signalled, in advance, the role that the Albanian working class was to play a few years later in organizing national resistance.

My perception that the Kosovo events represented a watershed in Yugoslavia's post-war history was confirmed in January 1986, when several prominent *Praxis* intellectuals added their signatures to an anti-Albanian petition. As soon became clear, the organizing of this petition marked the beginning of an open struggle inside the Serbian party and state leadership – a struggle which, by the end of 1987, would be won by Slobodan Milošević and his supporters. I remember the feeling of fear provoked by seeing the signatures of Mihailo Marković, Ljubomir Tadić and Zagorka Golubović on this petition – a fear produced by my realization that such a rallying to nationalism of Serbia's progressive intelligentsia meant that civil war was now on the cards. There followed the first of many sleepless nights. 'This unexpected, indeed astonishing, alignment of *Praxis* editors with nationalism has aroused considerable dismay among their friends and sympathizers, for it delineates a complete break with the political and philosophical tradition represented by the journal,' I wrote at the time. There was an immediate angry response from the three which, quite apart from its intellectual and moral poverty,[1] was also highly instructive in that the arguments they used were drawn from the Memorandum of the Serbian Academy of Arts and Sciences – a document that provided the blueprint not only for Serbia's onslaught upon the entire Federal order, but also for the 1991–92 war.

The subsequent political evolution of the three *Praxis* editors was as follows. Ljubomir Tadić became a member of the Democratic Party, which in the elections of 1990 acquired a few seats in the Serbian parliament. This party, nationalist in orientation, was characterized from the start by opportunistic vacillation on two central issues of the time: the aggression against Slovenia and Croatia, and how to achieve the democratic constitution of Serbia. Tadić himself was to the forefront in denouncing Serbian anti-war activists as national traitors. Mihailo Marković, who turned out to have been one of the authors of the above-mentioned Memorandum, in 1990 became a vice-president of Milošević's Socialist Party of Serbia, and a noted scourge of various non-Serb and Serb 'national enemies': Slovenes, Croats and Albanians; Serbian students demanding democracy; peace activists and draft-dodgers; prominent members of the Serbian opposition. Zaga Golubović alone regained something of her earlier democratic vocation: she joined the anti-war Association of Independent Intellectuals and, as this book was being prepared for publication, was visiting Kosovo to engage in a dialogue with the Albanian 'democratic alternative' there.

Note

1 For an effective demolition of the propaganda myths on which they relied in their arguments, see *Kosovski Čvor: Drešiti ili Seći* (Report of an independent commission of inquiry established by the Union for a Yugoslav Democratic Initiative), Belgrade 1990.

Wrong Turn in Kosovo

Six months have gone by since a wave of mass demonstrations shook towns and villages throughout the Socialist Autonomous Province (SAP) of Kosovo, demanding republican status for the province. Kosovo is one of the eight federal units of Yugoslavia, which is made up of six republics and two provinces.

SAP Kosovo, which occupies some 4 per cent of Yugoslavia's territory and contains around 8 per cent of its population, is overwhelmingly inhabited by ethnic Albanians. Though the Army moved in with tanks early last April, and the Province has been *de facto* under a state of emergency ever since, the situation remains in the official language 'complex'. Security is now in the hands of special detachments of the Yugoslav paramilitary police: one wing is organized at the federal level while the other, the All Yugoslav Security Forces, is organized by the republics and the provinces. The latter, armed with modern riot control equipment, in uniforms clearly differentiating different republics and provinces, has never been used before. The men patrol the towns and the countryside mainly after nightfall. Together with the local police, they also guard roadblocks which have been set up on all roads into the province: nobody is allowed in unless on clearly specified and approved business. The initial intervention of the police and the army claimed officially twelve dead and over 150 wounded, but the real total is no doubt larger (although probably not as high as the hundreds and even thousands claimed by the emigré press).

Two months of open confrontation gradually gave way to a passive but nevertheless tangible resistance, which still flares up, in occasional – though by now rare – demonstrations, but most often takes other forms: the painting of slogans on public buildings (some 20 feet long), almost invariably demanding republican status for Kosovo; the distribution of leaflets; and, more serious, industrial sabotage and the destruction of agricultural fixed assets (the burning of forests, felling of fruit groves, etc.).

Most worrying to the authorities is the industrial sabotage; because of its high degree of concentration, Kosovo's industry is particularly vulnerable to this form of attack. Consequently, the Province's Territorial Army, locally recruited and commanded by an Albanian, Major-General Fadil Qaranoli, guards all factory gates and each new shift is accompanied by a small unit – the TA members often working their machines in full uniform, arms handy.

The policy of repression for which the authorities have opted has been exceedingly harsh: quite apart from the initial dead and wounded, 140 people have so far been formally tried and sentenced to prison for a disturbing total of 999 years. Many others have been dealt with summarily by magistrates' courts, which can imprison for up to ninety days; these minor sentences go largely unreported. Direct reporting of the trials has not been permitted, with the state press agency Tanjug (accused at one point by the provincial government of being biased) supplying all material to the daily papers. The harshness of the sentences, particularly where young people are concerned – and indeed the whole analysis and interpretation of the Kosovo events – has upset and divided Yugoslav public opinion.

Sentences of from ten to fifteen years have been quite common for those accused of belonging to some irredentist organization or for committing some act of violence (though it is worth noting that nobody has as yet been accused of killing or wounding a member of the police or the army, or indeed anybody else). Two-thirds of those sentenced have been students, high-school pupils, teachers, less often workers and peasants (again, mainly young, though a few in their forties and fifties) who organized or participated in demonstrations. Few of the slogans heard on these occasions had either an anti-Serb or secessionist character; most merely demanded republican status within Yugoslavia for Kosovo.

All those brought to court were treated with exceptional severity. Thus on 21 May at Skopje, capital of Macedonia, five people were given gaol sentences ranging from seven to thirteen years for forming an illegal organization, the National Party of Labour, whose aim was the unification of Albanian-inhabited areas of Yugoslavia with Albania. Of the five, three were workers, one was a teacher and one a private builder. All but one were in their mid-thirties.

On 3 August, a group of eleven was tried in Priština, the provincial capital. They were charged with organizing demonstrations in a number of local villages, erecting a roadblock and disarming a police car. After a day of weapons training in the woods, they gave themselves up. They were gaoled for between one and thirteen years. Of the eleven, five were peasants, two high-school pupils, two workers and two unemployed.

On 8 August, ten students and high-school pupils were sentenced to between four and eight years in prison for organizing demonstrations and shouting 'We want a republic! Long live the Socialist Republic of Kosovo!'. One of them, an eighteen-year-old from a village in the district of Lipljane (the scene of a considerable ferment among secondary-school – and even primary-school – children), was charged, in addition with writing these slogans on the blackboard in his classroom and throwing stones at a police car. He received a five-year sentence.

On 31 August, three youths were gaoled for two, four and six years for painting the slogans: 'Arise, brother Albanians!' 'Down with Yugoslav revisionism!' and 'Long live the Republic of Kosovo!' on eight houses and an electric substation. This is the picture which, with individual variations, has been repeated throughout the summer months in courthouses across the Province.

Those identified as having been involved in any way with the events of last spring have in most instances been dismissed from their schools, colleges and workplaces. Since in Kosovo (which in any case has a low proportion of its population in employment) wage-earners often support large families, the sentences and the dismissals have often caused enormous hardship. What is more, any help to families left unsupported is rigorously discouraged. The authorities, in desperation, have recently announced a measure (of doubtful legality) which will make parents responsible for their children's behaviour, and the first charges of this kind have been lodged with the public prosecutor.

All in all, the Yugoslav state has decided on a policy of exemplary punishment, despite the fact that it is clearly understood (and indeed often publicly repeated) that the events demand a political response, including a good deal of self-criticism by the political leadership at all levels. In the words of Mehmed Maliqi, an old partisan until recently president of the region's War Veterans' Association and now the new police chief: 'We must above all win the battle for our children.' More recently, Mitja Ribicic, president of the Slovenian branch of the Socialist Alliance, declared himself against a 'legalist-administrative approach' which condemns to long-term imprisonment eighteen-year-old youths instead of 'influencing them by different methods, above all of an educational kind'.

In the meantime, the wounds which oppression has inflicted on the Albanian community will take years to heal; a chasm of suspicion and hostility has opened up between the Slav (mainly Serb) and Albanian population in the area. Since the demonstrations first took place, more than four thousand people of Serb origin have left or applied to leave the Province. The Albanian population, on the other hand, has been exposed to hostility from much of the press printed in Belgrade in a manner which bears all the marks of traditional Serb anti-Albanian chauvinism.

The thinking behind the policy of heavy repression is, no doubt, that the crushing of any actual or potential opposition for a decade or so will buy the time in which to tackle some of the more acute socio-economic problems of the Province. This policy, however, represents an irresponsible flight from reality: far from being a temporary solution aimed at stabilization, it is sowing the seeds for an even greater future threat to the internal cohesion and stability of Yugoslavia.

Alongside the judicial reprisals, around six hundred people have been expelled from the Party and this process of 'political differentiation' is still continuing. Mahmut Bakalli, head of the provincial party; Dušan Ristić, president of the Assembly; Mustafa Sefendi, secretary of the interior; Imer Jaku, secretary for culture and education; Gazmend Zaymi, rector of the University; Shaban Hyseni, head of Kosovo television; Ali Hadri, director of the Albanian Institute and a noted historian, have all been replaced. It is interesting that most of the above-mentioned have not been expelled from the Party, and this lenient treatment contrasts vividly with the long sentences handed out to the youth. Although the number of those so far affected by the purge is far below the figure reached in Croatia and Serbia in 1971–72 (particularly in Croatia following the days of 'national euphoria'), this may be just a matter of time. However, as even a superficial examination of the events would show, the central slogan raised in the demonstrations – 'a Republic for Kosovo' – enjoys widespread support not only in the population at large, but also among cadres of both Party and state, particularly at the base: there has been a general closing of Albanian ranks in the face of the Federal government's iron-handed policy.

The demand of the Albanians in Yugoslavia for their own republic has roots in the awakening of a sense of intense national pride which until not long ago was denied to them, though tolerated in other Yugoslav nationalities. The spring explosion is in many ways a product of this delayed consummation of national equality and rights. Their size and ethnic compactness are, in the eyes of the Albanian population, sufficient reason for changing Kosovo's status from that of a province to that of a republic.

According to the Yugoslav constitution, however, national minorities cannot have their own republics; despite its size, the Albanian population is a national minority by definition. The constitution also specifies that provinces must be integrated into republics: Kosovo is a province of the Republic of Serbia.

Due the the historic conflict between the Albanians and the Serbs during the era of formation of their respective states, a conflict which the revolution was able only partly to transcend, the Albanians find it difficult to accept the nominal tutelage of Serbia. This tutelage is indeed nominal, because the 1974 constitution grants the two Yugoslav provinces effectively the same rights and responsibilities as it does to the republics.

Kosovo, like the other federal units, has its own party organization, National Assembly, constitution, high court, police, flag and other state symbols, university, academy of arts and sciences, own bank, etc. The change so universally desired would make in a sense little difference; this is an argument used by both sides.

On the one hand, given that provinces and republics are *de facto* equal and that, according to at least one interpretation of the Yugoslav constitution, republics but not provinces have the right of secession, is not the demand for republican status in effect a demand for secession? And would this not just be the first step towards the disintegration of the entire multinational state, something which, due to the mixed ethnic distribution, would inevitably lead to a civil war? On the other hand, the size of the Albanian minority – both in relation to that of other Yugoslav nationalities and in relation to Albania itself (whose population is around two and a half million) – makes it qualitatively different from any other in Yugoslavia, probably in Europe. In recognition of this fact, Kosovo was given autonomy and made a federal unit on a par with others.

This compromise solution, however, appears not to have worked: there is a a widespread conviction in the Albanian population that nothing short of a republic would guarantee them equality with other Yugoslav nationalities. Speculation as to whether such a step might not at some point in the future lead to secession is insufficient as a response to this conviction, particularly as few irrendentist slogans appeared on the demonstrations.

Albanian nationalism becomes quite understandable when one surveys the economic position of Kosovo, and the size of the gap which separates it from other republics and SAP Vojvodina. Kosovo is lagging far behind the others and this gap is increasing. Its birthrate, among the highest in Europe, is one cause of its falling behind, but it is not the only or the fundamental one. Deeper reasons are to be found in postwar history (Kosovo was included in the category of the underdeveloped and therefore given additional grants only after a significant delay): some in the nature of the Yugoslav economy (market socialism has increased regional inequalities), others in the international context within which it has to operate (the high price of industrialization exacted by imperialism).

The ideology of neighbouring Albania's ruling Party of Labour, with its emphasis on egalitarianism, finds among the poor, the unemployed and the low-paid a natural audience. Many of the social and economic problems confronting Kosovo are present also in other parts of Yugoslavia, only here they are thrown into sharper relief by the greater poverty and backwardness. The federal government has so far failed to take appropriate measures to tackle the very special case of underdevelopment presented by Kosovo. Making Kosovo a republic might be a necessary condition.

Paradoxically, Kosovo's industrial infrastructure is more modern than is the case anywhere else in the country – it is far more automated even than Slovenia's. This is due partly to its more recent origin, but also to its high concentration. Much of Yugoslavia's reserves of lead, zinc, nickel and half of its coal lies in Kosovo and this mineral wealth is exploited by real industrial giants: one of the biggest, the Trepča complex, employs over 19,000 workers. The next five-year plan envisages a diversification of its industrial base in order to create more labour-intensive branches (though even if all the plans are put into operation there will still be 100,000 people looking for a job in 1985). To raise greater income within the province, more processing plants are to be built and more money spent on agriculture, which in turn will demand more extensive irrigation of this generally fertile but dry land. Between now and 1985, the Province is due to receive 140,000 million dinars (over £2,000 million), a sum comparable to the total received over the last fifteen years. However, what has also been learnt from the failure of the last five-year plan is that money alone is insufficient to break the vicious circle of economic underdevelopment. Consequently, the current plan envisages a more extensive integration of Kosovo's industry with enterprises in other republics and Vojvodina, through joint economic ventures and sharing of risks.

Economic investment apart, the political response which the state can make to its troubled province will necessarily be conditioned by the quality of its relations with the People's Republic of Albania. After diplomatic relations were restored in 1971, trade rapidly expanded to reach $116 million in 1980, four times the figure for 1978. A lively cultural exchange was initiated, particularly after 1978, the year of Albania's final break with China. Theatre and folk-music ensembles travelled back and forth, professors from Tirana lectured at the University of Priština, and the Yugoslavs published modern Albanian (from Albania) literature not only in Albanian but also in other Yugoslav languages; some of this literature was included in Kosovo textbooks.

In 1978 there was a joint celebration of the hundredth anniversary of the founding of the League of Prizren, the historic watershed of Albanian national revival in the nineteenth century. The occasion was of immense significance for the growing warmth between the two neighbours. The initiative came largely from the Yugoslav side. Though welcoming visitors from Kosovo, the Albanian government never allowed their nationals to travel unofficially to Yugoslavia, nor did they permit non-Albanian Yugoslavs to travel in Albania. Yet for a whole period Belgrade turned a deaf ear to the unremitting anti-revisionist propaganda beamed from Tirana, which possesses one of the strongest transmitters in Europe and whose television is received on 60 per cent of the territory of Kosovo.

The Albanian Party of Labour clearly felt that this increased cooperation should not stand in the way of its duty to 'wage ideological struggle in the defence of Marxism-Leninism and against revisionism' because among other things 'the Yugoslavs wage their ideological struggle against the Albanian positions even if they do not say so'. The Yugoslavs, including in particular the Albanians in Kosovo, clearly hoped that better relations would ultimately give them some say in Albania after Hoxha's departure, while the Albanians feared that closer ties could also prove subversive to the APL conception of the Albanian road to socialism. Although there is no evidence that Tirana has masterminded recent events in Kosovo, it has for the first time openly backed the demand for republican status raised in the demonstrations of the past spring.

This demand the Yugoslavs for their part have termed 'anti-constitutional', 'irredentist' and 'counter-revolutionary': people caught writing it in public are liable to two years of imprisonment. In this new climate there is a danger that the very real progress of the past decade is being rolled back: textbooks are being re-written, literature originating from Albania expunged from them, the history taught in Kosovo's schools restyled – all in the name of combating 'romantic nationalism'. One of the consequences has been that many schools, even faculties of the University, had to start the new academic year without adequate books or the necessary number of teachers.

It is notoriously difficult to draw the line between national affirmation and nationalism, and for a country like Yugoslavia it is extremely dangerous to confuse the two. But one of the paradoxical results of current repression in Kosovo has been to put Kosovo on the Yugoslav map. The average Yugoslav citizen is for the first time learning something about Kosovo's past and present, and the country as a whole has been firmly reminded that Yugoslavia is not a country of South Slavs but the homeland of a number of different Balkan nationalities.

(November 1981)

News has just arrived of a thousand-strong demonstration in the capital, Priština, to mark the first anniversary of the initial disorders on 11 March 1981. On the eve of the anniversary the police had arrested several students in the town of Vitina, closed a number of schools and shops in the capital and severed its telephone links with the rest of Kosovo, thereby testifying to the continued unrest among the ethnically Albanian population. Already on 3 February 1982, the provincial secretary for internal affairs, Mehmet Maliqi, had referred to various 'complications of the security situation' and to a number of indications that 'hostile activity' was on the increase. He further claimed that the police had uncovered no fewer than thirty-three 'illegal groups', describing as 'massive' the Marxist-Leninist Group of Kosovo and the Marxist-Leninist Communist Party of Albanians in Yugoslavia. The character of the official propaganda offensive in recent months also seems to suggest that Albanian nationalism, often tinged with the distinctive ideology of the Tirana régime, continues to have considerable resonance in the social and economic conditions of the province.

(March 1982)

Students Demand Amnesty for Albanians

In October 1981, more than a hundred students from three different Yugoslav republics signed a petition demanding political amnesty for those jailed in the aftermath of the spring events. This was a development of major importance, being the first such concerted action by Yugoslav students in support of their fellow students and citizens in Kosovo.

Belgrade–Zagreb–Ljubljana
October 1981

To the:
Presidency of the Socialist Federal Republic of Yugoslavia
Presidency of the Socialist Republic of Serbia
Presidency of the Socialist Autonomous Province of Kosovo

We propose the opening of an initiative to re-examine juridical policy in SAP Kosovo, with respect to the current trials of participants in the demonstrations and persons who in some other way expressed their political positions in Kosovo in the course of March, April and May 1981. The reasons for this initiative are as follows:

1. The greatest number of cases involve exclusively political charges over which, in principle, courts have no jurisdiction.
2. The massive number of people sentenced in the first stage (222 up to now) and the unusually high level of sentences (from 1 to 15 years) point to clear legal arbitrariness in the service of a momentary political interest, which directly brings into question the principle of independence of the judiciary.
3. The protection of the legal rights of the accused, and therefore the very impartiality of the legal process, have in the majority of cases been brought into question by staging collective rather than individual trials; by the unusually short duration of the trials; by the fact that charges were always proved *in toto* and in all cases; and by the complete absence of information offered to the wider public in the course of the court proceedings.

4. The clearly discriminatory approach in the criminal proceedings, directed in the main against young people of Albanian nationality, principally schoolchildren and students, creates a situation in which greatest political responsibility and punishment is being reserved precisely for those who have least political power or institutional protection.

In a situation in which the national-economic instance is used as the key to social power and income, a situation of increasing republican and social etatism, nationalist deviations were bound to occur, above all among those in positions of responsibility in the League of Communists. One is therefore surprised by the difference in the kinds of punishment which have been meted out, on the one hand, to the leaders in the LC of Kosovo and, on the other, to young people who have grown up in such a climate and who for years have been indoctrinated in the idea of national emancipation which, though an essential precondition of human emancipation, cannot be seen as the highest or only form of emancipation. It is doubtful whether the legally established aim of punishment can be served by such trial proceedings at all.

In saying this we do not, of course, advocate that the previous political leadership of SAP Kosovo should be put on trial, but rather that the problem should be tackled at its socio-economic roots and solved by democratic means. We expect that the proposal for this initiative will be accepted also in the interest of safeguarding human rights and developing democratic relations within Yugoslav society.

The undersigned students of the:
University of Belgrade
University of Zagreb
University of Ljubljana

2

Kosovo between Yugoslavia and Albania

On 2 April 1981, massive demonstrations took place in the Socialist Autonomous Province of Kosovo, an area of Yugoslavia inhabited mainly by ethnic Albanians, to demand republican status within the Yugoslav federation. By the end of the next day, the Army had moved in with tanks and armoured personnel carriers to institute martial law, the first time this has happened in the country since 1945. The party leadership declared that they were fighting counter-revolution. Yet they offered no evidence to show that Kosovars were demanding restoration of capitalism in this poorest of Yugoslav provinces, plagued by far the lowest standard of living and highest rates of unemployment. The April demonstrations were not peopled by remnants of the old order suddenly resurrected by the approaching anniversary of Tito's death. On the contrary, most of the protesters were extremely young, many still in secondary and some even in primary school.

The trouble started on 11 March with an action by students protesting against poor living conditions in university hostels at Priština, capital of the Province. Discussions with the university administration followed, in which the students aired a whole number of grievances concerning the state of their Province – high unemployment, poverty, backwardness, social differences, etc. – and put forward the demand for republican status.[1] They then marched to the provincial party headquarters in the centre of the city, but the police broke up this demonstration with relative ease. The whole affair would probably have ended there, had it not been for the fact that on 23 March the city was to celebrate Tito's official birthday and the local party leaders – nervous about the possible repercussions of any breakdown of order upon Kosovo's place in the federation, in the uncertain atmosphere of the first year after Tito's death – were desperately anxious for the occasion to pass off without incident. They therefore ordered the police to round up all potential troublemakers, including student leaders, prior to the celebrations. The result was the exact opposite of what they had intended: students and others collected on

23 March in the streets leading to the city's main square, with banners demanding the release of their comrades, denouncing Kosovo's inferior status and demanding a republic. Ordered to prevent their entry into the square, and badly prepared for a crowd that size, the police behaved with considerable brutality: tear gas was used to break up the demonstrations, shots were fired and more arrests followed. By 2 April demonstrations had spread throughout the Province, in an explosion of popular anger unseen since the war. Reports from a variety of sources agree that the chief demand everywhere was that Kosovo should be made a republic.

The local party, keen at first to deal with the disturbance without recourse to outside aid, imposed a news blackout, which only made things worse, allowing the wildest rumours to circulate (e.g. that Priština was burning) – reflecting the widespread fear of a return to the Ranković era.[2] By 2 April, faced with what amounted to a generalized revolt, the party called up Belgrade and asked for help. On 3 April the Province was put under martial law. Extra security forces were rushed in: troops with armour; police units from other republics and Vojvodina (in their seven respective uniforms); and above all detachments of the All Yugoslav Security Forces, a federal paramilitary body here seen in action for the first time. They proceeded to re-establish order. By the time they had finished, the final toll – by official figures – was twelve dead and over 150 wounded. The actual numbers, however, were certainly far higher – perhaps as many as three hundred dead – suggesting that the AYSF, in particular, had been explicitly given a free hand in suppressing the disorders.

Martial law was lifted some two months later, but extra security forces remained encamped outside the main towns. They are still there. The open confrontations of March, April and May gave way gradually to passive resistance. Even today, after hundreds of arrests and long prison sentences,[3] after fifty-five different illegal groups belonging to four different organizations have been uncovered and disbanded, the situation has not returned to normal. A fall in industrial production, far beyond anything attributable to economic crisis, cannot but be related to the systematic purges which have taken place in the party and state administration, and to the general sense of sullen bitterness following the repression.

Contours of the Problem

The Socialist Federative Republic of Yugoslavia is a state composed of six Socialist Republics (Bosnia-Herzegovina, Croatia, Macedonia, Montenegro, Serbia and Slovenia) and two Socialist Autonomous Provinces (Kosovo, Vojvodina). The two Provinces are also formally a part of the SR

Serbia: of the two, Vojvodina is ethnically very mixed, Kosovo predominantly Albanian. The national question in Yugoslavia is defined by the
following structural elements:

1. The country is a multinational state in which no single nationality
   claims a majority. If one takes the figures of 600,000 (the approximate
   size of the Montenegrin group) as the lower benchmark, there are seven
   main nationalities, of which one – the Albanian – is non-Slav. The
   country has no common language: although a large part of the
   population (over 70 per cent) speaks Serbo-Croat, the fact that this
   language appears in two major literary variants makes the whole
   sphere of public communications even in Serbo-Croat an arena for
   nationalist contestation.
2. Most nationalities are not located in geographically discrete areas, but
   commingle in the six republics and two provinces, giving each federal
   unit a multinational character in turn. The degree of ethnic heterogeneity varies (see Table below), but the presence of these minorities is
   often a vociferous reminder of the interdependence of Yugoslavia's
   constituent parts.
3. The Yugoslav nationalities are also internally separated by history, so
   that the existing ethnic map is overlaid with historic frontiers which
   further complicate (or enrich) national loyalties. The strength of
   historic versus ethnic frontiers is shown in the separate existence of
   Bosnia-Herzegovina and Vojvodina, in spite of the fact that these have
   large Serb populations on the borders with Serbia proper, Croat
   populations on the borders with the Republic of Croatia, etc.
4. Finally, the relatively late formation of the Yugoslav state, well after
   rather than before the arrival of its ethnic components to fully fledged
   national consciousness, has infused the state with a perception of
   distinct and sometimes conflicting interests as between Yugoslavia as a
   whole and its separate component nationalities.

The Albanians in Yugoslavia inhabit an ethnically compact and continuous area, which includes Kosovo[4] (where three-quarters of them live),
western Macedonia and southern Montenegro. In Kosovo, they form close
to 80 per cent of the total population. This is why any discussion of the
Albania national question in Yugoslavia starts with the status of Kosovo
within the federation. The sheer size of the Albanian ethnic group, in
relation both to other Yugoslav nationalities and to the population of
Albania itself, makes it difficult to treat it as a national minority pure and
simple. Equally, the concept of 'autonomous province', a state form
chosen for areas of mixed population, is not really applicable to Kosovo
with its overwhelmingly Albanian majority: in this respect Kosovo is more

Yugoslavia's Ethnic Composition in 1981 (thousands)

	Serb	Croat	Moslem[a]	Slovene	Albanian	Macedonian	Yugoslav[b]	Montenegrin	Hungarian
Yugoslavia	8136	4428	2000	1754	1731	1341	1216	577	427
Bosnia	1320	758	1629	3	4	2	326	14	1
Montenegro	20	8	78	1	37	1	31	399	0
Croatia	532	3454	24	25	6	5	379	10	25
Macedonia	45	3	39	1	378	1281	14	4	0
Slovenia	42	57	13	1712	2	3	26	3	9
Serbia (proper)	4861	31	151	8	72	29	271	77	5
Vojvodina	1107	109	5	3	4	19	167	43	385
Kosovo	210	8	59	0	1277	1	1	27	0

a. 'Moslem' as a national category refers to South Slav population converted to Islam during Ottoman rule.
b. 'Yugoslav by nationality': this category has increased 943,000 since 1971.

Source: NIN, 28 February 1982.

like the other republics (excluding the special case of Bosnia-Herzegovina) than it is like Vojvodina.

The poverty and backwardness of the Province accounts for much of the dissatisfaction and rebellious effervescence in the Albanian population – no such unrest visits, for example, the Hungarian-inhabited areas in the more developed northern Province of Vojvodina. As a federal unit, Kosovo is lagging far behind the others economically and the gap is increasing. In spite of the funds poured into the Province – and these have been considerable over the past fifteen years – no relative improvement has been achieved. Slovenia, Yugoslavia's most advanced republic, is today six times more developed than Kosovo; at the end of the war the ratio was 3 : 1. According to the 1975–79 plan, the Province's economy should have grown at a rate of 10 per cent above the average for Yugoslavia; instead its growth was 10 per cent slower. In 1975 its *per capita* income was 33 per cent of the Yugoslav average; by the end of the five-year period it had slipped to 29 per cent. Whatever figure one chooses to consider, the Province is a case *sui generis* in Yugoslavia today. Its birthrate, close to 26/1000, is one of the highest in Europe, so that it is the *per capita* figures which are so devastating. A young population (more than half under the age of twenty, one third still at school) puts additional strain on social services, while fewer people are wage-earners (one in ten) than in Yugoslavia as a whole (one in five). As the most densely populated area of Yugoslavia, pressure on the land is high and hence unemployment in the cities greater than elsewhere. Of the total population of over one and a half million, there are only 173,000 wage-earners, while 71,000 are looking for jobs and a further 80,000 work outside the Province. In Kosovo, unemployment is three times the Yugoslav average.[5] What has been happening there, however, transcends the purely economic framework and signals a more general political problem for the country as a whole. The massive and persistent desire of the Albanians for their own republic within Yugoslavia, and the refusal of the authorities in Belgrade even to consider it (choosing instead extreme measures of repression), indicates that more is at stake than a simple amendment to the present constitution.

The Yugoslav constitution of 1974 blurred the previous distinction between South Slav and other nationalities. This is most visible in the status of the autonomous provinces, which since 1974 have enjoyed *de facto* equality with the republics. Though formally remaining part of the Republic of Serbia, their relationship with the latter is now based on *consent*: the constitution forbids the Republic to intervene in provincial affairs against the will of the assemblies in Priština and Novi Sad. Furthermore, their presence within the republic is conditional upon the latter remaining in the Yugoslav federation: the provinces are directly constitutive units of the federal state, and their legitimacy is 'original', not formally conferred upon them by the federal centre; it is seen as *won* by their people, through their participation in the revolutionary war.

Because of this constitutional status of Kosovo, the Albanian population plays a role in the federation directly comparable (even if not quite identical) to that of the six South Slav nations. This in spite of the fact, and here lies the essential ambiguity, that it is officially only a 'national minority', i.e. a segment of a nation with its own independent state elsewhere. The Yugoslav state and party praesidiums have equal representation for republics and provinces, with rotating presidents (so that the Yugoslav Head of State 1984/5 will be an Albanian from Kosovo). Kosovo flies its own flag (which is also the flag of the People's Republic of Albania) on all state occasions, and its Albanian children, overwhelmingly Geg-speaking at home, learn the new standard Albanian language (heavily influenced by Tosk) just like their counterparts in the People's Republic.[6] Nevertheless, one insistent demand has surfaced repeatedly since the mid-sixties in the province (and has been supported by Albanians living outside the latter's boundaries in western Macedonia and southern Montenegro): *de jure* recognition of the Albanians' equality with the Slav nations, in the form of a republic of their own, with the corollary of a wholly voluntary participation in the Yugoslav community of nations.

The essential difference, of course, between the country's Albanian and Slav nationalities lies in the fact that, while the latter are overwhelmingly concentrated within the Yugoslav borders, the former are divided by them: almost as many Albanians live in Yugoslavia as in Albania (over 40 per cent of the total). Consequently, the national unrest in Kosovo, where most Yugoslav Albanians live, immediately raises the spectre of irredentism, of a redrawing of state frontiers and Albanian national unification. Clearly, the Albanian question in Yugoslavia, by its very nature, transcends the purely Yugoslav framework and directly involves the People's Republic of Albania. Speaking to foreign journalists a few days after the introduction of martial law, Stane Dolanc, a leading Slovene member of the Yugoslav Party, currently Federal Secretary for Internal Affairs, said that the Yugoslav state had no intention of giving republican status to Kosovo and thereby creating a second Albanian state. Citing the two Koreas and two Germanys as unhappy examples, he suggested that two Albanias would be a danger to the future stability of the Balkans.

These parallels obscure a very important fact, which is that in the case of the 'two Albanias' the physical frontier does not separate two different and fundamentally antagonistic social systems. The very existence of the Albanian national question, therefore, can be understood only in the context of the revolution which took place in Yugoslavia and Albania in the period 1941–45 and its subsequent evolution. In 1948, however, the special bond between the two countries, created by the common revolution, was broken when Yugoslavia was expelled from the Cominform. The double bind of intimacy and alienation which has linked Albania and Yugoslavia since 1941 and throughout their formative period – in the course of which the two countries have acquired very different physiognomies – finds its proper explanation, it will be argued, in the failure of a Balkan Socialist Federation to get off the ground in the aftermath of World War Two, thus confirming the previous frontiers and allowing the Yalta Agreement to be imposed on the Balkans. But this first revolution after October did not, in any case, take place in the pure space of the class struggle, but was burdened by the need to solve certain elementary tasks bequeathed it by the previous socio-political order. In particular, it confronted problems pertaining to the specific state/nation nexus established in the Balkans by the bourgeois 'revolutions' of the first decades of this century. It is thus relevant to our understanding of the Albanian national problem in Yugoslavia to recapitulate the role played by Kosovo in the formation of the Albanian and Yugoslav states.

The Balkan Heritage

Kosovo is the cradle of the Albanian national renaissance: here the more recent history of bourgeois-led movements for independent statehood takes precedence over the mediaeval glories of vanished empires.[7] From the second half of the nineteenth century right up to the proclamation of Albanian independence in 1912, Kosovo played a central organizing role in the Albanian national struggle. The historic watershed was the formation of the League of Defence of the Rights of the Albanian Nation at Prizren in 1878, which signalled the arrival of the Albanian nation to political maturity. Kosovo towns became the centres of resistance to Ottoman rule and repression. It was in Kosovo that the Albanians first declared their support for the Young Turk revolution of 1908, and later organized a generalized rebellion when the new administration in Constantinople reneged on its initial promise of cultural and administrative autonomy for the Ottoman subject nationalities. The subsequent bloody repression helped shift westward the Albanian national struggle to what is today Albania proper.

Kosovo, however, with its significant Serb minority and its past association with the mediaeval empire of Dushan, was also an area where Albanian and Serbian nationalisms clashed directly and continuously from the mid-nineteenth century.[8] The Serbian bourgeoisie, keen to escape the economic domination of Austria-Hungary, which controlled Serbia's access to the markets of Central Europe, premised its independence on the acquisition of a maritime outlet, either to the Aegean at Salonika through

Macedonia or (increasingly) to the Adriatic through Albania: both directions led across the Kosovo plain. These economic interests were commonly wrapped in a heady rhetoric evoking the battle of Kosovo and recreation of the empire destroyed some five hundred years earlier.[9] Serbia's plans, however, depended on its neighbours' intentions: the last decades of Ottoman rule in the Balkans witnessed a major competition between successor states for the territories soon to be vacated by the Porte. Two wars were fought in rapid succession for the Balkan inheritance. These so-called Balkan Wars expelled Turkey effectively from Europe, cut Albania approximately in half and partitioned Macedonia between Serbia, Bulgaria and Greece. The frontiers established by the Balkan Wars of 1912–13 have proved durable, surviving two world wars and a socialist revolution.

The wars effectively doubled the size of Serbia, increasing its population by 50 per cent. It acquired a large part of Kosovo and Macedonia, but was at Austrian insistence evicted from northern Albania and thus denied access to the sea. Montenegro, Serbia's sister state, doubled its population and grew by a half, incorporating the rest of Kosovo and the south of the present-day republic of Montenegro. The two states for the first time acquired a common border, a factor of some significance in the subsequent formation of Yugoslavia. Belgrade failed to win itself a port, but it could claim it had regained 'Old Serbia' – an incalculable boost to national pride which was to serve it well in World War One which followed within a year.[10] The acquisition of a large irredenta in its south was, however, to have an important effect on the future Yugoslavia, since the need continuously to repress a deeply antagonistic population pushed the military to the forefront of the new state, further weakening its already fragile democratic potential.

Serbia's and Montenegro's gains were, of course, Albania's loss. Arriving late to national consciousness, the Albanians, like their Macedonian neighbours, had to wage their struggle for national independence not only against a decaying empire but also against more powerful neighbours who had already won their own. The constant threat of partition among these would-be predators had a profound effect on the Albanian national struggle. It acted so as to accelerate the process of national coordination, but at the cost of subjugating all other issues to the needs of national survival. More specifically, the freezing of the internal class struggle at this crucial juncture meant that the liberation of the peasantry from the hated *chiflik* system, that anti-'feudal' revolution which provided much of the internal strength and cohesion of states like Serbia and Bulgaria, did not occur in Albania.[11] Consequently, the chances of the weak Albanian bourgeoisie establishing its political leadership by way of an agrarian reform were considerably diminished in the circumstances of the country's arrival at independence. In the end this independence was not won but granted by European powers to a rump Albania in 1913.[12]

Once the question of its frontiers was settled, moreover, the internal contradictions exploded, plunging the country into chaos. Its survival, in fact, remained an open question until the arrival of the revolution in 1944. More than this: the new frontiers were drawn in a way that could not but have a devastating effect on the economy of the new state. The loss of the fertile plain of Kosovo and of access to the valley of the river Vardar stunted and deformed its prospects. Cut off from its traditional town markets, the already deeply impoverished peasantry of the Albanian north saw its standard of living decline even further. Excluded from its natural hinterland, and thereby from the Balkans as a whole, Albania became a country dependent on whoever controlled the lower Adriatic. At the end of World War One that power was Italy: by 1925, Albania was an economic satellite of Rome and in 1939 Victor Emmanuel III assumed the title of King of Albania.

Serbia's gains in the Balkan Wars were confirmed and consolidated by the outcome of World War One. It was able, therefore, at the end of 1918, and weeks before the creation of Yugoslavia, to occupy Montenegro: in the merger that followed, the latter lost not only its unpopular dynasty but also its centuries-old separate state identity.[13] Enlarged in this way, Serbia went on to effect a fusion with the embryonic 'State of Serbs, Croats and Slovenes' which had been created out of the now vanished Habsburg empire. The outcome was the Kingdom of Serbs, Croats and Slovenes, confirmed by the Great Powers in the peace treaties, which ten years later (January 1929) would assume the name of Yugoslavia.

Without the Bulgars, however, the new country's eventual name was something of a misnomer. The old competition between Serbia and Bulgaria for control of the Vardar valley and Macedonia, which had culminated in the Balkan War of 1913 (and was to line them up on opposite sides in both world wars), had dissipated the dream of unification of all South Slavs. Curiously, therefore, in that it excluded the Bulgars and included a large number of neighbouring non-Slavs (well over half a million Albanians and almost as many Hungarians), Yugoslavia as created in 1918 was a state which prefigured – albeit in a truncated and distorted fashion – the Balkan federation which socialists of both the Second and Third Internationals had called for as the only proper way of solving the national question in the Balkans. The unresolved problems of Albanian and Macedonian national unification, however, were to be a heavy burden on the revolution unleashed by World War Two in this part of Europe.

State versus Class and Nation: 1918–41

The establishment of Yugoslavia at the end of World War One was the culmination of several analytically distinct processes, accelerated by the war, each of which bestowed on the new state it own christening gift. Key, of course, was the desire of Serbs and Montenegrins, Croats and Slovenes to free themselves from foreign rule and/or unite with their co-nationals within the frontiers of the same state – thus escaping partition of the kind which befell their neighbours further south.[14] But assisting the birth of Yugoslavia (which, for reasons just mentioned, could hardly be described as an artificial creation of Versailles) were those European powers who had been victorious in the war, together with its main beneficiary, the USA. Their interest was to block the German *Drang nach Osten* by erecting in its path a large Slav state; a state, furthermore, which in the wake of the October Revolution would seek its support not in the East but in the West, in Britain and France, and which would indeed actively combat the revolutionary appeal of the young Soviet state in this troubled part of Europe.[15] At the same time, the frontiers of this latecomer to the European political map, shaped by these two factors – desire for national unification and foreign plans – incorporated also the earlier expansionist acquisitions of Serbia and Montenegro: Kosovo and Macedonia.

When the Kingdom of the Serbs, Croats and Slovenes was created, only Serbia possessed an army and, just as importantly, international recognition, so that the new state was from the start dominated by the Serbian bourgeoisie. Throughout the interwar period, this particular fraction of the Yugoslav ruling class governed the country through a policy of national oppression so crude and violent that, within a few years, all internal political life (with the important exception of the Communist Party, condemned after a brilliant electoral start to an underground existence) was polarized along ethnic lines: Slovenes flocked to the Slovene People's Party, Croats to the Croat Peasant Party, Moslems of Bosnia to the Yugoslav Moslem Organization. In Macedonia and Kosovo, where no pretence of bourgeois democracy was maintained, terrorist organizations substituted for political parties. Only in Serbia, because of its dominant position, did a multi-party system survive – although, in practice, the smaller parties did little but tail the Great Serb policy of the dominant Radicals.

After 1928, the country could be ruled only by dictatorship (somewhat modified after 1935). By the time the Second World War engulfed the country, in April 1941, the name of Yugoslavia for most of the population had long since become little more than a synonym for a Greater Serbia – hence, a cause not worth defending. The result was not just military defeat and partition among German, Italian, Hungarian and Bulgarian invaders. It was a far more intimate disintegration of the interwar bourgeois state. The new Yugoslavia which emerged in the revolution that followed has thus rightly refused to claim the dubious parentage of its bourgeois predecessor.[16]

Was the state born in 1918 inherently unstable because it was multinational? Such a claim would be a great oversimplification. It is true that the national conflict dominated the politics of the interwar period, but it would be quite incorrect to conflate the two. In the first place, to do so would ignore the more crucial dimension of class struggle. No legal channels for this existed for most of the period in question; nevertheless, without this dimension it is impossible to understand the Yugoslav bourgeoisie's inability to 'put its house in order' and thus avoid its revolutionary destruction in 1941–45. The instability of the state created in 1918 was a result of the capitulation of a more advanced northern ruling class to Serbia's state demands: a political compromise conditioned as much by the panic which the dissolution of the repressive state apparatus, following the break-up of Austria-Hungary, induced in its ranks as by fear of territorial losses to the foreign invaders. The October Revolution, then barely one year old, and the destabilizing effects of the international conflagration, had produced a pre-revolutionary situation in Yugoslavia's northern areas, with political ferment in the cities, the takeover of large estates in the countryside, and wholesale desertion of soldiers from the front. The Yugoslav bourgeoisie, caught like its Russian counterpart (of February–October 1917) between military pressure from abroad and popular pressure from below, at the very outset relinquished the burden of its historic tasks: solution of the national question and creation of a democratic republic. A symbolic victim of this compromise was the right of women to vote, dropped from the constitutional platform at the insistence of the deeply patriarchal ruling class of pre-war Serbia.

In the second place, by the late 1920s bourgeois politics itself was breaking out of the national pattern and falling into an essentially bipolar contest: on the one hand, the economically stronger bourgeoisie of the ex-Habsburg lands keen to claw back some of its losses; on the other, the political machine centred on Belgrade and the court, manipulated by the propertied strata of the old Serbia. The parliamentary era ended in early 1929 not because of some inorganic intolerance between Yugoslav nations, but because a stalemate developed between these two camps, one favouring a reorganization of the state on federal lines, the other insisting on maintenance of the status quo.

Whether, in the absence of war and revolution, some sort of limited resolution of the national conflict would have been possible within bourgeois Yugoslavia, is a debate best left to the scattered remnants of the old Yugoslav ruling class living in emigré communities around the world. There are good reasons to believe (and the years of the civil war here give ample evidence) that the Yugoslav bourgeoisie was congenitally incapable of solving the national problem, even in the limited sense in which it conceived it – not least because of the ethnic heterogeneity of the territories claimed by each bourgeois fraction as its 'historic right'. It is no accident that the Yugoslav emigration is in fact not Yugoslav at all, but irrevocably split into national components still bitterly antagonistic to each other.

When, in 1941, Yugoslavia was dismembered following the invasion by Germany and its allies, the violence done to the country from above – a complete territorial partition[17] – thus combined destructively with the disintegrative process emanating from below. No political force at this point spoke for Yugoslavia, except for the government-in-exile: its voice, however, was invalidated by its 'Royal Army in the Homeland' which took the notorious name of Chetniks. The Chetniks saw their mission as being to wreak vengeance upon Croat, Moslem, Albanian, etc. 'traitors', clearing away all renegade nationalities from 'Serb' territory. Meanwhile, in the monstrous 'Independent Croat State', physical annihilation of the Serb population was embarked upon as the most urgent task.[18] In Kosovo and other Albanian-inhabited areas, now merged with fascist-controlled Albania, systematic retaliation was conducted by the puppet régime against Serb and Montenegrin minorities. In Macedonia, occupied by Bulgarian troops, the Serb population – numbering some 100,000 – was evicted across the border into German-occupied Serbia. Moslems from Bosnia, Germans and Hungarians from Vojvodina were recruited to fight the Nazi war in the Balkans. Only in Slovenia, ethnically homogeneous but now partitioned among its neighbours, was violence from the start confined to the duel between pro-fascist and anti-fascist forces. Until the formation of the Communist-dominated government in late 1943, there was little evidence that Yugoslavia could ever be reconstructed in anything like its previous form.

This apparently impossible task fell to the Communist Party of Yugoslavia, the only party which spoke in the name of the working class as a whole – even if not always in the name of Yugoslavia. In fact, until approximately mid-1942, CPY proclamations rarely mentioned Yugoslavia, concentrating instead on anti-fascist resistance and class revolution. Objectively, however, Yugoslavia was inscribed in the very nature of the Party's organization, since it existed and could continue to exist only as an all-Yugoslav institution. Defence of the Party's physical existence made it imperative to resist the combined pressures of partition and national/religious strife. That much of the organization survived the onslaught of the war was to be the first great achievement of Tito's leadership, and the first step in forging Yugoslav unity. But this time round, in contrast to 1918, this unity was to be sought not on the terrain of some common Yugoslav *nation* but around common class interests: bourgeois-democratic tasks were to be seen as the springboard for a leap into a new society, and there was to be no 'middle stage' between old and new Yugoslavia.[19] With the emergence of the Communist-led resistance movement, national differences were submerged into a wider class war splitting each nation in turn. World War Two was to cost the country 10 per cent of its population, yet by the end of it Yugoslavia emerged truly united for the first time in its history.

Nationalism versus Internationalism, 1941–48

The CPY, founded in early 1919, took a considerable time – in fact all the vital years of 1919–28 – to arrive at a policy sensitive to the multinational character of the new country. Through much of this period its position was that the national problem could be solved by local decentralization of government.[20] It therefore found itself in active opposition not only to the non-Serb population's intense reaction against Belgrade's iron-fisted rule, but also to the Comintern, which saw Yugoslavia as an artificial construction and called upon the CPY to support national struggle against it and in favour of a Socialist Balkan Federation. Under the Comintern's constant and vigilant pressure, the CPY came to recognize the right of national self-determination, including secession, of the different nationalities – this line acquiring its fullest elaboration at the Fourth Congress held in exile in Dresden in 1928. By that time, however, the national unrest in the south had died down, while in the north it came under bourgeois leadership. Between 1929 and 1934, during the dictatorship of King Alexander, all political rights were suspended and the Party almost destroyed by police terror. When a revival of political liberties of a limited kind did take place, after Alexander's assassination in 1934, the Comintern line on Yugoslavia had changed and with it the nationality policy of the CPY. No longer hostile to the European status quo, Moscow under Stalin responded to the Nazi rise to power by emphasizing collective security and the politics of popular fronts.

The Party now stressed Yugoslav unity: the right to self-determination was put to one side, and advocating the secession of disaffected regions condemned once again as nationalism. Tito's accession to the general secretaryship in 1937 was followed by the important step of returning the whole party leadership back to Yugoslavia – for the first time since 1921. The new leadership now adopted a policy which in many respects has remained operative to this day. On the one hand, a concession was made to national aspirations by creating separate communist parties (starting in the north, where the pressure of the bourgeois parties was the greatest); on the other, these separate parties were kept under firm control by the all-Yugoslav centre. A principle was thus established, which was followed right through the war and after, of linking the establishment of separate party organizations with recognition of autonomous national existence. Slovene and Croat parties were formed in 1937, separate parties for Vojvodina and Macedonia in 1943, others were formed after the war, in the period 1946–48. At the 5th Party Conference, the last before the war, a gesture was made towards the Albanian population by detaching the Regional Committee of Kosovo (itself formed in 1937) from the Montenegrin Provincial Committee and placing it under direct control of the CPY's Central Committee. Implicit in this measure was a recognition of the territorial autonomy of Kosovo and of the separate and distinct status of the Albanian population in Yugoslavia. It was felt that this step would not only facilitate recruitment of Albanian cadre, but also assist Communist groups in Albania itself – a task for which the CPY was directly responsible to the Comintern and into which it put considerable effort, prior to the founding of the Communist Party of Albania in November 1941.

Under the impact of the civil war, the CPY's nationality policy took a sharp turn to the left in the course of 1942: the Party appealed to the oppressed nationalities for their support, reminding them that any return of the old régime would also be a return to national oppression. It argued that 'Versailles Yugoslavia oppressed Croats, Slovenes and Montenegrins' and that it 'enslaved and exposed to extermination Macedonians and Albanians'. Writing in the Party's paper *Proleter*, Tito spelled out party policy as follows: 'The current national liberation struggle and national question in Yugoslavia are inseparably connected. . . . The expression "national liberation struggle" would be only a phrase, indeed a fraud, if it did not have in addition to its Yugoslav meaning also implications for each of its nations in turn . . . for Croats, Slovenes, Serbs, Macedonians, Albanians, etc.' The CPY, he went on to say, 'will never depart from the principle stated by our great teachers and leaders, Lenin and Stalin, which is the right of every nation to self-determination including secession.' Warning that the Party would also 'fight against the misuse of this right by the enemies of the people', Tito emphasized: 'The question of Macedonia, Kosovo and Metohija, Montenegro, Croatia, Slovenia, Bosnia and Herzegovina, will be easily solved, to the general satisfaction of all, by the people solving it themselves, gun in hand, through the struggle.'[21] Within the next few months separate parties for Macedonia and Vojvodina were set up, while Tito sent an envoy to the Bulgarian, Greek and Albanian parties to discuss the military and political coordination of the revolutionary struggle in the Balkans. The idea of a Balkan federation of socialist states now acquired a tangible reality and made frequent appearances in party propaganda.

However, in mid-1943 the Party quite suddenly veered away from the federal idea, in favour of discrete national revolutions in the Balkans and the preservation of existing frontiers until after the war.[22] One can only offer conjectures not incompatible with the documentary evidence so far published as to why the Yugoslav leadership changed its position so suddenly. Three factors must have influenced its policy in this direction. One of these was the dissolution of the Comintern in May 1943, absolving Moscow *de jure* of any internationalist obligations. Secondly, there was the British disapproval of a Balkan federation in any form (the early phase of the future Yalta agreement).[23] Thirdly, the Party feared at this time a British landing in the Balkans, possibly in Albania or Dalmatia.[24] The leadership was convinced that a partition of Yugoslavia was being planned by the Allies, to separate the Communist-dominated centre and west from an east hardly touched by Partisan activity during much of 1942 and 1943.[25] The Allied landing in Sicily in July 1943, which increased the military importance of guerrilla forces in the Balkans (symbolized by the arrival of a British mission at Partisan headquarters one month earlier), helped focus the CPY's mind on the future regional settlement. By forming a new government, they were to challenge directly 'in state-legal form' the royal government-in-exile and also 'create a basis from which to prevent plots by great powers against the national liberation struggle of the Yugoslav peoples'.[26] The CPY, in other words, was to put on the state mantle of Yugoslavia in order to prevent the revolution from succumbing to the British–Soviet compromise in this part of Europe.

Once its position was secure within the Yugoslav frontiers, however, the CPY turned its attention once again to the project of Balkan federation, as a guarantee in the last instance of collective security against the designs of both Moscow and London. In the same month that Tirana and Belgrade were liberated, November 1944, Kardelj visited Sofia and discussed the project with Dimitrov and other Bulgarian leaders, and similar discussions were held with the new Albanian government. By 1947, treaties of friendship had been signed with the two countries, preparing the economic and political framework of the federation. On a visit to Romania, in early 1948, Dimitrov spoke of Greece joining as well, once 'popular democracy' was installed there.[27] By now the evident independence of the CPY was increasingly worrying Stalin, particularly as it appeared that the germ of autonomy was spreading to Bulgaria and Romania; he was also greatly concerned by the British reaction to Balkan assistance for the communist side in the Greek civil war. (In January 1945, the British government had formally informed its Bulgarian counterpart that any agreement with the Yugoslavs on federation would be met by Western opposition.) In June 1948 Yugoslavia was expelled from the Cominform and isolated from Eastern Europe. This automatically put an end to the project of the Balkan federation. Specifically, Macedonian and Albanian unification was once again postponed to the distant future, as relations between Bulgaria, Albania and Yugoslavia changed into overt hostility.[28] The final crushing of the Greek revolution was the most tragic direct consequence.

A proper assessment of the correlation of subjective and objective factors which put paid to the project of Balkan federation at this time is outside the scope of this essay. It is my opinion that conditions for it did exist, certainly in 1943–44 and probably again after 1945. True, the Yugoslavs and the Bulgarians already appeared to be drawing apart *before* the great powers vetoed the project. But in 1947 both sides nevertheless resumed talks, leading to the signing of the so-called Bled agreements (to be annulled when Yugoslavia was expelled from the Cominform).[29] This essentially optimistic assessment cannot, however, obscure the fact that real problems and differences did emerge in the course of the negotiations, particularly where national unification was concerned, because of the frontier changes that would be necessary. Territorial disputes were much less amenable to rational or indeed principled resolution, once the various parties began to speak in the name of 'their' states. It could be argued that by leaving the issue of federation until after the war, rather than building it on the immediate and clear needs of the common Balkan revolution, an important chance was missed to create an alternative revolutionary pole in south-east Europe to the political hegemony of Moscow and so prevent imposition of the Yalta agreement in this part of Europe.

Kosovo in War and Revolution

At the start of the war, Kosovo, western Macedonia and southern Montenegro were attached to Albania, which had itself been formally incorporated into fascist Italy two years earlier. The bitter memories of Yugoslav rule meant that initially Italian occupation was experienced as a liberation. The interwar Yugoslav régime had conducted a policy of aggressive denationalization, forbidding schools and publications in the native language.[30] The agrarian reform which followed the end of World War One had been used to 'correct' the national composition of 'Old Serbia': Montenegrin and Serb peasants from hunger-prone areas of Croatia, Herzegovina and Montenegro were brought in as colonists to what was already one of the most densely populated areas of the Balkans. Between 1918 and 1941, when World War Two intervened, some 11,000 settlers were given land in Kosovo. The colonists received almost three times as much land as local families, a fact visible even today in the pattern of land ownership in the province; they were freed from all state and local taxes for three years, and helped with housing and essential facilities.[31] In the situation of land-hunger characteristic of pre-war Yugoslavia, the colonization was deeply resented – which is why, in the words of Veli Deva, the present Kosovo party chief, this was the only region which could boast 'more prisons and police stations than schools'. Furthermore, the state used systematic terror to make Albanians emigrate to Turkey and

Albania proper: 'hundreds of thousands' were sent to desolate regions of Anatolia between 1939 and 1941.[32]

With the Italian occupation, however, Albanians found themselves for the first time since 1912 within the frontiers of a common state. Mussolini appealed to Albanian nationalism by establishing schools, a radio and a press in the Albanian language, and by a degree of Albanization of the administration. After replacing Italy in late 1943, Germany pursued the general policy of its predecessor, even granting Albania a degree of self-government under the domination of Kosovar landowners.

According to Emin Duraku, an Albanian member of the CPY's Regional Committee for Kosovo in 1942, the Albanian population was 'unable to distinguish between the Yugoslav people and the Yugoslav government: it welcomed any change which would end twenty years of exploitation and national oppression'.[33] Tempo, Tito's envoy to Kosovo and Macedonia in early 1943, recalls that the conditions for armed struggle in Kosovo were worse than anywhere else in Yugoslavia, partly due to the nature of the terrain, but also because of the population's fear of a return to Serbian rule.[34] The party reorganization which had put the regional committee under the direct control of the CC CPY did not increase Albanian membership in any spectacular manner: new members continued to come mainly from among the children of Serb and Montenegrin settlers, whose wretched state after 1941 further encouraged the Slav inflow.[35] The Slav preponderance was a grave problem for the Party operating in this strategically important zone during the war, precisely because Serbs and Montenegrins were a minority in relation to the Albanian population. Prone itself to one (Slav) form of national chauvinism, it found it hard to contest another (Albanian) form propagated by bourgeois nationalists. It was therefore unable to intervene at the crucial moment, from around the end of 1942, when after the initial euphoria at unification the masses turned against the occupier, encouraged by the emergence of anti-fascist resistance in former Albania itself.[36] The only solution was for the young Communist Party of Albania to be drawn into 'the work of mobilizing the Albanian masses' in Kosovo too.[37]

The CPA, formed in 1941 with direct assistance from the Yugoslav Party, claimed no jurisdiction over former Yugoslav territory now in occupied Albania. Indeed, it was hardly in any position to do so, not only because of the great influence exercised over it by the CPY,[38] but also because, until mid-1943, it was little more than a pressure group confined to southern Albanian towns. From mid-1943, however, as the Italian military presence contracted to urban centres, the CPA spread into the countryside and began recruiting from the peasantry, thus transforming its fighting strength. Parallel to this growth, however, the Party acquired an increasing awareness of its national constituency, if only because of the rival presence of Balli Kombetër, a bourgeois nationalist formation whose programme included retention of the new borders, and which for this reason could hope for support from Yugoslav Albanians. In August 1943, one month prior to the Italian capitulation, the CPA held a meeting at Mukaj with Balli Kombetër at which the two organizations agreed to seek ethnic frontiers at the conclusion of the war. Under pressure from the CPY, however, the agreement was rescinded within days, opening the way for civil war in Albania.

This split between the bourgeois and communist-led resistance movements, which forms the starting moment of the Albanian revolution, compares with Tito's break with Mihajlović in 1941; in both cases, the Moscow-proffered strategy of revolution by stages was rejected in favour of permanent revolution. The Albanian Party at Mukaj faced the classic issue of twentieth-century revolutions: should the bourgeois-democratic tasks (in this case national unification) be undertaken *against* or *together with* the national bourgeoisie: as an integral part of a wider social revolution or as a first stage towards it? In Yugoslavia the CPY, faced with the same choice two years earlier, had taken up the former alternative. It was, therefore, in a strong position to intervene against an agreement whose upholding would have spelt the end of the Albanian revolution. (That the agreement was a strategic mistake has been recognized ever since by the CPA.[39]) Armed with its own experience of dealing with competing nationalisms, which only an iron discipline often oblivious to previous national injustice could keep under control, the CPY came out against the Mukaj agreement with some authority: the national question was to be subordinated to the needs of the common revolution.[40]

The break with Balli Kombetër made it even more urgent for the two communist parties to adopt a clear and principled position on the Albanian national question, not only for political but also for military reasons: Kosovo, bordering with Serbia, Macedonia and Montenegro, was important for the German takeover of collapsing Italian positions in the south-western Balkans in late 1943; Balli Kombetër in Kosovo and Chetnik formations in the Sandjak alike helped the German efforts to keep the area clear of Partisan forces. Miladin Popović, the CPY representative with the Central Committee of the CPA, urged the Yugoslav leadership to make public its commitment to Albanian postwar self-determination.[41] His advice, which Tempo accepted as realistic, was for Serbs and Albanians in Kosovo to be placed under separate command, with the latter coming under the direction of the military headquarters controlled by the CPA.[42]

In the course of its preparations for the Second Session of the Anti-Fascist People's Liberation Council of Yugoslavia (AVNOJ), at which the new Yugoslavia was to be announced to the world (that is, the

Allied leaders about to meet in Teheran), the CPY had set up a number of regional governments corresponding by and large to the the postwar federal division of Yugoslavia, precisely in order to build the new state right from the start on a federal basis. Accordingly, at the end of December 1943, the Regional Committee for Kosovo organized a civilian gathering with the aim of setting up a Regional People's Liberation Committee as the civilian authority for the area. The meeting took place just across the border in a liberated zone of Albania proper; forty-nine delegates from Kosovo took part, of whom forty were ethnic Albanians. Even this vetted body declared its wish for unification with Albania. The delegates, having welcomed the creation of the new Yugoslavia at Jajce that November, went on to adopt the following resolution: 'Kosovo and Dukagjin [Metohija] form a region in which the Albanian inhabitants preponderate: they, as always, still wish to be united with Albania. The only way for the Albanians of Kosovo and Dukagjin to unite with Albania is through common struggle with the other nations of Yugoslavia against the invaders and their forces, because this is the only way to win freedom, when all nations, including the Albanian, will be free to choose their own destiny, with the right of self-determination including secession.'[43] The CC CPY responded with heavy criticism of the parts referring to unification with Albania, as well as of the change of name from Metohija to Dukagjin. It instructed the Regional Committee not to form an Anti-Fascist Council out of the People's Liberation Committee, for fear of legitimizing the desire for unification.

The Yugoslav Party preferred to keep open the question of the future of this area of Yugoslavia. Two weeks after the Second Session of AVNOJ, Tito sent messages to both Tempo and the CC CPA, in which the question of self-determination was set to one side: 'Slogans about the union of Kosovo and Metohija with Albania today, which Miladin [Popović] supports, also the position on the command of the Albanian General Staff over Metohija, would in fact play into the hands of the enemy . . . who are trying to slice off, piece by piece, the democratic movement of the peoples of Yugoslavia and who are putting in the first place not the struggle against the fascist occupiers but the delineation of boundaries between antagonistic nationalities.'[44] 'The new Yugoslavia which is in the making will be a land of free nations, and consequently there shall be no room for national oppression of the Albanian minority either . . .'[45] However, the Albanian Party was to be asked to help Partisan mobilization in Yugoslav areas; not surprisingly, numerous clashes developed in practice – as illustrated by the taking of Debar, a town on the Macedonian–Albanian border.[46]

Throughout the war, the Yugoslav Party's policy on the national question was dictated by what it saw as the needs of the revolution. 'Was the national question in Yugoslavia to be a lever for the national liberation struggle or a lever for the occupiers and the allies? In the individual areas of Yugoslavia this question was posed differently, so that the tasks of our propaganda, even though in essence the same, were to a certain measure specific for individual cases.'[47] In Kosovo, however, the line of the party ran contrary to the national aspirations, and the CPY never gained the kind of political influence and hegemony there which it won elsewhere in the country. The result was that at the end of the war, in spite of 50,000 Albanian Partisans who had by then joined the Yugoslav People's Liberation Army, an open revolt developed in Kosovo against its return to Yugoslavia – the only instance of actual armed rebellion against the new state – and this lasted well into February 1945. Thus only six weeks after the departure of German troops the region found itself once again under military rule, this time imposed by some 30,000 soldiers of the PLA.[48] The suppression of the militant Albanian irredenta was to write one of the least glorious chapters of the Yugoslav revolution.[49]

At the end of the war, when the future of Kosovo was discussed behind closed doors by the Yugoslav leadership, it would appear that – the option of immediate full autonomy having been excluded – two alternatives were considered: partition between Montenegro, Serba and Macedonia, or limited autonomy within one of the republics. Rejecting the idea of partition, which would have meant a flagrant denial of national rights, the alternative of autonomy within Serbia was chosen. There were apparently two reasons for this choice: the sheer size of the Albanian population, and the presence of a significant Serb minority in Kosovo.[50]

Weighing different costs, including the military-strategic ones, the Party in 1945 chose to appease Serbian nationalism: separation of Kosovo would have demanded a head-on confrontation over one of the most potent nationalist symbols in the Balkans. In the difficult but also hopeful period immediately after the war, the Party chose to avoid it. The creation of the republics of Montenegro, Macedonia and Bosnia-Herzegovina, and the approaching provincial autonomy of Vojvodina, had put a final end to the dream of a Greater Serbia which had infused so much of modern Serbian history, and which even Serbia's entry into Yugoslavia in 1918 had not dispelled, given the political supremacy of its bourgeoisie within the new state. The integration of Kosovo into Serbia in 1945 was to play an important role in winning Serbian acceptance of the new constitutional order which was to divide – more in form than in fact – the Serb nation inside post-revolutionary Yugoslavia.[51]

At this stage, whatever solution was to be adopted was in any case considered to be a temporary one, because until 1948 the Yugoslav Party was hoping that creation of a Balkan federation would finally solve the Albanian problem: on joining the federation, Albania was to incorporate Kosovo.[52] However, after the Cominform resolution of June 1948, this plan came to an abrupt end. The bloody purge of the pro-Yugoslav faction inside the Albanian Party which followed, and the general persecution of all those with any Yugoslav connection whatsoever (resulting in the exodus of some four and a half thousand refugees across the border into Kosovo), helped initially to dampen disappointment at this newly confirmed division of the Albanian nation.

In the Yugoslav constitution of 1946 Kosovo was given only a limited regional autonomy, which meant concretely that internal security as well as managerial appointments were to be controlled from Belgrade. In the absence of pre-existing frontiers, new ones were drawn for the region, based on a combination of ethnic and supposedly historical criteria.[53] A significant number of Albanians were left outside it, most of them in the newly created republic of Macedonia (though this was not in itself strange, if one remembers the multi-ethnic character of most of the republics created at the end of the war). Of course, from the mid-1940s to the mid-1950s republican and provincial boundaries were in any case little more than administrative divisions, because the Party ruled tightly from the centre.

From Unitarism to the Constitution of 1974

The effect of Yugoslavia's post-1948 isolation was to weaken the federative principle established in the revolution and the perception of the country as a multi-national entity. A strong centralism – demanded by the country's acute sense of insecurity – was combined with an attempt to forge a *Yugoslav* national identity; a policy, destined to last for more than a decade, whose ideological underpinning, indebted to the Soviet concept of a 'socialist nation', derived to a great extent from the Stalinist formation of the CPY cadre (not erased overnight by the break with Moscow). This Yugoslav unitarism was grudgingly accepted by the federated South Slav nations as a measure of necessity; it fell especially hard, however, on national minorities, viewed by the state security services (in view of the propaganda emanating from Moscow) as potential fifth columns. The Albanian population, in particular, suffered greatly during this period.[54]

However, the introduction of self-management and economic reform, in a process which lasted from the early fifties to the mid-sixties, was paralleled by a political and economic decentralization that ultimately crystallized in the 1974 Constitution, which gave republics *and* provinces state autonomy. This process was not homogeneous or linear, as many rules had to come from in practice, tested or rejected according to criteria which were themselves exposed to change. But there is no doubt that the Albanian population was its main beneficiary. The region became a province (as Vojvodina had been since 1945), and both were accorded the status of constituent members of the Yugoslav federation. The provinces were seen not merely as administrative devices, but as unique products of the revolution – significantly designated as 'socialist'. The new constitution's stress on Yugoslavia as a state created by revolution, rather than a national state of the South Slavs, underlined the newly proclaimed equality of national minorities with the South Slav nations.

These constitutional changes drew, in practice, a clear line of distinction between the Albanians and other national minorities: their ethnic predominance made the Socialist Autonomous Province of Kosovo a *de facto* Albanian state, whose population could participate in the federation on a basis of equality with the Slav nations. Albanian became – alongside Serbo-Croat – an official language in the Province, and in practice predominant. The so-called 'national key' system of proportional ethnic and/or republican/provincial representation on Yugoslav public bodies was used as an instrument of positive discrimination, leading to a rapid Albanization of the provincial party and state. Kosovo acquired its own university at Priština and this, together with the Albanological Institute created soon after, played an important role in forming a qualified Albanian cadre fully conscious of their national rights.[55] The political emancipation of the Albanian nationality in the period 1968–81 was almost vertiginous, creating whole new strata of state and party officials, industrial managers and university lecturers, teachers and policemen, radio and television personalities. An enormous expansion of newspapers and journals in the Albanian language responded to the rapidly growing needs of a newly educated population. In this period too, a large number of peasants left the countryside to look for jobs in the towns, creating a new layer of young Albanian workers. Already, under the terms of the Second Five Year Plan (1952–56), Kosovo had been accorded priority as an underdeveloped region in the government allocation of funds; after 1968, its special degree of underdevelopment was recognized in the form of direct grants and particularly favourable conditions of borrowing from federal banks.[56]

The ethnic weight of the Albanians in Yugoslavia, meanwhile, was increasing steadily, putting them numerically ahead not only of Montenegrins but also of Macedonians, and on a par with Slovenes and Moslems. But the constitutional changes of 1974, however beneficial and welcome, failed to satisfy the widespread desire for an Albanian republic. For throughout the late sixties, when a public discussion of the forthcoming constitutional changes had been initiated and encouraged by the Party across the whole country, something close to a national movement had developed in Kosovo around this issue. The Kosovo leadership had finally decided not to press the demand, on the grounds that it was 'unrealistic', since unacceptable to the Serb and Montenegrin minorities, hence also to the Republic of Serbia. Without Serbia's consent, the other republics and Vojvodina would have been unwilling to endorse any such change.[57] Disappointment at the failure to make Kosovo Yugoslavia's seventh republic spilled into the streets in 1968, and there were demonstrations again in 1974–75 (though the rapid Albanization of the administration since 1968 was reflected in the gradual disappearance of anti-Serb slogans).

Clearly, political decentralization was important in strengthening national rights. It was also an acknowledgement of the essentially polycentric character of the Yugoslav state. In the post-1974 Yugoslavia, the Party took over from the state the necessary unifying role, by organizing and remaining the focus of loyalty of the Yugoslav working class as a whole. However, the rise of nationalism in Kosovo and Serbia showed the current limits of the Party's ability to perform this function: hence the extreme use of force in the province. As in Poland, this was symptomatic of a general political crisis.

Over the past fifteen years, the emergence of republican/provincial centres as spokesmen for individual national rights has often been blamed for any resurgence of nationalism. In the immediate aftermath of the Kosovo demonstrations, the Yugoslav political arena witnessed an alignment of the traditional centralizers: the unitarist current in the Party and Serbian nationalism. The presence of sizeable Serb minorities in Croatia, Bosnia and Kosovo, which naturally see themselves threatened by any growth of local particularism, has provided the material basis for a conjunction of these two forces in the history of the Yugoslav Party. Those who had always seen increased national rights as weakening Yugoslav unity could now use Kosovo as a warning about 'too much' regional independence as well as a link to the latent force of mass nationalism, now revived by the combined efforts of the Orthodox Church and a part of the 'traditional intelligentsia'.[58] This nationalism was also fanned by the outflow of the Serb population from Kosovo, which – though determined predominantly by economic factors and paralleled by movements of populations from other regions (e.g. Bosnia) – no doubt reflecting a real increased sense of insecurity among the Slav minority in the province.[59] The result has been an evident rise of nationalism in Serbia. Unable as yet to attack directly the system of self-management – itself weakened by current economic problems and, more importantly, by the continuous tendency to bureaucratization – Yugoslav unitarism has instead concentrated on advocating increased centralism of party and state, and the restriction of all forms of unfettered democracy. In this it has been aided by Western financial institutions which, concerned with Yugoslavia's ability to repay its $20,000 million foreign debt, are calling – in addition to severe deflationary measures – for greater centralization of political and economic management.

For the time being, as was shown by the Twelfth Party Congress of May 1982, this tendency is being kept in check. The Congress confirmed the status quo, rejecting attempts to return to previous modes of party organization and centralized methods of rule, as well as measures which, by weakening Kosovo's status in the federation, would have made a first step towards weakening the federal nature of the state as a whole. But it is difficult to see how this position can be maintained for much longer, and regression can be only be averted by moving forward. This must mean the creation of an Albanian republic in Yugoslavia, based on Kosovo.

It is increasingly untenable to treat a population which will within ten years be the third largest nationality as a 'national minority'. What happened in the spring of 1981 was a reminder that a solution to the 'Albanian problem' has become urgent. The alternative is to resort to periodic repression, which though it would be technically possible in the short run for the Yugoslav state, would involve enormous political cost. On the one hand, it would cause an ultimately irrepressible growth of Albanian irredentism – a phenomenon which has up to now been confined to small groups – particularly if an internal liberalization in Albania following Hoxha's departure were to provide a viable alternative pole of political identification. On the other hand, permanent repression would pose an obvious threat to the internal political stability of the country as a whole, since few could view with equanimity the armed forces putting down a popular national movement. Creation of a political climate in which the transformation of Kosovo's status is seen not as a threat to the Serb national identity but as a gain for intra-national solidarity is a necessary precondition.

Such a move is important for the future of Yugoslav–Albanian relations as well. When, after the invasion of Czechoslovakia by Warsaw Pact forces in August 1968, Albania made a first tentative attempt to mend its severed links with its northern neighbour, it met with a ready and immensely positive response. Yugoslavia opened its frontiers with Albania, and Kosovo became the host for many cultural and scientific exchanges with Albanian artists and intellectuals.[60] The growing warmth between the two countries throughout the seventies found its symbolic peak in their joint celebration in 1978 of the centenary of the foundation of the League of Prizren. Clearly, however, these developments were also seen as something of a threat to the Hoxha régime in Tirana, which restricted the entry of Yugoslavs into Albania and never allowed its own citizens to visit its neighbour freely. Thus the 1981 events in Kosovo, and the rapid cooling of Albanian–Yugoslav relations, must in reality have come as a relief to the dominant tendency inside the Albanian Party. Tirana broke a precedent by officially supporting the creation of a Kosovo republic within Yugoslavia, thus laying itself open to the charge of interference in its neighbour's internal affairs. Kosovo became a weapon to use against any opposition tendency in the Albanian Party. The sudden death in December 1981 of Mehmet Shehu, the last member apart from Hoxha of the original leadership which led the country to revolution and independence, only confirms this. In November 1982 Hoxha was to accuse his closest comrade-in-arms for almost forty years of having been an agent of both the CIA and the KGB, entrusted by Belgrade with the task of poisoning him and delivering Albania into Yugoslav clutches!

Conclusion

From the point of view of the 1941–45 revolution's programme, the Albanian cause should have fared no differently than that of other Yugoslav nationalities, since the principle of national self-determination which the programme enshrined – and on which any lasting solution rests – is universal and not selective, refusing any distinction between 'state-building' and apparently 'marginal' nations. The Albanian national question became a 'problem' in the second decade of this century, and has since vitally affected both Yugoslavia and Albania: in this common history, the Communist-led revolution represented a vital discontinuity, opening the perspective of its final resolution within a Balkan-wide socialist transformation. In an effort to ward off nationalist incantations from both sides, an attempt has been made in the preceding pages to draw a balance-sheet of the interaction between 'subjective forces' and 'objective resistance' which made this solution finally impossible, giving the problem its present form and posing it as a challenge to Yugoslav socialism. Against the argument that nationalism is a force stronger than socialism, or that Yugoslavia is inherently condemned to periodic nationalist explosions, one need only point to the original revolution which was won against both an internal intra-national war and international reaction because it was posited on the firm ground of proletarian solidarity. Its articulation at that time was the YCP. If this articulation is no longer functioning, then this points to a deep malaise in the body politic of Yugoslav socialism.

It would indeed be impossible to conclude this analysis without a direct reference to the role the Party has played in the current revival of nationalism in Yugoslavia. In a very real sense, as indicated by many of the debates that have raged in the country over the past two years, the national question has been used as the screen behind which a major inner-party struggle is taking place, thus paralysing the political institutions at a time when Yugoslavia faces its most serious economic crisis since 1948. The limited possibility for the working class to assert independently its own transnational interests combines negatively with the Party's determination (especially since 1968) to stifle any wider growth of socialist critique of its practice, be it outside or inside its framework. In a situation thus defined, nationalism can and will grow – indeed, it may be fostered consciously as a substitute for class identification. The rebellion and repression in Kosovo, therefore, speak of a generalized political crisis much more serious even than the accumulation of economic problems confronting the country in the current decade. Self-management in the hands of the bureaucracy, and national equality championed by regional party bosses, have shown themselves an ineffective medium for tackling the acute needs of this poorest area of Yugoslavia. As in Poland in the same year, the answer to a political crisis was sought in the use of the army, special police and the institution of martial law. And as in Poland, surely, a positive answer cannot be envisaged outside a framework of properly functioning proletarian democracy.

Suspended between a belated national emancipation and persistent economic backwardness, the demand for an Albanian republic in Kosovo has acquired great symbolic power, further cemented by the bloodshed of last year and the continued imprisonment of some six hundred students, workers and peasants from the province. What is at stake is not only a completion of the process started by the defeat of unitarism in 1966, but also the whole image of the Yugoslav state and the revolution that had brought it into being. It is a sharp reminder of the urgency of a radical re-examination of the state of socialism in Yugoslavia today. For Albania as well, friendly relations with its socialist neighbour are vital for ending the great isolation and internal repression which have become synonymous with the revolution there: any hope of Albania's reintegration into its Balkan hinterland is inexorably linked to improvement of relations with Yugoslavia. Kosovo, between Yugoslavia and Albania, holds the key to their common future.

(July 1983)

Notes

1. Kosovo student demands echoed those put forward a decade and a half earlier in 1968 – an *annus mirabilis* in Yugoslavia as in many other countries in the world – when students in many centres attacked the increasing bureaucratization, high unemployment and wide social differentiation caused by an uncontrolled introduction of market mechanisms, in the name of an authentic self-management. This radical student movement reached its apogee with the occupation of Belgrade University, renamed the '*Karl Marx' Red University*. See D. Plamenić. 'The Belgrade Student Insurrection', *NLR 54*, March–April 1969.
2. Alexander Ranković was Yugoslavia's Interior Minister continuously from 1945 until his fall from power in 1966. He was subsequently held personally responsible for atrocities committed against the Albanian population and other minorities in the years between 1952 and his fall, and indeed for many other abuses of power during this time. In addition, he became a symbol of Serb dominance in the postwar period, though little

conclusive evidence has been produced to show that he was indeed a Great-Serb chauvinist. He did, however, resist both decentralization and liberalization in the 1960s, in favour of a unitarist Yugoslav state, with limited freedom to dissent. This stance (and his use of the security apparatus to further his policies) ultimately caused his downfall.

3. For a detailed account of the harsh sentences handed out in the first six months after the spring events, see 'Wrong Turn in Kosovo', Part I, Chapter 1, in this volume. In October 1982, several hundred students at the universities of Belgrade, Zagreb and Ljubljana signed a petition protesting at the political nature of the Kosovo trials (pp. 13–14 above).

4. Throughout this text Kosovo refers to the territory of the Socialist Autonomous Province of Kosovo, which before 1968 was called 'Kosovo and Metohija' (or Kosmet), Metohija being the Serb name for the western part of the Kosovo plain, once the property of the bishopric of Peć. Geographical names are given in their Serbo-Croat form, as recognized by international convention, though there are good reasons for Yugoslav practice to adopt Albanian spelling.

5. Most of these figures are to be found in Martin Shrenk et al., *Yugoslavia – World Bank Country Economic Report*, London 1979, chapter 11.

6. The Albanian language has two literary forms, Geg and Tosk, based on the respective dialects spoken by the eponymous two main peoples making up the Albanian nation. Geg is spoken by the Albanians in Yugoslavia and in the northern part of Albania (north of the river Shkumbi), while Tosk is spoken in the south of the country as well as by Albanians in Greece. In 1969 both Kosovo and Albania adopted the so-called New Standard Albanian, which combines the two variants, as the language of instruction.

7. The epicentre of Serb mediaeval history is located in Kosovo. In 1348 the Serbian prince Stephan Dushan crowned himself Emperor of the Serbs, the Greeks, the Bulgars and the Albanians and established his capital at Prizren. A national church, an indispensable condition of independence from Byzantium, was created at this time by the transformation of the Peć bishopric into a patriarchate. In 1389 the final vestige of Serbian independence was crushed by the Ottoman army on the plain of Kosovo (quite close to Priština) in a battle in which much of the Serbian ruling class was destroyed. This battle was subsequently commemorated in a cycle of epic poems which, passed orally from generation to generation, preserved the memory of Serbian statehood. The ethnic composition of the area in the fourteenth century, and whether and how this changed in the centuries that followed, is subject to dispute: a dispute which often pits Serbian against Albanian historians. A division of historical schools along ethnic lines is not, of course, solely a Balkan phenomenon. But debate on this subject has acquired a new lease of life in Yugoslavia since the recent events in Kosovo, and what once seemed simply a factual disagreement has now become a terrain for nationalist propaganda on both sides.

8. Dushan's empire was not a national state in the modern sense, and the formation of the modern Serbian nation bears little direct relation to Kosovo and the empire of Tsar Dushan. The movement of Serb population from Kosovo and Macedonia to the north and, more importantly, from the karst areas of Montenegro and Herzegovina to the northeast, round the end of the seventeenth century became a steady flow. But it was the emergence of a merchant bourgeoisie, playing the role of cadet partner to its more powerful Austrian neighbour in the gradual opening of the Ottoman lands to European goods and capital in the late eighteenth and early nineteenth century, that saw the creation of a new national centre of gravity in the north.

9. Dushan's heritage was also important in providing legitimacy for the newly created institution of monarchy (1882) in what was a predominantly peasant and relatively egalitarian society. A mystical fusion of Kosovo, Orthodoxy and 'Serbdom' inspires Serbian nationalism to this day. In May 1982, *Pravoslavlje (Orthodoxy)*, official organ of the Serbian Church, published an 'Appeal for Protection of the Serb population and its Holy Places in Kosovo'. Addressed to the highest organs of the state, the Appeal refers to Kosovo in the following terms: 'There is no more precious word for the Serb nation, no dearer reality, no more sacred object past, present or future, than the existence and holiness of Kosovo. . . . The Serb nation has been fighting its battle of Kosovo without a break, fighting for just a remembrance of its being, for its conscious presence and survival in these lands, from 1389 until today.' *NIN*, 23 May 1982; *Danas*, 1 June 1982.

10. Leon Trotsky, reporting from the front during the Balkan Wars, records this experience of a young Serbian officer: 'When the soldiers entered the plain of Kosovo, they became very excited. I was even surprised at the way they reacted. Kosovo, Gračanica, – these names were handed down from generation to generation, repeated over and over in folksongs. The soldiers started to ask whether we should soon reach Bakarno Guvno – that's near Prilep [in southern Macedonia]. Apparently, this was the furthest limit of the old Serbian kingdom. I must confess I had not known that. But the soldiers were firmly convinced that when they got to Bakarno Guvno that would mean that our task was completed.' *The War Correspondence of Leon Trotsky*, New York 1980, pp. 123–4. Trotsky gives a grim picture of the scorched-earth policy practised by the Balkan armies in the newly 'liberated' areas; more brutal than the regular Serbian army were the auxiliaries or *Chetniks*. As Dimitrije Tucović, the great pre-1915 Serbian socialist, bitterly commented, not only did thousands of Serbian peasants drafted as soldiers give their lives for the colonizing ambitions of their bourgeoisie, but they also earned in the process great hatred from the Albanian people. *Srbija i Arbanija*, Belgrade 1914.

11. To be sure, the break-up of the large estates would in any case have been more difficult here since, unlike in Serbia or Bulgaria, the landowners were of the same faith and nationality as the peasantry and did not depart with the Turkish administration. The Albanian pursuit of independence was fatally impaired by the beys' fear lest the transfer of power unleash social unrest in the countryside – as it indeed did.

12. The formation of Fan Noli's government in 1924 provided the occasion for the only serious attempt to conduct an agrarian reform in Albania prior to the revolution of 1941–44. Noli's government lasted only six months: a reactionary coalition of tribal chiefs and landowners, aided by Yugoslav and White Russian units, as well as by the British Ambassador to Tirana, sent Noli into exile and replaced him by Ahmet Zogu, later King Zog I. Fan Noli was one of the rare Albanian leaders who favoured the country joining a Balkan federation. His fall marked the start of the growth of Communist influence among the Albanian intelligentisia.

13. Though the idea of a union with Serbia was widely popular in Montenegro (outside the narrow circle of King Nikola's supporters) for historical, economic and political reasons, the manner in which it was carried out and the suppression of Montenegro's state identity together made the merger appear more as an annexation to Serbia than as a voluntary entry into the newly created South Slav state. Consequently, a large-scale rebellion soon broke out, which lasted in guerrilla form well into the mid-20s and resembled resistance movements of the same period in Kosovo and Macedonia. See Dimitrije Vujović, *Ujedinjenje Crne Gore i Srbije*, Titograd 1962.

14. In this they were only partly successful, because large parts of the Yugoslav coast were used as a bribe to entice Italy to enter the war on the Allied side. Much of this territory was regained during World War Two, with the important exception of Trieste.

15. The strongly anti-communist Serbian monarchy was intended to play an important role in keeping the red menace out of southeastern Europe – for much of the interwar period Yugoslavia had no diplomatic relations with the Soviet Union. The constitution of 1921 gave the king extensive powers – republicanism was not the birthmark of the Slovene and Croat bourgeoisies either.

16. Is the legitimacy of contemporary Yugoslavia derived from its bourgeois predecessor or from the revolution of 1941–45? This is a question still debated within the country today. In June 1982, for example, a seminar was organized by the League of Communists of Serbia around the theme: 'Federalism, Autonomy and Self-Management'. Some of the participants argued in favour of the former thesis: Yugoslavia is the expression of a centuries-old South Slav desire for unification; hence the provinces of Vojvodina and Kosovo are part of the Republic of Serbia by historic right; the legitimacy of the federal units, particularly of the APs, has been conferred upon them by the central state and the existing constitution should be corrected to take this into account. This open challenge to the principles of the revolutionary founding of the new Yugoslavia and national self-determination – two principles which underpin the constitution of 1974 – not surprisingly was vigorously challenged, particularly by the participants from the APs. The seminar was reported in *Danas*, 22 June 1982 and *NIN*, 27 June 1982.

17. Germany incorporated one-third of Slovenia, while the other two-thirds, including the capital Ljubljana, went to Italy. Italy also took most of Dalmatia with its principal ports and the Adriatic islands; Montenegro became an Italian protectorate; parts of Croatia, Bosnia and Herzegovina were occupied by Italian forces; and Kosovo and western Macedonia were given to Italian Albania. Hungary was awarded the Bačka, Baranja, Medumurje and Prekomurje regions of Vojvodina and Croatia. Serbia was reduced to what it had been before the Balkan Wars, and occupied by German troops: a quisling government was set up under General Milan Nedić. The Banat region of Vojvodina remained nominally part of Serbia, but was given its own administration in which the local German minority ruled. An Independent State of Croatia was set up (comprising historic Croatia, Slavonia, Bosnia-Herzegovina and part of Dalmatia) and put under the control of Ante Pavelić's fascist Ustashe mcvement; an Italian duke was made its king. See Jozo Tomasevich. *War and Revolution in Yugoslavia 1941–5: The Chetniks*, Stanford 1975.

18. The Ustashe, an extreme Croat nationalist movement fostered by Italian fascism in the thirties and numbering no more than a few hundred supporters, were hoisted to power by the invading German army and proceeded to 'govern' this puppet state in accordance with the military needs of the occupation forces. The bloody nature of Ustasha rule is explained not only by an ideology of 'blood and soil' borrowed from fascism and concepts of social organization harking back to the Middle Ages, but also by its lack of popular roots. The truly macabre story of this experiment is lucidly analysed by Fikreta Jelić-Butić, *Ustaśe i NDH*, Zagreb 1972.

19. 'We did not want to stop halfway: to overthrow the king and destroy the monarchy, come to power and share it with the representatives of the capitalist class. . . . This was the will neither of the working class nor of the great majority of the Yugoslav people. We decided, therefore, to enter boldly on the road of complete liquidation of capitalism in Yugoslavia' (Josip Broz-Tito, 'Political Report', *Fifth Congress of the CYP*, Belgrade 1948). Quoted in Michael Löwy, *Combined and Uneven Development – The Theory of Permanent Revolution*, London 1981, p. 140.

20. There were many reasons for the CPY's early disregard of the national question, of which the following are perhaps the most important. First, it had inherited the positive response of social-democracy in the majority of South Slav areas to the national liberation and unification achieved through the creation of Yugoslavia. Secondly, the Party was worried about the deleterious effects of nationalism on its ability to act on straight 'class issues'. Thirdly, it was dominated by Serbian socialists who identified more intimately with the creation of the new state. A chilling illustration of where this attitude sometimes led it is provided by an incident on 2 August 1923 at Skopje, when 'Serbian gendarmes had fired into an assembly held to commemorate the Ilinden uprising [of Macedonians against Ottoman rule in 1903]. Ten persons were killed. On the following day the Skopje Party Committee organized a demonstration against "Great Serb hegemony and Belgrade terror". The CC CPY expelled eight Skopje ringleaders from the Party, characterizing them as chauvinists and enemies of the working class. To ensure that the culprits had learned their lesson, the Party published their names in a leaflet. The eight were arrested and allegedly passed away in Belgrade's Glavnjača Prison' (S. Palmer and R. King, *Yugoslav Communism and the Macedonian Question*, Archon Books 1971, p. 29). This attitude led to violent inter-party struggle around the national question.

21. *Proleter*, December 1942.

22. Svetozar Vukmanović-Tempo, sent to discuss the idea of Balkan Federation and, related to this, the creation of a Balkan General Staff, was caught in mid-flight by the change in line and had to revise his positions, notably with respect to the unification and autonomy of Macedonia (where he was when he received his new instructions). Some of the relevant correspondence is quoted in Palmer and King, op. cit., pp. 102–6.

23. 'After the dissolution of the Comintern, any organ of coordination and cooperation of the communist parties and "resistance movements" on a regional basis became increasingly unacceptable to Moscow, and therefore also to the Greek communists under its influence. This idea was also unacceptable to Great Britain, whose government

feared all forms of organization of anti-fascist forces in the Balkans outside its control, especially under communist influence. This is something the leadership . . . had to take into account' (Branko Petranović, *AVNOJ-Revolucionarna Smena Vlasti*, Belgrade 1976, pp. 182–3). An authoritative account of Allied wartime policy towards the Balkans is Elizabeth Barker, *British Policy in South-East Europe in the Second World War*, London 1976.

24. In preparation for the Allied invasion of Italy, the British High Command organized a number of diversionary actions in Greece, whose idea was to persuade the Germans of an imminent Allied landing in the Balkans – in which they were successful. F. W. D. Deakin, who led the first British mission to the Partisans, writes: 'As to Tito, his analysis followed closely that of Hitler, but its confirmation, in his eyes, lay in the "50–50" so-called agreement between Churchill and Stalin. He was convinced that a political division of Yugoslavia had been decided on this occasion and would be implemented, before the end of the hostilities, by the advance of the Red Army from the east, and the landing of Anglo-American forces from the west.' See 'The Myth of the Allied Landing in the Balkans', in P. Auty and R. Clogg (eds), *British Policy towards Wartime Resistance in Yugoslavia and Greece*, London 1975, p. 93. In fact, the British did push for an Anglo-American occupation of the Balkans at this time, only to have their plans vetoed by the Americans, who remained determined to concentrate instead on north-west Europe. See Barker, op. cit., p. 116.

25. Colonel W. S. Bailey, British representative with the Chetniks, proposed in February 1943 a line of demarcation which 'would run roughly from the Yugoslav–Bulgarian frontier on the Danube in the north-west, to the Montenegrin–Albanian border in the south-west' (S. W. Bailey, 'British Policy towards General Draža Mihajlović', in Auty and Clogg, op. cit., p. 73). How the British were to enforce this plan short of sending in troops was, of course, a mystery. But it was fear of such developments that led the Partisans to make a desperate (and unsuccessful) break into Serbia in Autumn 1943. Petranović, op. cit., p. 180.

26. Petranović, op. cit., pp. 207–8.

27. Robert Lee Wolff, *The Balkans in Our Time*, New York 1967, p. 320.

28. The unification of Albania and Yugoslavia was seen by a significant part of the Yugoslav leadership as the only way to solve the Albanian question in Yugoslavia. This view is expressed by Milovan Djilas: 'I considered, as did many others, that unification – with the truly voluntary agreement of the Albanian leaders – would not only be of direct value to both Yugoslavia and Albania, but would also finally put an end to the traditional intolerance and conflict between the Serbs and the Albanians. Its particular importance, in my opinion, lay in the fact that it would make possible the amalgamation of our considerable and compact Albanian minority with Albania as a separate republic in the Yugoslav–Albanian federation. Any other solution to the problem of the Albanian national minority seemed impracticable to me, since the simple transfer of Yugoslav territory inhabited by Albanians would arouse violent opposition in the Yugoslav Communist Party itself' (*Conversations with Stalin*, London 1962, p. 130).

29. The documents signed by Tito and Dimitrov at Bled in August 1947 and Evksinograd the following month have been published in Slobodan Nešović, *Bledski sporazumi (The Bled Agreements)*, Zagreb 1979.

30. Already, under Ottoman rule, Albanians were the only nationality enjoying the dubious distinction of being denied schools in their own language. Consequently, illiteracy was very high: the 1921 census found 97 per cent of the Albanians interviewed to be illiterate. See British Foreign Office, *Yugoslavia*, Geographical Handbook Series, 1944, vol. 2, p. 244.

31. 350,000 hectares were apparently earmarked for colonization, but the reform was ultimately limited here, as in other areas, by political horse-trading between the local landowners and the main Serbian parties. See Milovan Obradović, *Agrarna reforma i kolonizacija na Kosovu 1919–1941*, Priština 1981; and Jozo Tomasevich, *Peasants, Politics and Economic Change in Yugoslavia*, Stanford 1955, pp. 358–61.

32. Peter Prifti, *Socialist Albania since 1944*, MIT Press 1978, pp. 226–7. Yugoslav inter-war governments tried to solve the Albanian problem by mass expulsion into

Turkey. To encourage the peasants to leave the land, the police were allowed complete freedom of action. Methods used involved refusal to recognize old land deeds, ruthless tax collections, religious harassment, destruction of Albanian cemeteries, distributing weapons to the colonists, inciting riots which would then be bloodily suppressed, setting fire to Albanian villages and town quarters, etc.

33. Svetozar Vukmanović-Tempo quotes this in a letter he sent to the central committees of the Leagues of Communists of Kosovo, Serbia and Yugoslavia, protesting an unfavourable review by Ali Hadri, the well-known Kosovo historian. Hadri had accused Tempo of confusing the pro-fascist sentiment of the Albanian beys with the antifascist mood of the masses. Tempo's reply to Hadri was never published in full. Only after the Kosovo events of 1981 did a popular and chauvinistic Belgrade weekly publish some parts (see *Ilustrovana Politika*, 9 June 1981). Hadri's counter-reply was neither sought nor published; in October 1982 he was expelled from the Party and dismissed from his post at the University of Priština for his refusal to cooperate with the authorities in purging staff and students.

34. Svetozar Vukmanović-Tempo, *Revolucija koja teče – Memoari (Revolution in Flow – Memoirs)*, Belgrade 1971, p. 338.

35. In 1942, when Duraku was writing, out of 343 members of the regional party only 52 were Albanian. Of these 52, 17 were from Albania itself, having emigrated there before the war, usually in search of education. Fadil Hoxha, present-day Kosovo's representative on Yugoslavia's eight-person state Presidency, was one of these.

36. In his report to the CC CPY of 8 August 1943, Tempo argued that it was essential to organize the Party so that it 'could successfully cope with the great chauvinistic hatred which indeed exists between the Albanians and the Serbs' (quoted in Palmer and King, p. 95).

37. 'The extent of chauvinist hatred of Albanians against the Serbs is made clear by the fact that one of our units, which was composed of Albanians, was surrounded by over two thousand armed Albanian peasants and the battle went on for several hours until the Albanians saw that it was an Albanian unit. They then departed and left the Italians holding the bag' (Tempo, ibid.).

38. It is no exaggeration to say that all the key decisions made by the CPA in the war years were made under Yugoslav influence. These include: formation of the People's Liberation Committees and of the Anti-Fascist People's Liberation Council of Albania as new and alternative state institutions; the setting up of a proper military structure for the People's Liberation Army, and of the so-called Proletarian Brigades which were the shock troops of the revolution; non-cooperation with the British and nationalist forces. Worried that the Allies might land in Albania, Tito encouraged the Albanian Party in October 1944 to set up a Provisional Democratic Government, which would confront the Anglo-American troops with a *fait accompli*; Hoxha became the first Prime Minister. See Stephen Peters, 'Ingredients of the Communist Takeover in Albania', in Thomas T. Hammond (ed.) *The Anatomy of Communist Takeovers*, Yale 1975. Peters was a member of the American military mission to Albania in 1944–45.

39. See, for example, *History of The Party of Labour of Albania*, Tirana 1971, pp. 168–71.

40. But subordination does not mean suppression: the Yugoslav Party after the summer of 1943 was guilty of treating the Albanian right to self-determination as an essentially tactical question rather than an inalienable right. This attitude not only hampered the development of the revolution in the Albanian-inhabited areas of Yugoslavia, it also helped to fan nationalism inside the CPA itself. The CPY, in other words, shares with the Hoxha faction inside the Albanian Party responsibility for the success with which Stalin, five years later, severed links between Albania and Yugoslavia that had been forged in a common revolution.

41. 'We have always postponed the question of self-determination to the future. But it is impossible to mobilize the Albanian masses to fight against their "liberators" without the CC [CPY] giving some concrete declaration in support of the self-determination of the Albanian people in Yugoslavia.' Miladin Popović, Archives of the Albanian Party of Labour, *Zëri i popullit*, May 1981.

42. Tempo commented: 'I think that both of these measures would indeed facilitate the

rallying of the Albanian masses to the national liberation struggle', but he warned that they might provoke a nationalist backlash which could be exploited by the Chetniks. Palmer and King, op. cit., p. 96.

43. This resolution, together with other conference materials, was duly sent to the CC CPY with the request that the Party popularize the newly established committee over Radio Free Yugoslavia (stationed in Moscow), and that the latter sometimes mention the Albanian struggle. See Ramadan Marmullaku, *Albania and the Albanians*, London 1975, p. 143 .

44. Palmer and King op. cit., pp. 105–6.

45. Marmullaku, ibid.

46. Debar (Dibra), a town with a predominantly Albanian population on the Yugoslav side of the Albanian–Macedonian border, was liberated in October 1943 by an Albanian Partisan detachment commanded by Haxhi Lleshi, subsequently President of the People's Republic of Albania. A People's Liberation Committee was set up, but this provoked a sharp reaction from the Yugoslav side, which accused Lleshi of pandering to Albanian chauvinism by excluding Macedonians from it. Writing to Lleshi about this incident, Hoxha complained: 'In the present situation . . . it is impossible for us to implement our correct line concerning the question of the border, for if we were to act according to Tempo's advice and leave Dibra, not only will the Macedonians be unable to control the situation, but the [Balli Kombetër] reaction will strike heavily against them and us together.' *Selected Works*, Tirana 1974, pp. 206–7.

47. Milovan Djilas, *Fifth Congress of the CPY*, op. cit., p. 271.

48. Branko Petranović, *NIN*, 31 May 1981.

49. Paul Shoup, *Communism and the Yugoslav National Question*, New York 1968, p. 103.

50. According to Obradović, 34.4 per cent of the Kosovo population in 1939 was Slav, of which 9.2 per cent were newly settled (op. cit., p. 223).

51. Speaking after Kosovo was established as an Autonomous Region of the People's Republic of Serbia, Ranković declared at a meeting of the Anti-Fascist Council of Serbia in April 1945 (the first of its kind held in Serbia) that the measure was the best answer to those who trumpet the danger of partitioning Serbian territory, who make accusations that the National Liberation War will weaken Serbia to the advantage of Croats and others. *Borba*, 8 April 1945.

52. When Enver Hoxha visited Belgrade in 1946, he was apparently told by Tito that 'Kosovo and other regions inhabited by Albanians belong to Albania and we shall return them to you. But not now, because the Great Serb reaction would not accept such a thing.' See editorial in *Zëri i popullit*, 17 May 1981. Yugoslav party officials have subsequently denied that such an exchange ever took place.

53. The boundary between Macedonia and Serbia (hence Kosovo) closely follows the line advocated by IMRO after 1934. See H. R. Wilkinson, *Maps and Politics*, Liverpool 1951, pp. 232–310.

54. Albanians were not allowed to designate themselves as Albanians, but were called 'Šiptars', a vulgarized term for Shqipëri. Up to 1966, any Albanian showing his national flag was liable to imprisonment. Only primary education was conducted in the Albanian language. 'Serious violations of legality and constitutional rights of citizens of Albanian nationality took place, and individuals were physically maltreated and even killed' (Stipe Šuvar, *Nacije i medunacionalni odnosi*, Zagreb 1970, p. 122). During the notorious search for arms in 1956, some 30,000 people were manhandled and around one hundred killed by the state security forces. The memory of police terror conducted against the Albanian population prior to 1966 is still alive in their collective memory. This is illustrated by the recent court case involving Amrush Sailevksi, Albanian street vendor of taped music in Skopje, a crippled father of nine children. He appeared in court in May 1982 charged with fomenting counter-revolution. What he had done was to sell cassettes in which 'figured not only the distant and terrible Albanian history, the sins of ousted feudal lords and the bourgeoisie, but also the injustice and the excesses of the Ranković period'. One of the songs told the story of 'Ranković and his friends'. 'In the [1956] attack on Kosovo, he conducted black torture and maltreated the people, seeking rifles

and machine-guns from those who had them and those who did not. Our sons were left bleeding in side-streets. You Ranković, who put the Yugoslav people to shame, and even more the people of Kosovo and Metojija, why did you leave mothers with broken arms, fathers without sons, sisters without brothers? Tito calls from his office: Why, in the living God's name do you not obey and why do you torture the Albanian people in Kosovo? Then one day something else happened: the UDBA [secret police] hit with the police and killed two young heroes [including] Shaban Sadiku, that young man. You, Ranković, let the darkness swallow you, your body I want to cut with a knife. Did the Party teach you so? This was not taught by the Party, which fought to give us the right to make this our home.' Sailevski was also charged with tearing Tito's picture and swearing at him for not giving Kosovo its own republic before he died. *Danas*, 25 May 1982. *Danas* does not report what happened to Sailevski.

55. 'The proportion of children undergoing elementary education in Kosovo today equals that for the whole country, i.e. 96 per cent. The total number of pupils and students amounts to 470,000, which means that every third inhabitant is attending school. With its 50,000 university students, or 300 for every 10,000 inhabitants, Kosovo is in the first place in the country and among the first in the world. The University has nine faculties, an Academy and seven higher schools of learning.' 'Events in the SAP Kosovo', *Review of International Affairs*, Belgrade 1981, p. 8. The high number of university students in Kosovo is a consequence of the relative youth of the population; if one relates the absolute figures to the size of the relevant age group, Kosovo conforms to the all-Yugoslav pattern.

56. 'Between 1961 and 1965, 403.5 million dinars, or 28.8 per cent of total resources, were allocated to Kosovo from the fund for the Development of Underdeveloped Regions. In the next medium term period, the sum allocated from the Fund to Kosovo came to 2,667.2 million dinars, or 30 per cent of the total reserves of the Fund. For the five year period between 1971 and 1975 the Province received from the Fund 8,181.6 million dinars: Kosovo's share in the Fund's resources increased to 33.2 per cent. In the medium term period which has just ended (1976–80), the Fund set aside for Kosovo 28,467 million dinars or 37 per cent of the Fund's total resources for the development of underdeveloped republics and the Province of Kosovo' ('Events in SAP Kosovo', p. 8).

57. Marmullaku, op. cit., p. 150. Ramadan Marmullaku, an Albanian from Kosovo, at the time of his book's publication occupied the post of Secretary-Counsellor on the LCY Praesidium's Commission for International Relations. A specialist in Balkan affairs and particularly those concerning Albania, he was dispatched in 1982 as Yugoslav ambassador to Nigeria.

58. Albanian history is often treated in a narrowly nationalist manner by Serbian historians. This is illustrated by the often acrimonious debate which has accompanied the production of the second edition of the *Encylopaedia Jugoslavica*. Since the 1981 demonstrations, the Albanian entries have come under heavy fire, particularly the Illyrian origins of the population and the denomination of the Prizren League as historically progressive. Matters became quite absurd when the CC of the League of Communists of Serbia, meeting before the Twelfth Party Congress, addressed itself to these problems often in the most inappropriate terms. The Albanian members were accused of falling, by their insistence on the ethnic specificity of the Albanian nation, into the same racial trap as Hitler with his Aryan myth! *Danas*, 11 May 1982; *NIN*, 6 June 1982.

59. Some 15,000 Serbs left Kosovo between 1968 and 1971, and another 30,000 (estimated) left over the next decade. Since the unrest, a further 9,000 have either left or applied to leave, which represents an acceleration of the outflow – up to 1981 the numbers had not gone beyond the general pattern of inter-regional migration. See Miroslav Lalović, *NIN*, 11 and 15 August 1982. The exodus of the Serb population from Kosovo has become a principal rallying cry of Serb nationalists, and compares with the similar reaction in Croatia when, in the 1960s and 1970s, hundreds of thousands of Croats left to look for work in Western Europe. The Albanian leadership in Kosovo could be criticized for not taking early and energetic measures to prevent anti-Slav incidents in the province.

60. After diplomatic relations were restored in 1971, trade expanded rapidly to reach $116

million in 1980, four times the figure for 1978. In spite of the Kosovo events, economic exchange has continued to improve, until today Yugoslavia is Albania's single largest trading partner. The proposed Shkodër–Titograd railway line, for which the two governments have already allocated funds, will for the first time connect Albania into the international railway network.

Nationalism Captures the Serbian Intelligentsia

(a) Petition by Belgrade Intellectuals

In January 1986 some two hundred prominent Belgrade intellectuals signed a petition to the Yugoslav and Serbian national assemblies of an obscurantist, nationalist and anti-democratic character. The petition effectively accused the authorities of national treason in Kosovo: 'Everyone in this country who is not indifferent has long ago realized that the genocide in Kosovo cannot be combated without deep social . . . changes in the whole country. These changes are unimaginable without changes likewise in the relationship between the Autonomous Provinces and the Republic of Serbia . . . Genocide cannot be prevented by the . . . gradual surrender of Kosovo and Metohija – to Albania: the unsigned capitulation which leads to a politics of national treason.'

Belgrade, 21 January 1986
To the Assembly of SFRJ
To the Assembly of SR Serbia

In October 1985, 2,016 Serbs from Kosovo and Metohija sent a petition to the assemblies of SR Serbia and SFRJ, subsequently signed by further thousands of signatories, in which the unbearable condition of the Serb nation in Kosovo was described, and which demanded radical measures that would ensure it all constitutional rights and prevent its forced exodus from its ancient hearths.

All those who have been shaken by the suffering of Serbs and other nationalities in Kosovo and Metohija, all those who are concerned for the destiny of Serbia and Yugoslavia, all those in whom conscience and sense of responsibility are not dead, were amazed and dejected by the authorities' reaction to this petition: by the threatening response of the officials in Kosovo and by the attitude of the highest Serbian and all-Yugoslav authorities.

Those whose first concern should be for the destiny of their nation have shown themselves to be deaf to its desperate cry and its awoken consciousness – they have shown neither sympathy for its sacrifices nor determination to prevent its sufferings, contesting its right to express the feeling of historic desorientation to which the nation has been brought through no fault of its own – its right to seek help and protection from its own state.

The demand for justice and equality expressed in this Petition-Plebiscite has been condemned as an enemy act and qualified as rebellion, instead of being taken by the government as an encouragement to re-examine itself, come to its senses and understand that time is running out for these people stripped of their rights, and that they now are trying to organize themselves and take responsibility for their own destiny. No nation willingly gives up its right to exist and the Serb nation is not and will not be an exception.

In the last twenty years, 200,000 people have been moved out of Kosovo and Metohija, more than 700 settlements have been ethnically 'purged', the emigration is continuing with unabated force, Kosovo and Metohija are becoming 'ethnically pure', the aggression is crossing the borders of the Province.

The political condemnation of the Petition has therefore moved us, the undersigned, to turn to public opinion with an appeal to support its demands for a radical change of the situation in Kosovo and Metohija. Political reason insists that emergency sessions of the assemblies of SFRJ and SR Serbia should be convened to consider the Petition of Serbs from Kosovo and undertake immediate and effective measures to put an end to this chronicle of one long, destructive genocide on European territory. As is known from historical science, from still unextinguished memory, the expulsion of the Serb people from Kosovo and Metohija has already been going on for three centuries. Only the protectors of the tyrants have changed: the Ottoman Empire, the Habsburg Monarchy, Fascist Italy and Nazi Germany have been replaced by the Albanian state and the ruling institutions of Kosovo. In place of forced Islamization and Fascism there is Stalinized chauvinism. The only novelty is the fusion of tribal hatred and genocide masked by Marxism.

The methods have remained the same: the old poles now carry new heads. The new Deacon Avakum is called Djordje Martinović, the new Mother of the Jugoviches – Danica Milinčić. Old women and nuns are raped, frail children beaten up, stables built with gravestones, churches and historic holy places desecrated and shamed, economic sabotage tolerated, people forced to sell their property for nothing . . .

Not only are individuals exposed to this persecution – Serbia, Yugoslavia and peace in the Balkans are endangered as well. If an 'ethnically pure Kosovo' is achieved, new national and state confrontations are inevitable, which will turn the Balkan space into a potential crucible of war and endanger the peace of Europe.

Under cover of the struggle against 'Great-Serb hegemonism' a rigged political trial of the Serb nation and its history has been going on for decades. The first goal is an ethnically pure Kosovo, to be followed by further conquest of Serbian, Macedonian and Montenegrin territories. There is no national minority in the world which has greater constitutional rights [than the Albanians in Yugoslavia], but its leaders and ideologues are leading it into a national adventure in which it can lose all.

The absence of law; the authorities' sympathy for the crime and the criminals; the categorization of serious criminal acts as mere misdemeanours; the organization of violence; the hushing up and passing over in silence of injustice; the unequal status of citizens in employment and education; the 'pacification' of public opinion by means of false statements, 'ideological explanations' and the covering up of violence; equating the victim's cries for help with deliberate crimes and similar acts – all this, in essence, constitutes abuse of the constitutional right to autonomy. The case of Djordje Martinović has become that of the whole Serb nation in Kosovo. Even among crimes it would be hard to find a crime like this; but the fact that the entire legal-constitutional order of a country has been harnessed to hide such a crime is surely without precedent.

The enemy is being encouraged; his 'arguments' and goals are being legitimized. As if the truth were on the other side; as if we had no firm conviction or clear goal. Giving credence to a lie and casting doubt on the truth also means confusing international public opinion, which seems to show greater understanding for the genocide of the persecutor than for the fate of the persecuted.

In 1981 it was publicly admitted that the real situation in Kosovo had been hidden and falsified; the hope was encouraged that this would cease to be the case. However, for five years now we have witnessed permanent anarchy and the crushing of any hope for a transformation of social and national relations in Kosovo and Metohija. Draconian measures meted out to young people, verbal 'differentiation' and ideological babble simply serve to provide the ideological leaders with an alibi for maintenance of their positions.

Everyone in this country who is not indifferent has long ago realized that the genocide in Kosovo cannot be combated without deep social and political changes in the whole country. These changes are unimaginable without changes likewise in the relationship between the Autonomous Provinces and the Republic of Serbia, hence also of Yugoslavia. Genocide cannot be prevented by the politics that had led to it in the first place: the politics of gradual surrender of Kosovo and Metohija – to Albania: the unsigned capitulation which leads to a politics of national treason.

The Serb people, in the course of its own wars of liberation, fought also for the Albanians; with its unselfish aid since 1945 and up to the present day, it has given sufficient proof that it cares for the freedom, progress and dignity of the Albanian people. We stress that we do not wish harm or injustice to the Albanian people, and that we support its democratic rights; when we demand equality for the Serb and other peoples in Kosovo, we see among them the Albanian people also. We disavow and condemn all the injustices that were ever committed from the Serbian side against the Albanian people.

We demand the right to spiritual identity, to defence of the foundations of Serb national culture and to the physical survival of our nation on its land.

We demand decisive measures, and that the concern and will of all Yugoslavia be mobilized in order to stop the Albanian aggression in Kosovo and Metohija; democratic reforms, in order to establish a firm juridical order and ensure equal rights for all citizens; an end to the internal undermining of Yugoslavia's frontiers; and, by guarantees for civil security and political freedoms, the confidence and winning of support from Europe and the world at large.

(b) The End of an Era

Quite apart from the absurdity of its charges of genocide, surrender of the Albanian-inhabited areas of Yugoslavia to neighbouring Albania and so on, the Belgrade intellectuals' petition is remarkable for its failure to relate national tensions in Kosovo to any social or economic causes. Instead, they are viewed as part of a supposed centuries-old feud between Serbs and Albanians – presented, what is more, as a transcendental struggle between good and evil. Evoking 'the right to spiritual identity, to the defence of the foundation of Serb national culture and to physical survival of our nation on its land', the petition demands 'decisive measures . . . in order to stop the Albanian aggression in Kosovo'. The petition then goes on to call for support of the fifteen demands raised in another petition, signed a few months earlier by some two thousand Serbs from Kosovo, which sought fundamental alterations to the present political system and parallel changes in the constitution: notably, doing away with the autonomy of Kosovo and Vojvodina, making Serbo-Croat the official language throughout the Republic of Serbia, expelling all immigrants from the People's Republic of Albania (claimed to number 200,000 whereas official statistics show only 2,000) and purging the Party of all those who disagree with such policies.[1]

Particularly surprising was the fact that the January petition was signed by three former editors of *Praxis*: Zaga Golubović, Mihailo Marković and Ljuba Tadić – joined subsequently by Milan Kangrga, another well-known former *Praxis* editor, who gave an interview to the Belgrade literary and oppositional journal *Knjizevne novine*, once again overtly anti-Albanian in message.[2] This unexpected, indeed astonishing, alignment of *Praxis* editors with nationalism has aroused considerable dismay among their friends and sympathizers, for it delineates a complete break with the political and philosophical tradition represented by the journal.

This process of internal differentiation of the intelligentsia on a national basis goes back to the early 1970s, but has accelerated in the 1980s. Complex in origin, it also reflects strains induced by severe contraction of the economy, an increasingly uneven development of the regions, and a considerable loss of morale in the Party. The latter's inability to cope, in any but a passive manner, with the elements of real crisis in recent years has particularly affected the generation to which the *Praxis* editors belong. There has been a somewhat disingenuous feeling that the Party has betrayed them (most evident in the preoccupations of the novelist Dobrica Cošić, another signatory) and a search for alternative ideological shores. The appearance of *Praxis* signatures on the Kosovo petition, signalling a *de facto* absorption into the nationalist bloc, thus represents not only the final denouement of the *Praxis* venture but also a generational rupture within Yugoslav Marxism. The importance of the petition, however, goes well beyond this. The fact that it was signed by a highly representative section of the Belgrade intelligentsia and professional middle class (including Orthodox priests and retired army officers) suggests the consolidation in the Yugoslav capital of a political gravitational centre outside the Party and to its right, promising a rerun of the nationalist upsurge in Croatia in the late 1960s – but now in the very different context of the mid-1980s.

To be sure, the country as a whole has up to now suffered from the lack of any but a purely administrative policy (largely ineffective at that) to deal with its accumulated social and economic problems (a dramatic index of which is an inflation rate of close to 100 per cent this year). Faced with apparently intractable economic stagnation, the party leadership is visibly on the defensive. Unsure where to look for allies, it is increasingly inclined to seek 'purely' economic solutions, which in practice involves giving greater power to enterprise managements, which in turn means remodelling Yugoslav self-management as it emerged from the social and political battles of the 1960s. The last, 13th, party congress, held in June 1986, has firmly postponed all plans to regenerate the 'socialist content' of the system until after the end of the economic crisis (!) and has instead ushered in an era of political and economic 'realism'. Lip-service continues to be paid to self-management, yet at the same time the new government under Mikulić, soon after it was constituted, introduced a law (an unprecedented and unconstitutional measure) to regulate wages; and right now it is planning to amend the Basic Law of Associated Labour in a manner that will radically curtail workers' rights in the enterprises in favour of those of managers. The workers, for their part, having already suffered a cut in living standards probably unsurpassed anywhere in Eastern Europe except in Romania, have resorted to the classical weapon of the strike: the last two years have witnessed a qualitative increase in the number, duration and scope of strikes right across the country. The new law on wages, moreover, gave the increase a strong upward push.

The mid-1980s situation in Yugoslavia thus exhibits many of the features of the mid-1960s: economic stagnation, mass unemployment, rising inflation and labour unrest. Each of these trends, however, is more strongly present today than twenty years ago. But whereas in the 1960s the working class found support in a radical student movement – a combination of forces powerful enough to end further planned liberalization of the economy – this time things are different. Party and non-party intellectuals alike have largely trimmed their reactions to the perceived interests of their own republics or provinces; even those on the left, mesmerized by economic indicators, have largely remained silent in the face of this latest attempt to make workers pay the price for bureaucratic incompetence.

The new climate of 'realism' is propitious to opportunistic, ad hoc decisions. These, not surprisingly, have extended also to the national domain. In this multinational state, official attitudes to the national problem have always had a high degree of visibility, and the Belgrade petition has made its own – by no means insignificant – contribution to opportunistic decisions made over the past months regarding national policy on the territory of the Republic of Serbia. The Serbian wing of the League of Communists of Yugoslavia, squeezed between its federal responsibilities and the nationalist ferment at its base (though not in the working class: there is little evidence of nationalism among Serbian workers), has for several years now avoided anything but cosmetic changes in the formal relationship between the republic and its provinces laid down in the 1974 constitution – despite considerable pressure to do more. Its recent decision to sail closer to the nationalist wind reflects not only the increased agitation on the issue of Kosovo, but also the incapacity of the LCY as a whole to act as a united party, providing a commonly agreed alternative. The recent party congress seems to have done little to put a brake on the tendency of the republican and provincial parties to seek separate answers to the problems of 'their' regions.

Many of the recent decisions of the Serbian government – like, for example, the restriction it has placed on the sale of land and the movement of population in the Kosovo province – are said to be of limited duration only. Others – such as building a factory in a Serb-only village, in a predominantly Albanian province which suffers one of the highest unemployment rates in Europe – can be seen as one-off gestures, acts of desperation. But one recent decision could have more serious implications, for it relates to those sections of the penal code that deal with 'hostile intentions against the state'. According to reports in the Belgrade press, the Serbian government has now adopted a draft amendment to the republican penal code that would allow acts of common crime (such as theft, damage to property, assault, rape, murder, etc.) to be treated as anti-state activity, in instances where the ethnic origin of the victim differs from that of the perpetrator. There has also been a drive by Serbian representatives urging similar changes in the federal penal code. Juridical experts – such as

Ljubo Bavcon from Ljubljana – have publicly remonstrated against this further subjectivization of the criminal law, pointing to the strong possibility of its 'misuse according to momentary political need'. Such a change, he has argued, will 'unavoidably add fuel to the fire of nationalist and chauvinist conflicts, unnecessarily creating "martyrs" and "heroes", instead of calming irrational passions with common sense, patience, and above all with suitable measures of political, economic and social policy'.[3]

The proposed amendment – aimed once again at the Kosovo problem – is in direct conflict with the Yugoslav constitution, which states that citizens are equal before the law irrespective of their ethnic, religious or sexual membership. The adoption of this draft amendment to the Serbian penal code by the republican government suggests that the Serbian party has decided to ride the tiger of 'irrational passions' – as its Croatian counterpart did so disastrously at the end of the 1960s. At that time the editors of *Praxis* condemned nationalism in Croatia and elsewhere in the name of an all-Yugoslav vision of democratic socialism. This time, in contrast, some of them have decided to support a political stance that elevates 'the destiny of the nation' to a supreme political and moral imperative: in the petition which they have signed, 'socialism' appears not once among its 3,500 words.   (September 1986)

Notes

1. *Mladina*, Ljubljana, 28 February 1986.
2. *Knjizevne novine*, Belgrade, no. 700. Kangrga's interview was followed by a lengthy reply from the Kosovo Albanian writer Rexhep Qosja.
3. *Delo*, Ljubljana, 7 June 1986.

(c) Editors of *Praxis International* Defend their Position on Kosovo

To the Editorial Collective of *Labour Focus on Eastern Europe*

Dear friends,

In November 1986 you published an article by Michele Lee under the title *The End of an Era*. The article seems to have three purposes: (1) to condemn former editors of *Praxis* (Zaga Golubović, Mihailo Marković and Ljubomir Tadić) for betrayal of their former socialist views and alignment with nationalism, (2) to inform about the real nature of the problem of the Yugoslav province Kosovo, and (3) to explain the present-day crisis in Yugoslavia, concerning which former progressive intellectuals have allegedly remained silent.

The publication of the article violates some basic principles of your editorial policy, published on page 2 of your journal. We are aware, of course, that, as you say in your *Statement of aims*, signed articles need not necessarily represent the view of the editorial collective. However, the author of the article, Michele Lee, is a member of the editorial collective. More importantly, the article is preceded by a comment which adds insult to injury and is not signed – therefore, can hardly be anything else but the *editorial* comment. That is why we address this letter to you and not just to the author, convinced that, as a consequence of your commitment to democratic socialism, you will publish it without delay, and allow the possibility of a dialogue, which is the only possible means to resolve an obvious conflict of opinions.

Let us, first, explain in what sense the publication of Michele Lee's article violates the principles of your editorial policy. In your *Statement of aims* you insist on the labour movement's responsibility to 'take a stand against the suppression of democratic rights in the Soviet Union and Eastern Europe'. And you say that the mass media largely ignore campaigns run by socialists concerning victims of repression in Eastern Europe. Now, the petition on Kosovo signed by two hundred leading Belgrade intellectuals, including the best-known independent democratic socialists, raises essentially the issues of the suppression of human rights of the minority groups in the autonomous region Kosovo, it defends victims of repression. There is not a shred of doubt that the repression in question really exists. On this factual issue there is no controversy: Yugoslav federal authorities, even Albanian authorities from Kosovo, do not at all disagree with the signatories of the petition that the Serbian, Montenegrin and Turkish families are increasingly forced either to leave the region or to get assimilated, and that the force in question is: threat of violence, appropriation of land, destruction of harvests, attacks on people and domestic animals, rapes and murders. Everything else is controversial: the causes, the consequences, the speed of the transformation of a multinational region into an ethnically pure one – in a socialist and allegedly internationalist society. That people suffer in a direct, brutal, tragic, unexplainable way is an irrefutable fact. All Yugoslav mass media report about it regularly. That governments are responsible that tolerate crude violations of elementary human rights for a prolonged period of time is rather obvious. That socialists must raise their voice of protest against such injustice and in defence of the victims – no matter which nationality they belong to – should also hardly be controversial. And yet the journal identifies the protest against repression of national minorities – as nationalism. It effectively defends the regime against 'the accusations' of its radical critics. Since when is this your policy concerning the bureaucratic régimes in Eastern Europe?

Another principle of your editorial policy is to provide *reliable comprehensive information* about events in Eastern Europe and the Soviet Union rather than to 'debate on the nature of those states or recommend a strategy for socialists in Eastern Europe'. Do you really believe that Michele Lee's article offers a reliable and comprehensive coverage of either the Yugoslav crisis or the tragic developments in Kosovo? As we shall show this coverage is not only 'scanty' but also 'selective and slanted' – characteristics that you ascribe to the bourgeois press. As the title and the main thrust of the article clearly indicate, the main point of the text was to discredit and write off another group of former leftist friends. Another betrayal, another rupture, another break with 'fellow travellers' who 'get confused in the inevitable turning points of history'. Why should you continue with this most pathological, most insane feature of the traditional behaviour on the left?

Did we exaggerate? Have another look at the text. Before you say anything (and you say next to nothing) about the contents of the alleged petition, the signing of which constitutes 'the end of an era' (of the progressive era in our lives) – you stamp your judgement on it. This is a petition of an 'obscurantist, nationalist and anti-democratic character'. This style of passing such devastating judgements before and without any arguments and without any 'reliable and comprehensive' information about the subject and its context – sounds quite familiar. You must know at least theoretically where the source of this style and method is. And we know it from experience since that is how we have invariably been treated during the last quarter of a century by most dogmatic Soviet and Eastern European ideologues, by the worst Stalinists in our own country and by ardent admirers of Enver Hoxha and Kim Il Sung in the West. What on earth brings you into this company, how could you resort to this kind of treatment of your *Praxis* friends? You could have easily found out that, far from 'searching for alternative ideological shores' as Michele Lee has gently put it, we stay what we have always been. We continue to publish a truly internationalist journal committed to democratic socialism. (*Praxis International* is now in its sixth year.) All three of us are members of the *Committee for defence of freedom of public expression* in Belgrade and raise our voice against all forms of repression in our country, in defence of victims that belong to various social groups and to various nationalities: Serbs, Montenegrins, Albanians, Turks, Bosnians, Moslems, Croats. We are far from silent about the Yugoslav crisis and the possibilities of overcoming it, we are in fact more engaged on concrete issues of Yugoslav society now than in 1968.

Are we nationalists because we also write on national issues (which are very acute in Yugoslavia now), or because we, being Serbs, also defend Serbian victims of repression? Is it nationalism if we defend the same principle of national and human self-determination both in the case of Albanians and non-Albanians in Kosovo? Albanians constitute 8 per cent of the Yugoslav population but they have the right to their own autonomous government and to free development of their language and their national culture. However, there are 20 per cent of non-Albanians in the population of Kosovo (Serbs, Montenegrins, Turks, Gypsies) and this minority within the minority must also have all civil and human rights protected – which is *not* the case. We are willing to support a further step – from autonomy to full national self-determination, including secession. But then again, instead of aspiring to an ethnically pure Kosovo, Albanian leaders in the region would have to grant the right of self-determination, including secession to the non-Albanian minority. One of the essential characteristics of nationalism, whether Serbian or Croatian or Slovenian or Albanian, is that it refuses to recognize *equal rights* for all nations and national minorities. And that has never been our position – as anyone who claims to know the Yugoslav situation and to inform the world about it would have to know.

Showing in full detail how inadequate, superficial, selective and utterly biased is Michele Lee's account of either the problem of Kosovo or of the Yugoslav crisis would make a long story. It should suffice for the moment to indicate at least some areas of issues that are entirely missing from Lee's account and without which nothing could be understood about either Kosovo or Yugoslavia.

First, there is a century-old history of national conflict in Kosovo, a series of acts of aggression and counter-aggression, of acts of violence and bloody revenge – a story of true horror. It is only human to feel sympathy 'under the veil of ignorance' for the smaller Albanian people. But the little David had the upper hand most of the time because it was amply supported by overwhelming allies: the Islamic Ottoman Empire during five centuries until 1912, Austria-Hungary which occupied the entire territory during World War One; fascist Italy and Germany which did the same during World War Two; the Soviet Union and China after 1948; eventually a dominating anti-Serbian coalition in Yugoslavia itself over the last twenty years.

What happened during World War Two is especially relevant here. In contrast to the vast majority of Albanian people in Albania who fought bravely against the Italian occupation army, the Albanian people in Kosovo received the Italian army and later the Germany army as liberators in 1941 and 1943. This indicates how oppressed they felt in pre-war Yugoslavia. This also explains why there were fewer than one hundred Albanian partisans and Party members in Kosovo until 1944 and why dozens of thousands of Albanians from Kosovo joined the Italian and German armies (SS division Skender-beg was formed entirely of Albanians). Furthermore, this explains why the dominating political organization in Kosovo during the war was the pro-Fascist Balli Kombetër, and why this organization was able to organize a mass uprising against the new people's government during the winter 1945–46. Whatever happened later, the fact is that Kosovo was the only Yugoslav region where the socialist system was *imposed* from outside, by the victorious Yugoslav partisan army, and has *not* emerged as the result of a mass liberation movement by Albanian people in Kosovo themselves. The fact is that Balli Kombetër – which was completely destroyed in Albania – survived in Kosovo and still plays a formidable role there, supported financially and politically by its powerful organization in the West. This must be taken into account not only when one tries to understand the political problems in Kosovo after 1945, but also when one tries to figure out where a sovereign Kosovo state might end up. This could be a first and unique case of a region of a socialist state seceding and restoring bourgeois society governed by a pro-fascist right-wing régime. It is by no means an accident that in June 1986 the conservative American senator Robert Dole submitted to the US Senate a resolution demanding from the Yugoslav government that it grant Kosovo the status of a republic.

Another factor that must never be ignored is the policy of *Comintern* towards Yugoslavia between the two world wars. That was the policy of disintegration of the country (officially characterized as 'the prison of nations'), a policy of support for every separatist national movement. After a long period of vacillation this policy has, to a surprisingly large extent, been brought to life owing to the Yugoslav Constitution of 1974. Yugoslavia is now a loosely connected association of eight states, eight parties and eight economic systems. This madness of restoring feudal political and economic relations cannot be fully understood without taking into account this syndrome of Comintern's anti-Yugoslavism which has been transmitted from one to another generation of Yugoslav party leaders. Without an awareness of this syndrome one would fail to understand the strength of the Albanian bureaucracy in Kosovo, which is, in fact, openly or tacitly supported by the majority of the eight bureaucratic elites against the Serbian bureaucracy.

Only against this historic context may one also understand the economic causes of the tragic disaster called Kosovo. This is indeed the least developed region, with the highest unemployment, with still existing forms of abject poverty. Worst of all the gap between the developed regions and Kosovo is growing. This is the inevitable consequence of the restoration of the market economy in Yugoslavia after 1965. The leadership of the country cannot eschew responsibility for such a development. However, one must bear in mind that Serbia does not belong to the developed parts of Yugoslavia: according to all economic indicators it is now below the average Yugoslav level and lags behind, together with Kosovo. And when one hears the *altera pars* – the representatives of the three developed federal units (Slovenia, Croatia and Vojvodina) – one begins to understand better the complexities of the Kosovo economy. These three and Serbia have so far given enormous amounts of aid to Kosovo. Since 1945 Kosovo has received more than $10 billion from the Federal Fund for the aid to developing regions. The Kosovo authorities have autonomously decided the use of this aid. It could be shown in detail how those enormous means (like elsewhere in Yugoslavia) have been misinvested, and how Kosovo has wasted an opportunity of faster and more rational development. In spite of that the social product of Kosovo has increased 6.5 times since 1945. Furthermore, the Albanian bureaucracy in Kosovo has always supported a disastrous demographic policy. In most developing countries efforts have been made to decrease the population growth rate: China is probably the best example. In Kosovo the pursuit of a project of an ethnically pure Kosovo has resulted in a flat refusal of any policy of family planning. Albanians in Kosovo have the highest population growth rate in Europe. That is why indicators *per capita* give a far worse picture than indicators in absolute terms. This looks like a suicidal economic policy. But as national policy it does lead to its ultimate end. In 1940 there were 55 per cent

Albanians in Kosovo, in 1985 it is already 80 per cent. It is hardly possible to do anything about such a demographic policy, which greatly contributes to unemployment and poverty in Kosovo. But something can be done and must be done about the forceful assimilation and expulsion of the non-Albanian population from Kosovo. To qualify as nationalists those who raise their voices against this form of repression means either that one has a very peculiar idea of nationalism, or that one simply continues to follow the Comintern policy of the disintegration of Yugoslavia, involving full support for separatist national movements, no matter how chauvinistic and reactionary they may be.

This letter can hardly be an occasion for a detailed critique of Michele Lee's account of the Yugoslav crisis. She could learn a lot about that subject from the excellent work of another of your editors – Catherine Verla from Paris. To call the present policy of the Yugoslav leadership a policy of 'realism', to say that it is increasingly inclined to seek 'purely' economic solutions, to single out 'recent decisions of the Serbian Government' as the example of 'irrational passions' – is rather an example of unserious, irresponsible and systematically biased writing. The present Yugoslav policies resulting in an inflation of over 100 per cent, in the worst unemployment in the country's history, in the fall of the real standard of living to the level of the sixties, are anything but realistic. If its 'solutions' are, as a rule, hardly more than purely pragmatic compromises between eight political wills of eight oligarchies at loggerheads with each other – then they can be qualified as 'purely economic' only in a very peculiar sense of the word. Singling out the Serbian government – one of the weakest after great purges in 1966 and 1971 – as the main villain that has just decided to ride the tiger of 'irrational passions' – is hardly more than an indication of the author's bias and the expression of her aversion. Any sound political and economic analysis will be able to establish that, under the given external and internal conditions, the single most important causal factor of the present deep crisis of Yugoslav society was the 1965 complete reversal of the policy of socialist democratization, a restoration of the market economy, increasing reliance on Western capital loans and a growing division of political power among eight national or regional oligarchies. This was the policy that expressed particular, shortrange interests of the two developed republics Slovenia and Croatia. Every student of recent Yugoslav history knows who were the unchallenged leaders during this period and that there were no Serbs among them. The question, therefore, arises: what are the sources of Michele Lee's 'information'? They can hardly be found in any serious existing political, sociological and economic analysis of Yugoslav society. To a large extent they coincide with rumours that circulate in some bureaucratic and truly nationalistic circles in Yugoslavia. Even more surprisingly, the basic attitude towards the petition of Belgrade intellectuals concerning the repression in Kosovo fully co-incides with the attitude of the Yugoslav regime itself.

We regret that this letter is so long, but we hope that you will understand our desire to not only reply to unfounded accusations, but also to offer your readers some additional information so that they would be able to form their own judgement.

Zagorka Golubović, Mihailo Marković,
Ljubomir Tadić
Belgrade, 26 February 1987

(d) 'Michele Lee' Replies

Before taking up the arguments presented by Golubović, Marković and Tadić in their response to my article *The End of an Era*, it is worth recalling that *Labour Focus* has never shied away from criticizing the nationality policies of the East European states. It has published texts on Bulgaria, Romania and Albania that have condemned the ruling parties' nationalism – be it, in the case of Bulgaria, directed against a specific ethnic group (the Turks) or, as in the Albanian case, providing a key underpinning of the official ideology. So it should come as no surprise to our readers to see Yugoslavia's attitude towards its Albanian minority critically scrutinized following the events of 1981 – the more so since that country has a far better record on the national issue than any of its neighbours.

Let us set aside all the insinuations about my supposed Stalinoid sectarianism,[1] and concern ourselves with the substance of the arguments put forward by the three authors. They argue, in effect, that a state of complete lawlessness exists in the Yugoslav province of Kosovo, aided and abetted by the Provincial authorities with varying degrees of complicity on the part of the Federal state itself and the seven other Republican (or Provincial) governments. They speak of the 'threat of violence, appropriation of land, destruction of harvests, attacks on people and domestic animals, rapes and murders'.[2] The petition which they signed speaks of 'genocide' suffered by the Slavs in the Province; of national treason, expressed in the conscious surrender of parts of Yugoslavia to Albania.

These are all very serious charges. Yet what evidence do the three authors produce for them? None at all. They convey an impression of continuous anarchy in Kosovo, such as would require the introduction of direct administration by the Federal authorities: suspension of the Province's political autonomy in favour of yet another dose of emergency rule. But is this the true picture? Let us examine briefly the three most serious charges they make, concerning murder, rape and the land issue.

Murder and Rape

How many actual murders of Slavs have been committed in Kosovo over the past five years? The Yugoslav press has reported exactly one: the outcome of a dispute among neighbours over land, of the kind that is unfortunately still quite common in Yugoslavia. The judicial investigation showed no indication that the crime had been committed out of nationalistic hatred. The perpetrator was speedily executed, to the great consternation of all those Yugoslavs who have been actively campaigning against capital punishment.

How about rapes? Official statistics show that the incidence of rape is, if anything, smaller in the Province than, for example, in neighbouring 'Serbia proper' (i.e. Serbia excluding the autonomous provinces of Kosovo and Vojvodina) or in Slovenia (the most advanced republic in economic and cultural terms). Furthermore, the figures do not show any particular national bias: the overwhelming majority of both perpetrators and victims are Albanian.

In spite of this, the Serbian republican government has recently adopted amendments to its criminal code (which has force also in Kosovo) that make the ethnic origin of the accused in rape cases (indeed, in other forms of common crime as well) a matter of legal relevance. That this change was anyway quite redundant in view of actual court practice is shown by the case of a young Albanian who, only a few months before the new law was introduced, had received a *ten-year* prison sentence for molesting – not raping! – a Serb woman. So it seems clear enough that the change in the law was made not so much to meet a real problem as to appease nationalist agitation and, perhaps, to silence the voices calling for the reimposition of a state of emergency in Kosovo.

Yet we are told by the three authors that to criticize this legal innovation is to show bias: 'Singling out the Serbian government . . . is hardly more than an indication of the author's bias and the expression of her aversion.' Here we see one of many attempts to dress up all criticism in national colours.[3] Why should Lee in particular be biased against the Serbian government, or have any particular aversion against it? After all, condemnation of the legal amendments was widespread in Yugoslavia itself. It came not just from the prominent jurist Ljubo Bavcon, but from many other quarters within the legal profession. Thus we read in the press that a Belgrade lawyer, Toma Fila, protested last April to the Constitutional Court of Yugoslavia on the grounds that the new laws were unconstitutional. Similar criticism has been voiced in such important journals as the Belgrade weekly *NIN*. Furthermore, other republican governments have declined to follow Serbia's lead (which, of course, does not absolve them of responsibility in the matter, given the constitutional issues raised). One can only hope that the Federal Constitutional Court will come to the aid of the Serbian government, by annulling this obvious blunder.

In reality, if one takes into account the fact that, whereas Albanians form only 8 per cent of the country's population, they provide (according to Amnesty International) some 75 per cent of all 'prisoners of conscience', it is quite obvious that the Yugoslav authorities, from the Provincial administration up, have been showing extremely little leniency in dealing with any real or imagined Albanian nationalist threat. If anything, the zeal with which people are sent to prison for 'political offences' in Kosovo, often without any proof whatsoever, suggests a lawlessness of quite a different kind from that alluded to by the three authors. Their arguments beg the real question, which they nowhere openly confront: what kind of 'radical' policy could the Yugoslav state adopt that would meet the demands of the petitioners (including themselves)? Would they be satisfied by a further sharp rise in the already quite unacceptable number of young Albanians in prison (unacceptable from the point of view of the victims, but also from that of Yugoslavia's own long-term interests)? Or are they seeking more fundamental changes, such as the elimination of Kosovo's status as an autonomous province? Even as a temporary measure, this would lead only to disaster.

Land and Emigration

It is worth paying some attention to the question of changes in land ownership in Kosovo, since these are often cited as the main axis of Albanian nationalist pressure on the Slav (mainly Serb) minority population there, not to speak of 'proving' the deliberate alienation of national territory. An official survey of land sales in the Province was recently conducted by the Kosovo internal security organs, under the supervision of the Serbian government, and its results were published in April 1987. It shows no evidence for any nationalist design in the buying or selling of land in Kosovo. Judging by comments in the Yugoslav press, the survey's results had been expected. Yet the three authors signed a petition which refers to 'national treason' and the 'surrender' of land to Albania (not just to Yugoslav Albanians!). Such attitudes prevent any true understanding of what is happening in the Province. Their only contribution is to further inflame national tensions.

Increased migration of Serbs out of Kosovo in recent years is an undeniable fact. But if one is to gauge its significance and understand its real causes, it must be viewed first of all in an all-Yugoslav context. Yugoslav statistics show the existence of a general tendency for internal migration to be directed towards national centres: Serbs from Bosnia tend to move to Serbia, Bosnian Croats to Croatia, Macedonian Albanians to Kosovo and so. This tendency is overlaid with economic pressures arising from uneven regional development: for example, the whole South Morava region (the poor southern area of 'Serbia proper' adjacent to Kosovo) is becoming depopulated, as the young and able leave their villages in search of jobs in the industrial centres further north. In all, some 4.5 million Yugoslav peasants have left the land over the past fifteen years, flooding the cities in pursuit of employment. Kosovo, a largely agricultural area and the poorest as well, has predictably suffered most in this respect. The Province, moreover, is one of the most densely populated areas of Yugoslavia, with highly subdivided land the price of which is probably the highest in the entire country: the already quoted survey of land sales gives this as one of the main reasons for the sale of land. It is worth pointing out in this connection that the Yugoslav public, well acquainted with the figures for Slav emigration from Kosovo, has been given no idea of the scale of Albanian emigration in the same period.

To be sure, these purely material causes of Serb migration from Kosovo are not the whole story. There is little doubt that, since 1966, the rapid (because belated) Albanization of the Kosovo administration, the new ascendancy of the Albanian language and the accompanying cultural-national shift in the Province's schools, media etc. – rendered more dramatic by the fast growth of the Albanian population – have been very hard for the formerly privileged Slav minority to come to terms with. Yugoslav, and Albanian, policy-makers have clearly failed to anticipate the substantial problems necessarily associated with such a change. Positive discrimination favouring the formerly disadvantaged Albanians has been experienced by other national groups as real injustice, so that a growth of insecurity among them has paralleled the growth of a new Albanian national self-confidence. In some quarters, moreover, the fear grew that this advance of the Albanians was dangerous for Yugoslavia – which did not help matters.

The souring of inter-community relations following the repression in and after 1981, together with the violence of the economic crisis in recent years (which has produced, for example, an unemployment rate in Kosovo of around 50 per cent in 1987), have made the process of change far more strained. In the absence of any positive strategy by party or state, the resulting frustration only too easily spills over into petty violence across ethnic boundaries. Even recent attempts by the Kosovo and Serbian authorities to encourage the return, or indeed new settlement, of Slavs in the Province by promising jobs and accommodation – goods in acutely short supply throughout Yugoslavia and pre-eminently so in Kosovo – have inevitably generated new tensions.

History and the Position of Serbia

Let us now turn to some other arguments put forward by the three authors. We are told we cannot understand what is happening in Kosovo today without surveying the last hundred years of Serb–Albanian relations in the Balkan context (the petition they signed actually takes the story back three hundred years). The authors begin by speaking of 'a series of aggressions and counter aggressions' – a fair assessment. But then we are quickly introduced to the idea that 'the little David [the Albanians] had the upper hand most of the time', because over the past century he has been supported by such powerful allies as the Ottoman Empire, Austria-Hungary, Fascist Italy, Nazi Germany, the Soviet Union and China – and, most recently, also by the 'dominating anti-Serbian coalition in Yugoslavia . . . over the past twenty years'.

As any reader of Balkan history will recognize, this is a highly tendentious account. To take just one example: in the last decades of its rule, the Ottoman state allowed its Serb, Bulgar and Greek subjects education in their own language; but it always denied this right to the supposedly privileged Albanians – a policy continued after 1918 by bourgeois Yugoslavia, leading to an estimated 90 per cent illiteracy among the country's Albanian minority at the start of World War Two. However, one part of the three authors' argument 'from history' is more relevant to the real issues under discussion: the 'anti-Serbian coalition' supposedly in power in Yugoslavia over the past twenty years. A quick calculation shows that the date of its installation would have been the removal from office of Alexander Ranković, in 1966. But why should one accept – even from such eminent Marxists as Golubović, Marković and Tadić – the idea that the fall of Ranković was a blow against Serbia? After all, however one chooses to define the post-1966 leadership, it soon showed itself able to purge the local party and state apparatuses in Croatia, Serbia, Slovenia, Macedonia and most recently Kosovo with equal vigour.

The authors find themselves on firmer ground when they ascribe the worsening situation in the Province to the long-term effects of the economic reform launched in the mid-1960s. This promising line of argument, however, is once again compromised by their national *parti pris*. We are told that the market reforms were introduced without Serbian consent, so that their ill-effects can be placed at the door of the 'short-range interests of the two developed republics of Slovenia and Croatia'; indeed, 'every student of recent Yugoslav history knows who were the unchallenged leaders during this period and that there were no Serbs among them'. But this is simply untrue. On the contrary, there is absolutely no doubt whatsoever that the market mechanisms introduced in the 1960s very much involved the Serbian leadership. Were not the younger generation of party leaders purged in Croatia and Serbia in the early 1970s alike accused, *inter alia*, of giving free reign to 'technocracy'? To view the debate on the economy – or the constitution – solely through national spectacles only serves to cloud the essential issues related to regional underdevelopment.

In a recent memorandum produced within the Serbian Academy of Arts and Sciences, which was leaked to the press without its authors' consent, it is argued that after the fall of Ranković power passed to the Slovene Kardelj and the Croat Tito, who – because of their ethnic origins – inflected Yugoslav politics to serve the interests primarily of the republics of Slovenia and Croatia. It would appear from the above that this view is shared by Golubović and her co-authors, Academicians Marković and Tadić. Moreover, the 1974 Constitution is presented by them as 'a policy of support for every separatist national movement'. But though many justified criticisms can indeed be levelled at that document, surely socialists should in fact support that part of it which endorses very substantial national rights for Yugoslavia's minorities – and especially the Albanian one. There is no justification at all for presenting this as an encouragement to separatism. One the contrary, national equality has been one of the main pillars of Yugoslavia's cohesion.

'Enemies'

Another claim of Marković and his colleagues is that violations of Kosovo Slavs' human rights are intimately linked to the presence in the Province today of Balli Kombëter, the wartime bourgeois and collaborationist Albanian nationalist front. Apparently, this organization 'has survived in Kosovo and still plays a formidable role there, supported financially and politically by its powerful organization in the West'. What is the source for this bizarre notion? The Yugoslav press over the past years has reported the discovery of dozens of secret organizations in Kosovo (reports which, of course, may or may not have a basis in reality). The security services have uncovered nest after nest of 'Marxist-Leninists', 'irredentists' and generic nationalists. Yet, for all their tireless vigilance, they have not detected any such active presence of Balli Kombëter. We are, however, informed categorically by the three authors that it exists.

Because of it, moreover, a 'sovereign Kosovo state' would produce a pro-fascist régime: 'this could be a first and unique case of a region of a socialist state seceding and restoring bourgeois society governed by a pro-fascist right-wing régime'. Who are they trying to scare? It is astonishing to hear it so blandly asserted that a population overwhelmingly raised in socialist Yugoslavia (and Albanians are the youngest of all Yugoslav nationalities) would – at the nod of King Zog II or Senator Robert Dole – embrace fascism.[4] In the eyes of those with such febrile imaginations, all the two million ethnic Albanians living within Yugoslavia's borders must automatically be suspect. No doubt this extraordinary assessment of the country's Albanian population is made easier by an 'appropriate' view of the People's Republic of Albania: in the petition which the three authors signed, Albania is placed on the same footing as Nazi Germany!

In the three authors' presentation of the situation, enemies without are joined by enemies within, and also by enemies from the past: by the Comintern tradition, with its supposed responsibility for the 1974 Constitution.[5] 'Comintern's anti-Yugoslavism . . . has been transmitted from one to another generation of Yugoslav party leaders. Without an awareness of this syndrome, one would fail to understand the strength of the Albanian bureaucracy in Kosovo, which is . . . openly or tacitly supported by the majority of the eight bureaucratic elites against the Serbian bureaucracy.' Without going into the whole history of early Comintern policy towards Yugoslavia, it is enough to point out two facts. First, Tito's appointment as leader of the Yugoslav Communist Party coincided almost exactly with the Comintern's endorsement in 1935 of the Popular Front policy, which entailed defending the European status quo – including the territorial integrity of Yugoslavia. Secondly, in all the discussion between Stalin and the Western Allies from 1941 on, the integrity of Yugoslavia was never questioned. And in 1948 Yugoslavia split with the Soviet Union on the issue of Yugoslav independence.

So why on earth should the Yugoslav League of Communists today be charged with 'anti-Yugoslavism'? How many of its cadres can really have been moulded immutably in a *pre-1935* Comintern tradition? There is no need for any such far-fetched theory. For what is 'anti-Yugoslav' about the bureaucracy's support for its wing in Kosovo? Or does the problem for the three authors really lie in the fact that in Kosovo we are dealing with an *Albanian* bureaucracy? Are the Kosovo Albanians somehow less Yugoslav than Serbs or Croats? Surely such a view would lead one to reject altogether the Yugoslav federation as presently constituted and conceived, in a favour of a reduced, more ethnically pure South Slav state? After all, given that some 80 per cent of the Kosovo population is Albanian, is it surprising that the administration there should be staffed largely by Albanians, as it has been since 1966? Why should this not be seen as only right and indeed desirable, as much by South Slavs as by non-South Slavs?

Population Control

Finally, let us take up the question of the population policy supposedly being pursued by the Albanian authorities in Kosovo, as part of a grand design to make Kosovo an all-Albanian land. 'In Kosovo the pursuit of a project of an ethnically pure Kosovo has resulted in a flat refusal of any policy of family planning,' write Golubović, Marković and Tadić. Given the high Albanian birthrate and the Province's poverty, 'this looks like a suicidal economic policy. But as national policy it does lead to its ultimate end.' Now it is true that Albanians have a higher birthrate than any other nation in Europe (excluding Turkey). It is equally true that the population of Soviet Central Asia is growing more rapidly than that of European Russia, and that this has produced considerable anguish among Russian chauvinists. But as in Central Asia, so too in Yugoslavia, the high birthrate need not be part of any sinister nationalist plot. The Albanian birth rate today matches those obtaining among South Slavs before World War Two. We are dealing here with the completion (the birthrate is actually falling) of a demographic cycle undergone by all European nations in their more or less recent past – the Albanian case just happens, for socio-economic reasons, to be the last in Europe.

The Yugoslav state, for its part, has never pursued a population policy of any kind, other than making abortion available on demand. It does not have any particular need to do so: its area is that of Great Britain, while its population is less than half Britain's. Given this context, the birthrate is essentially a question of industrialization and modernization. As a Kosovo demographer has put it succinctly: the fertility of Albanian women is in the last instance a function of their lack of social emancipation. Now Golubović, Marković and Tadić do not argue that the overall Yugoslav birthrate is too high, like that of China, but that the birthrate of the Albanian minority is too high. They say that the Kosovo economy in and of itself cannot sustain the existing rate of population growth in the Province, so the Kosovo authorities would be well advised to introduce a policy of limiting births. But the truth is that no multinational state could countenance a policy of ethnically selective restriction of births without being rightly charged with racism.

The Principles at Stake

In conclusion, let us move from particular arguments to a more general assessment of the response to my article from Golubović, Marković and Tadić. It is conducted at two different levels. On the surface, their argument is the following: we were moved to sign the petition criticized in 'The End of an Era' because the situation of Serbs and Montenegrins in Kosovo is so bad that to protest against it is a socialist and democratic imperative. However, the fact that they signed not a *petition*, but *this particular petition*, together with the concerns expressed in their response to my article, make it clear that beneath the surface they see other, essentially national, issues as being at stake in the 'Kosovo question'.

This is why the three authors' solution is sought in terms of strengthening one (Serbian) bureaucracy against another (Albanian) bureaucracy. Their text is quite devoid of any idea that Serb and Albanian peasants, workers, intellectuals, women, students, etc. – all those who have shared, in a truly democratic manner, the effects of the Province's parlous economic situation – might *jointly* deal with the provincial, republican and federal powers, on the basis of a programme that asserted certain basic rights of all Yugoslav citizens. The trouble is that, at the precise moment when a socialist and internationalist outlook was most necessary to combat rising national prejudice, the editors of *Praxis International* simply joined the fray.

In their response, Golubović, Marković and Tadić speak of their equal commitment to Albanian and Serb national rights, and to such rights for all other nations. I do not wish to dispute the sincerity of their feelings. But it is their practice which has been so disquietening. When in 1981 a state of emergency was declared in Kosovo – for the first time in postwar Yugoslavia – in order to quell popular demonstrations, did they protest against such undemocratic action by the state? Did they condemn the shooting of twelve demonstrators (even by official figures) or the subsequent draconian measures taken against hundreds if not thousands of Yugoslav citizens of Albanian origin, in a whole string of political trials that have scarred Yugoslavia's internal life over the past six years?

When an anti-Albanian rampage took place in Belgrade last year – it was immediately and correctly condemned by the authorities, but the sentences handed out were a fraction of what they would have been in Kosovo – did the three authors speak out against such an outrage? When factories were built in Kosovo which, in a break with the whole tradition of socialist Yugoslavia, excluded workers because they were Albanian, and when families were forced out of villages because these were seen as exclusive Serb property, did they sign a petition against such infringements of the national and democratic rights of these Yugoslavs? When legislation was brought in which, contrary to the Yugoslav constitution, made ethnic origin a relevant factor in common crimes, did they protest against this departure from all democratic norms? The purging from Kosovo school textbooks of some of the best Albanian novelists and poets, simply because they were born or are living in the People's Republic of Albania, was likewise passed over by them in silence.

Golubović, Marković and Tadić, formerly professors at the University of Belgrade, over a decade ago now were themselves the victims of a political purge, the original motive for which was their support for students during and after 1968. Their removal from the University was rightly felt as a loss by all progressive Yugoslavs, in the same way that the closing down of the journal *Praxis* impoverished the Marxist and socialist thought of the country as a whole. At the time there was an international campaign on their behalf. Yet when professors at the University of Priština in Kosovo were dismissed after the 1981 events for refusing to condemn their students, or for their stated (or more often merely alleged) beliefs;

when students were excluded from the university and secondary-school pupils denied entry to higher education, on the grounds that some member of their extended family was deemed by the state to be politically suspect: when these things happened the former Belgrade professors and *Praxis* editors remained silent. Their only public act in relation to Kosovo has been to put their names to a petition whose content and preoccupations have nothing to do with the democratic socialist principles that have been the hallmark of the *Praxis* tradition.

Democratic Initiatives and Nationalism

Kosovo raises issues that go well beyond individual human rights. The argument that the three authors present – that their signing of the petition was governed by the same set of concerns as their participation in the work of the *Belgrade Committee for Defence of Freedom of Thought and Expression* – is contradicted by the text of the petition itself. My dispute with them is not about whether or not they should have signed *any petition*, on behalf of the rights of any particular group of Yugoslavs. Nor is it about whether non-Albanians in Kosovo do or do not suffer acts of discrimination. Clearly all acts of discrimination, at whatever level, must be condemned and petitions are entirely legitimate forms of public protest. The problem lies in the nature of the particular petition they chose to sign, in the present Yugoslav political context.

The case of the above-mentioned Committee is a good example of how democratic initiatives can have only a limited impact in a multinational state if their initiators are seen to make compromises on the national question. As far as one can judge from official and unofficial publications, the Committee drew initially upon two strands of public resistance: one coming from within the Serbian Writers' Association and the Serbian Academy of Arts and Sciences in response to the trial of the Serbian poet Gojko Djogo, who in 1982 was sentenced to two years in prison for poems judged to be insulting to the recently deceased President Tito; the other formed out of defence activities related to the trial of the Belgrade Six and that of Vojislav Šešelj in Sarajevo. When the Committee was set up as a permanent body – its platform was presented in an open letter to the Federal Assembly and the Yugoslav public in October 1986 – it found it impossible to attract members from outside Serbia. This doubtless says something about the national-regional limitations of the critical intelligentsia in Yugoslavia. Yet it is difficult to avoid the impression that the past passivity of the Committee's founding members in the face of the repression carried out by the Yugoslav authorities in Kosovo, i.e. on the territory of their own republic of Serbia, has contributed also to its present predicament: its confinement to Belgrade. The Committee is now seeking to overcome this predicament to some extent, by enlarging the scope of its activities to include defending individuals from other national groups. This is a positive development. For that very reason, it is all the more disheartening to see the signatures of some of its most prominent members (not just Golubović, Marković and Tadić) on a nationalist petition.

The End of an Era

My aim in 'The End of an Era' was not to 'inform about the real nature of the problem of . . . Kosovo', nor to 'explain the present-day crisis in Yugoslavia', as Golubović and her colleagues seem to think. Nobody serious would have attempted all that in such a short text. Nor did the title of my article refer to them personally. It referred in fact to an era in Yugoslav politics. Against the background of a continuing political and economic crisis, certain new developments as 1987 drew near were particularly worrying: (1) The government's move to freeze workers' wages and in some cases even push them below the December 1986 level (in a situation of 100 per cent inflation) opened up the possibility of a frontal clash with workers for the first time since the war. (2) Official endorsement of 'ethically pure' Slav factories and villages in Kosovo, and legal changes making ethnicity a relevant factor in judging common crimes in the Republic of Serbia (including the autonomous provinces), could not fail to fan further the flames of nationalism and counter-nationalism. (3) The petition signed by two hundred Belgrade intellectuals – an unprecedented event – signalled the alignment of a key social layer behind what can most charitably be called an anachronistic view of the Kosovo problem. (4) The failure of socialists among them to provide the necessary corrective facilitated the emergence of a consensus right across the political spectrum which works against any positive (as opposed to police) resolution of the Kosovo problem.

Thus the title 'The End of an Era' suggested that the Yugoslav crisis has evolved to a point where it is no longer possible for any of the social forces to behave in the old way. It did not imply that Golubović, Marković and Tadić were no longer socialists in the sense in which they have been up to now, any more than it implied that Yugoslavia itself was no longer a socialist country in the sense in which it has been up to now.[6]

A clarification may help here. After the Revolution the Yugoslav Party proclaimed the rule of the working class, at a time when this class was only a small minority in society as a whole: this constellation of forces was to be one of the main motors of subsequent bureaucratization. Furthermore, national equality was endorsed as one of the Revolution's main achievements, in a situation characterized by a very sizeable degree of regional (hence also national) economic and social inequality. Forty years on, the situation has changed considerably. The working class has grown in size and self-awareness, which today poses more sharply than ever the need for a radical democratization of political life. At the same time, the growth and national emancipation of the Albanian population, in particular, has placed on the agenda the need for their proper integration into the Yugoslav community – hence the need to shift popular identification of the federation with the South Slavs in favour of what Branko Horvat calls a 'federation of Balkan peoples'.[7] Such integration, indeed, is a necessary condition for overcoming Kosovo's economic and social backwardness – something which is vital for Yugoslavia as a whole.

The Yugoslav crisis has negative aspects which are obvious to all. But it can also contribute something positive: by making many of the country's systemic problems stand out more clearly, it can assist their future resolution. At least potentially, it can encourage a more ambitious and advanced conception of Yugoslav socialism. Which of these two dimensions of the crisis will prevail depends upon Yugoslav socialists themselves.

Thus what above all moved me to write 'The End of an Era' was a real concern that, if such well-known socialists as Zaga Golubović, Mihailo Marković and Ljubomir Tadić were to join the nationalist cause, all hope of seeing the emergence of a genuinely democratic alternative to the present quagmire of bureaucratic and nationalist discord would be set back.

(July 1987)

Notes

1. Or about my 'scanty', 'selective and slanted', 'inadequate, superficial, selective and utterly biased', 'unserious, irresponsible and systematically biased', approach.
2. It is simply not true that there is an all-Yugoslav consensus concerning the state of lawlessness in Kosovo. Moreover, a concerned propaganda campaign in the Yugoslav press is no proof either of the existence of such a consensus or of the truth of the campaign itself. Who should know this better than the three former Belgrade professors, themselves once the target of just such an onslaught?
3. At the same time as I am accused of 'bias and aversion towards the Serbian government', my criticism of the petition and those who signed it 'fully coincides with the attitude of the Yugoslav régime itself' and my article 'effectively defends the regime against the "accusations" of its radical critics'.
4. A concern over the US Right's designs in the Balkans, directed impartially against socialist Yugoslavia and socialist Albania, has already been voiced by me. See M. Lee, 'Albania's journey into isolation and US plans to end it', *Labour Focus*, Vol. 7, No. 1 (Winter 1984).
5. Searching for 'enemies' seems to have become a passion in certain Yugoslav circles. See, for example, the approach followed by Miloš Misović in his recent *Who Wanted a Republic: Kosovo 1945–1985*, Belgrade 1987.
6. Regress on the vital issue of national equality is much more evident, in fact, in the case of these three authors than it is for the LCY. As is shown by their reply, moreover, their signatures on the petition cannot unfortunately be regarded as a momentary aberration. This is confirmed by a recent intervention of Mihailo Marković at a Round Table

discussion on demographic policy in Yugoslavia organized last May by the Serbian Academy of Arts and Sciences. Here is part of the report published in the Belgrade weekly *NIN* of 14 June 1987:

'According to Academician Macura, the high natural birthrate of the Albanian population is creating an exceptionally strong population pressure. Serb, Montenegrin and other populations are disappearing in Kosovo in the demographic sense . . . Dr Musa Limani from Priština said that development was the most effective form of contraception. . . . the high birthrate is a consequence not a cause of Kosovo underdevelopment. . . . "Attributing political intentions to the Albanian population in regard to its birthrate is inappropriate and unreal", said Dr Aslan Pushka from Priština. He found an important reason for the high birthrate in Kosovo in the lack of education and employment of Albanian women, which he illustrated with many statistical data. . . . '*In the spirit of laissez-faire, unrestrained demographic growth is continuing in Kosovo and the bill for it is being submitted to the Federation*, said Academician Mihailo Marković. *With the Federation's material aid, Kosovo is supposed to draw closer to the Yugoslav income per capita. In a situation where the Kosovo population is doubling every few decades, this is like throwing money into a bottomless pit.*'

One is reminded of an incident a few years ago in Britain, when a Tory cabinet minister, Sir Keith Joseph, complained publicly that the poor were a drain on the resources of the state and said they should be encouraged to limit their families. His statement was widely condemned, not just by socialists. In Yugoslavia, at least, the current constitution, framed by the LCY, specifically guarantees couples the right to choose the size of their families.

7. See Branko Horvat, 'The Kosovo Question', *Labour Focus* vol. 9, no. 2 (July–October 1987).

PART TWO

Interregnum (1980–88)

Introduction

The 1980s began in Yugoslavia with the announcement that Tito was seriously ill – he was to die in May 1980. The Western media were speculating a great deal about whether the country would survive his departure. Tito's replacement was already in place: the eight-member state presidency, the nine-member executive bureau of the League of Communists, and the Committee for Protection of the Constitutional Order. The Army had its representative on two of these three bodies, though not on the state presidency which was to replace Tito as its commander-in-chief. At that point in time the country was already experiencing economic difficulties. Its future, I believed, depended on the one hand on maintaining national equality, on the other on the Communist Party's relationship to the working class. My prognosis was that mass industrial unrest rather than national tensions would come to the fore in the short term. I maintained this view even after the events of Kosovo.

The introduction of martial law in Poland, in December 1981, rang warning bells also in Yugoslavia, particularly since the Yugoslav authorities did not condemn Jaruzelski's act outright. Public opinion, by contrast, was undoubtedly on the side of the Polish workers: hundreds of Yugoslav intellectuals and students signed petitions protesting against military rule, and a further demonstration in solidarity with Solidarnosc was held in Belgrade on the first anniversary of its introduction. By the early 1980s there were clear signs of growing authoritarianism in Yugoslavia, culminating in the spring of 1984 with the arrest of six Belgrade intellectuals and the mysterious death of a young worker. I helped to set up a defence committee in London to press for their release, since it was important to prevent what was shaping up to be the first important political trial since Tito's death. I ascribed the political tightening up to the growing economic and political crisis. On the other hand, disunity within the leadership was increasingly coming into the open, posing the question of the durability of the central institutions. The country as a whole, and its youth in particular, was gripped by a sense of disorientation.

1987 brought many of the negative trends into focus. In April 1987, coalminers in Croatia began what turned out to be the longest strike in Yugoslavia's postwar history, while in Serbia Milošević's star began to rise with an inflammatory anti-Albanian speech in Kosovo Polje. There followed a sustained and well-organized anti-Albanian campaign, leading to a fundamental political realignment in Serbia and Yugoslavia as a whole. '1987 will be remembered in Yugoslavia as the year in which the systemic character of this crisis was made so evident that any hope of a partial solution to the country's troubles has been buried for good,' I wrote at the end of the year. I agreed with Gajo Petrović that democratization of the ruling party was of key importance. In Croatia, eminent economists talked of Yugoslavia becoming a member of the Common Market 'while retaining its socialist system'. In Slovenia, spokesmen for a new generation spoke in far more radical terms, demanding a revolution in the 'old social and political relations' so as to recognize formally the growing 'dominance of capitalist economic categories'.

The interregnum that formally opened with Tito's death ended with Milošević becoming the undisputed leader of Serbia, and Slovenia escaping what looked like a military coup. On my visit to Yugoslavia in the late spring of 1988, the sense of Yugoslavia's disintegration was already strong, as was the feeling that major clashes could not be avoided in the near future.

1

Tito's Deluge

Although Tito does not appear to be fatally ill, it is not surprising that the entry of Soviet troops into Afghanistan should have provoked a new round of speculation on the future of Yugoslavia. Yet NATO intelligence reports no Warsaw Pact troop movements near Yugoslav frontiers; and the fact that the Yugoslav army has been placed on low alert is neither more nor less than one would expect. They Yugoslavs themselves have reacted strongly against suggestions that they need any external protection. Indeed, such speculation has more to do with making political capital out of the Soviet dilemma in Kabul than with safeguarding Yugoslav national independence. However, if it is the case that the invasion of Afghanistan was caused by a 'fraternal' country's growing instability, then do not the Yugoslavs have some cause for concern?

Certainly, Tito's death will mark the end of an era in Yugoslavia's history. He is identified, in the eyes of his countrymen and the world, with the successful war of national liberation and social revolution in 1941–45, which in turn enabled the Yugoslav Communists to defy Stalin in 1948 and embark upon a 'Yugoslav road to socialism'. Most Yugoslavs know of this period only at second-hand: already by the mid-1960s, the vast majority of the Yugoslav population – and more than two-thirds of the party cadres, staff officers and administrative bureaucrats – had been born or reached adulthood in postwar Yugoslavia. With Tito's own departure imminent, the last link with the revolutionary birth of Yugoslavia will be broken. Following the deaths of Kidrič, Pijade and Kardelj; the purging of Žujović, Hebrang, Djilas and Ranković; the retirement of Popović and Vukmanović-Tempo, Tito is (apart from the old and sick Bakarić) the last of the original Central Committee which led the anti-fascist struggle and turned it into one for social revolution. Yet, as Mayakovsky once wrote:

Of the courage of our fathers we know from books
And their dream is what warms us
But today and beyond is our concern.

By continuing to hold power at the very top of the state and party apparatus for so long, Tito and his small circle of veterans ensured that those who came afterwards would, by comparison, be relatively unknown. When Tito finally departs, it is intended that political power should pass to a collective leadership, based on the twin principles of rotation of all elected officials and equal representation for the six component republics and two 'autonomous provinces' that make up Yugoslavia. There will be three supreme organs: the State Presidency, with eight members, one for each republic and province; the similarly constructed Executive Bureau of the Party; and a special committee set up in 1975 to safeguard the new Federal Constitution adopted a year earlier at the 10th Party Congress – and which includes the ministers of defence and the interior. By checking and balancing each other, these three bodies should, in theory at least, enable the new leadership to continue smoothly along the established road, and maintain equitable relations between the country's diverse ethnic groups.

History has taught Yugoslavs bitter lessons on the importance of such relations to ensure that their country survives intact. The virtual disintegration of the country four decades ago, followed by four years of bloody civil war, was due above all to the fact that the legitimacy of the old monarchist state rested essentially upon a single nationality (albeit the largest), the Serbs, and that it trampled on the national rights of the remaining Yugoslav peoples. In pre-war Yugoslavia all political parties were ethnically based, with the exception of the illegal Communist Party. The latter was thus alone capable of uniting the different nationalities, not only to fight successfully against Nazi occupation, but also to overthrow the corrupt and incompetent old social order in the name of a federal, socialist Yugoslavia. Yet despite this achievement, the late sixties saw a revival of nationalist politics, halted only by the ousting first of the Croatian and then (for somewhat different but not unrelated reasons) the Serbian party leaderships, in 1970 and 1972 respectively. The events of those years showed that, under certain conditions, nationalist intolerance could rise once again to dominate domestic political life.

These conditions had been provided, first of all, by the uneven economic development of the country. 'Market socialism', first introduced in the 1950s and given full rein with the economic reforms of 1965, increased the gap in the standard of living between the richer provinces in the northeast and the poorer southeastern regions. Meanwhile, on the political front, the development of 'market socialism' was accompanied by a redefinition of the role of the Party. Power was nominally devolved, on the one hand, to workers' councils (self-management) and, on the other, to the constituent republics. The Party changed its name to the League of Communists, and proclaimed that it was moving away from direct administration to the more modest role of a guide. The result was something of a vacuum at the centre. The key political role continued in reality to be played by the Party, but now the essential locus of its power became the regional centres, with their extensive economic autonomy. Strong local party bosses emerged who provided an institutional funnel for the growth of nationalism.

It was a sad reflection on the Yugoslav revolution that the second generation of party leaders were apparently able to establish themselves only on a petty-national basis (i.e. as Croats, Serbs, etc.), threatening in the process the country's stability. Tito, with the army's support, threw his personal weight into the fray and managed to defeat those powers in 1970–72. Thereafter, at the 10th Party Congress in 1974, he repudiated much of the course followed in the preceding two decades, and attacked 'liberalism' and nationalism in the name of Marx and Lenin and proletarian dictatorship. By means of these purges, and the partial recentralization of party and state which followed the 10th Party Congress, the spirit of nationalism was exorcized – at least for the time being. Yet the whole experience suggested that the ghost could rise again, if circumstances changed.

As Tito emphasized at the time, there was another reason why nationalist tendencies had to be kept in check. After the removal of the Croatian party leadership, Tito gave a speech to Zagreb workers in which he said that, if the Yugoslavs could not put their house in order, 'somebody else' would do it for them – unmistakeably the Soviet Union. Fearful for their independence, the Yugoslavs have always been quick to condemn armed interference in the affairs of other countries, whether by capitalist or communist governments. Recently they have criticized the Vietnamese invasion of Cambodia, the Chinese of Vietnam and the Russian of Afghanistan. In reality, short of some direct threat to the existing social order in Yugoslavia, it is highly unlikely that the Russians would intervene militarily. But the mere possibility acts as a powerful stimulus to the maintenance of a relative internal harmony.

Though nationalism was thus stripped of any respectability in Yugoslav political life, the leadership has not been able to find a serious solution to the economic contradictions which stimulated its revival. The country's foreign debts are huge, and its balance of payments showed a $3 billion deficit in 1979. By virtue of its extensive integration into the international market, it is much more exposed to the cold winds of depression in the West than are some of its sister-states in Comecon. The budgetary deficit for 1980 is in the range of $5 billion. Inflation will probably continue at least at the official rate of 25 per cent.

In the 1970s, the problem of economic growth or of stagnation could easily be interpreted in terms of 'developed' versus 'undeveloped' sectors, but the current economic situation has produced a sharp differentiation of interests within each of these.

Although the period since 1974 has seen a revival of economic planning 'in the context of self-management', the absence of effective institutions at the federal level can only hamper planned direction of the economy. In Yugoslavia today, there has to be much talking in the provincial and regional assemblies, and much bargaining in Belgrade, before the centre can act. And in the face of universal need, who is to decide priorities? The economic problems of today have deep roots in the structural under-development that was allowed to become endemic when consumer industries were being promoted in the sixties. Ageing industry, neglected agriculture, an inadequate road and railway system, significant unemploy-ment and low productivity – these could only be tackled by a massive increase in public investment and a consequent holding down of the standard of living for some time to come. Even if such a policy were adopted now, would the new Yugoslav leaders have sufficient political authority to persuade Yugoslav workers and peasants of the new scale of priorities?

The working class, the ultimate arbiter of Yugoslav stability, can at present find only a muted voice in the maze of institutional and constitutional structures that regulate political life. The system of self-management was a subject much discussed by socialists in the 1960s. But the workers' councils, even if they do represent a genuine attempt to escape rigid state control of the Soviet type, in fact have only limited scope while political power is monopolized by a single party which also provides the main channel for recruitment of the country's administrative cadre. Moreover, the League of Communists, though a large organization, is predominantly one of the technical and administrative intelligentsia: officials, professional people and highly skilled workers. The manual working class accounts for only about a third of its membership, with peasants making up another 7 to 8 per cent.

The role of Yugoslav trade unions was redefined in 1976, when a new Law of Associated Labour gave them a greater independence from party and state, and demanded more action from them on behalf of their members' material interests. Yet their true basic function is still to seek out and diffuse conflicts at the base, before they develop into full-scale strikes. In spite of this, strikes are common. Usually confined to a single plant or enterprise, and of limited duration, they are almost all concerned with wages and work conditions. They normally end in victory for the workers – and in replacement of the party, trade-union and factory officials who had allowed the strike to happen in the first place.

It is to relations between Yugoslav workers and the state that one should look for possible causes of social instability in the coming period, rather than to the national question or to Russian designs on Yugoslav territory. The working class has grown in size and culture: only 36 per cent of the population now live off the land, compared to over 60 per cent in 1948. Yet the working population is in a considerable state of flux. Almost 10 per cent work abroad; 14 per cent are unemployed (largely blue-collar workers). Perhaps as many as 40 per cent retain direct links with the land (the so-called worker-peasants), where there is widespread underemployment. There are large numbers of seasonal workers (in tourism and agriculture for example), and a massive migration from the poorer to the richer republics (14 per cent of the total population of Montenegro works outside its borders, 12 per cent in the case of Bosnia). Up to now, the Yugoslav régime has been able, by means of persuasion and partial concessions, to avoid generalized industrial unrest. But it is not clear how long it can continue to do so, if the underlying economic problems are not confronted.

(January 1980)

Reverberations of the Polish Coup

(a) Reactions, Official and Otherwise

The Yugoslav government has condemned the introduction of martial law but in measured terms, emphasizing the need for the Polish people to sort this problem out by themselves. Yet it has allowed very critical comments to appear in the press and on television, so much so that the Polish Embassy found it necessary to protest. (*The Times*, 18 December 1981) Here are a few:

- Belgrade *Politika*: 'What the Polish people want is national independence, free choice of their own road and defence of authentic progress.'
- *Borba*, the paper of the Socialist Alliance: 'The fundamental struggle is between the democratic forces in the working class and in the workers' vanguard against bureaucratism and a dogmatically imposed model, but not against socialism as such. Of course, the struggle against counter-revolution, which in the general disturbance did raise its head, is self-understood, but it is difficult to believe that it was anything but secondary.'
- The Yugoslav trade unions have expressed their deep concern for the working class in Poland after the introduction of the state of war.
- *Student*, paper of Belgrade university students: 'The PUWP has admitted its impotence by introducing martial law. The Party was unprepared for the problems, and perhaps did not really want to tackle them. The Polish working class has raised these problems in 1956, 1968, 1970, 1976, 1980. The only time the Party appeared willing to change its ideas about the way forward for socialist construction was in August of last year. Those who visited Poland in that year saw for themselves that the Polish people forgot to be frightened, that they were pressing for a qualitative change.' Punning on the word 'real socialism': 'The Polish real utopia is in fact the world real utopia. Can committees dispense with people?'
- *Start*, Zagreb bi-weekly: 'It is irrefutable that Solidarity had emerged as

the authentic representative of the Polish working class, that the working class trusted it and that a vast majority identified with it and its struggle. All those who summarily condemn Solidarity as anti-socialist and counter-revolutionary argue at the same time also that the Polish working class itself (that is, its 80%) is anti-socialist and counter-revolutionary. . . . It is clear that the Polish working class, after so many attempts and disappointments, had become distrustful and demanded firm guarantees, but it was also ready for dialogue and agreement. Those who were not ready for that, who clung with desperation and dishonesty to their monopoly and privileges, were the domestic and foreign conservatives. They are guilty for the fact that the struggle of the Polish working class and the great majority of the Polish people for better, more democratic and more human socialism, has once again been confronted with such difficult problems . . .'

● *NIN*, the Belgrade weekly: 'Not even the military government of the day disputes the fact that the main resistance to its act of 13 December came precisely from the working class. Therefore an essential question for understanding the Polish drama remains: can workers be counter-revolutionary? Can they struggle against their own essential class interest? The question of the socialist model, which so many times and with such measures of force and violence had to be defended from the workers, has to be posed once again. There is only one answer to this question, in our opinion. If the action of the Polish army had as its aim the maintenance at all costs of this model in its old form then, in the long run, its chances of success are negligible. To think otherwise is to go against the fundamental messages of history and of the Marxist way of looking at the world.'

Petitions on Poland

Around 400 Yugoslav intellectuals have signed petitions condemning General Jaruzelski's introduction of martial law. One such petition was read out at a meeting called at the Belgrade Student Centre a few days after Jaruzelski's move and around 150 people put their names to it after the meeting. A demonstration was called for a few days later in front of the Polish Embassy but the Secretariat of the Interior refused to give the necessary permission. When, in spite of this, a couple of dozen people still turned up, fifty policemen were waiting for them; a number of people were subsequently questioned by the police. Below are the texts of three such petitions circulating throughout Belgrade last December, showing many similarities but also significant differences in language and emphasis. Among those who signed the third petition were Milovan Djilas, Srdja Popović, a Belgrade lawyer who often defends political dissidents, and

Dobrica Ćosić, the well-known Serbian novelist. Nebojša Popov and Ljubomir Tadić, two ex-professors of Belgrade University, who were fired from their posts after the government moved against *Praxis*, signed the second petition.

1. To General Wojczek Jaruzelski, Warsaw

Expressing full solidarity with the trade union Solidarity, which at this moment represents the Polish people, we strongly protest against the introduction of military rule in Poland under your command and demand an immediate end to it in the interest of peace and democratic Polish renewal. All political prisoners should be immediately released.

2. To General Wojczek Jaruzelski, President of the Military Council of National Salvation, President of the Government of the People's Republic of Poland, the First Secretary of the Central Committee of the PUWP

It has fallen to you to enrich the inglorious arsenal of bureaucratic counter-revolution by bringing to it the experience of military rule. The efforts you are investing in covering up for your acts before European and world public opinion speaks volumes of its nature. Your attack on the Polish people confirms once again that in its fear and hatred of the authentic movement of workers, intellectuals and youth, of freedom and democracy, the usurping bureaucracy does not lag behind the most militant bourgeois reaction. Leonid Brezhev could have hardly hoped for a better birthday present.

We strongly condemn your brutal attack on the democratic achievements of the Polish people and demand an immediate end to the state of emergency, the freeing of all those arrested and the recognition of all the democratic rights which have been won since August 1980.

3. To Poland, the Polish people, the independent trade union Solidarity and all political and democratic currents

On 13 December 1981 a cruel military régime has been imposed by means of an unwarranted declaration of martial law. Such a drastic and fraudulent misuse of an army against its people, its historic and living strivings, is unprecedented. With it the democratic movement and national dialogue in Poland has been ended. This act, in addition, has disturbed international relations and endangered peace in Europe and in the world as a whole.

We greet the suffering and heroic people of Poland and its struggle for democracy and independence and join with others who have been shaken and disturbed by the Polish tragedy with this demand: for an urgent and immediate ending of the state of war, for the freeing of all arrested Polish patriots and democrats, for an end to all foreign interference in Polish affairs, for an urgent resumption of dialogue and negotiations with the patriotic and democratic forces in Poland, for resumption of the work of the independent trade union Solidarity.

(Spring 1982)

(b) Solidarnost with Solidarnosc

The Yugoslav daily *Borba* (the official organ of the Socialist Alliance) reported on 16 July 1982 that eight people – Pavluško Imširović, Gordan Jovanović, Dragomir Olujić, Jovica Mihajlović, Veselinka Zastavniković, Branislava Katić, Radmila Krajović and Bojadin Vizintin – had been sentenced to between twenty-five and fifty days in prison.

What happened and why is described best in a letter sent to the Belgrade weekly *NIN* (18 July 1982) by Dušan Bogavac, a journalist with *Komunist*, the official paper of the League of Communists of Yugoslavia. He writes of an 'unpleasant and unfortunately unreported incident' which took place during a demonstration organized quite spontaneously by various Belgrade youth clubs and organizations in support of the Palestinian national struggle at the height of Israel's attacks on Beirut last July.

> I must explain, in view of what I am about to say, that I was not sent to do a story but was simply drawn by the compulsive enthusiasm of the young people. Coming from all directions towards Marx-Engels Square, they created an atmosphere well known and dear to us older people. Who says that our youth is apolitical? . . . I was feeling rather pleased that I had come, when an unexpected drama developed involving six participants. This took place at the centre of the crowd and a high point of the meeting, when a PLO representative was about to speak. . . . What crime did these two girls and four boys commit that the SUP [police] boys should want to remove them them in such a brutal manner . . . and keep them isolated in a nearby building before driving them away in handcuffs once the demonstration had dispersed? Four of them did nothing more than hold banners with the name of the Polish independent trade union Solidarity. To be precise, the word Solidarity on their banners was written as it should be in Polish: *Solidarnosc*. As for the other two, all they did was to take photographs of the public meeting.
>
> To continue an account of the facts, ten or so plainclothes policemen masterminded the snatching of the youths from the crowd in front of the speakers' platform and temporarily placed them . . . where else but in the *Komunist* Readers' Club (!). They executed all this quickly and efficiently, swooping in twos and threes on individual men or women and dragging them across the square, the street and the pavement into the building.
>
> Although this is meant to be a limited statement by a witness, I cannot but ask some questions. Why should such an ugly event be allowed to take place during a demonstration dedicated to freedom, in the middle of our capital city, and before the eyes of a thousand shocked onlookers? Who had the idea of arresting our young people because they peacefully expressed solidarity with the Polish comrades of the trade union Solidarity? Why and how was this decision reached? Which laws did they break, which official political positions did they violate, which national and working-class feelings did they insult?

A few days after this incident, during the student radio programme Index 202, the organizers of the demonstration in Marx-Engels Square expressed their indignation at these arrests. Ljubomir Kljakić, director of the Belgrade Student Centre, felt 'a moral and material responsibility to speak out against this incident, which is totally unacceptable and politically damaging in every way'. His colleague, Milorad Vučelić, added that 'the sentences cannot be defended and those responsible for them should be named'.

When a *NIN* reporter interviewed Bora Pantelić, the chief Belgrade magistrate, he was told that the sentences were 'much too light' and there were hints of further arrests and trials. In Pantelić's opinion, the six should not have been tried by a magistrates' court at all since it was a question of a 'criminal act'. And he complained of the fashion apparently spreading through Belgrade according to which 'everybody and anybody feels entitled to question court decisions'. The legal article under which the six were tried refers to those who 'insult and denigrate the socialist and national feelings of Yugoslav citizens or Yugoslavia's socio-political form'.

Concluding his report, the *NIN* journalist Jovanović writes: 'This was not the only attempt during the demonstration (to change its aim and character). At one moment someone set alight a straw effigy on whose back was written *Juden*. This confusion of anti-Semitism and anti-Zionism must surely also insult the socialist, patriotic and national feelings of our citizens. Particularly since only a few metres away from the burning straw dozens of young Jews were giving their blood for the Palestinian fighters.'

Following on this incident, widely reported in the Yugoslav press, several more people were arrested for holding a silent vigil for their imprisoned comrades on the very spot where the six had been grabbed by the 'SUP boys'. They were condemned to one month in prison and only released after spending a week on hunger strike.

Meanwhile, in another capital, Ljubljana, the publishing house *Komunist* had released a book written by six well-known Slovenian intellectuals, most if not all members of the League of Communists of Yugoslavia. This book, called *Crisis under a Steel Cover*, is an account of the Polish martial-law regime in which cool realism mingles with warm sympathy for the Polish nation and working class. Once again Yugoslavia appears to speak with (at least) two tongues.

(November 1982)

Onset of the Crisis

(a) The Radović Affair and its Menacing Consequences

On 20 April 1984 the Federal police raided a flat in Belgrade (belonging to Dragomir Olujić). Those present were arrested, questioned and soon released. Four were physically assaulted while in custody. Several of the participants were subsequently rearrested for questioning, and released. One of these, Radomir Radović, disappeared after his second release, on 23 April. One week later he was found dead at a house outside Belgrade.

In the first week of May, Miodrag Milić and Dragomir Olujić (of the original group) were arrested in Belgrade and committed for trial. They have been charged with dissemination of hostile propaganda. In the second week of May, Vojislav Šešelj, another participant, was arrested in Sarajevo and charged with attempting to bring down the constitutional order. Šešelj has been on hunger strike ever since. His lawyer, the well-known Belgrade man Srdja Popović, has been denied access to him.

In the last week of May, three more people were arrested in Belgrade: Milan Nikolić, Vladimir Mijanović and Pavle Imširović. Mijanović will be charged with forming an illegal organization – a Free University – the others with being members of one. All three at once went on hunger strike and are now in the prison hospital, where they are being fed intravenously, apparently against their will. In mid-June Nikolić suffered a heart attack. All three are reported in poor health. Their families believe that the effects of the hunger strike will be permanent.

The four hunger strikers are demanding unconditional release, since they have broken no law. Amnesty International has adopted all six as prisoners of conscience.

Although the Yugoslav media have not even registered these arrests (with the exception of that of Šešelj), a number of petitions on their behalf are now circulating in Belgrade, Zagreb and Ljubljana, such as that published below.

It would appear that the Yugoslav authorities have decided to use this method to frighten unofficial critics, at a time when the country is undergoing its most severe economic crisis since the war. We are worried that this may be only the first wave of a more general repression of *all* critical opinion. We are therefore urging friends of Yugoslavia, and people on the left in general, to write or otherwise contact the Yugoslav Ambassador to express their concern, in an attempt to obtain the release of those imprisoned, and the clarification of the circumstances of the death of 33-year-old Radomir Radović.

Death of a Worker's Tribune

Radomir Radović was taken to the Central Police station for 'investigation', but released on the following day, 21 April, at 4 am. His interrogator was Ranko Savić.

On the following day, 22 April, he was rearrested. This time he was questioned by Mirosavljević and Petrović. He was released the next day, 23 April, at l pm. His family says he was quite calm. He had lunch, slept for half an hour and went to meet his girlfriend (they were soon to be married). Before saying goodbye to her, he told her he was going to visit a joint friend a few hundreds yards away. This was the last time he was seen alive.

On Monday, 30 April, he was found dead at a cottage outside Belgrade by his aunt, Jelena Radović. He was in his sleeping bag, lying on his back, arms crossed. His face was relaxed, and he had a bruise or scratch on his temple. On the floor of the house were a lot of spilled insecticide and and other agricultural poisons, human excrement and vomit. The family promptly called the police, who carried out only a superficial investigation (for example, the cup from which he was supposed to have drunk the pesticide was not taken away). The family lawyer asked for another investigation. It was agreed that he should be present at the autopsy. But when he came for the appointed meeting, he was informed that the autopsy had already been completed and was ushered out of the room. The day after Radović's burial, the results of the autopsy were still unavailable to his family and its lawyer.

The lawyer, Vitomir Knezević, was told that the technical analysis would take at least three weeks. Yet, as early as 10 May, the Under-Secretary of the Internal Security Service (ISS) of Serbia, Obren Djordjević, told a press conference that 'the autopsy . . . found no sign of violence on the body and death occurred as a result of an overdose of sedatives'. Also, the Chief of the ISS of Serbia told the official new agency *Tanjug* that Radović had been arrested only once and promptly released. This was then transmitted by *Tanjug* to all Yugoslav media. At the same time, Knezević was told by the Institute of Judicial Medicine that the results of the autopsy were as yet unknown.

A subsequent article in the Belgrade weekly *NIN* had the family describe Radović on the day of his disappearance as being in a state of great nervous tension, sorry for ever taking part in the discussion meetings, and saying that he was going to break off with those people and turn over a new leaf. Also, the lawyer was purported to say that the campaign by friends for clarification of the circumstances of Radović's death was most unhelpful. All this was subsequently denied both by the family and by its lawyer.

Radomir was 33 years old. He was first a building worker, later a technician. He helped to organize a petition, circulated by the workers of the Belgrade engineering enterprise *Minela*, demanding the replacement and punishment of one of the directors, Radoje Stefanović, for misappropriation and theft. An investigation was started but soon dropped – the signatories being informed that Stefanović had been appointed to head the executive of the Belgrade city council (which post he still occupies). Radović was sacked. He then found a job at 'Hidrotehnika', where he was also involved in a workers' petition against Mikaina Savić, a judge in the Court of Associated Labour, known for her anti-worker stand and various abuses of her position. The petition led nowhere – the city's new top executive moved in to protect her. Her cousin Ranko Savić, who is 'responsible for the University and the intelligentsia' in the Belgrade section of the ISS, was Radović's first interrogator!

Radović was known at Belgrade meetings for his courageous defence of workers' interests and of the principle of social equality and democracy. His funeral was attended by his family, several dozen plainclothes policemen and several hundred friends and comrades. His comrades laid a wreath at his grave with a big red star at its centre, because Radomir was a communist in the old and best tradition of the word – a workers' tribune.

(June 1984)

Open letter to the Assembly of the Socialist Federative Republic of Yugoslavia (SFRJ) and to the Assembly of the Socialist Republic of Serbia

Ever since 20 April this year, when twenty-eight people were arrested for meeting at a private flat in order to talk about the national question in Yugoslavia, the Enemy Number One has become the Free University. One outcome has been the tragic death of the young worker Radomir Radović. The arrests are continuing. On 23 May the Belgrade Investigating Court issued a warrant for the arrest of three more people: Vladimir Mijanović Pavluško Imširović and Milan Nikolić, whose names are now added to the previous three arrests – those of Miodrag Milić and Dragomir Olujić, and the synchonized arrest of Vojislav Šešelj in Sarajevo. All are being charged with 'the criminal act of association for enemy activity'. At this moment, four young lives are also in danger since, in protest against these illegal acts by the authorities, Mijanović, Imširović, Nikolić and Šešelj have started an unlimited hunger strike.

The authorities are behaving sternly, pretending that they are dealing with a dangerous group of terrorists which is a threat to the security of the state and its citizens – the indictment speaks of 'acting in the period from 1977 until April 1984 in creating, organizing, recruiting and consolidating a group of persons for the purpose of a counter-revolutionary action against the social organization, designed to destabilize and anti-constitutionally change the existing socio-economic system and overthrow the existing system of government'. No proof is offered other than these meetings which took place in private flats, the various topics which were discussed, the number of participants, and the number of these meetings. These meetings have been declared illegal. Yet everybody knew about them since they have always been open: those who took part in them considered them to be perfectly legal, indeed guaranteed by the Constitution of the SFRJ. Indeed, while declaring them illegal, not a single theme discussed at them has been mentioned by the authorities as proof of this, no doubt in order to cover up the true character of these occasions.

We, ourselves, have organized such seminars, known as the Free University, in the past – though these could not be 'advertised', because we could not use public places, which were closed to us, so we had to meet privately. As such we protest against this loathsome misuse of law which, playing with the lives and security of Yugoslav citizens, tries to construct a political process against imaginary enemies.

For the sake of public information, and in order to show what 'hides' behind these 'illegal meetings', we shall quote to you the themes discussed at them, together with the names of the main speakers, so that you may understand the nature of the 'counter-revolutionary activities' with which these people are being charged today.

Between 1972 and 1982 we organized and participated in the following meetings: L. Tadić, *Once More On the Concept of Enlightenment*; S. Stojanović and Z. Golubović, *An Attempt at a Marxist Analysis of Stalinism*; M. Marković, *The Distribution of Power in a Just Society*; V. Rus, *A Comparative Investigation of Industrial Democracy and Workers' Participation*; D. Mićunović, *The Idea of Humanism in Post-Classical Philosophy*; Discussion of Bahro's *The Alternative*; D. Ćosić, *About the Conflict between Realism and Modernism*; Discussion on the theme of *Philosophy and the Transformation of the World*; D. Bosković, *The Problem of Ideology in the Early Works of Yugoslav Marxists*; L. Veljak, *The Actuality of the Theory of Reflection*; B. Burzić, *Youth Between Movement and Organization*; K. Cavoški, *The Legal System in Real Socialism*; D. Grlić, *The Theory of Creativity*; T. Indjić, *About Spain*; N. Popov, *Ideas, Movements, Ideologies*; B. Jelovec, *Problems of Ideology and New Experience (Psychoanalysis and Phenomenology)*; M. Nikolić, *High Technology and the Possibility of a Telemathic Civilization*; M. Belančić, *Speech and Power*; Z. Golubović and M. Marković, *On Human Needs*; L. Stojanović, *Modern Art and the Humanist Idea*; Debate about the Solidarity movement in Poland;

S. Knjazeva-Adamović, *Man as a Natural Being*; Debate on the crisis of Marxism with respect to the work of Kolakowski.

Among those present at all these 'subversive' meetings were the above-mentioned comrades who, because of this, have been arrested and charged with 'organizing against the social system' and with counter-revolutionary activity. That which even the Polish authorities did not dare to do between 1975 and 1980, when the so-called Flying Universities were operating as a first alternative to the existing institutions of learning, the Yugoslav authorities are now arrogantly doing, breaking all international conventions on human rights and civil liberties that have been signed by our country. The idea of the Free University was naturally born too, at a time when everywhere in the world, under the influence of new social movements, 'alternative forms' are increasingly being sought and created in parallel to the institutionalized ones, expressing a general dissatisfaction with the latter. This is how we conceived the Free University and how we practised it for several years at different discussion meetings. We consider we have done nothing illegal. We have used only rights guaranteed to its citizens by the Yugoslav Constitution, which allows them personal initiative in the organization and improvement of their intercommunication. The above themes – and similar ones covered at other seminars of the Free University – best show its nature. Only a sick mind or an obscurantist conservatism could 'discover' counter-revolutionary activity and 'criminal acts' for the overthrow of the existing order behind this kind of activity.

We turn, therefore, to the general public and to you with a warning that a dangerous situation is now being created, which will have unforeseeable consequences not only for the future of these innocent people but also for the future of a free and democratic Yugoslavia, if *urgent* measures are not taken to put an end to this arbitrary exercise of power and if the necessary dignity is not returned to the court and judicial system in this country.

Therefore, in the interest of the possible and necessary democratic development of this country – which is the only real way out of the state of deep crisis in which Yugoslav society finds itself today – we demand an end to this hate-fuelled campaign, this hunting of people, and that those arrested – Miodrag Milić, Dragomir Olujić, Vlada Mijanović, Milan Nikolić, Pavle Imširović, Vojioslav Šešelj – be released. The charges against them have been invented, and their elementary civil rights have been withdrawn.

Since their lives are in danger, we demand *immediate* action. Otherwise their personal tragedies may become a very great shame for the whole of Yugoslav society.

Signed: Zagorka Golubović, Nebojša Popov, Miladin Životić, Svetozar Stojanović, Mihailo Marković, Dobrica Ćosić, Dragoljub Mićunović Ljubomir Tadić.
Belgrade, 30 May 1984

(b) Yugoslavia between the IMF and Socialism

The recent wave of repression in Yugoslavia has come as a rude shock. The raid on an informal political meeting, the manhandling of some of the arrested, the death of the young worker Radomir Radović, and the arrest of six intellectuals (five in Belgrade, one in Sarajevo), undoubtedly represents a novel development.[1] Nothing like this has happened since 1971 when a number of student leaders (including Mijanović, Imširović and Nikolić) were given two-year prison sentences for political activity. What explains these arrests and what are their implications? What follows is a sketch of the economic and political conjuncture against whose background they occurred.

Any analysis must start with the specific insertion of Yugoslavia's current problems into the wider international context. The post-Tito period, in which the Party has had to find a new internal balance after the departure in 1980 of its charismatic and long-serving president, has coincided with the first postwar economic slump. Its effect in fact began to hit Yugoslavia before Tito died; but any willingness to conduct the necessary economic and political reforms was lacking also in the period dominated by his departure. The present party leadership, constituted after the large-scale purges of the early 1970s, proved to be weak and divided, not only in response to the first wave of economic troubles, but also in its response to the accumulation of national, economic and social frustration which exploded in Kosovo in the spring of 1981. This tangible warning of the gravity of the problems faced by the leadership broke the charmed existence in which the Party had lived throughout the 1970s.

The three pillars upon which the Party's policy had rested up to the late 1970s – borrowing abroad in order to extend the industrial base, without sacrificing the standard of living or civil freedoms of the current generation; East–West détente, which reduced the pressure on the country's independence; and the non-aligned movement, which gave it a positive place in international politics – were all structurally weakened by the end of the decade. But it is the economic crisis which has proved most immediately intractable.

The Yugoslav economic crisis started in earnest in 1979, with shortages of elementary consumer goods. The scope of the problem was initially hidden from the Yugoslav public – and indeed from the highest bodies of state and Party! Even two years later, when the foreign debt climbed to $20 billion, neither the federal nor the republican assemblies, nor the equivalent Central Committees, were told the dreadful news. The truth emerged only in 1981 when, in the wake of the Kosovo events, the Belgrade press in a great heave broke through the traditional embargo on information. Other sections of the media pushed through the now opened door, and a period of considerable press freedom began. The party leadership, its confidence now badly bruised, responded with verbal self-criticism in order to assuage public wrath. With the 12th Party Congress looming (it took place in 1982), it managed to cobble together a kind of compromise on how to deal with the economic crisis – the so-called *Long-Term Programme of Economic Stabilization and Development*.[2]

Yugoslavia's economic problems have, no doubt, been aggravated by the high cost of money characteristic of the international finance markets since the oil crisis in 1976. Yet their roots are structural: they are to be found in the great imbalance created over the past two decades between an extractive industry which has been systematically neglected (along with other infrastructural investments like agriculture, transport, energy and health) and a bloated processing industry, mostly financed by foreign loans, dependent on imported raw materials, primary industrial goods and machine spares – all of which have to be purchased in hard Western currency.

In 1983 alone $900 million were added to the country's $20 billion foreign debt. To service this debt, and in order to be able to borrow more, the government has been cutting down imports and stepping up exports 'at all costs'. Import reductions have in turn produced a great shortage of essential materials. The result has been great industrial stagnation: depending on the branch, only between 30 per cent and 60 per cent of industrial capacity is at present being utilized.

This means that enterprises are increasingly operating at a loss. Industrial losses have in fact doubled each year over the past three years: 30 billion dinars in 1981, 62 in 1982, 118 in 1983. They climbed to 89 billion dinars in the first three months of this year. The main loss-makers are to be found in basic industry – energy, chemicals, black metallurgy, construction – all of which have created large processing plants without an equivalent extractive foundation. Yugoslavia's underdeveloped republics and province (Kosovo, Macedonia and Montenegro) suffer particularly from these problems.

One consequence is that industry now shows manifest over-employment, estimated at 900,000 workers out of a working population (employed in the social sector) of 6.7 million. Outside the factory gates, officially registered unemployment totals 1 million. Further increases are expected as some of the loss-making enterprises are forced into liquidation, and as social services are cut down.

Expensive primary industrial goods, a low level of utilization of industrial capacity due to shortages, low productivity of labour and high taxation of industry have all been fuelling inflation, which last year reached the record level of 58 per cent. For the only way that enterprises have been able to survive is by passing some of the increased production and operating costs on as higher prices. The rest is covered by borrowing. The pressure to borrow has drastically limited the availability of internal capital, 80 per cent of which is kept in the country's 175 banks. As the IMF terms begin to bite this year, problems of internal liquidity will increase, thus further deepening the already grave industrial stagnation.

What are the IMF terms? The IMF, working in tight coordination with 600 Western banks and 16 Western governments, has agreed to postpone Yugoslavia's current annual repayment of some $2 billion and to provide the government with a standby credit for this year's imports, on condition that Belgrade implements the following:

1. Strict downward movement of the dinar (at quarterly intervals!) with respect to a 'basket' of currencies of the main industrial countries.
2. 'Realistic' internal borrowing rates which, within the current financial year, should reach a level of 1 per cent above the rate of inflation.
3. Free market formation of prices of most goods and services.
4. Drastic lowering of individual and social consumption. With some amendments, the government has capitulated to these demands.

The crude monetarism of these terms spells nothing but further trouble for the Yugoslav economy. In 1983, when interest rates were at 18 per cent and inflation at 58 per cent, industry was already finding it difficult to sustain repayments on its internal borrowings. Its indebtedness rose by 68 per cent from the 1982 level (which was already a bad year), to a sum of 266.8 billion dinars. In fact, in order to keep production going and hence pay wages with some regularity, enterprises were borrowing without asking for terms – over 50 per cent of loans today are short-term. 396 billion dinars went from the economy into the banks last year to pay interest on short-and long-term loans, a sum only 11 billion smaller than what was put into its capital reserve fund. 1983 was the year in which 4614 out of 9597 larger enterprises had their bank accounts frozen, as a result of their inability to service their debts.

In this situation, the rate of inflation becomes all-important. According to the government's current plan, the rise in inflation will be 40 per cent, and new interest rates are being calculated accordingly. Such a rise in inflation will add 800 billion dinars to industry's debt burden, which means that outgoings will surpass accumulation. As industrial losses increase, so will the pressure on prices – indeed, the possibility of a 100 per cent rate of inflation this year is not ruled out by respectable economists, both Yugoslav and foreign. If this happens, the government's economic strategy will break down, as it will be forced to breach the fundamental principle of the deal with the IMF – positive interest rates. In fact, nobody in the government – nor, indeed, in the party leadership – knows what will happen if the level of inflation goes above 50 per cent. Whether this will happen – and there are some indications that it is in fact already above that figure – will be known in the autumn. If it does happen, Yugoslavia like Poland before her will be entering *terra incognita*. The press is already speaking of the possibility of recourse to Paragraph 267 of the Constitution: the suspension of self-management and direct rule by the nine-person state presidency.

In actual reality, of course, self-management – after a long period of increasing suffocation by the bureaucratic cancer – has already effectively been terminated. Reflecting on the circumstances of its demise, it is instructive to note that it was the West rather than the East which dealt the final blow. But self-management has not been the only victim. The grip which the IMF now exercises over the country's economy needed a fulcrum and found it in the increased power of the federal state, not only over the republican and provincial centres, but also over the main levers of the economy. As the government in Belgrade becomes the main arbiter of who is going to prosper and who go under, national intolerance has once again been placed on the country's agenda.

In a recent survey of Yugoslavia by the *Financial Times*, it was noted that 'Yugoslavia's protracted economic crisis, now in its fourth or fifth year, is beginning to change the political system.'[3] More than that, Yugoslavia's national independence, always an important factor of its internal stability, has come to suffer as well. Its non-alignment looks increasingly like a Yalta-type division of spheres of influence: last year Yugoslavia exported more to Comecon than to the West. Yet, as the commentaries in both *The Times* and the *Financial Times* noted last June, the country's acceptance of capitalist economic principles – exclusive reliance on monetary mechanisms – is seen as implying that 'the West is ahead ideologically' of the Soviet Union.[4] This year, furthermore, Yugoslavia has agreed to move away from the barter trade with Comecon towards greater exchange with the West. Current agreements with the IMF and the World Bank show Yugoslavia's commitment to liberalize controls, which still cover over 80 per cent of all imports, to relax the terms under which foreign capital can invest, and to open (for the first time) the service sector to it as well. In return, the banks are promising patience and tolerance.[5]

However, it is obvious that this addiction to foreign loans, which the LCY leadership has acquired over the past decade or two, will have to be paid for by the Yugoslav working class. If one examines the economic effects of the current crisis on this social layer, the most visible is the drop in its purchasing power: 30 per cent over the last three years, and the trend is continuing. A part of revenue destined for the workers' pockets has instead gone to maintain production. A tight squeeze on wages was enforced last year, with the federal government's decree which tied the growth of personal incomes to the growth of *net* income in the enterprises. This blatantly anti-self-management measure was found unconstitutional by the Constitutional Court, yet the government has simply ignored its ruling! As a result, the drop in real income of those employed in the social sector – 12.7 per cent last year – was the only part of last year's economic plans which was fulfilled (all the other predictions dealing with the rate of inflation, exports and industrial growth have already gone badly astray). This year further wage cuts are being planned. In compliance with IMF demands, the income of workers employed in loss-making enterprises, or in those which find themselves unable to maintain their tax and bank interest rate burden, will be cut further.

The following will serve as an illustration. Between 50 per cent and 60 per cent of workers working in the communes of Zagreb and Belgrade, the two largest Yugoslav cities – i.e. some 200,000 workers – will suffer direct wage cuts. In Titograd, the capital of Montenegro, 7,500 workers are employed in loss-making enterprises and will be similarly affected. As a trade unionist reported to a recent meeting of the trade-union Federal council, the first question you are asked when you go to the factory to explain the need for sacrifices is: 'When did you last receive a wage and how much was it?'[6]

According to a trade union research study, 70 per cent of the earnings of the lowest paid category of workers today goes on food. For those in the middle wage bracket the equivalent proportion is 46 per cent. Can their standard of living be forced down much further? Recent announcements in the press speak of rents and council service charges going up between 30 per cent and 90 per cent. Yet the government has done nothing to protect the low-paid. Last year's agreement in the Chamber of Republics and Provinces to protect the living standard of the worst off was merely a piece of paper, since no sources for funding this relief programme were ever specified. Not only individual but also social consumption has been under attack, and further cuts are on the way.

The press reports economic and political pundits as saying that it is precisely large social expenditure that has been the main barrier to increased productivity and hence to a healthy competitiveness of Yugoslav exports. There are even suggestions to privatize consumption completely – what one paper called 'a monster idea spawned by the tide of conservative economic ideologies coming from the West'. Jakov Sirotković, a member of the Central Committee, attacked the government's monetarism in the press in the following fashion: 'Concepts borrowed from bourgeois economics which see profit as the fundamental moving principle, interest rates as the main regulator of extended reproduction, and the labour market as the economically rational criterion of consumption, are once again being popularised.'[7]

Mitja Ribičič, a member of Yugoslavia's top leadership, has commented in response that the critics of monetarism have not come up with a better, 'acceptable' solution. What is 'acceptable' is precisely the key to the present debate in Yugoslavia. A young Zagreb economist has recently put the matter bluntly: 'It is true that the workers have not eaten the accumulation; but they will nevertheless have to pay for all the wrong investment made by borrowing abroad. Somebody must pay, and it must be industry. . . . The belief that industry's trouble can be solved by redistribution of capital sitting in the banks is absurd. For there is no capital there at all, only huge debts which do not appear thanks only to various bookkeeping machinations.'[8] It is now time to turn to the workers' vanguard, the League of Communists (LCY) and its leadership.

The Long-Term Programme was cobbled together, as we noted earlier, in time for the 12th Party Congress, when the leadership needed a substantial answer to public concern about the economy. Adopted as the Party's programme, it was voted in by the Federal Assembly and taken as the main framework of the government's economic policy. Under the impact of a rapidly deepening social and economic crisis, however, marked differences in the leadership developed around its underlying conceptions, its aim and its general orientation. The conflict is about what is a *socialist* economy and hence also about the nature of socialism.

Six out of twelve meetings of the Central Committee since the 12th Party Congress have been devoted wholly to the economy without any of them producing a workable unity. These meetings 'have become instead a series of monologues, prepared several weeks ahead'. A broad division between the proponents of the market (and the IMF terms) and those in favour of a 'socially agreed' response and greater self-reliance has been established. This division is by no means neat. Many who adhere to the *Long-Term Programme*, because they fear that any other alternative will increase significantly internal repression, dislike for similar reasons the strengthening of the central state which has accompanied the adoption of the monetarist policies. Those on the Party's Left, who are preoccupied by the effects of the current economic approach on workers' living standards and on the position of the working class in general, and who would like a more centrally managed economy, do not like to align themselves with the Stalinists ('the bureaucratic right') and their demand to return to the situation which existed prior to the 1965 economic reforms. For example, Alexander Grličkov, a prominent 'liberal' member of the Central Committee, has expressed concern with the fact that there is no worked out 'self-managing way' out of the crisis. His party colleague, Sirotković, quoted earlier, said recently that 'never before have vulgar apologists for the economy of state socialism, of state capitalism, tried with aggress-iveness and such misuse of their status to impose their views on society'. Dragoslav Marković, the current head of the Yugoslav Party, complain-ing of the lack of unity in the Central Committee, stated in a recent in-terview: 'We seem to have adopted under pressure an attitude of waiting in order to gain time. It is once again 1965 when, influenced by social demagogy and left posturing, we had in fact capitulated. Today there is no alternative.'

The Yugoslav press has registered the fact of leadership disunity and reacted accordingly. In fact, since its breakthrough in 1981, this press has in more than one sense become an honourable substitute for the banned journal *Praxis*. It is true that the influence of most of the alternative ideas that appear in print is limited; nevertheless, the readi-ness of the press to debate problems and solutions to the current crisis has been remarkable.

Under pressure from below, but also from within the Party, the press has opened a wide discussion on the main themes of economic and political life. It has publicized the fact that the Party's disunity has affected the government's ability to act in any but an *ad hoc* manner, and has turned its attention therefore also to the question of the democratization of the state institutions, 'discovering' in the process a widespread desire for direct (as opposed to the present laborious indirect system of) elections to all state bodies, with multiple candidacies.

The obvious impotence of the Federal Executive Council, the im-pression that nobody really knows what will happen when prices are finally unfrozen at the end of June, have been seen as ominous. 'There is no analysis, nor any competent predictions, of what kind of social earth-quakes may occur, nor is there a programme for what can serve as social shock absorbers when this happens.' Indeed, the vacillations of the Yugoslav Party contrast badly with the determination of the IMF. 'Federal ministers admit privately that the IMF has given them support they have hitherto lacked from other institutions in the country.'[9]

The state of health of the LCY has therefore come under an unpre-cedented scrutiny. This is so not only because it has been proved that 'the LCY was no better at foreseeing global social events than ordinary Yugoslav citizens, so that instead of the vanguard ambushing the crisis, the crisis has ambushed the vanguard'. It is also because of the Party's disunity. What level of differences can be tolerated without any move to do anything to overcome them? Are the differences in the Party more fundamental, or is it divided only on how to implement its programme? Is it possible to overcome the differences? What is specific to party action that distinguishes it from being a mere tail to chaotic administrative regulation of the economy? These are some of the questions put to the

LCY. Calls are being made for an extraordinary party congress. 'These days the party forums are busy organizing their own discussions and submitting their reports to themselves. Nobody mentions the position of the working class, the unemployment, etc. as the relevant criteria for judging the Party's efficacy.' Such statements can be found scattered in the press, showing the deep demoralization of the party membership.

According to Ivica Račan, a member of the Central Committee, an extraordinary congress of the LCY would serve no useful purpose. 'If this CC is unable to put into practice the decisions of the 12th Congress, why expect it to be able to prepare a congress which would solve anything?' Speaking before the June meeting of the CC, which was to consider the current role of the LCY, Račan predicted rather accurately what was going to happen: 'We shall again have sterile expositions, sterile discussion and sterile conclusions, which will move nobody to action.'[10] Only after a thorough debate in the membership, he believes, can one hope to have a productive CC plenum.

Under the heading 'The Membership must be given a chance', the Zagreb weekly Danas wrote last May: 'The pressure of the problems is too great. It is impossible to go any further in stabilizing the economy without a public debate. The question is: is it politically wise today to avoid a wide and democratic discussion of the state of the LCY?' Commenting on the view of Franc Šetinc (the Slovene party leader) that the Party should go to the people, the paper wrote: 'If among the most responsible people of this country there is no unity on the programme [for a way out of the crisis], what will the leadership take to the base? What will win the people, motivate them to shoulder the burden? A functionary's appearance is no substitute for a programme of action.'[11]

In spite of the clamour for an open and public debate, the head of the Party, Dragoslav Marković, does not see any need for it. He favours a 'scientific-professional discussion' instead. 'What are the questions around which we need to conduct a public or party debate? The problem is not that we have no answers to the economic crisis, but that we do not have the strength to put them into practice.' Indeed, he was worried that 'insufficiently thought-out and precipitate social action may only worsen the great difficulties ahead: social and other misfortunes could force us to retreat.'[12]

The LCY leadership, in other words, while presiding over a first step in the thoroughgoing transformation of Yugoslav socialism into something more acceptable to its capitalist creditors, is unwilling to go to the country to justify itself. The Party has been accustomed to governing with a large measure of popular support; it knows today that such support escapes it. Squeezed between the IMF and the working class, between crude expediency and its historic association with this class, the Party has proved unable to move. Instead, as a result of this basic and inescapable contradiction, it is splitting into a number of different and opposing currents which cut across national boundaries. The question is: how long can the centre hold?

The recent repression must be understood in this context. The Party's centre, in its desire to contain internal party differences, has now moved sharply against an active dissident intelligentsia. The city's Free University forums have in the past three or four years been speaking with varied and dissonant voices. Interventions of a purely bourgeois character, un-restrained in their dismissal of all achievements of the Yugoslav Party; nationalist sentiments mingling with Southern European populism; anarchist visions of post-industrial society; social-democratic critique of the Leninist tradition; syndicalism influenced by the Polish *Solidarnosc*; trenchant Marxist critique of the state of socialism in Yugoslavia – all these and many other preoccupations have been registered in these forums. The socialist intelligentsia, under a continuous economic and political pressure from the authorities, has taken all this time to recover its élan of the late 1960s. The rise of the working class movement in Poland was very important in this respect. Social tensions generated by the increasingly formidable economic crisis, and the immobilism of the Party in the face of it, have further strengthened its growing involvement with the present status and the future prospects of the Yugoslav working class.

The battle in Yugoslavia today to maintain and extend freedom of speech, writing and assembly is not, therefore, of concern just to restricted intellectual circles. It is of vital interest for the socialist future of the country itself.

(June 1984)

(c) Trial of the Belgrade Six

In August 1984, six Yugoslav intellectuals – Pavle Imširović, Gordan Jovanović, Vladimir Mijanović, Miodrag Milić, Milan Nikolić and Dragomir Olujić – were charged jointly with forming a 'counter-revolutionary organization aimed at the overthrow of the constitutional order'. Three of them – Imširović, Mijanović and Nikolić – went on hunger strike until they were released five weeks later, following wide-spread protests both within the country and from an impressive constell-ation of forces abroad, spanning West European trade unions, the Italian Communist Party, the German Greens, French, German, Austrian and Scandinavian Social Democrats and the British Labour Party, as well as numerous artists and writers from the West European and North American Left. Mindful of the country's complicated national pattern, the

Western Left has often neglected the Yugoslav authorities' tough treatment of 'nationalists' (most recently following the repression of a revolt against poverty and backwardness in the Province of Kosovo), which has given the country a place near the top of the European league table so far as the number of its political prisoners is concerned.[13] This time, however, things were different, not just because the repression was directed against socialists – the three hunger strikers had been leaders of the student movement in 1968, for which honour they had paid with two-year prison sentences in the early seventies – but also because the trial of the Belgrade Six, and the arrests which preceded it, signalled the danger that, twenty years after the fall of Ranković, a much more authoritarian regime might once again be established.

The trial began on 5 November 1984 and closed four months later. In the week preceding sentencing, Imširović was freed unconditionally, while the case against Jovanović and Mijanović was postponed to a later date. Despite the fact that only the prosecution had been allowed to call witnesses, the accusation of 'counter-revolutionary organization' had collapsed. The remaining three defendants were now charged with 'hostile propaganda', on the basis of papers from their flats. The case against Nikolić rested on two texts: a seminar paper he had written for Ralph Miliband while on a postgraduate course at Brandeis University in 1982, and a copy of the article by 'Michele Lee' on Kosovo which NLR published in the following year. On 4 February 1985 Milić was sentenced to two years, Nikolić to one year and a half, and Olujić to one year in prison – all pending appeal. The NLR text was dismissed from the charge against Nikolić. He was found guilty not of 'hostile propaganda' but of 'incorrectly' portraying social and political conditions in Yugoslavia: of not being sufficiently patriotic before a foreign audience. His wife's serious illness, the judge said in his summing up, alone had been responsible for lighter sentence.

Milan Nikolić's speech on the last day of his trial was at once testimony to Yugoslavia's achievements and a harsh indictment of its leadership's failures.[14] Addressing himself to socialism's great and abiding need for democracy, Nikolić is clear that only socialism can secure democracy's full flowering. His message, and the programme he charts for socialism, transcends Yugoslavia's frontiers and speaks directly to Western and Eastern Marxists alike. His insistence on the responsibility of the intelligentsia for seeing through the historic project of socialism recalls the promise of 1968, when – under the impact of the Cuban and Vietnamese revolutions – the Left in both East and West appeared to wake up to its political tasks. In 1968 the Yugoslav authorities chose to ignore the voice of the country's youth. In 1972 they sent its leaders to prison. A decade later they have condemned them to prison once more. But the message will not go away: either a democratic, self-managing socialism or a return to some variant of Stalinist or capitalist barbarism.

(March 1985)

Notes

1. See foregoing texts under (a).
2. For some of the debate provoked by this programme, see *Labour Focus*, Winter 1984 (vol. 7, no. 1). In this period, faced with increasingly combative assemblies, the government has developed an art, reminiscent of Westminster, of dodging uncomfortable questions. For example, when asked to clarify the statement made by then Finance Minister Petar Kostić at the end of 1982 that Yugoslavia faced 'a collapse', it set a precedent by answering fifteen days later – in writing! At this time, however, it was still possible to hear government ministers describe the IMF as 'international finance gendarmes', whose task was to make sure that debtors paid in full and on time. By the end of 1983, as the economic crisis went into full swing, such direct naming of the *force majeure* became more or less impossible – 'democratic centralism' took care of that. The more the IMF bled the Yugoslav economy, the greater were the attempts to present them as paragons of sound economics and honest living. The 'gendarmes' turned into 'our foreign partners'!
3. Of 18 June 1984.
4. Ibid. Also, *The Times*, 16 June 1984.
5. The decline in the value of the dinar has made Yugoslav labour power very cheap. This has encouraged, for example, the influx of the modern version of putting-out from Austria, Italy and West Germany. Foreign businessmen bring in material, machinery and even supervisors and return with finished goods. Done occasionally in the past, as a measure of dire necessity, in the textile industry, the practice is now much more common and has entered other industrial branches. It has been attacked in the Yugoslav press in a language very reminiscent of pre-war CPY writings.
6. See *Start*, 8 October 1983.
7. *Danas*, 2 April 1984.
8. Ibid.
9. *Financial Times*, ibid.
10. *Danas*, 2 April 1984.
11. Ibid., 25 April 1984.
12. *NIN*, 27 May 1984.
13. See the Amnesty International report *Yugoslavia: Prisoners of Conscience*, London 1982.
14. For Nikolić's speech, see *NLR* 150 (March–April 1985).

A New Stage in the Crisis

1987 will be remembered in Yugoslavia as the year in which the systemic character of the crisis was made so evident that any hope of a partial solution to the country's troubles has been buried for good. The debates over the distribution of power among the republics and provinces that have been taking place during the past year, in preparation for possible changes to the 1974 Constitution, have been unable to conceal the true problem: the gravely eroded legitimacy of the party and state apparatus in the eyes of the population at large – and above all in the eyes of the working class.[1]

The Yugoslav press highlighted this problem particularly in its detailed coverage of last April's strike by miners at Labin in north-west Croatia, the longest strike in Yugoslavia's postwar history. The miners stayed out for two months, braving a concerted barrage of hostility from managerial, trade union and party/state functionaries at the regional level, struggling to provide their families with the bare necessities of life (attempts by Slovenian miners to collect aid were blocked). Deserted by their own Workers' Council, the Labin miners showed that self-organization, discipline and solidarity could prevent the imposition of a quick solution at the workers' expense.

The very length of the strike and the unanimity of officialdom's attitude to it (though it did enjoy a largely sympathetic press coverage, with reporters clearly shocked by the conditions in which the miners were supposed to live and work, and by the gulf between the miners and local functionaries) produced a new awareness of how inadequate the existing system of self-management is in representing and defending the interests of the self-managers. The system was challenged at all levels: the power of workers to decide on their own living and working conditions; investment policy; control by managers, officials and party or trade-union bodies. Always presented as expressing the socialist essence of the Yugoslav state, in the light of this strike self-management was shown to be its opposite: an instrument for exploiting the workers. This is not, of course, to say that self-management could not be given a different content. But in an overall situation in which emphasis is increasingly laid on the right of the market to determine the mode of operation – and indeed viability – of an enterprise, the question is automatically posed as to whether the workers too should not be free to determine the price of their labour-power in the marketplace, by their self-organization and using all the traditional means of working-class struggle.[2]

Srdja Vrcan, a sociologist of national repute, has expressed this plainly: 'I must admit I have always been suspicious of the idea that true self-management, which ought to mean more than complete autonomy of economic management, can be harmonized with the treatment of workers as wage labour, as a commodity. It seems to me now [i.e. after the strike] that refusal to recognize the status of workers as labour-power is only too easily translated into denial of their right to influence independently the price of their labour.'

The Labin miners' grievances were not just the abysmal level of their wages or the arduous conditions in which they lived and worked, they were also the fact that recent unprofitable investment by the Republican government in two new pits had had to be paid for largely out of their own pockets. The unequal distribution of this burden was registered graphically by the media, which contrasted the comfortable lifestyle of the local functionaries with the dire poverty of the workers, one of whom told a reporter: 'I work in a pit and live in a hovel.' Many of the pit workers in fact come from Bosnia-Herzegovina and remain totally unintegrated into the local community based on tourism, where life is geared to making a quick buck out of this particular exchange with the wealthier West.

The workers had no difficulty in calculating the difference between their wages and the price that coal fetches on the market; but no Republican politician came to explain to them how the surplus was being used. Energy prices are a matter of increasingly heated dispute between producers and consumers, and the final settlement is left to the powerful chamber of republics and provinces within the Federal Assembly. The remoteness of the Republican government from the men who actually dig the coal was pointed up sharply by the strike.

The miners asked for members of the Federal government to visit Labin, to see how they lived. In 1986, in fact, all Yugoslav wages had actually been allowed to rise, after a four-year decline; this was due to the 13th Party Congress which took place that year. In 1987, however, the rise of inflation to a new high of 120 per cent was used as a pretext to claw back some of this gain (a reduction in the value of their work norms provided the immediate motive for the Labin miners to come out on strike) and the Federal government imposed an all-round wage cut, except for administrative workers. Throughout the country, industrial workers responded by taking strike action, in the most extensive wave of strikes since the war.

The Republican and Federal governments chose to treat the strikes as problems of local self-management. What was particularly conspicuous was the total abstention of the Party from any involvement at that level. Indeed in the case of the Labin strike, the Party quite simply attempted to break it, by calling upon its members to return to work, provoking many bitter comments on the new role of the Party as strike-breaker. Threats to dismiss the striking miners prompted the press to quote Brecht: since the people have lost the confidence of the government, the people should be dismissed.

The Bosnian miners digging coal in Croatia did not feel that their problem had to do with their national origin, for they knew that the local bureaucracy had used similar methods to break the strike by the largely Croat dockworkers in the nearby port of Rijeka, following which all the strike leaders were sacked. The Labin miners ensured that the same thing would not happen to them by insisting on total democracy and on the participation of all in the conduct of the strike. Similarly, in the second wave of strikes which took place over the summer, Serb and Albanian workers in Kosovo struck together, giving the lie to the daily propaganda in the Belgrade press about the supposedly unbridgeable ethnic tensions in the province.

The very durability of the Labin strike allowed a sustained press coverage that gave the Yugoslav public a glimpse into the organization of power at the local level. But the enormous clout possessed by local government bodies was most graphically illustrated at the beginning of August, in the Macedonian village of Vevčani in the commune of Struga. The cause of the conflict that arose there was the decision of the commune authorities to tap into Vevčani's water system, installed by the village's own efforts, in order to supply a neighbouring cluster of new dachas built by Macedonian Republican functionaries. Worried that there might not be enough water to irrigate their own fields, the villagers organized an effective civil resistance and prevented the new pipes from being laid on their land. The authorities responded by sending in a squad of specially trained riot police: armed with dogs and electric prods, they attacked the inhabitants, including small children in their mothers' arms. Several ended up in hospital. While the pipes were then being laid, the youth of Vevčani organized a hunger strike. Thanks to the press in other republics, the enormity of what had happened at Vevčani was made public; and the intervention of a Slovene delegate to the Federal Assembly ensured that the Federal government's responsibility could not be passed over in silence.[3] Slovene writers, moreover, attending the yearly poetry festival at Struga, used that forum to register their strong condemnation of the police brutality at Vevčani, and they were subsequently joined in this by their Serbian counterparts. But the total absence of any comparable protest from within Macedonia itself allowed the authorities there to brush off the writers' protest as merely an example of 'intolerance towards the Macedonian nation' – a perfect vindication of the charge commonly heard among left intellectuals that the main purveyor of nationalism in Yugoslavia is the bureaucracy.

The vital need to stand up to the nationalism of one's own bureaucracy (which provided the main theme of the debate [see pp. 52–73 above] between the present author and the editors of *Praxis International*) was stressed in a recent interview carried by the Zagreb weekly *Danas* with Vladimir Milčin, one of the most talented young Macedonian theatrical directors.

> For us in Macedonia, the present moment opens a perspective of decline into barbarism . . . we are gathering the fruit of a situation in which part of the intelligentsia has been richly rewarded for its silence and for its applause . . . part of the Macedonian intelligentsia has played the role of a shock-absorber, silencing possible incidents which could have caused it to raise its voice and ask: what are these politicians doing to our country? The economic situation is inevitably going to radicalize society, and the idyll – which has even been theorized – that the intelligentsia and the political establishment cannot come into conflict because of the external danger [i.e. to the nation] will no longer be able to function effectively.

Commenting on the silence of most Macedonian intellectuals following the police assault on the people of Vevčani, Milčin went on to say:

> The intelligentsia believes that the repression is directed against concrete individuals and that it will stop there. But in fact repression never stops there, it is increasing both in terms of the numbers affected by it and in terms of the range of measures employed. The more silence and collaboration there is, the more it gathers momentum. The silence of the Macedonian intellectuals in the case of Vevčani gives the political establishment, the bureaucracy, the right to use equally drastic measures against all protests, in all parts of Yugoslavia . . . Things went so far that people made statements saying that nobody had been injured there, that women had gone into hospital just to have a good time. Macedonian participants at the Struga poetry festival never contemplated boycotting it. They all agreed to the official blasphemy. The Macedonian intelligentsia agree to applaud those who lie, persisting in their hope that all would end there, that they themselves would not fall victim. . . . Something terribly important happened there [i.e. in Vevčani]. It showed above all that the Macedonian bureaucracy can with impunity raise a truncheon against the Macedonian people. The people of Vevčani have taken away from it the right to speak on behalf of the Macedonian nation . . . We are in a situation in which everybody is trying to save their soul . . . I mean, all of us have to find individual answers, though the space for such

expression is narrow. So we are left with the necessity of taking risks as individuals, reacting as individuals – which is more difficult and dangerous than speaking through a collective. But it seems that there is no other way.[4]

Milčin's words do not merely show the specific predicament of a Macedonian intellectual, they also express a general need for Yugoslav intellectuals to transcend the confines of their national cultures and to end collaboration with republican and provincial bureaucracies that try to present their own interests as 'national interests'. A new awareness of Yugoslav solidarity in the face of a common threat of bureaucratic reaction has been one important contribution of this troubled year.

Instructive in this respect has been the reaction to the political infighting in the Serbian party, which erupted into the open in dramatic fashion at the end of September. In an unprecedented move Dragiša Pavlović, head of the Belgrade party – the largest party organization in the country, numbering almost a quarter of a million members – was dismissed overnight. This followed a talk he held with the editors of the newspapers and journals published by the Politika publishing house, in which he criticized the nationalist tone that had been present in several of their organs (notably Politika, Politika Ekspres, Duga and Intervju) and emphasized the danger presented by the growth of Serb nationalism.

The difference between the two wings of the Serbian party – that led by republican Prime Minister Ivan Stambolić, to which Pavlović belonged and whose principal organ in the recent period has been the weekly NIN; and that led by Serbian party leader Slobodan Milošević, whose flagship in the past months has been the daily Politika – has most evidently centred on their different approaches to national problems in the autonomous province of Kosovo: should these be tackled with or without the collaboration of the Kosovo provincial leadership; consensually or by more drastic means including reliance on Serb nationalism?[5]

The print-runs of the papers criticized by Pavlović, which have increasingly been specializing in the exposure of supposed instances of Albanian nationalism and irredentism (often through the pens of dis-credited former policemen from the Ranković era before 1966, who seem to be in possession of many secret party and administrative files), have been rising vertiginously, making them a powerful and independent instrument of policy-making vis-à-vis Kosovo.

When in early September a young Albanian recruit called Aziz Kelmendi went berserk in a barracks of the Serbian town of Paracin, killing five of his fellow soldiers (one Serb, one Croat, two Bosnian Moslems and one Slovene) and wounding a dozen more, the door was opened for an orgiastic assault in sections of the Belgrade press on the Albanian population as a whole, an assault which spilled over into actual (and in places seemingly coordinated) violence against Albanian citizens and their property in towns throughout Serbia (similar incidents also occurred in Macedonia and Montenegro). A dangerous link was emerging between militant nationalism and the 'firm hand' ideology associated with Ranković's period: the no-nonsense approach of the authorities at the time is increasingly being contrasted with the supposedly soft policy of today towards the Albanian population in Kosovo. Resurgent Serb nationalism was thus carrying in its wake the danger of a slide into undemocratic methods of political rule.

It seems likely that the differences between the two wings of the Serbian party in reality go well beyond the issue of Kosovo. Yet it is characteristic of the present climate that Kosovo was used as the pretext to settle differences. It did not matter that Pavlović, in drawing attention to the danger of Serb nationalism, in fact said nothing contrary to the proclaimed position of the Yugoslav Party; nor that the methods used to remove him and a number of his co-thinkers (including two leading functionaries of the Politika publishing house) were openly undemocratic; at the end of a two-day public debate, the Central Committee of the Serbian party voted overwhelmingly for the dismissals, in the full knowledge that this was only the first stage of an extensive purge. Only a handful of contrary votes were cast, while a small number of delegates mainly from the Provinces abstained.

Milošević in reality won his massive victory on the promise of strong leadership at a time of mounting economic difficulties and growing social unrest. The precarious state of the Serbian economy, which is officially admitted to be on the point of collapse, had produced a fear of popular demonstrations in a city in which one quarter of the republic's industry is concentrated. Yet Milošević offered no alternative programme for solving either the national problem in Kosovo or the perilous state of the Serbian economy – nothing other than insistence on 'unity' and unquestioning respect for the authority of the party leadership. He has now gained the reputation of being the country's leading neo-Stalinist (an honour once coveted by the Croatian politician Stipe Šuvar).

The bulk of the Yugoslav press published in the north has registered its concern at events in Serbia with unwonted unanimity. The Slovene youth weekly *Mladina* denounced the particular marriage of nationalism and neo-Stalinism that brought Milošević his victory. In more measured tones, the Zagreb weekly *Danas* expressed similar anxieties. In Belgrade, the weekly *NIN* – which had been among the first in the capital to draw attention to the increasingly unacceptable face of Serb nationalism, and whose editors will for that reason soon be replaced – has, together with *Danas*, provided the best coverage of the Serbian party's new course. Party leaders in other republics, however, have for their part remained silent. Public comment would have broken the accepted norm according to which politics within the different republics is the prerogative of the local party leaderships. But more importantly, perhaps, they had nothing to say on the key nexus of problems: the state of the Serbian economy, the plight of its people and the fear of mass demonstrations in the country's capital city. Their silence points to the missing centre of the country's politics: the Central Committee of the League of Communists of Yugoslavia and its 'executive' officers. The authority once enjoyed by Tito was never transferred to the federal party organs and this provides an important clue to Yugoslavia's current political disarray.

It is not just Serbia's economy, of course, which is in a critical state. Most recently, the precarious economy of the entire country was given a massive jolt by the Agrokomerc affair. Agrokomerc, based at Velika Kladuša in north-west Bosnia, was until August 1987 considered to be one of the most successful of Yugoslav enterprises, having grown from a small chicken farm to an agro-industrial unit employing 13,000 people. In August, however, it began to emerge that much of its phenomenal expansion was due to the extensive issuing of false promissory notes, costing unwitting creditors right across the country as much as $500 million. The rise and fall of Agrokomerc cannot be explained simply in terms of economic crime, though it was also that. In many ways it was Yugoslavia in miniature, combining such elements as: shortage of liquidity, which is strangling the economy; desire to escape from backwardness and underdevelopment; integration of party chiefs, state functionaries and managers into a form of concentrated power specific to Yugoslavia's decentralized system; development as a springboard into prestigious public office; localized Stalinism, the sense of both total control over economy and men and loyalty of a population lifted out of traditional backwardness; as well as a degree of national pride, in this case linked to Bosnia's two-million-strong Moslem nation. One dramatic outcome of the affair was the resignation of Federal Vice-President Hamdija Pozderac – a tactic of damage-limitation so far as the high functionaries of Bosnia-Herzegovina were concerned.

The big holes which have emerged in the capital of many banks and enterprises (some of which could not pay their workers in August or September) have caused consternation throughout the country, and there has been a concentrated attempt to present Agrokomerc as the sole responsibility of the Bosnian republican government. Yet it is in fact clear that responsibility for this greatest of postwar financial scandals rests with the entire Yugoslav political establishment, since Agrokomerc simply behaved in a manner which has become the norm in the country as a whole. 'Fikret Abdic [director of Agrokomerc] made only one mistake: he overreached himself. Otherwise, Fikret's innovation is not new in the Yugoslav economy as a whole: whenever somebody issues a false promissory note, the officials of the commune, the republic or the Federation – depending on the importance of the Potemkin village in question – come to his aid and cover the losses. This time there is no power in Yugoslavia which could cover this up, quite simply because Abdić inscribed the whole of Yugoslavia on his promissory note. That Agro-komerc was a motley lie was known by all. Those who did not know – did not wish to know.'[6]

The fall of Agrokomerc exposed a fundamental truth of the state and organization of the Yugoslav economy. In his interview quoted above, Milcin spoke of the vista of barbarism opening up. For the population of Velika Kladuša, the bankruptcy of Agrokomerc brought barbarism to their doorstep. As creditors sought to make good their losses, the entire regional economy simply closed down. The empty vaults of the social bank meant that 13,000 workers – as well as many others in the area – could not be paid. Shops were closed down since there were no goods in them: they simply had no money to buy stock. At the extensive Agrokomerc farms, millions of turkeys and chickens, left without food, have turned to cannibalism. Local rivers are full of dead birds, and the Army has been called in to plough up a square mile of land to bury the victims. Sixty thousand inhabitants of Velika Kladuša and its surroundings have been suddenly abstracted from the rest of Yugoslavia and left in limbo. The republic's authorities did provide some money to prevent actual mass starvation, but they have not dared send any representative to talk to the local population. Nobody in the end has taken responsibility for remedying the catastrophe that has hit the area. Practically overnight, a large part of north-west Bosnia was thrown back into its age-old existence of poverty and unemployment. The traditional exodus of local men to the industrial centres of the north has been resumed.

The rapid deterioration of the country's overall political and economic situation has been becoming a matter of public concern for the Yugoslav Army. Back in 1981, the Army was called in to put down mass demonstrations in Kosovo; it made it clear that it did not like the task. Defence Minister Admiral Branko Mamula warned in September that Yugoslavia's friends abroad were becoming increasingly concerned about the fact that 'our country's problems are growing in an unbridled manner, to a level which exceeds any possibility of control by the leadership'. He criticized the League of Communists for remaining at the margins of social reality, devoid of the necessary unity on the basic question of how to tackle the crisis, and without any secure basis on which to reform and organize. The Army has declined any autonomous role for itself in resolving the country's problems. Yet the possibility cannot be excluded that it may feel obliged to assume such a role, if only on behalf of the beleaguered Party. There are certainly signs that the Army is quietly beginning to organize the necessary infrastructure within civil society, in order to facilitate the imposition of law and order if and when it feels that this has become imperative.

One medium of the Army's presence within civil society is provided by the peculiar structure of the Committees of General People's Defence and of Social Self-Protection. These were established by decision of the 11th Party Congress in 1978, when it had already become clear that the crisis was there to stay. Committees are formed at all enterprises, and at all levels of the state administration. They are composed of party and trade-union leaders, representatives of the state administration, Army and police commanders. Thus they concentrate political and state power at the different levels of society, though it is not at all clear to whom they are responsible.

In September 1987, Nenad Bucin, a member of the Federal Conference of the Socialist Alliance, called for outright abolition of the committees on the grounds that they not only act outside the norms of the system, but are also deeply unconstitutional. 'Not only does no organic link exist between them and the state, i.e. a self-managing and socio-political mechanism, but their members also feel themselves to be free, under no obligation to integrate themselves into or act within that system. With the exception of the highest party bodies, socio-political organizations [i.e. party and state organs] have practically ceased to follow and analyse in depth the political situation, not to speak of what should follow from such an analysis – e.g. action, influence, leadership. . . . It is open to dispute whether these committees have assumed non-transferable rights and obligations; I personally believe that they have. The important thing is that the state, enterprise, political and other social bodies are no longer concerned with this delicate and important work.'[7]

The editor of *Danas* commented pertinently: 'The essential truth contained in this proposal [of Bucin's] begins to shine forth once one understands that a whole series of the "black spots" in Yugoslavia's current reality are due not to any nefarious activities by some internal enemy, but to the suspension of the system's legitimate institutions and to the exercise of political power by way of silent prohibitions, through which an increasing number of political decisions are being taken with ever-decreasing responsibility.' The bureaucracy is increasingly engaged in a kind of double-talk: what individual state and party leaders cannot do in public, because it may be unpopular or open to question, they do under a different hat through the committees, which are not susceptible to outside control.

This question, together with others, is likely to be discussed at the forthcoming Party Conference, scheduled for 1988. Whether this conference will be productive remains to be seen.

(December 1987)

Notes

1. Working-class membership of the LCY continues to decline. The Belgrade party lost 4,389 members during 1986, most of whom were workers. The rate at which workers are leaving the Party trebled over the last year. There are also fewer peasants. The Belgrade youth organization, moreover, registered a loss of 10,601 members during this period. *Politika*, 15 October 1987. Only in Macedonia, Montenegro and Kosovo has the party membership grown over the last year.
2. Since 1980, the number of strikes in Yugoslavia has been doubling every year. In the course of 1987 alone there were over 900 strikes involving over 150,000 workers. Strikes increasingly involve whole enterprises: although most of them are aimed at higher wages, an ever larger number demand the replacement of managers and functionaries, and take up wider issues of economic policy and declining living standards. For an account of the vigorous strike wave in Macedonia in 1987, see *Labour Focus* vol. 9 no. 3 (December 1987).
3. Vika Potočnjak asked for the formation of a commission of enquiry to establish what happened in Vevčani. The assembly's Committee for Internal Policy decided against this; instead the commune of Struga and the Macedonian republican assembly will be asked for additional information. In the meantime, Vevčani holds daily public meetings.
4. *Danas*, 22 September 1987. Milčin could have taken up the question of the Macedonian republic's attitude towards its Albanian minority. In a letter to *Mladina* on 9 September 1987, a number of Albanian intellectuals drew attention to attempts by the Macedonian authorities to reduce educational opportunities for the Albanian population. It seems that the commune of Struga is once again taking a leading role here. 'In recent years, the number of Albanian children attending secondary schools has been decreasing, as has the number of secondary school children receiving education in their own language. Silently, through a system of unspoken quotas, closure of Albanian classes and reallocation of Albanian children to mixed classes, educational discrimination is being practised against Albanians. In Skopje, where 3,000 children finished primary school, only 140 of them were enrolled in the erstwhile Albanian "Zef Lush Merku" gymnasium. If this trend continues, we can expect that in the near future secondary school education in the Albanian language will practically disappear in Macedonia.' Albanians form some 17 per cent of the population of Macedonia.
5. For an extended account of the struggle inside the Serbian party, see 'The Spectre of Balkanization', Part III, Chapter 2, this volume.
6. Alexander Singer, in an interview in *NIN*, 4 October 1987.
7. *Danas*, 6 October 1987.

Awaiting the Future

On 15 March 140 years ago, two weeks after the publication of *The Communist Manifesto*, a revolution erupted in the Habsburg Monarchy which was both national and democratic in content: on that occasion, the Monarchy's South Slavs declared themselves in favour of unification within a common Yugoslav state. Today, on the anniversary of the 1848 revolution, the Western press reported the concern of France and West Germany that Yugoslavia may actually disintegrate, both economically and politically. The main problem, according to foreign ministers Delors and Genscher, is that the central government in Belgrade is simply too weak to tackle the problems of an insolvent economy.[1]

In March 1988 a whole number of pressing issues – ranging from competing national claims via the collapsing economy to the nature and scope of the common state – are firmly present on the country's political agenda, not least because of the ruling party's impotence, flounderings and determination to avoid every opportunity for self-reform. Only the apparatus of repression seems to be intact – its activities, however, increasingly questioned by a press that reflects not only internal differences in the country's leadership, but also the uneven political and economic development of Yugoslavia's constituent republics.

Characteristic in this respect is the current dispute between the Federal and the Slovene public prosecutors, following a wave of criticism in sections of the Slovene press of a recent visit made by Branko Mamula, the Yugoslav Minister of Defence, to Ethiopia. *Mladina*, the weekly paper of the Slovene Socialist Youth Alliance, has questioned the rightness of selling arms to a government that is at war with its own people, arguing that the Ethiopian masses need not arms but food.[2] Confusing Admiral Mamula's civilian with his military function, *Mladina* aimed its criticism at the Yugoslav People's Army itself: fear that Yugoslavia may be nurturing its own Jaruzelski has become widespread in the northernmost republic.[3] This prompted the Federal government to lean on the Slovene judiciary to institute criminal proceedings against *Mladina*'s editor, Frani

Zavrl, and another Slovene journalist, Andrej Novak of *Teleks*, for their 'attack' on the army. The Slovene public prosecutor complied and countered the ensuing public outrage by referring to his own impotence before the constitutional powers of the Federal instance. Irritated by this lack of bureaucratic solidarity, the Federal prosecutor responded by publicly denying any role in the affair, thus in effect calling his republican colleague a liar. Hence, what began as a case of 'the state versus the press' turned into a case of 'the Federation versus the Slovene Republic' – and inevitably also into one of the 'Slovene national problem'.[4] For its part, *Mladina* has remained unbowed: its print-run has almost doubled in the last year, to 30,000 copies, which is a staggering number given that the Slovene nation in Yugoslavia numbers less than two million people and that *Mladina* is a youth paper.

The fact that the official press had called precisely for such action (i.e. criminal prosecution of Slovene editors and journalists), with the once great Belgrade daily *Politika* – now reduced to the role of local party rag – even accusing *Mladina* of state treason, is not accidental. This is because the leadership of Serbia has nailed its flag firmly to the mast of a new centralism. What is more, the party in that republic is today headed by a man widely perceived as a neo-Stalinist. The spectre of a recharged authoritarian state, under the guise of Yugoslav unitarism, today haunts the entire Yugoslav critical intelligentsia, irrespective of its regional and ethnic provenance.

This fear is fuelled by the continued fall in the gross national product: unprecedented economic stagnation and high inflation have remained impervious to the various 'reforms' undertaken by successive governments.[5] It is universally acknowledged that last year was like its predecessors, only worse; and that this year will conform to the same pattern. However, this response does not take into account the tectonic shift which has taken place in Yugoslav politics, transforming the familiar landscape into a wholly new terrain. Postwar Yugoslavia was built on a consensus between two main forces: the working class and the Party. Today, this consensus no longer exists. A visible aspect of this momentous development is the growing militancy of workers in industry and social services. Workers today are better organized and increasingly ready to take their demands for a living wage and responsible government onto the streets and before government buildings. The time when workers on strike remained within factory walls is gone for good; today they are marching and occupying city squares. To be sure, workers' self-organization is only at its initial stage, but one should not underestimate the damage which this growing self-reliance is inflicting upon the party bureaucracy, unaccustomed as it is to open confrontation with its historic base. As a result, the Party is in disarray: the rising pressure exerted at its base can no longer be accommodated by the apparatus. The greater the gulf between the two, the more profound and systematic does the crisis become. Workers' strikes should not be seen as only defensive: they are a necessary stage of the class's positive self-definition.

The vacuum opened up by this breach is today being filled by increasingly radical (though not necessarily left-wing) programmes drawn up by the country's intelligentsia. Their comprehensive character, however, contains a central vagueness regarding the question of who is to be the agent of the necessary reform. The choice of the agent and the character of the reform are intimately related: no assessment of the latter can be made without reference to the former. Notwithstanding considerable differentiation, one can speak today of the existence of two broad fronts – both of which, however, share the premise that political democratization is vital if control is to be re-established over the rapidly deteriorating political and economic life of the country. One approach seeks, on the one hand, removal of the state from control of the economy (regulation of the latter being left basically to free market forces) and, on the other, removal of the Party's control over the state, replacing it with a system of parliamentary democracy. Whether such a system should be multi-party or not is a matter of debate: while some argue that democracy depends on freedom to organize, others fear that freely constituted parties would become vehicles of national strife, citing the history of pre-war Yugoslavia as a negative example. There are differences regarding the extent to which the electoral system should be adjusted to reflect the multi-ethnic composition of the country: in Slovenia, for example, the idea of replacing the existing federation with a confederation has been rapidly gaining ground among otherwise quite dissimilar political currents; this reflects above all Slovene industry's frustration with the rising demands made upon it by the Federal government, especially in order to subsidize the latter's foreign currency obligations, but also the fear of centre-led bureaucratic counter-revolution. Similar frustration exists in Croatia, another big exporter to the West. In Serbia, on the other hand, it is almost part of the local common sense that Yugoslavia is already not a federation but a confederation, and that the main task lies in amending the 1974 Constitution in favour of greater centralization. Whereas, in Slovenia and Croatia, there is the emergence of a working relationship between intellectuals and party leaders on what is called 'modernization' of the economy and the state, in Serbia the basis for this is increasingly provided by nationalism.[6] The developments in Serbia over the past few years can best be described as tragic for the country as a whole.[7] Likewise, in the three federal units which only a year ago declared themselves bankrupt (Macedonia, Kosovo and Montenegro), dependency on a redistributive Federal centre is the starting-point of any discussion on political reform.

Whatever the differences, however, democratization of the state and liberalization of the economy – with the workers having the right to organize free trade unions – commands practically universal agreement. That this project heralds an end to the Yugoslav system of self-management is either implied or positively argued. Indeed, given that one is dealing here with affirmation of the market in both goods and labour, and that the reform is likely to lead to an increase in the already high level of unemployment (some 1.2 million out of a working population of 6 or 7 million, unevenly distributed among the Yugoslav regions), it is obvious why the working class is ruled out as the main carrier of the reform. The choice falls instead on state institutions, such as the Federal/republican assemblies. Even the idea of an imposed constitution and a government of 'good men and true' has been mooted. In an economy plummeting below the level of subsistence, it is assumed that workers would not resist such changes, even if they did not approve of them: the majority might even welcome an extension of democracy coupled with a promise of economic revival.[8]

The other broad current seeks change also through democratization of the Party. Such a position was recently expressed, in a rare public appearance, by Gajo Petrović, one of the most respected of Yugoslav philosophers and a founding father of the journal *Praxis*:

In recent times one increasingly hears the opinion that the situation inside the Yugoslav League of Communists is so hopelessly bad that the organization should be left to die its own death. It is argued that one should instead try to create outside and independently of the Party – through some other existing (or new) institution or body, or outside all institutions and bodies – if not a socialist democracy, then at least some kind of civil society or legal state. Some of these ideas undoubtedly have merit. But it is wrong simply to leave the Party out of such thinking. The LCY is, not only factually but also constitutionally, the ruling state party (which I do not approve, but merely point out), so without its democratization and de-bureaucratization no serious democratization of the whole society is possible. A bureaucratized LCY will fight by all means to maintain its political monopoly. Only a democratized LCY would consent to 'political pluralism' in any form. This is why the struggle for democratization is a necessary moment of the struggle for democratization of society as a whole; and it is the right and duty of every citizen of the Socialist Federal Republic of Yugoslavia to criticise the bad situation in the LCY and to support the democratization of that organization.[9]

This is advice that cannot be faulted. Indeed, one of the most surprising aspects of Yugoslav politics today is the absence of suggestions regarding this most pressing and important task. The character of the reforms being undertaken in the USSR and China seems, if anything, to have strengthened public lack of interest in the condition and affairs of the Party. Even those 'liberal' and left-leaning currents within the LCY who, only a year ago, were advocating the creation of a 'progressive bloc' of anti-bureaucratic forces in and out of the Party, or the transformation of the Socialist Alliance into an 'oppositional' force, have fallen silent. The few gains made in Croatia, where the last election of the republican party's central committee involved a choice of candidates, have turned out to be quite ephemeral. In Serbia proper, a substantial regression has been registered with the recent change in leadership. Only in Slovenia is the space for alternative tendencies and programmes actually being enlarged. The weakness of the Federal government, moreover, is an expression of this uneven political development: it is due, in the last instance, to the collapse of the LCY as a party in any meaningful sense of the word; to its implosion into a purely bureaucratic, state-dominated core. Democratiz-ation of the LCY, both organizationally and politically, is therefore a *sine qua non* of any positive resolution of the Yugoslav crisis. Again, this poses the question of who is to be the agent of de-bureaucratization of the LCY. For Petrović, this should be the Yugoslav citizens. To judge by the Polish experience, however, it is more likely to be the increasingly self-confident and self-organized working class.

No programme which does not appeal to the latter's class interests is likely to succeed: the party bureaucracy, with its long experience of governing, is fully aware of this, which is why it feels itself impotent. The economic crisis has grown out of the long-term conflict between its own privileges and the interests of this class: the result is the growing disintegration of Yugoslavia as a political and economic unity. Unable to make a radical turn either to the right or to the left, since both threaten it with loss of power, its ideological machinery is churning out programmes and documents that satisfy nobody. Though considerable differences exist within it,[10] they are balanced by the equally strong tendency to close ranks. The key to the balance of power within the Party lies, in the last instance, in what the working class does in the period ahead.

The reform that is necessary for ending the Yugoslav crisis must be as comprehensive as the crisis itself. However, no successful blueprint for a thoroughgoing reform of the sclerotic institutions of the Yugoslav state and politics can be drawn up unless it is pivoted on the working class, hence also on the historic interests of that class. At least one can say that some green shoots are visible today in the bleak landscape of Yugoslav politics. This is because the ground itself is changing, in conformity with the tectonic shift itself.

(April 1988)

Notes

1. *The Guardian*, London, 7 March 1988. This is a year of several anniversaries for the Yugoslavs: seventy years ago Yugoslavia came into being; forty years ago it broke with Stalin's Cominform; twenty years ago the student movement provided the glimpse of a political revolution.
2. *Mladina*, Ljubljana, 12 February 1988.
3. Though this fear may not be realistic, recourse to the army at some future date cannot be excluded. An actual military coup is highly improbable, though candidates may be found among the large number of retired military officers, of whom as many as 10,000 live in Novi Sad, 7,000 in Split; there are apparently 800 retired generals and 18,000 retired colonels living in Belgrade. Organized in their own associations, and with time on their hands, they have been busy recommending a policy of the 'firm hand' as a universal medicine for the country's ills. *Mladina* in particular and the Slovene Socialist Youth Association in general have been their favourite targets. There are some signs also that the middle layer of active army cadre is getting restless now that their living standards are falling, along with those of other citizens.
4. The editors of the army journal *The People's Army* joined in this campaign. They argued in favour of legal proceedings on the grounds that *Mladina*'s articles are 'only one expression of anti-socialist and anti-self-management destructive activity on the position of nationalism and separatism. [*Mladina*'s] attack on the army is an attack on Yugoslavia'. Quoted in *Danas*, 1 March 1988. Mamula's own response, in contrast, was more tempered. As the campaign against *Mladina* grew to include calls for a purge of the Slovene leadership, the leadership decided to comply with the Federal request.
5. In 1987 investment fell by 16 per cent; capital reserve funds to 16.5 per cent of the GNP; losses in the economy in the first nine months were up 135 per cent; inflation was at 170 per cent. 'The two years of Mikulić's government have been catastrophic. Between 1987 and 1988 the economy has practically collapsed under the combined effects of falls in production, exports, imports, investment, capital reserves and personal incomes. The effects of this collapse may not look dramatic, since we do not have a stock exchange and people are not throwing themselves out of windows, but everybody knows that we have become the sick man of Europe.' Cedo Zić, *Start*, Zagreb, 5 March 1988.
6. The 'ethnocentric' bloc in Serbia is, of course, not a monolithic entity. Optimists argue that some of its elements, such as the Belgrade Committee for Freedom of Thought and Expression, even provide welcome humorous relief. When not concerned with the Albanian birthrate, its members are busy redrawing internal Yugoslav frontiers. Its suggestions for amending the current Yugoslav constitution include 'elevation' of the Republic of Croatia's regions of Istria, Dalmatia and of the erstwhile Habsburg Military Border to the status of Autonomous Provinces, to balance the two in the Republic of Serbia. They also argue against the principle of national equality at the federal level: it is, apparently, unjust that one Montenegrin vote should have the same weight as eighteen Serb ones.
7. This is evident in the Belgrade press. The daily *Politika* and the weekly *NIN*, once leading Yugoslav journals both in quality and readership, are now in the service of a parochial dogmatism. Only in the last few months, the circulation of *NIN* has dropped from 200,000 to 70,000 copies. The back pages of *Politika* are today given over to interminable obsessive features on Serbia's past: its battles, its dynasties, its unique sufferings. This change is all the more serious given that Belgrade is Yugoslavia's capital city.
8. For two – politically very disparate – articles belonging to this current, see *Labour Focus*, April 1988 (Vol. 10, no. 1).
9. *Danas*, Zagreb, 23 February 1988.
10. The brutality with which the struggle within the bureaucracy is waged, at meetings and in the press, is degrading the country's public life on a daily basis. Today, it is a common occurrence for journals published in one republic to be banned in another: the recent arrest of the *Mladina* street vendor in Zagreb was paralleled by the confiscation of another Slovene youth paper, *Katedra*, in Belgrade. In a ringing denunciation of this

practice, a well-known Belgrade journalist wrote recently that 'protection' of the readers of one region from information coming from 'foreign' territories elsewhere in the country is turning all Yugoslavs into foreigners in their own land. Alexander Tijanić, 'The Art of Disintegration', *Danas*, Zagreb, 1 March 1988.

6

Brief Notes on a Visit to Yugoslavia, 18 May to 1 June 1988

Belgrade

My luggage is left behind in Split, courtesy of JAT, bringing inevitably the suspicion that this was intentional. As a result, several hours' wait at the airport. A chance to talk to Milan N.

He and his friends feel themselves isolated by the nationalist wave that has swept Belgrade. The new leadership has contributed to a dramatic decline in the quality of the press. Unlike myself in London, Milan no longer reads the daily *Politika* or the weekly *NIN*: he is unaware of what is being written there. Nevertheless, Milan believes that the nationalist tide is now in retreat and that people in general and some intellectuals in particular are getting tired of the Kosovo business. For ordinary people, the struggle for daily existence is becoming the paramount concern. Milan fears that the coming cuts in wages, combined with rising prices, might easily trigger a mass workers' demonstration in Belgrade (which is the major industrial centre of the republic). He fears this, on the grounds that the result would be bloodshed and a general tightening up on the domestic front. In other words, he does not place much hope in worker unrest ameliorating the situation.

Milan is highly critical of Ljuba Tadić and Mihailo Marković, who he feels have behaved opportunistically in regard to the Albanian issue and have thus contributed to the rise of nationalism in Serbia. This in order to be received into the well-organized nexus of Belgrade intellectuals gathered in the Serbian Academy of Arts and Sciences and the Writers' Association. Milan says that the times have produced their own men: the obnoxious stuff printed in the press is written by nobodies – but it brings money and instant fame. He refers in this context to a Serb participant in a recent (unsuccessful) meeting of the Serbian and Kosovo writers' associations, who told his Albanian colleagues: 'Gentlemen, our nations are at war and that is all I wish to tell you.' This outburst (which brought the orator much applause) was reported only in *NIN* and nowhere else in

Serbia proper. It is such happenings which are making Zaga Golubović nervous: her unhappiness with the activities of the Human Rights Committee to which she belongs is apparently growing by the day. She is, I am told, horrified by the growth of the lunatic fringe which is demanding military rule in Kosovo and the elimination of the Province's autonomy. She is, apparently unhappy with the Committee's proposed amendments for the current constitution, in which a drastic redrawing of internal frontiers is called for. Yet she has signed the document in question.

During my stay in Belgrade, another delegation of Serbs from Kosovo visited the republican and federal assemblies, handing in a petition with the above-mentioned demands signed by at least 50,000 people. Milan believes that what is happening in Kosovo is influenced if not outrightly organized from Belgrade.

The isolation of the Left in Belgrade is tangible. The city (which has tidied up its centre and looks more handsome than ever before, its superb position on the confluence of the two rivers breathtaking in the beautiful spring weather) radiates claustrophobia. The bookshops are marked by the new emphasis on traditional values, history and religion. A chance conversation with an activist of the Solidarity Fund (set up two years ago to support journalists and others suffering repression for their political views) brings this into focus. Highly intelligent and articulate, he has been organizing citizens – owners of small plots of land on the city outskirts – threatened with expropriation without compensation. He vividly evoked the indifference and brutality of the local magistrates. He had led the plot owners in a march to the Assembly buildings and spoken on their behalf to those who had received them there. (The central government buildings, situated on Marx-Engels Square, are now an almost daily target of marches and visits by aggrieved citizens and workers.) The proud father of a small son (who participated vigorously in the conversation, much more than his mother!), his intolerance towards other nationalities was open, despite protestations to the contrary. (I am told by a young historian, another chance acquaintance, that nationalism tinged with xenophobia has penetrated deeply into the masses.) He repeated the now usual refrain that 'since Ranković, we Serbs have not had a proper leader'.

This is, after all, what Marković and Tadić – who should know better – have been saying for the last two years or more. I am told by Mladen L. (a sociologist from Belgrade, long resident in Zagreb) that, at this year's Inter-University Conference, Marković openly lauded the new party head Milošević as 'the best leader we Serbs have had since Ranković'. (This was subsequently confirmed by Tomaz M., a well-known Slovene dissident philosopher, who maintains contact with Belgrade intellectuals.) How is one to explain this posthumous embrace of Yugoslavia's best-known policeman, and the present-day endorsement of a party leader widely rejected elsewhere in Yugoslavia as neo-Stalinist, as symbols of a (which?) national cause – by men and women whose life has been dedicated to the struggle against bureaucratic deformations? The only explanation is that Ranković was, and Milošević is, a convinced centralist and that this is seen as favouring Serbia and these national leaders *manqués*.

Suspicion of Slovenia (and of Croatia, but there is less to be said for the moment about this central republic) is widespread. Even those who, like Milan, welcome democratization there and are committed to maintaining links with Slovene activists, nevertheless speak in sorrow of Slovenia's 'separatism'. There is a conviction that Slovenia wishes to turn its back on Yugoslavia and integrate itself into some sort of Central European community. There is much criticism of its nationalism and supposed sense of superiority – the feeling that Slovenia is doing too well borders on exasperation. There is a sense of bitterness that Slovenia does not understand Serbia.

That evening I am taken by Milan and Sonja L. to a meeting between the Belgrade section of the Helsinki Watch and the organization's representatives from the United States and the European centre at Vienna. (A diversion: One of the Viennese present was Schwarzenberg, scion of the princely family that once dominated the politics of the Habsburg Monarchy. There is an element of irony here, since 140 years ago Prince Schwarzenberg helped to put down the 1848 revolution in the Habsburg lands: as the Foreign Minister of Franz Joseph, he was responsible for the Monarchy's adventurist policy in Germany, which ended so ingloriously. A young Dutchman, who works at the centre in Vienna, complained bitterly of the atmosphere of nostalgia that permeates Vienna, thanks to which he is frequently corrected when forgetting to add the 'Fürst' before 'Schwarzenberg', despite the fact that the present-day Schwarzenberg, he says, cares little for the title.)

Milan and Sonja have been actively engaged in organizing this event, and were concerned that the Slovene branch, which had been invited, would not be able to attend, due to the sudden change of schedule. They were relieved by the fact that, after some hesitation, the Belgrade authorities allowed the meeting to proceed. It took place in the expensive Hotel Yugoslavia – an incongruous setting (green baize covers on the tables; a row of crystal glasses arranged in front of the seats; mineral water, white wine and other beverages served by discreet waiters) for the sorry tales of state repression. Those who attended must represent the core of Belgrade 'dissidence': ex-*Praxis* editors Marković and Golubović; lawyers Srdja Popović and Ivan Janković (who had initiated a campaign against capital punishment); Vesna Pešić, human rights activist; Kršmanović, a lawyer (?) from Belgrade, who has initiated a campaign against abuse of psychiatry; Svetlana Slapšak from Slovenia, a contemporary of

Milan and Sonja and a talented sociologist; Croat lawyer Vladimir Šeks; Zagreb ex-prisoner of conscience Dobroslav Paraga; and many others – altogether about thirty people present. There were general reports on past activities, but no discussion on current events in Yugoslavia. Only Marković touched upon the contradictory aspect of Yugoslav reality: the increase in human, i.e. democratic, rights has been paralleled by a decrease in social rights (employment, standard of living, etc.). The younger generation was, however, absent from this highly dignified occasion. The other noticeable aspect of it – the instances of popular mobilization in defence of democratic or social rights – were not mentioned. The mobilization of the village of Vevčani in Macedonia against police armed with dogs and electrified cattle prods; the rebellion in the Bosnian village of Moševac against the local oligarchy; collective and individual struggles against dismissal from the workplace for organizing strikes, etc. were not brought into the sphere of concern of Helsinki Watch. (The Slovene representatives, who were unable to attend, assured me later that they were going to bring this up.)

In Belgrade, as elsewhere, people do not read the press appearing in other republics. The capital city, its intelligentsia turned back towards the Serbian past, is nevertheless besieged daily by visits and marches from all parts of Yugoslavia. One would think that this should provide a golden opportunity for the Belgrade Left to meet and discuss with the visitors. However, the younger Left is isolated or is turning towards such activities as Helsinki Watch, while their erstwhile teachers have become senior national spokesmen. It seems clear that, generally speaking, a peace has broken out between the bureaucracy and the intelligentsia in Belgrade since the purge of the liberal current, and this is contributing further to Belgrade's isolation from the other republics (especially Croatia and Slovenia), as well as from Serbia's provinces of Vojvodina and Kosovo.

Zagreb

A long talk with Vjekoslav M., a senior academic and party member, active in joint intellectual ventures with Serbian colleagues (he is one of the organizers of the Cavtat conferences). He was extremely worried about what was going on in Serbia, both at the level of official politics and in regard to the intelligentsia. In regard of the former, he fears what he perceives as neo-Stalinism and unitarism, combined with a strong dose of Serb nationalism and Orthodoxy. He kept saying: they are entering the twenty-first century armed with Saint Sava (Serbian patron saint, founder of the Serbian autocephalous church). Indeed, the country's largest and strongest nation has suddenly turned irrational, threatening dire consequences for what he believes are two most important contemporary tasks:

democratization and a sound economy, based on the market. (That Serbia, Montenegro, Macedonia and now also Bosnia-Herzegovina favour the introduction into the Federal Assembly of a Chamber of Associated Labour – which would represent industry chiefs rather than the workers, of course – he ascribes to their desire to be able to influence the economy by recourse to the state. There is probably a good deal of truth in this, since the better off republics and Vojvodina are against it.) He finds himself unable to talk to his Serb colleagues about Kosovo and the Albanian issue. Yet the Albanian question is an all-Yugoslav one: as the Albanian population migrates to northern and western areas (Croat and Slovene), the need to establish general principles for their accommodation and integration (for example, schooling in their language, which in turn demands active collaboration of the Kosovo authorities) is urgent. Yet this is impossible as long as Albanians are treated as potential irredentists and enemies of Yugoslavia. Albanians today, he tells me, form one-third of military recruits and by the end of the century this proportion will rise to about a half. Yet the army is encouraged to treat them with the utmost suspicion – which often spills over into open humiliation of the young peasant soldiers.

A chance conversation with a Zagreb student, Igor, currently doing his military service. One third of the men in his unit are Albanian. Of this number, half do not speak the Serbo-Croat language, which is the official language of the Army. My interlocutor was given the task of teaching them some Serbo-Croat, but there are no textbooks nor an established procedure for this, and he had to find his own. These young men, leaving, often for the first time, their villages, in which the male code of honour is well defined and particular, suffer painful humiliations. Such treatment comes from several sources. There is the military's suspicion of the Albanian nationality, reaffirmed after the recent killings in Paracin when a young Albanian, clearly deranged, killed several of his colleagues before committing suicide. Frequently, also, local authorities hand over to the Army the names of Albanian 'troublemakers' before they are called up. This means that the young soldiers are constantly under surveillance. Then there is national chauvinism, either of the individual ethnic or the Slav variety. Can the Albanians be considered true patriots? Did they struggle against the Turks, etc. like we Bosnians, Serbs, etc. did? And so on.

Here is one example of the Army's insensitivity towards its Albanian recruits. Igor was once given the task of writing the names of a new contingent on their lockers. Croats, like Slovenes and Albanians who also use the Latin script, do not transliterate individual names (of persons, countries, rivers, cities, etc.). He therefore wrote the Albanians' names as they are spelt, not pronounced. The Albanians warned him that there would be trouble, but in any case felt terribly pleased to see their names written as they should be. A superior officer, checking that the task had been executed, removed all these names and substituted for them new, transliterated, versions. The Croat soldier chose not to feel insulted by this rejection of the Croat language – but then there would be no problem with his own, Slav, name. It must be a problem for the Albanians, however – one, furthermore, that could be avoided. As a result, the issue of the language of command in the Army is kept alive and those nationalities, like the Croats and the Slovenes, which have the strength to complain, do so. The Albanians, of course, do not.

To return to my conversation with M. He certainly feels that Serbia today is the biggest block to progress in Yugoslavia. This attitude seems to be universal in Croatia and Slovenia. Even in Dalmatia, which has traditionally lacked the anti-Serb edge present in parts of northern Croatia, I heard complaints that the Serbs have gone 'crazy'. Serbia is in dispute with its Provinces, and also with Macedonia – both on religious matters (the Serbian Orthodox Church, now very much in favour, is refusing to recognize the autonomy of its Macedonian counterpart), and on issues pertaining to history: e.g. the current Belgrade–Skopje polemic on how to assess the Balkan Wars, the First World War, etc. Then there are frictions with Slovenia, Croatia and Bosnia on a wide range of subjects. As a general rule, people outside Serbia find Serbian politics today, particularly in regard to the Albanian issue, quite incomprehensible. It is indeed incomprehensible.

I have heard two interesting observations in regard to the Kosovo issue. The first is that it in fact has little to do with Kosovo and everything to do with the internal political fight, in Serbia as much as in Yugoslavia. With reforms coming whose outcome cannot be foreseen, everybody is fortifying their positions, awaiting the inevitable storm. Whatever the cause, it is a fact that Serbian policies towards the Albanians (now copied by the Macedonians, though the Macedonians seem to be learning also from the Bulgarians) are destabilizing the whole country. In this context, the second observation makes sense. It relates to Croatian politics on the Albanian question. Branko Horvat's courageous act in publishing a book on the Albanian question in Yugoslavia (which has earned him much personal abuse in the Serbian press, along the lines of 'paid agent of Albanian fascism and irredentism') was apparently tacitly encouraged by the Croatian leadership, in the hope that a wide public debate would somehow lead to a new and less destructive consensus. This may well be the case: the Zagreb bi-weekly *Start* keeps publishing superb investigative pieces on Kosovo and Macedonia. In Slovenia, criticism of the treatment of the Albanian nation is widespread, and I am told that the Ljubljana weekly *Teleks* has also recently published several serious articles on the situation in Kosovo and Macedonia – the two parts of Yugoslavia where unemployment is at its highest and national tension at its worst.

My Zagreb interlocutor feared also the consequences of the new unitarist mood in Belgrade for the status of the republic of Croatia and the internal balance of forces there. The Croatian intelligentsia has a reasonable *modus vivendi* with its party and state leadership – having got rid of the local neo-Stalinist Šuvar by sending him to a federal post (he represents Croatia in the party presidency). Only a few years ago, while active in Croatia, Šuvar became famous through his attempt to initiate a witch-hunt against dissident Yugoslav intellectuals – the affair known under the name of the 'White Book' (which spelt out the names of state 'enemies' and their 'crimes'). Unlike that of Milošević – whose victory in Serbia was assured by mobilization of provincial cadres (who, by bringing their weight to bear at the 8th Plenum of the Serbian CC, managed to crush the Stambolić faction), and whose unitarism seems primarily directed against the Provinces – Šuvar's unitarism is based on all-Yugoslav state institutions such as the Army. Šuvar has warmly endorsed Milošević's victory and has been busy creating the ideological basis for eliminating critics of the system: in a recent speech, he threatened the rebellious intelligentsia with the Army. Thus Zagreb fears that Belgrade may become the base of bureaucratic reaction also in Croatia. The Zagreb weekly *Danas* is the best journal in the Serbo-Croat language, and is now read everywhere. My friend is worried that moves are afoot to replace its editorial board, thus extinguishing this last voice of liberalism outside Slovenia. Furthermore, there is also a concern that the new unitarists may succeed in curbing republican autonomy and hence also the national rights of the Croats and others. A debate on the name of the official language in Croatia has resulted in vivid polemics bringing up the whole history of Croat–Serb relations. The official position of the Croatian party is that the current name 'Croat literary language' be replaced by 'Croat or Serb' or some other variant that involves the Serb name; this is being resisted by all cultural institutions in Croatia. This polemic could have a serious effect on Croat–Serb relations in Croatia, but I am told by my Serb friends in Zagreb that there are no national tensions there. This shows the other side of the Croatian leadership's political caution.

To Vjekoslav I put forward as a tentative proposal the idea of starting a journal whose aim would be to drive a wedge into the nationalistic bloc in Belgrade, splitting off the 'Left' from it. A policy of killing two birds with one stone: weaken the nationalist consensus, prevent isolation of the Belgrade intelligentsia. It turns out that this has already been thought of: maybe a journal that would deal with the problems of economic reform and democratic restructuring (though this latter may be more dicey, since it necessarily relates to the Albanian question). For such a journal to get off the ground, however, money is required, hence also a degree of official support, which does not exist. The Croatian leadership is wary of anything that might push it to the front.

There seems to be a consensus in Slovenia and Croatia as to why the Croatian leadership behaves in this manner, i.e. timidly. The massive purge of the younger generation of Croat leaders in the early 1970s has produced – I am told everywhere – a politics of caution. Discussing Slovenia with another Zagreb friend, an industrial sociologist originally from Belgrade, Mladen L., and making the inevitable parallel with Croatia (to the detriment of the latter), I was asked to consider the following. In Slovenia, democratization has occurred by way of national mobilization and it would be impossible to imagine that it could have been successful otherwise. This means that the Slovene leadership is ready to lend its authority and protection even to its own (Slovene) critics, since it sees in Slovene national unity a strong protection against policies emanating from Belgrade that are injurious to Slovenia. Indeed, the unity of the Slovene leadership is remarkable, given the pressure exerted on it, and given that there exists in Slovenia also a hard-line current, associated with Stane Dolanc. Such a policy of national homogenization would be impossible in Croatia with its considerable (12 per cent) Serb population and where Serbs occupy important places in the political hierarchy. Why not a movement centred on democratic and social demands? It seems that Croatia does not wish to move too far ahead of events in Serbia, which means that the local bureaucracy is unwilling or unable to offer reasonable protection to political activists on the Slovene model. My friend assured me, however, that the intelligentsia is active and engaged in concrete projects, albeit on a modest scale. He himself has recently started to organize a petition for a democratic reform to be signed by intellectuals from all of Yugoslavia. It is interesting that some signatories come from Kosovo. On the issue of Kosovo, however, Mladen's democratic inclinations are checked by a strong sense of ethnic identification.

The youth press in Zagreb (in Belgrade, incidentally, the critical paper *Mladost* had its editorial board replaced soon after Milošević's victory) is held on a tighter leash than in Ljubljana. The editor of the university youth paper *Studentski list* was recently sacked for describing the visiting Mobutu as a bloody dictator. After meeting the new editor, the whole editorial board resigned, on the grounds that they could not work with him. Another youth paper, *Polet*, supports *Mladina*. The issue I read analysed local party election results (part of the preparation for the party conference) in a serious and competent manner, and also republished parts of the leaked minutes of the meeting of the Slovene CC held after the news broke of possible military intervention in Slovenia.

Zagreb – Yugoslavia's most industrialized city – thus gives the appearance of stability and calm. However, this is also deceptive; as in

Slovenia there is an atmosphere of battening down the hatches against the next round of economic policies to be adopted by the federal government. I ask Mladen whether he expects massive upheavals, following the new government measures designed to lower working-class standards. He believes not: the system is sufficiently flexible to accommodate itself to individual workers' actions. In Croatia, the party and state leadership is anxious to maintain good relations with the intelligentsia and is ready to do its own bit to prevent social upheavals. The current Croatian state leadership has been recruited from major industrial enterprises located in Zagreb and knows very well the situation there. The head of the Croat party, Ivica Račan, has the reputation of being a liberal. Šuvar is quite another matter, however. It is now Croatia's turn to occupy the post of Federal party president and various tactical moves to prevent Šuvar from occupying it have failed. Hence, anxiety about what the new Yugoslav party leader may do. Everywhere references are made to a possible 'Rumanization' of Yugoslavia.

Ljubljana

Yugoslav prices have gone haywire: the price of a return rail ticket Zagreb–Ljubljana costs the same as a decent bunch of flowers and much less than a modest meal in a restaurant. As a result the trains are overcrowded, the customers made up mainly of workers, peasants and soldiers. I sit in the compartment and listen to horror stories regarding rail travel in Yugoslavia. Often passengers have to stand for 6–7–8 and more hours, unable to move, so hard are they pressed against each other. People faint on such journeys and there are problems with satisfying simple natural needs.

In my compartment, workers exchange information regarding work in foreign countries, this time mainly in the Middle East. (Yugoslav applications for work permits abroad have soared over the past few years.) They are young, most of them in their twenties, and speak with bitterness about how socialism has failed while capitalism seems to be flourishing. The hatred of those responsible for the Yugoslav 'mess' is open – no names are mentioned but everybody knows who is who. At some point an older worker intervenes to warn that things are not so rosy in the West either, and that workers have also taken a great battering there. The compartment listens in silence – none of that immediate protestation that one gets as a rule when talking to the Yugoslav 'middle classes'. Class anger and hopelessness hang in the air.

My first act in Ljubljana is to buy a copy of *Mladina*. It contains a longish interview with Slovene party leader Milan Kučan, who is questioned on the recent affair involving a threat of military intervention in Slovenia. The paper reports also the formation of a Peasant Alliance (the first autonomous peasant organization in Yugoslavia since the war), under the umbrella of the Socialist Alliance, and also of a Young Peasant Alliance which has joined the Socialist Youth Alliance. We are also told that the new Minister of Defence, Kadijević, already has a villa, so the soldiers will be spared the work of building him one (as they had to do for his predecessor Mamula)!

The papers give – in all the Yugoslav languages – advance notice of new wage cuts and price increases. I read with interest that shipyard workers in Split will have their wages lowered by 40 per cent. Average wage cuts: 20–40 per cent. Average price increases: 30–100+ per cent. The prices of black bread, milk and cooking oil will be protected. The IMF has demanded a drastic cut in domestic consumption and the closure of loss-making enterprises. Hundreds of telexes arrive daily at the door of the Federal government in Belgrade protesting against wage cuts. They are motivated in one of the three following ways: unconstitutional since against self-management; penalization of enterprises that have been keeping wages down; workers just cannot take any further degradation of their living standards.

Characteristic is the story of the Bosnian miners who, after a four-day strike, resolved to go the federal assembly. The commune authorities refused to help and the men walked for some 60 kilometres (older men falling out after a while) until, by courtesy apparently of the local police, they were provided with buses. Along the road the marchers confiscated a Yugoslav flag and a café owner gave them his own portrait of Tito. Thus armed, they arrived in Belgrade, where they became guests of the local trade unions. The following day they marched to the federal Assembly, situated on Marx-Engels Square, with the flag and the portrait of Tito – a scene evoking Petrograd 1905. The television filmed their encounter with the federal trade union president and some of the federal functionaries. The Yugoslav public thus had the opportunity to see the miners crying – but the sound was cut. The papers reported in some detail what they had been saying. Despite fulfilment of their work norms, their wages were being cut by around 40 per cent. How were they to feed their families? They were told to return home – the Federal government would send a telex rescinding the wage cut. Is this an example of what Mladen had in mind when he talked of the system's flexibility?

Ljubljana is preoccupied with the affair of attempted military intervention. Stenographic accounts of the Slovene CC meeting circulate, as well as information from 'reliable' resources. The Slovenes are convinced that the Military Council (an all-military body, formed to advise the Yugoslav presidency – which is commander-in-chief – on technical issues) was planning the arrest of several hundred Slovene intellectuals and activists, bypassing the local party and state bodies. One is told that only a vigorous protest by Kučan and Dolanc prevented this. The Yugoslav presidency has denied that anything happened outside legal routine. Even if one disbelieves that a coup was intended, the above denial does not hold water. Something highly worrying did happen. There is no doubt that the intelligentsia is now feeling extremely insecure. Letters demanding a formal explanation from party and state authorities, and threats of resignation from the Party by prominent individuals, are printed in the local press. The Belgrade *Politika* denounces *Mladina* for publishing such 'provocative stories'.

Slovene 'alternative politics' seems to resolve around two poles. One is provided by the 'traditional' intellectuals, gathered around the literary journal *Nova revija*, and places the accent on the nation. These have recently put forward their own amendments to the constitution: closing of national ranks, sanctity of life, the family as the basic social unit. This highly conservative programme is combined with demands for full democracy, etc. This current is also engaged in a rehabilitation of the Slovene Christian Social tradition – my friend Tomaz M. is critical of this and worried that, for example, no mention is made of the fact that its chief ideologue, Janez Krek, was strongly anti-Semitic. The other pole is provided by *Mladina*, which is strongly anti-nationalist – though *Mladina*'s pages are opened to alternative views.

I ask whether this is always wise. Take, for example, these new peasant associations, senior and junior. There is no doubt that the Socialist Youth Alliance activists have taken part in this venture, but equally there is no doubt that the desire and need was already present among the farmers, who have been badly hit by the growing disparity between agricultural and industrial prices. In a characteristic speech, Šuvar said that he had nothing against peasants organizing, providing that they did so as a guild – he warned, however, against the intelligentsia coming in to provide subversive, and indeed any, support. The peasant organizations have joined the Socialist Alliance. *Mladina* published a long article by a member of *Nova Revija* group attacking this move on the grounds that 'communists' have always been hostile to peasants and have done nothing for them. This is not the view of *Mladina*, of course. Is it wise, then, to publish articles that suggest the possibility of an 'anti-communist' role of the new association? I am told that, despite problems, *Mladina* must maintain open pages if it is to retain its leading role in the formation of Slovene public opinion.

I suggest to Tomaz, who occupies a position somewhere between the two poles mentioned above, but is closer to *Mladina* for which he frequently writes (he is certainly not a nationalist), that the entry of the peasant association into the Socialist Alliance was a good step. He is not so sure: it is important for further democratization of the system that alternative movements retain their distance from official organizations. He tells me, nevertheless, that Slovene intellectuals support the Slovene party's efforts to widen democratic rights.

I ask what the reasons are for the lack of interest in working-class issues on the part of the critical intelligentsia throughout Yugoslavia. He tells me that the explanation is very simple: the disappointing performance of socialism has also removed the notion of the working class as a vanguard class. In addition, the workers will cling to the Party and the memory of Tito – witness the fact that workers almost everywhere march with Tito's portraits, shout 'Tito-Partija', and sing old revolutionary songs that maintain the man's cult ('Comrade Tito, we swear to you that we shall follow your road', etc.). On the other hand, concrete workers' demands are supported by the intellectuals, despite the latter's concern about the workers' 'conservatism'.

I ask about Yugoslavism – endorsement of a Yugoslav 'community'. His answer is that often this expression 'Yugoslav community' is a cover for unitarism. The belief that Slovenes are bent on separatism is absurd, but attempts to impose on Slovenia a common educational programme, for example, with its strong Serbo-Croat component, would be resisted to the point of Slovenia walking out of the federation. Is he worried that Slovenia, by developing in a way so different from the rest of Yugoslavia, may remain isolated and hence open to repression? Yes, of course, and the most worrying thing was Croat timidity. He asks in turn: why are the intellectuals there not supporting Slovenia more openly? That they may lack the local party's support is no excuse; the Slovenes too have been threatened with persecution and imprisonment.

Recapitulating later this part of my conversation with Tomaz, I realized that I had never heard a single word of criticism of Slovenes in Croatia: nothing but warm support, and criticism of Croat officials for not supporting the Slovenes more openly. My Serb friends tend to be far more critical. Yet I heard on my return home that, following the arrest of Janez Janša, a candidate for the presidency of the Slovene Youth Alliance, a protest has been organized in Belgrade and signatures collected on a petition for his release. A similar protest was mounted also in Zagreb. Democracy in Slovenia will therefore be defended also as an integral part of Yugoslav democracy – it is a good omen for the future.

25 May is the official Youth Day: I go with my friends Nada and Srečo K. to the Student City, where rock music and alternative happenings are provided. Among the participants, children abound: there are balloons and dragons and clowns. My problem is my ignorance of the Slovene language, though I meet with much kindness: people translate and make an effort to keep the conversation in Serbo-Croat, not an easy task amidst lively encounters. The well-known Bosnian film director Kusturica was

present at this event, and there is an attempt to talk to him. Kusturica recently gave an interview to *NIN*, in which he spoke of 'Nazi-style' developments in Slovenia. I am worried about the effect of such words on the Serbian public. It turns out that he was misquoted. He was referring in fact to a small minority. Kusturica was recently making a film in a small Slovene town, situated just inside the Yugoslav border with Italy, about the sale of Gypsy children to petty gangs operating in Italy. The local population attacked the actors and the crew, shouting anti-Gypsy and anti-Bosnian slogans. The talk with Kusturica thus served also as an opportunity for an apology, a condemnation of Slovene nationalism and expression of solidarity.

We talk of the Slovene working class. I am told that the workers are already electing their own stewards and that strike committees frequently remain in place after strikes end. In any case, both the management and the workers are aware that the vital decisions regarding industrial policy are now the prerogative of the federal government. This means that the tendency to take protests to Belgrade will continue.

I talk to a Slovene deputy to the Federal Assembly, Vika Potočnjak, an intelligent and courageous young woman who has gained fame throughout the country by insisting that the federal government investigates the Vevčani affair. She tells me that the Macedonian authorities have tried to blacken her, circulating rumours that the inhabitants of Vevčani have built her a house in Slovenia (Vevčani is a wealthy village, its men traditionally working abroad.) She has also raised other issues such as the case of Moševac, or matters relating to the Albanian problem. She told me of a document produced by Serbian deputies, aimed at reducing the Albanian birthrate by drastic means (reminiscent of the younger Gandhi). In the end they managed to defeat this move. Deputies who wish to take a more active role suffer from a lack of facilities. In preparing her cases, she has been very much helped by the unpaid work of Belgrade young intellectuals as well as others, but such help is ultimately limited, since these people, however much they are willing to help, have their own work and obligations. Did I know that documentary films have been made about Mosevac and about Vevčani?

The deputy complains bitterly about the anti-Albanian feelings of Belgrade intellectuals. She once joined a discussion organized in the Writers' Club, and dropped out of it after four hours. She was told: 'It is easy for you Slovenes. Your children will be playing with computers, while ours will be fighting Albanians.' She has also been at the receiving end of anti-Slovene sentiments. There was for instance one incident when a young Serb woman was attacked only because she carried under her arm a copy of the Slovene daily *Delo*. Belgrade press hostility towards Slovenia worries her. The Slovene 'problem' lies also in the language, which

Serbo-Croat speakers do not understand (though the 'kaj'-speaking Croats do). How about producing a Serbo-Croat version of, say, *Mladina*? I am told that there is a suggestion that the Slovene daily *Delo* print a Serbo-Croat version. The amount of money involved would not be very great, but the editors are as yet undecided. There would be problems with distribution.

The conversation turns to Šuvar (newly elected president of the Yugoslav party): everybody agrees that he is a dangerous man. Šuvar is also an intellectual and has developed a tactic of winning over younger and more energetic party members. The deputy is worried by his success with them, which she cannot explain. Šuvar has a prodigious memory and an amazingly detailed knowledge of the family and personal backgrounds of individuals with whom he comes into contact. My friends are worried that the liberal political philosophy of people like Slovene party leader Kucan or Croat party leader Račan may be no match for Šuvar's neo-Stalinism.

Slovene public opinion has recently been agitated by the idea of rehabilitating the Slovene leaders purged in 1971. This is seen as part of a more general attempt to review the all-Yugoslav party purges that took place then. *Časopis za kritiko znanosti* has just published memoirs of the best known of them, Stane Kavčič, who recently died in almost total political obscurity. Igor Bavčar, Igor Omerza and Janez Janša have been busy promoting the book, hoping to sell as many copies as possible before the inevitable new explosion of prices that is scheduled for after the party conference. There is a lively debate, from which I am unfortunately almost immediately excluded thanks to the language, on whether this rehabilitation has been one-sided. During Kavčič's reign, several students and intellectuals were imprisoned and journals closed. Clearly, this is an important debate on tactics. There are those who argue that, in the context of today, it is more important to emphasize Kavčič's positive contribution. Is it not the case that, thanks to the revival of the memory of 1971, Andrej Marinc, a bureaucrat who was involved in Kavčič's demise, had to withdraw from running for the Slovene presidency? The man who won, Janez Stanovnik, was also the official candidate. Characteristically, one of Stanovnik's first public pronouncements was to warn Slovene intellectuals not to go too far too fast: 'Remember what happened to the "Prague spring".' Here, of course, the invasion would be an internal affair. The candidate of the Youth Alliance was defeated, I am told, as a result of undemocratic voting procedures. Those arguing here are all close personal and political friends, but there are important differences separating them as well, regarding basic questions of Yugoslavia's future. Is the economic reform fundamentally an economic or a political problem? What about the working class? Can one dismiss self-management just like that? The pro-Kavčič 'faction' (which I must stress is not nationalist) argues that the regional unevenness of Yugoslavia's economic development precludes any centrally defined economic policy, and that economic recovery can be based only on an arithmetic sum of individual policies. For this reason, the federation should be reorganized as a confederation. This is a sorry fact of reality.

Take the question of aid to the underdeveloped republics and Kosovo. These days, even the small percentage of revenue that goes into this aid has become a major burden on industry, where often a relatively small sum determines the viability of an enterprise and hence also the level of workers' wages, which are now tied strictly to the enterprise's performance and which are being constantly lowered. At the same time, the money poured into these areas is showing no results, and the corruption of the local bureaucracy, which diverts a proportion of this money to maintain its own privileges, is well known. In other words, the current policy of aid to the underdeveloped regions is producing nationalism within the working class, here specifically the Slovene one. Here the government has tried to spare the weaker enterprises by redistributing the burden and allocating it to a small number of better-off enterprises – which in turn is choking the 'engines' of the local economy. Once more, the policy is producing nationalist reaction against the 'underdeveloped nations'. A confederative organization of the joint state would also allow different approaches to the all-Yugoslav problem of uneven economic development, in that it would take out of the reach of the bureaucracies of the underdeveloped regions the right to direct all-Yugoslav support to their own self-preservation.

I raise here once more the idea of a new, all-Yugoslav journal which would try to unite the Yugoslav intelligentsia around concrete common problems and where issues of economy and society could be discussed in an open and rational manner. Such a journal would be attractive: particularly, Srečo argues, if it would openly tackle problems of uneven development; only in this way would the intelligentsia of the underdeveloped regions be drawn to it. For Srečo, the most important problem of contemporary Yugoslavia is its uneven economic development.

And so it is. Travelling through the northern part of the country, one is struck by an awareness that Yugoslavia as such exists only at the level of the federal bureaucracy and the army. In reality, the country has been divided into separate units, each living its own life, each burdened with its own specific problems. In the most pessimistic scenario, it is only a matter of time before a major explosion occurs and the only question is whether this will be on a national or a class basis. Will the first blood be spilt as the result of a pogrom directed against a local national minority, or will it occur as the result of suppression of a mass workers' protest? If the former, then the country will become even more split. If the latter, it may provoke a sobering up in the country as a whole.

7

Democracy and the National Question

Analysis of Yugoslav history and politics has traditionally veered towards two opposite extremes: exclusive preoccupation either with class or with nation. The Left, for its part, has tended to undervalue the importance of the national question, treating it at best as of secondary importance and at worst as a 'bourgeois deviation' from the class struggle. More frequent, however, has been an inclination to concentrate on the supposedly eternal national 'problem' in Yugoslavia: in the West, academic works and media alike almost invariably describe the country's multi-national character, and its consequent decentralization, as the main cause of its problems.

Both tendencies have shared a common premise: that national self-government and socialist order somehow stand in fundamental contradiction with one another – or, to put it differently, that multi-national states are inherently unstable. Yet history has offered widely different options to multinational states. At the end of World War One, while Austria-Hungary disintegrated in favour of independent national states, the Union of Soviet Socialist Republics was being born contemporaneously from the ashes of Imperial Russia. Indeed, the end of the former was signalled by the arrival of the revolution which, in the guise of the Petrograd Soviet of Workers' and Soldiers' deputies, as early as March 1917 had endorsed the principle of self-determination as the solution to the national problem in Central and Eastern Europe.[1] In 1941 the unitary Yugoslav monarchy fell apart, only to be replaced a few years later by the Socialist Federative Republic of Yugoslavia. In both the Soviet Union and Yugoslavia, national liberation was a necessary condition of social revolution. Hence, their federal constitutions, based on the principle of national self-determination, were essentially revolutionary class acts. Socialist democracy and national equality have remained inseparably connected – it is not accidental that political dispossession of the working class, and with it of the population as a whole, has gone hand in hand with the rise of state-sponsored nationalism and the persecution of national minorities in countries like the Soviet Union (despite its constitution),

China, Romania, Bulgaria – and today also in Yugoslavia. Political, economic and cultural equality of the nationalities has remained a visible indicator of the state of health of Yugoslav democracy. Bureaucratic reaction, in contrast, has preferred to present itself as 'class-based' and a-national (albeit with a strong Slav bias).[2] The same is true of the regional bureaucracies which, following the suppression of the country's Left in 1968, have been putting themselves forward as champions of individual national interests – and the more so as the economy has increasingly been sliding towards anarchy. The absence of democracy – both within the Party (appointment from above, rather than election from below, of the Federal and Republican Central Committees; ban on tendencies within the Party) and in society at large – has prevented the political integration that only a free, all-Yugoslav debate around alternative political programmes could achieve. The result has been a tacit legitimation of nationalism, while at the same time the 'struggle against nationalism' has been used as an ideological cover in inner-party struggles and for suppressing critics outside the Party. In the 1970s, a campaign against 'Croat nationalism' was used to purge the Party of its liberal wing, and the opportunity was taken to send several student leaders to prison as well as to close down journals like *Praxis*. In the 1980s, the main fire was directed against 'Albanian nationalism' – as the leadership struggled to contain the effects of Tito's death which coincided in time with the 'discovery' of a $20 billion foreign debt and a catastrophic economic situation. Today it seems to be the Slovenes' turn to join Croat and Albanian 'separatists' as the universal enemy.

The political ferment in Slovenia – and in particular the official toleration there of explicit opposition – has caused considerable consternation in the centres of power elsewhere in the country (with the partial exception of Croatia). There, the effects of economic and political crisis have resulted in a growing authoritarianism, which in certain areas has acquired a strong nationalist form. Only a year ago the liberal wing of the Serbian party was unceremoniously removed for refusing to sanction an openly nationalist campaign to strip Kosovo and Vojvodina, the two Provinces of the Republic of Serbia where most of the country's minorities live, of their autonomy.

The critical forays of the Slovene youth paper *Mladina* have instilled real fears among conservatives, who prefer to stifle criticism by recourse to more traditional methods. Their problem is that the growing democratization of public life in Slovenia enjoys official sanction. In the cold war now raging within the country's leadership, the attitude to the developments in Slovenia has become a totemic symbol of divide between liberals and conservatives. Harangues against *Mladina* in particular, and Slovenia in general, provide the daily staple diet in sections of the media under conservative control. The Slovene party leadership has clearly underestimated the subversive effect their own local experiment in democracy is having on the rest of the country. Not only *Mladina*'s refusal to respect republican frontiers, but also the readiness of Slovene deputies to take up in the Federal Assembly cases of police repression in the conservatives' own backyards,[3] have inevitably exposed the vulnerability of the Slovene party's strategy of seeking an all-Yugoslav agreement on economic reform while leaving the degree of 'internal' democracy to be decided by individual republican leaderships. A response was bound to come.

The military's intervention this spring and summer against democratic tendencies in Slovenia, described below, has left much egg on the generals' faces: a strong element of farce was introduced by the Army's attempt to justify its action on the grounds that a 'counter-revolution' was taking place in Slovenia. A spontaneous mass solidarity with the victims ensured that what began as a trial against three *Mladina* journalists and a pacifist sergeant of the Yugoslav People's Army was soon turned into a people's trial of the Army itself. Chief coordinator of this democratic mass movement has been the Committee for Protection of Human Rights.

Given that a virtually total mobilization of the Slovene nation has occurred, a most interesting debate on the relationship between nationalism and democracy has begun in the Slovene press, on which I report below.

The Ljubljana trial, and the spontaneous mass mobilization which it has provoked in Slovenia, have occurred against the background of quite different developments further south. In the Yugoslav southern regions, the tragedy of ethnic conflict seems set to repeat itself, as anti-Albanian chauvinist hysteria is being fanned by the resident bureaucrats and all those who are profiting from the current system of distribution of material and political privilege. A Committee of Kosovo Serbs and Montenegrins has emerged, with official support from the current Serbian party and state leadership, as a political force in its own right: the first time in Yugoslavia's postwar history that an openly nationalist formation has enjoyed open official backing. The trade-off is clear: Serbian official politics presents these bigots as 'freedom fighters', while the 'freedom fighters' organize mass meetings to press for full support for the Serbian bureaucrats' attempt to strip Kosovo and Vojvodina of their autonomy. For the time being, Yugoslav unitarists and Serb nationalists have joined forces in persecuting all those who show insufficient respect for the state and the party. The press in Belgrade, with few exceptions, has become the organ of this unholy alliance, as its daily and weekly editions churn out an endlessly repeated litany of nationalist and authoritarian demands.[4] Not a single Serbian politician has distanced himself from those of their supporters who paint slogans on the walls of Romanian houses in Vojvodina saying:

'Mother Serbia Rules Here!' or adorn the public buildings there and else-where with the more popular 'Kill Albanians!' and 'Hang Vlassi!' (the Kosovo party leader of Albanian origin), or raise the call for arms at mass meetings.

To be sure, the Serbs have no monopoly on nationalism in Yugoslavia. In Macedonia, for example, state-sponsored nationalism has been used quite cynically to divert popular attention from the Republican leader-ship's economic mismanagement: the Republic's bankruptcy has co-incided not only with mass workers' strikes, but also with an onslaught on education in the Albanian language, designed to confine tens of thou-sands of Albanian children to a future of manual labour or unemploy-ment. The specific danger of Serb nationalism lies in its unique potential power to affect a restructuring of the state – thus opening the door to lasting political instability and possibly also to counter-revolution.

The rise of Serb nationalism, and of unitarist tendencies in parts of the state apparatus, are fanning fear among Yugoslavs of all ethnic groups that their national rights are in danger, and that a victory of bureaucratic reaction could result in the removal of what liberties they today enjoy. In Slovenia, this fear has encouraged spontaneous mass resistance to Army pressure against the 'Slovene Spring'. During the trial of the Ljubljana Four, the emphasis within the solidarity movement was on unity in action. Once the trial was over, however, differences regarding the re-lationship between nationalism and democracy could once again be pub-licly debated.

Let us start at the beginning, however. Last March, following a public row, the Yugoslav Federal prosecutor forced his Slovene Republican counterpart to start proceedings against two journalists: Franci Zavrl, the chief editor of *Mladina*, official journal of the Alliance of Socialist Youth of Slovenia (ASYS), and Andrej Novak of the Ljubljana bi-weekly *Teleks*, on the grounds that they had insulted Branko Mamula, the Yugoslav Minister of Defence (now retired).[5] Following an impressive show of support for the accused in Slovenia the two journalists were acquitted. The Federal prosecutor responded by appealing against this verdict, but his appeal was rejected at the end of July. By the time this small victory was registered in the daily press, however, it no longer seemed relevant, for by then Zavrl was being sentenced to eighteen months in prison by a different court – a military one – concluding a long sequence of events that had started at approximately at the same time: March 1988.

At the beginning of May, rumours spread through Ljubljana that in March the Army had planned widespread arrests of Slovene intellectuals and activists, and had been stopped only by a vigorous protest from Slovenia's highest party and state officials. The rumours proved to have a solid foundation, as was shown by the leaked minutes of a closed meeting of the Federal party presidency which had taken place on 29 March.[6] This meeting had been called specifically to discuss the situation in Slovenia, and in particular increased criticism of the Army in the pages of *Mladina* and other Slovene journals. In advance of the meeting, a Draft Statement had been produced for adoption by the presidency. This statement mirrored the position already expressed by a body called the Military Council[7] four days earlier, namely that a 'counter-revolution' was taking place in the Republic. In an unprecedented gesture, the Military Council had made its conclusion public on 28 March, i.e. on the eve of the presidency meeting.[8] The Draft Document also, it seems, included references to Slovene 'separatism'.

At the meeting itself, Milan Kučan, Slovene party leader, in the name of the Republican leadership, rejected the Draft Document as 'unacceptable': 'We cannot take responsibility for such a document. It will be impossible to reach unity in the League of Communists of Slovenia on such a basis, above all with respect to the assessment that there is a counterrevolution taking place in Slovenia.' He argued that although 'the general socio-political situation in Slovenia' was 'very complex', the Document was biased against that Republic, since the problems found there were actually common to the country as a whole. The root of these problems lay, in his opinion, in the economy: 'This document does not deal with the problems of economic development, which are nevertheless decisive.'

That the economic crisis was not confined to the poorer Yugoslav regions, but had also struck Slovenia, Kučan illustrated with a telling paragraph: 'We have advance notice of general strikes being organized in the health service, in the building industry, and in education. We have been told that managers in the engineering and textile industries are planning to resign collectively.

We do not have the resources for a technological renewal, for a structural adaptation of our economy; yet this is a developmental imperative, without which we shall come to a standstill . . . We are no longer dealing with stagnation, but with regression and with a whole series of economic, social and political problems which are causing, unfortunately, also intra-national tensions. This is because the first to be hit will be blue-collar workers, among whom there are around 100,000 workers from other republics. . . . Big confrontations have already begun.'

Kučan reminded those present that in this situation the Slovene leadership was on its own: 'We cannot expect anybody to help us here. There is nobody to help. Two republics [Montenegro and Macedonia] are in the financial and economic situation in which they are [i.e. bankrupt]. Bosnia has its own additional problems [as a result of the "Agrokomerc" affair]. The same is true for Serbia. We know, therefore, that this is something we must undertake alone, and we shall do so. But we ask you that at least you do not hinder us in our political action.'

Adoption of the Draft Document would, in Kučan's opinion, also have a most negative effect on the coming Party Conference (which took place in May) diverting its attention from by far the most important question – the economy. 'Differentiation on the issue of economic development is essential, since without it there is no way out of the crisis.' The basic task of the Party Conference was 'the elaboration of a programme of economic development, which will foresee both social and political conflicts, but which, because of the persuasiveness of its orientation for the majority of the people, can acquire the majority consensus in each republic and province, and which can for this reason overcome conflicts and escalations.' By contrast, a 'confrontation articulated in the language of special war, of search for enemies, does not provide answers to the necessary development of socialism. This can be reached only by confrontation between different concepts of socialism.'

It was, after all, he argued, the crisis of the economies of 'real socialism' which had led to the communists' retreat. 'Communists are on the defensive [in Yugoslavia] because our policies are producing no results, no turn for the better, no promising perspective. This is why communists are silent and on the defensive under the assault of their critics and an opposition that uses arguments drawn from reality: the situation supplies them with ammunition, and arguments drawn from reality are more convincing than ones drawn from ideology.'

Kučan reminded his audience of what Gorbachev had said on his recent visit to Yugoslavia. 'He said . . . that he and the Army of the Soviet Union are attacked by the West because of fear of *perestroika*. And if crisis has to do with the [economic] development of socialism, then it cannot be solved primarily or exclusively by political means. For this very reason it is essential to trust those individuals, organs and forces which are trying to solve the crisis by economic means, including the state – since it is impossible to come out of this crisis without the intervention of the state in the economy. And this demands a reaffirmation of the role of the state, which is becoming increasingly weak, inefficient and incompetent. The state must begin to function like a real state, hence must free itself from political and bureaucratic voluntarism and pressure.'

Kučan was particularly insistent that the party leadership call off the anti-Slovene campaign currently being waged in Serbia, Montenegro and Macedonia, with the connivance of the republican leaderships: 'An anti-Yugoslav mood is growing in Slovenia in reaction to the growth of the anti-Slovene mood in the country. . . . there is no readiness [by the local leaderships] to calm the situation, which is now overheated.' The charges aired in the press that the editors of *Mladina*, and indeed the Slovene party leadership, were instruments of a special war being waged against Yugoslavia by world capitalism, were absurd. With this kind of argument, one could equally well ' "prove" that my positions and those of Vidoje [Žarković, head of the Montenegrin party] equal those of Ustashe and Chetniks[9] – one can use such methods to prove anything.'

Kučan went on to remind the Party Presidency of the multinational character of Yugoslav party and state organization. 'Our attention is drawn in particular to the statement [found in the Military Council's proclamation] that Yugoslavia is a *unitary* federal country. Not long ago one of our delegates was likewise told by the President of the Executive Council [Branko Mikulić] that we need a *unified* economic policy.[10] These are influential people. Is this not objectively an argument that the fundamental relations in the Federation, and the principles on which they are based, should be altered?'

The Slovene leader now came to the crux of his whole intervention: the status of the Military Council. It seems that neither the Party nor the state presidencies had been consulted by the Military Council before it took the decision to make public its views on the developments in Slovenia – on the eve of a Party presidency meeting convened to discuss the subject! 'Does this mean', asked Kučan, 'that this body has become an independent subject in the political life of the country? That it can independently make such far-reaching political judgements which – given its authority and the need to strengthen it – have enormous political weight?[11] In the same way that the words of Comrade Mamula, spoken at the political conference of the Yugoslav People's Army, had great political weight?' Having initially been tempted to go public with a dispute on this issue, the Slovene leadership had decided against it – apparently because they had not felt that a public confrontation would get them very far, while it would certainly have further 'inflamed' the already high local sensitivity on the question of the military's competence. 'But we are in favour of the Party presidency therefore making its position clear on this. For this is the only right place for such a discussion.'

At this point Kučan raised something that was not a purely formal question of the constitution or of party primacy, but a very concrete issue indeed. For what Kučan said next was to lead, just two months later, to a spontaneous mobilization in Slovenia which, in its scope and importance, is without precedent in postwar Yugoslavia. He raised 'a question' about

the instruction, which the commander of the [Ljubljana] military district has told us he received following the Military Council meeting, to make direct contact with the Republican Internal Affairs Secretary in regard to action to be initiated in the Republic. He asked if we were in a position to control the situation which might arise after the arrests, since it was assumed that people would come out onto the streets. He said that his main task was to safeguard himself, military barracks and military personnel, but that they were ready to help us.

Our comrades, the Secretary and Deputy Secretary, said that they could not discuss this without us. They searched for me and found me, and we spoke to him together with Dolanc.[12] Naturally we refused to discuss the matter, since we said we knew nothing about it. We also said that we were fully aware that any such action, which did not take into account the very subtle political situation in Slovenia, would have irreparable consequences for which the political leadership could not take any responsibility. . . . I told the Army Commander that our Committee for Social Self-Protection also knew nothing about the instruction he had received.

This is why I protest here most strongly against such a procedure. Not against the Commander, who was very correct, but against such a practice, since it would fundamentally alter relations within society and the position of its political subjects – their jurisdiction, their responsibilities. Such a procedure for solving relations and problems in the Federation is highly dubious and unacceptable, and we wish to have the Presidency's position on this.

The consternation in Slovenia following the leaking of this document was understandably great, and the conviction that the Republic had barely escaped a 'military coup' became widespread. This in turn explains the mass character of the mobilization that followed the incarceration by the military police of Janez Janša, a journalist of *Mladina*, well known for his critical writings on the Army,[13] on 31 May. Janša was followed within days by Ivan Borstner, a junior officer in the Yugoslav People's Army, and David Tasić, another journalist on the staff of *Mladina*. The three were charged with having in their possession a secret military document. Finally, two weeks later, *Mladina*'s chief editor Zavrl was charged with the same offence, though he escaped prison since the warrant for his arrest found him recovering in a Ljubljana hospital from a nervous breakdown following months of political harassment. Within hours of the news of Janša's arrest, the editors of several Slovene journals (*Mladina, Katedra, Tribuna*) and the producers of Radio-Student, joined by representatives of Slovene 'alternative movements', formed a Committee to Defend Janez Janša – which soon changed its name to the Committee for Protection of Human Rights. Since the Army initially refused all access to the accused, and since it also refused them civilian lawyers, the Committee came up with the following key demands: that the three be released from prison immediately; that they be allowed civilian lawyers; and that the public be admitted to the main part of the trial. The Army, referring to the letter of the Criminal Code, refused all of them. The Committee saw its task as including also the regular and accurate dissemination of news. All in all, the Committee became an indispensable public institution outside the control of the Slovene leadership albeit maintaining cordial relations with it.

As Yugoslav public opinion woke up to the fact that the Army has the right to hold and try civilians in peacetime, the Committee began collecting signatures in support of its demands. In under a month it gathered some 100,000, mostly – though not exclusively – in Slovenia. The Committee was joined also by over 500 organizations – schools and higher education institutions, hospitals, enterprises, cultural and professional associations, local party cells, etc. – covering all sectors of Slovene society.[14] The Republican Assembly, the Socialist Alliance of Working People of Slovenia, the Republican Presidency and even the party leadership voiced their support to differing degrees with the demands of the Committee. There is no doubt that the months of June and July saw a virtually complete national mobilization, carried out within strictly legal limits. At one point it seemed that the moment would give birth to an inner-party horizontal movement of reform, but although an Aktiv of Communists and Non-Communists for Democracy did get off the ground, it soon disintegrated under the weight of conflicting programmes and ideas. And an early offer by metalworkers to initiate a general strike was politely and firmly declined!

The peak of the Committee's activity coincided with the formal annual session of the Federal Assembly's legal subcommittee, at which the Federal public prosecutor complained that the Slovene judiciary, by failing to act against 'verbal crime' as defined by Article 133 of the Yugoslav Penal Code, had introduced 'deformations' into the all-Yugoslav penal practice! What is more, the Army added insult to injury by insisting – contrary to constitutional stipulations – that the trial be conducted in the Serbo-Croat language. The ridiculous and offensive spectacle of a Yugoslav Federal body trying Slovene citizens in the capital of the Slovene state in Serbo-Croat, against the express demand both of the defendants and of all popular and official bodies, could not but be seen as a form of national denigration and a unitarist provocation. It was understood as a sign of things to come.[15]

When, on 28 July, Ivan Borstner was sentenced to four years in prison, Janez Janša and Franci Zavrl to eighteen months and David Tasić to five months, the conviction grew that not only democracy but also the Slovene nation had been on trial. The Slovene leadership and the Committee at this point opted for different responses. The party and state leadership did throughout the trial express their desire that the four be defended by civilian lawyers and preferably in a civilian court, but they never questioned the legality of the Army's action. At the same time, they protested most vigorously to the Federal state presidency against the infringement that had taken place of the constitutionally guaranteed status of the Slovene language both in Slovenia and in the Federal institutions. Their appeal failed, since the Federation – in an act that can only increase the Slovene sense of alienation from Belgrade – took the side of the Army.

The Committee, for its part, while agreeing that the question of the language was important, also refused to accept the verdicts as legally valid, not only because it questioned the military's right to try civilians in peacetime, but also because the trial had involved numerous transgressions of legal norms. The Committee furthermore has demanded that the Slovene state presidency, together with the appropriate members of the Republican Assembly, should examine the secret document at the centre of the trial, since there was a justified suspicion that this document related to anti-constitutional activity by the Army. By mid-August, both the defendants and the military prosecutor had appealed against the sentences.

There is no doubt that the trial represented a defeat of the Slovene leadership's current strategy, elements of which can be gleaned from Kučan's speech quoted above. The Army's intervention in Slovenia has spelt out the limits of the Republican leadership's power, and this was confirmed by the Federal state's refusal to defend the constitutional status of the Slovene language. The Slovene quest for recognition of the right of minorities to exist in the Party – raised at the May Party Conference and supported there by the Croat liberals – has thus come to nothing. When the Slovene President Stanovnik – in an open bid to give the Slovene case the kind of nationalist justification which the Serbian leadership has used in its own quest for greater power – stated publicly that the Slovenes wished to be left to conduct their own affairs without outside interference, just as the Serbs wished to be 'masters in their own house', this was received with muted outrage by the neighbouring Croat party, where the liberal wing still holds a majority and which has therefore been supportive of Slovenia. Finally, the Slovene leadership's confidence in its ability to maintain a national consensus suffered with the emergence of a Committee for Protection of Human Rights frequently critical of official inaction. The idea that one could have agreement on the economy without an all-Yugoslav commitment to democratization turned out to be a mirage.

The Slovene Left, at the same time, became increasingly aware of the fact that, even though the Slovene party had been an important factor in the democratization of public life in Slovenia, it was unable or unwilling to formulate an all-Yugoslav democratic platform that would be acceptable to non-Slovenes. Without such a platform, it is impossible to defeat the growing bureaucratic counter-revolution; the latter's defeat, on the other hand, would open the way for a radical democratic transformation of the moribund political structures, as an indispensable condition for solving the economic and social crisis. In the interregnum created by the appeals – pending the outcome of which the defendants were released from prison – some of the Committee activists began to take stock of the new situation posed by developments not only in Slovenia but also elsewhere in Yugoslavia.

The debate was opened by Miha Kovač in *Teleks*, with an article entitled 'The Nation Will Prevail'.[16] In this article, Kovač contrasted the Slovene politicians' strong concern for the language with their meek acceptance of the Army's *diktat* on the legal and democratic issues raised by the trial. He argued, therefore, that the Slovene leadership, like its Serbian counterpart, views Yugoslavia solely through national spectacles:

What unites Slovene, Serb and Federal political forums is that they all behave as if the Yugoslav nations were homogenized and undifferentiated wholes. One immediate consequence is that this commitment to national sovereignty draws a veil over the responsibility of the individual [national] bureaucracies for the current social catastrophe.

The other consequence is that 'the [national] community's problems are sought outside of it. The various quarrels between the Yugoslav nations about who exploits whom are a direct consequence of the undemocratic social order', which – constituted around the nation as the main social subject – prevents an all-Yugoslav debate on the most vital issue of political democracy.

Therefore, paradoxically, it is nationalism that unites the Yugoslav nations. The more the Slovenes swear by their Central European heritage, which is supposed to differentiate them from other Yugoslavs, the more Balkanized do they become; the more they chafe against the stupid [Federal] government in Belgrade, the more they become blind to the foolishness of their own bureaucracy; the more independent they are, the less disturbed they are by the absence of democracy in Yugoslavia.

Kovač was answered in the following issue by Tomaz Mastnak. Mastnak's main argument revolved around the thesis that 'the homogenization of the Slovene nation differs from the homogenization of the Serb one.' Mastnak pointed out that the mass mobilization in Slovenia had been spontaneous, that it had emerged outside the official structures, 'although it did not treat the latter as something contrary or even hostile to it. The movement was at all times in communication with them and was prepared – when necessary and possible – to cooperate with them.' However, 'the initiative remained always with the people, who organized themselves politically and formulated their own exact and reliable criteria for judging the politicians' activity. So long as the politicians fulfilled popular expectations, the people saw in them their representatives.' In this interaction between the people and the political structures, therefore, official politics had

acknowledged the hegemony of the mass movement. The empirical evidence, however, is that the Slovene political structure only rarely fulfilled all the popular expectations... meeting the people only halfway. It also happened that individual politicians betrayed the hopes and expectations of the people, and the people responded by not recognizing them as their own. Each day the politicians' legitimacy was put to the test.

What had occurred in Slovenia, therefore, could not be described as a national homogenization:

> The people organized themselves by creating a political bloc which is not identical to the official, self-appointed structures. The effect of this crucial split has been a de-homogenization of the Slovene nation: now one can see more accurately than before who is who and what is what and this is valid as much for individuals as for institutions.

Herein, according to Mastnak, lies the fundamental difference between the mobilization in Slovenia and in Serbia. 'The platform for homogenization of the Slovene nation has been the struggle for political democracy, the defence of fundamental human rights, the battle for a legal state. The starting point of Serb mobilization has been *Blut and Boden*: Kosovo and the Serb blood spilled on that piece of land [in the fourteenth-century Battle of Kosovo]. Serb nationalism wishes to set itself up as a state-dominated community, whereas Slovene nationalism organizes as a society wishing to supervise the national state. This is why the former identifies easily with the Army, whereas the latter is anti-militarist. The former aims at state expansion, which it wishes to sanction with a new constitution; the latter limits itself to safeguarding the minimal constitutional guarantees of its state sovereignty. The greatest difference between Slovene and Serb nationalism is that . . . the social movement in Slovenia establishes the state as state whereas the pro-state Serb nationalism destroys the state as state . . . and transforms it into an instrument of the party.' For, 'the only Slovene politician for whom we can say that he has not only retained his credibility but also gained additional esteem has been the state president Stanovnik. In Serbia, on the other hand, at the centre of attention is the party chief Milošević.' And whereas the national movement in Slovenia 'never took a stand against any other Yugoslav nationality,' the Serb national mobilization 'has needed enemy nations'. Altogether, whereas the national mobilization in Slovenia 'was understood as a moment – today a key and decisive moment – of the struggle for democracy in Yugoslavia', Serb nationalism has emerged as an anti-democratic force: it 'demands military intervention (at least in Kosovo) and is not too bothered by constitutional norms'.

Mastnak, however, did not limit himself to empirical conclusions but sought to pose the difference between the two nationalisms also on a principled plane. He challenged the idea that all nationalisms were regressive, arguing that 'the political nature of nationalism is contingent'. Comparing Slovenia to the Soviet Baltic Republics, he contended that 'in that they [i.e. small nations] resist the totalitarianism of large nations', their nationalism inevitably has democratic consequences. 'To be sure, Slovene nationalism could become totalitarian [i.e. articulate itself as a substantialist ideology] if democracy were suppressed – if it did not succeed. Serb nationalism, however, would become definitely totalitarian if it were to succeed – for then democracy would be suppressed.' Pointing to the fact that people with different political positions worked together in the Committee for Protection of Human Rights without having to explore these differences, he saw it as symbolic of the kind of homogenization that had taken place within the Slovene nation as a result of the trial.

The fundamental objection to this way of looking at things, raised by Kovač in the following issue of *Teleks*, centred on Mastnak's distinction between democratic and totalitarian nationalisms. Kovač argued that Slovene nationalism, like all nationalisms, is a mixture of old and new ideological elements, not all of which bear affixed a democratic meaning. If one were to accept the premise of the essentially democratic nature of Slovene nationalism, then not only would this minimize the importance of internal differentiation within the Slovene nation – which has constituted the latter as a terrain in its own right of struggle between democratic and anti-democratic forces, and which has therefore played a dominant role in the national formation – but also 'the history of postwar Yugoslavia would appear . . . as repeated attempts by the Yugoslav bureaucracy to suppress the democratic tendencies of the Slovene party.' Such a 'democratic nationalism' would consequently 'be blind to the deeply undemocratic character of postwar Slovene history and to the rich contribution of Slovene national ideology to the formation of the existing Yugoslav socio-political system'. In other words, Slovene 'democratic nationalism' would be blind to its responsibility in establishing a system which is still able to produce 'a pogrom-like mentality ("Kill Azem!") and a cult of personality ("Slobodan, Freedom!")[17] in one part of the Serb nation.' Is Slovene 'democratic nationalism' not also responsible for the fact that 'in Serbia the barrier between "popular" and "official" nationalism has fallen – as when Kosovo Serbs march against all those who do not agree with the Serbian leadership?'

Suppose that we accept, Kovač argued, that Slovene nationalism is democratic because it defends a minority against the violence of the majority, then how can one explain the rightist tendencies within Slovene society which seek to replace a democratic model of social supervision by a corporatist concept of the state? 'A nationalism which is aware that the nation is not a homogeneous whole and acts in support of the latter's – and hence also its own – heterogeneity, is no longer nationalism. Why then call it so? Why should one clothe the democratic idea, which Mastnak supports, in national dress?' In the rest of his reply, Kovač expressed his doubt that mobilization on a national basis could be an answer to the

Yugoslav 'tragi-comedy'. 'It is impossible to articulate a democratic ideology in the language of democratic nationalism.' Only an all-Yugoslav democratic movement, capable of hegemonizing the disparate Yugoslav nationalisms, could prevent the triumph of the Yugoslav Right.

A final comment (for the time being) has come from a third Slovene intellectual, Lev Kreft. Noting that the debate between Kovač and Mastnak expressed a dilemma as to whether democratic rights or the Slovene nation's statehood should be defended as a priority, Kreft declared the counterposition to be essentially false: 'The importance of the national question in the present political moment lies precisely in the fact that it is dangerous to separate it from the whole question of democracy.' For once this is done, then the problematic is firmly back to where it was in 1848 and thereafter: 'trading away democracy in order to preserve a small domestic autocracy'. For Kreft, Mastnak was right to emphasize the democratic and spontaneous character of the mass movement of solidarity with the defendants; where he was wrong, however, was to introduce a distinction between democratic and totalitarian nationalisms in the contemporary Yugoslav situation. All nationalisms, Kovač was right to warn, are prey to totalitarian homogenization. Mastnak, in fact, had committed once again the mistake made by the young Marx in 1848.

'In the oscillation between extreme proletarian internationalism, which denies the importance of the national question, and state-sponsored national chauvinism, all that popular movements can do is to fight for all democratic rights.' Kreft emphasized how important it was for Slovene democrats to be aware of the dangerous ability of nationalism to co-opt any struggle for a 'legal state'. A Slovene who imputes an 'Asiatic' mentality to the Serb nation cannot be considered a democrat, any more than can a Serb who wishes to reduce Kosovo to the condition of a Bantustan within Serbia. The Slovene politicians, who acquired their current position of power in the early 1970s, have seen the crisis weakening the two elements of their distinct status within the Yugoslav bureaucracy: Slovenia's economic power and domestic national consensus. 'The homogenization which a "democratic nationalism" could bring about would work for them, and in the final instance only for them,' Kreft concluded.

If one compares this debate with a similar one which took place two or three generations ago, in the 1920s, within the young Communist Party of Yugoslavia, one is struck as much by the similarities as by the differences. Sixty years ago, such a debate would have been carried in an all-Yugoslav party theoretical paper, whereas today it is locally circumscribed.[18] In the current debate the operative categories are 'civil society' and 'legal state': the spontaneous mass mobilization in solidarity with the four defendants is seen as confirmation of the emergence of a 'civil society' in action for a 'legal state'. The young CPY spoke instead in terms of 'working class' and 'revolution'.

Yet some of the questions raised by the current debate in Slovenia have also confronted the socialist and democratic Left in the past – they were certainly present in the 1920s. Can nationalism at certain times play a democratic/progressive role? If so, what implications does this have for forming alliances with the classes/elites in power? Can one have a social/democratic transformation within a single Yugoslav nation without a simultaneous transformation of the kind in Yugoslavia as a whole?

The CPY emerged from its debates in the 1920s and 1930s with the understanding that the national question was a democratic issue of vital importance for the working class and that it had to be solved comprehensively. Furthermore, it posited the question of democracy not as an abstract category, but as a concrete problem of organization and power – hence the Party's commitment to a federal arrangement. Indeed, if one surveys the historical record of the CPY on the national question, its superiority over those of its nationalist and liberal competitors is undeniable. Unlike them, the CPY took as its starting position that nations did not exist as undifferentiated or harmonious entities, but were instead antagonistic totalities. It therefore subsumed the national question, without obliterating it, into the question of self-determination of one segment of the nation: the working class. The national problem in post-revolutionary society therefore emerges as an aspect of the relationship between the state and the class, or – to put it more precisely – as a consequence of the revolution's failure to redefine the national identity and the state in the manner and direction required for the establishment of a new socialist order.

Yugoslavia's multinational composition, and the consequent federalization of its state structure, has tended to obscure the class foundation of the state there, hence also the real roots of its current crisis: the political dispossession of the working class – which has guaranteed the political impotence of all other social layers. The Yugoslav bureaucracy has not as yet denied the historic role that the struggles and aspirations of this class have played in revolutionary or democratic (including national) gains at home and abroad. But it has consigned this role firmly to the past. For today, it seems, all is different: the class as such no longer has any positive role to play in society. Instead, the working class has become 'labour' (as in the phrase: 'we need a market not only in products but also in capital and labour'). No longer treated as the vanguard class, Yugoslav workers have instead become a 'problem' in couplets such as 'the unemployment problem', 'the problem of industrial restructuring', of 'industrial management', etc. Self-management is being quietly buried, without anything in particular being put in its place to stabilize the relationship between the workers and the state. Militant resistance by workers to the government's austerity measures – which have reduced their wages to an existential minimum – is feared by conservatives and liberals alike.

Over these past twelve months, the workers have, with increasing frequency, been travelling – on foot or in large convoys of buses and trucks – to demonstrate before the Federal Assembly building on Belgrade's Marx-Engels Square. Despite the absence of active support from the intelligentsia their slogans point to their growing radicalization. The legal right to strike has not figured among their demands, doubtless because the workers have already asserted this right in action. Despite this, the Federal authorities have shown a sudden readiness to consider inclusion of the right to strike into forthcoming constitutional amendments. This turn-about, after years of unproductive public debate, ensued after the occupation of the Federal Assembly last June by workers employed in the huge (22,000 workers) rubber and shoe enterprise of 'Borovo' in Croatia. Following a 30 per cent cut in their wages (stipulated by the Federal government's austerity measures), 2,000 'Borovo' workers appeared in Belgrade, where they demanded a meeting with Federal officials. After being left waiting for five or six hours in scorching heat to 'soften up' prior to the encounter, their patience finally ran out and they pushed past guards to invade the Assembly rooms – an act unprecedented in postwar Europe. Once inside the building, the first thing they encountered was the national mythologies of the Yugoslav nations, embodied in the statues of, respectively, the obscure mediaeval Slovene Prince Kocelj, the equally mediaeval and obscure Croat King Tomislav, the somewhat less obscure (since four centuries later) Serb Emperor Dushan, and finally Alexander Karadjordje, leader of the early-nineteenth-century Serb uprising against the Ottomans and perhaps most deserving of inclusion in this national Pantheon. These ancient national totems were erected after World War One – their living equivalents, however, were nowhere to be seen.

Outside the Assembly the 'Borovo' workers had been shouting slogans very similar to those voiced only weeks before by workers of the Belgrade truck factory 'Zmaj': 'Out with the thieves!', 'We want bread!', 'Down with the red bourgeoisie!'. Entering the Assembly and finding it deserted, their mood became quite ugly. Violence was avoided, however, by the belated appearance from hiding of Jovan Popovski, President of the Federal Assembly, and Nenad Krekić, an ex-manager of 'Borovo', who talked to the workers, promising to suspend the wage cuts. In a subsequent interview given to the press, Popovski talked warmly of the need to bring in strike legislation, since 'it is impossible to reason with workers when they are so enraged'; such legislation would also encourage the workers to limit their activity to their enterprises. If the Constitution is amended to include the right to strike, this will thus be done in a form and manner

manner designed to contain workers' freedom of action. However, given the parlous state of the Yugoslav economy, the immediate effect of such legislation could only be minimal.

The constitutional amendments currently being discussed include also the possibility of a more direct representation of citizens. The Yugoslav bureaucracy has quietly shed its professed earlier quest for a 'Yugoslav' socialist democracy, in favour of a research for a 'modern' state, 'adequate to the demands of the twenty-first century'. However, its problems would only begin here. For the kind of state to which its liberal wing today aspires was constituted historically in the form of a *national* state. Such aspirations thus carry within themselves an impetus towards the transformation of Yugoslavia into a confederation of national states – something which, of course, would be quite unacceptable to many of the Yugoslav nations.[19] It is also the case that the working class shows little interest in such a project. Over the past few years, the Federal Assembly has been visited by striking workers from Macedonia, Kosovo, Serbia, Bosnia and Croatia. But their slogans included no specifically Macedonian, Albanian, Serb, Moslem or Croat national demands. The workers instead denounced their political dispossession as a class, and demanded – in addition to amelioration of their rapidly declining living standards – the removal of those responsible for the country's crisis. Since the real value of workers' wages is continuing to decline drastically, beginning with this autumn the country is set to witness an even more powerful strike wave, possibly culminating in a general strike. In July 1988, police guarding the Federal Assembly buildings were instructed to allow workers to break their cordon: so far, an open physical confrontation between the workers and the repressive apparatus of the state has been avoided. It seems that this policy is now under review. There are warnings in the press that, were the policy indeed to change, a 'Polonization' of Yugoslavia would ensue.

The country's republican and provincial leaderships have been trying to co-opt their workers by fanning at best a sense of national self-sufficiency and at worst an atmosphere of nationalist revanchism. Herein lies the importance of the debate between Kovač, Mastnak and Kreft. It has come up with some important pointers for the future: the democratic movement must remain independent; it must hegemonize the national question; hence it must be not only Slovene but also Croat, Serb, Albanian, Macedonian, etc. – i.e. it must become all-Yugoslav or the rightist offensive will triumph. A 'Polonization' of Yugoslavia would be a catastrophe for the workers as much as for the Yugoslav democratic intelligentsia. An alliance between them would make such an outcome much more difficult.

(September 1988)

Notes

1. This principle was subsequently endorsed by the Western Allies, who limited it to Europe only. The Bolsheviks were alone in extending it to the European colonies in Africa and Asia. Their victory in Russia forced the Western Allies to sanction the break-up of the Habsburg Monarchy, thus ensuring the birth in 1918 of the Kingdom of Serbs, Croats and Slovenes (later renamed Yugoslavia).

2. Since state bureaucracy needs a national dress (cf. the great problem which 1848 and its aftermath posed in this regard to the Habsburg Imperial-Royal bureaucracy), the Yugoslav unitarists have been trying, unsuccessfully, to construct a Yugoslav nation out of bits of Panslavism, local folklore colour (peasant handicraft, folk poetry, etc.) and, of course, patriotism.

3. Vika Potočnjak, a Slovene delegate to the Federal Assembly, has become something of a Yugoslav heroine following her vigorous defence of the villagers of Vevčani (Macedonia) and Mosevac (Bosnia) against brutal police assaults sponsored by the local politicians. In both cases, popular resistance was organized by members of the Alliance of Socialist Youth, who showed exemplary courage and determination.

4. The Belgrade journal *Duga* recently published a special issue given over to the critics of Branko Horvat's book on the Albanian national question in Yugoslavia (see *Labour Focus*, vol. 9, no. 2). The cover of the issue carried a portrait of a mediaeval Serbian queen, with the following verses printed at her feet: 'They have gouged out your eyes, beautiful picture! . . . An Albanian has gouged out your eyes with his knife!' Shkelzen Maliqi, an Albanian intellectual with impeccable anti-nationalist credentials, commented on this lie by referring the reader to the mediaeval local Orthodox custom of using 'the holy dust of icons and frescoes to prepare medical potions and amulets'. *Danas*, Zagreb, 16 August 1988. The vast majority of the contributors to *Duga* are members of the Serbian Academy of Arts and Sciences. Not one of them has disassociated himself from the cover or its message – not even such former editors of *Praxis* as Mihailo Marković and Ljuba Tadić. Branko Horvat's endeavours to initiate an all-Yugoslav rational discussion of the subject has earned him in the Belgrade press the kind of vilification normally reserved for the country's outright enemies: his competence, personal integrity and motives have all been questioned, in a manner that goes well beyond civilized norms of discourse; while his ethnic origins have been sufficient to tar him with pro-Ustashe sympathies – this despite the fact that this particular Croat's Yugoslav orientation is well-known and beyond dispute. Branko Horvat was in his early teens when he joined the partisans.

5. See 'Awaiting the Future', above.

6. *Mladina*'s attempt to publish relevant sections of this document was stopped by official Slovene intervention. However, they were published in the Zagreb student journal *Polet* and the Belgrade weekly *NIN*. The contents of the leaked minutes were subsequently confirmed in a speech given by Milan Kučan, head of the Slovene party, at a July meeting of the Slovene party's Central Committee.

7. The Military Council is an advisory body (made up exclusively of military personnel) to the Minister of Defence, himself traditionally a soldier.

8. The Military Council stated that in Slovenia there was a 'harmonization of open attacks on the Army by enemies engaged in a special war against Yugoslavia. Their aim was: (a) to compromise the military cadre and thus break up the unity of the Army; (b) to alienate the youth from military service; (c) to prevent cooperation between the YPA and the armed forces of friendly non-aligned countries or national liberation movements' (a reference to *Mladina*'s campaign against arms sales to Ethiopia).

9. Ustashe and Chetniks were Croat and Serb nationalist and anti-communist formations which collaborated with the occupying forces during World War Two and were responsible for mass murders. In a March issue of the Belgrade main daily *Politika*, *Mladina* was accused of pro-Ustashe sympathies.

10. On this occasion, the delegates from Croatia and Slovenia unsuccessfully moved a vote of no-confidence in the current Yugoslav government.

11. At the conference in question, Mamula sharply criticized tolerance of 'enemy activity' in

Slovenia, particularly in the independent and semi-official media. Uniquely in eastern Europe, the Yugoslav Party is organized in the Army as a separate branch of the LCY, with the right to a seat in the Federal Party presidency. This has led one prominent Slovene intellectual, Tomaz Mastnak, to conclude that the Army is essentially the armed branch of the Party – i.e. that the Party and state are not only *de facto* but also *de jure* merged at the most crucial juncture.

12. Stane Dolanc, who enjoys the military's confidence, represents Slovenia at the Federal State Presidency, where he is responsible for liaison with the Army.

13. Janez Janša was a ASYS functionary in charge of relations with the Army (Yugoslav recruits are liable for a call-up as soon as they are eighteen) who helped to formulate the ASYA position on the Army, including such issues as greater social accountability of the Army, opening up military matters to public scrutiny. Thus *Mladina* took a public stand against the sale of arms to Ethiopia and other repressive states in the Third World, against the Army's desire to built itself its own supersonic plane, in support of conscientious objection, against traditional military parades on 1 May, for greater national equality in the Army, etc. Janša has a degree in People's Self-Defence, Yugoslavia's unique answer to a standing army.

14. A list of signatories was last published in *Mladina* of 29 July 1988.

15. This is not the first time, of course, that violation of defendants' right to be tried in their own language has taken place in Yugoslavia. The use of Serbo-Croat is quite common in trials of ethnic Albanians – and ethnic Albanians form four-fifths of Yugoslavia's political prisoners.

16. For an extended interview with Kovač, see *NLR* 171 (September–October 1988).

17. Slobodan is the first name of the Serbian party leader Milošević, etymologically linked to the word *sloboda* meaning freedom.

18. Various plans to publish *Mladina* and/or other Slovene journals also in Serbo-Croat have so far come to nothing. It is difficult to understand why, given the relatively small costs involved.

19. It would affect, in particular, the rights of the Serb nation, a substantial proportion of which lives outside the Republic of Serbia in the Republics of Bosnia-Herzegovina and Croatia. Like other Yugoslav nations, so also the Serb one is threatened by the rise of nationalism in the country as a whole.

PART THREE
Milošević Assails the Federal Order (1988–89)

Introduction

1988 was one of the most dramatic years in Yugoslavia's postwar history – indeed, in the month of October it seemed that the country might actually be falling apart. The foreign ministers of West Germany and France expressed their anxiety publicly, as Yugoslavia for the first time since Tito's death became front-page news. In the last days of the year the government resigned, as the decomposition of the League of Communists accelerated. The refusal, in August 1988, by the League of Communists of Serbia, led by Slobodan Milošević, to accept the authority of the League of Communists of Yugoslavia (which had instructed it to halt nationalist street demonstrations) drew a line under a whole historical period beginning in 1945.

By this time, the Yugoslav Communist Party had lost its traditional underpinning, with workers leaving in droves, and instead forming strike committees. In 1988 Yugoslavia was gripped by continuous working-class unrest. The divergence between Party and class was putting a question-mark over Yugoslavia's very existence as a unified state. The growing political vacuum was being filled with the politics of national chauvinism, especially in Serbia and Macedonia, often systematically fanned by party and state functionaries.

The local and Federal bureaucracies stubbornly defended their power, while all round them society and the economy crumbled, and one revolutionary ideal after another was jettisoned in favour of a naked struggle for survival. The problems faced by Yugoslavia and the ruling party, however, were no longer unique, forming part of a more general pattern of change throughout Eastern Europe. If anything, indeed, the class and national compact in Yugoslavia still seemed the more resilient. Demonstrations for national rights, strikes by public-sector workers, direct working-class interventions into party-state politics – all could be seen as a sign of its continuing vitality. Tito's Yugoslavia was clearly coming to an end, but it was not yet clear who was to inherit.

The whole of state and society was in fact living in a condition of acute schizophrenia. Thus, in November 1988, the Federal Assembly voted to adopt a nineteenth-century pan-Slav song *Hej, Slaveni!* ('Come, Slavs!') as the country's official anthem – a symbolic rebuff at once to the revolutionary founding of the state and to its sizeable non-Slav population. A few days later, there were solemn (albeit muted) celebrations to mark the forty-fifth anniversary of the wartime birth of that revolutionary state – one of whose pillars, of course, had been its commitment to national equality for Slavs and non-Slavs alike. To cap the whole thing, a few days later again the country commemorated – for the first time – the seventieth anniversary of the creation of the *first* Yugoslav state, against which precisely the 1941–45 revolution had been directed. By a bitter irony, the official chosen to preside over this occasion was notorious for having advised the pre-war Royal régime (and later the Socialist one) on the desirability of expelling most of the non-Slav population as 'unreliable'. The country as a whole became haunted by the spectre of an imminent break-up.

Two options seemed to be on public offer in Yugoslavia at this time. The first, associated with Slovene party leader Milan Kučan, advocated a programme – albeit only for Slovenia – of reform from above, in the direction of greater political pluralism married to a 'mixed economy'. The second, associated with Slobodan Milošević, clamoured for an authoritarian state in the language of populist nationalism. This latter vision relied heavily on 'enemies' – which it found in the Albanian population, and on the editorial boards of the country's student and youth journals. Bureaucratic reaction, not for the first time, was donning a national mask. In addition, continued workers' unrest and Albanian popular resistance, coupled with the collapse of the Federal party's authority, were gradually producing a third alternative: military rule.

Kosovo remained a focus of attention. Mass demonstrations by Albanian workers, in November 1988, were intended as a warning to both the Serbian and the all-Yugoslav leadership that proposed changes to the Serbian constitution, reducing Kosovo's autonomy and thereby Albanian national rights, would be resisted. Kosovo and Vojvodina lost the right of veto over any future alteration of the provinces' status within Serbia. Although their autonomy was still formally guaranteed by the all-Yugoslav constitution, the readiness of Yugoslav state and party leaders to accept Serbia's *diktat* made this provision worthless. The general strike in Kosovo in February 1989, and the mass character of Albanian defiance (for the first time women in Kosovo started to play a vital and indispensable role), gave Albanian resistance the character of an *intifada*.

Two hundred and fifteen Albanian intellectuals, including Shkelzen Maliqi, Isuf Berisha and Veton Surroi, addressed an open letter to the

Serbian assembly and the Yugoslav people, protesting against the undemocratic character of the planned constitutional changes in Serbia. The Yugoslav authorities answered their appeal by sending troop reinforcements, including federal paramilitary police, to Kosovo, violating in the process the country's Federal constitution.

Support for Kosovo miners, who played a leading role in the resistance, came from Croatia and above all Slovenia. A public meeting amounting to a national convention was held in Ljubljana on 18 February 1989, in support of the Albanian demands. In Zagreb, a newly formed Yugoslav Association for a Democratic Initiative issued a statement demanding a referendum in Kosovo on the province's status within the federation. In Moscow, meanwhile (at the request of a London-based committee which I helped to form), two members of the Moscow's People's Front – Boris Kagarlitsky (who had just won the Isaac Deutscher Memorial Prize for his book *The Thinking Reed*) and Sergei Stankevich (soon to be elected a People's Deputy of the USSR) – signed an appeal for a 'peaceful and just resolution of the issues at stake in Kosovo'.

Over a thousand Kosovo miners in Trepča went on hunger strike underground for eight days, demanding the resignation of three provincial officials imposed by the Serbian party. They were tricked into believing that this demand would be met, but as soon as they resurfaced mass Serb nationalist demonstrations took place in Belgrade, insisting on tough action against Kosovo. Milošević spoke to the crowd and promised arrests. The next day the strike leaders and several leading Kosovo politicians, most notably Azem Vllasi, were arrested. The Federal paramilitary police moved in and the province was placed under a state of emergency. In the Federal Assembly Lazar Mojsov, a member of the country's presidency, spoke in lurid terms about a plot hatched by Albania and foreign intelligence networks against the territorial integrity of Yugoslavia. The Federal police used tear gas and automatic weapons to quell demonstrations that now erupted throughout Kosovo. According to official figures, 'only' twenty-four deaths ensued. Journalists from the Ljubljana weekly *Mladina* and from the Italian Communist daily *l'Unità* reported operations by death squads against recalcitrant individuals. The Kosovo assembly at this point succumbed to extreme pressure and ratified the Serbian constitutional amendments, voting itself into oblivion. This allowed Serbia the following day to adopt a new republican constitution. Belgrade celebrated the event with street music, theatrical performances, funfairs and free refreshments. Ante Marković – Yugoslavia's new prime minister – congratulated Milošević and Co. In Kosovo, no public funerals or mourning for the dead were allowed. In contrast to what happened in Soviet Georgia after the Tbilisi massacre, no resignation of officials responsible occurred, nor was any public investigation into the shootings ordered. I wrote at the time: 'Under its current leadership, Yugoslavia is fast becoming a lawless and barbarous country.'

Will the Centre Hold?

The escalating Yugoslav crisis has further reinforced the ever-present tendency of the republican and provincial parties to entrench themselves in their local national constituencies. The outcome has varied considerably, given the wide economic disparities and differing national traditions.

(a) Slovenes Reach for Democracy

The Committee for Defence of Human Rights, established to defend four intellectuals arrested in May 1988 and sentenced for allegedly handling a secret military document, is today fast acquiring the character of a Slovene people's front.[1] It has remained in dialogue with the Party, maintaining a political consensus on all the main issues affecting democracy and Slovene national sovereignty. Yet the progress of Slovene democratization has by no means been a simple advance. At recent elections to a post on the republican (state) presidency, Igor Bavcar, a leading member of the Committee, was firmly 'filtered out' of the electoral procedure, despite the fact that he had won majority support at the base. The pretext given was that Bavcar had called for 'civil disobedience' to prevent execution of the sentence pronounced by the military court on Janez Janša, Franci Zavrl, David Tasić and Ivan Borstner (in fact, Bavcar's proposal had been heavily qualified: he had proposed direct action only to allow the Slovene republican assembly's special commission, set up to investigate the circumstances of the original arrests, to conclude its work). In protest against this undemocratic practice, some fifty of the best young party intellectuals resigned from the Party.

It was in this context that Janez Janša, one of the Slovene Four, wrote an open letter to the Slovene party leader Milan Kučan. In an astonishing indication of the democratic climate prevailing in Slovenia, this was published in the main Ljubljana daily *Delo* (5 November 1988), with a reply by Kučan. In his letter, Janša criticized a speech Kučan had given at

Poljce to trade-union activists just before the candidate list was to be approved, in which he had criticized Bavcar for calling for civil disobedience. Janša argued that this speech had opened the door to attacks on the Committee and also led to Bavcar's disqualification. Yet the original arrests, and the trial of the Four, had been 'an aspect of policy conducted by certain forces within Yugoslavia hostile to the liberalization in Slovenia'.

He also criticized Kučan for changing his position on the language. Initially, Kučan had argued that Slovenes could not feel loyalty to a state which did not respect their mother language. However, when the Federal authorities – the Federal state presidency and the Supreme Military Court – pronounced the use of the Serbo-Croat language during trial of the Four to be perfectly constitutional, he did nothing. Janša accused Kučan of 'naiveté at best and political opportunism at worst', arguing that unprincipled politics could only end in disaster. Slovenes lived with the fear that Kučan and Janez Stanovnik, the republic's state president, might be removed, since this would mark the end of liberalization in Slovenia. However, if the two were ready to give up their principles, then this amounted to the same. Kučan used to be described as 'progressive', Janša went on, but this description was now beginning to pale. 'One cannot assess how progressive ideas are solely in terms of the "relationship of forces"; it is a question of the vision they contain, which determines the aim. Without an aim, there is neither will nor way.' Without an aim that can inspire the people, it would be impossible to get out of the current crisis. But the electoral manoeuvre suggested that the Party's proclaimed reform would be only of a cosmetic nature.

Kučan began his reply by stressing that democratization in Slovenia was worthy of the name only if it provided space for people like Janša to state their views. While he refused to enter into a polemic, he nevertheless wished to touch on three important points raised by Janša.

1. 'I recognize the Yugoslav Federal state – as defined by the 1974 constitution – as my own. The key question today, however, is what kind of Yugoslavia?' Kučan argued that very wide differences existed in this regard, as was indicated by the trial. In his view, 'a Yugoslavia that was not socialist and democratic would not be possible.' But there were strong proponents of different options, and the battle over the character of the Federation would continue. The question of the language had to be seen in this context. This was not to say that one should give up the struggle: Slovene language and sovereignty depend, above all, on 'unity and determination in Slovenia'.
2. 'I do not share the opinion of those who say that Yugoslavia is not a legal state.' For Kučan, what was at stake was a strengthening of its

democratic content. This involved the elimination of arbitrariness and voluntarism on the part of the Party, which had turned the state into an alienated power over citizens rather than something belonging to them all. 'This must be the meaning of the reform of the political system.' This was why the Slovene Assembly had set up a commission to study all the circumstances of the trial, and why in July the Slovene party had given its support to the Committee for Protection of Human Rights. In the meantime, he was against calls 'to stop the execution of the legal sentence passed by the military court.'

3. 'Regarding my speech at Poljce, it would be unfair to suggest that the candidate commission was involved in manipulation. We in the League of Communists of Slovenia have the same visions and aims, and differ only about the means.' Just as in his speech he had not talked about the Committee's activity in general, it would be equally wrong to declare oneself for or against the Slovene party in general. He saw the call for civil disobedience as something that could 'stop the process of democratization and weaken the Slovene internal consensus, hence also Slovenia's influence on the formulation of an all-Yugoslav orientation.' A polarization in Slovenia – particularly on an issue such as respect for the law – could have 'tragic consequences'.

(b) 'Anti-bureaucratic Revolution'

It was in Serbia that the turn to the nation took the sharpest form: the primacy of class politics was formally abandoned in favour of national consolidation with the accession of Slobodan Milošević to unchallenged power in the League of Communists in Serbia, at the end of 1987, on a programme of re-centralization of Serbia.[2]

But the project of 'Serbia's unification' also subsumed a threat of expansionism and a recomposition – if not outright dissolution – of the country's federal structure. This is why the Federal party came so quickly to the defence of the beleaguered Montenegrin leadership (see below).[3] The Montenegrin workers' demonstration provided a backdrop for a determined attempt to replace the local leadership with Milošević's men. The Montenegrin events, it seems, were a substitute for something else: the overthrow of the Kosovo leadership, planned as a pendant of the successful putsch in Vojvodina. Belgrade was warned, however, that any such attempt in Kosovo would provoke mass resistance, which is why the organizers' accumulated energy was then turned in the direction of Montenegro. Indeed, as subsequent events in Kosovo show, the Serbian leadership's national and state plans have come up against a popular determination there that will be impossible to break without a long-term state of emergency in the province.

Cynically, the Serbian leadership, in response to criticism addressed to it from other parts of Yugoslavia that it is governed not by class but rather by purely national considerations, put considerable effort at the beginning of October into presenting itself as a friend to the workers.[4] This image will be difficult to sustain, since it is firmly committed to economic liberalism. At the meeting of the Serbian CC of 22 November 1988, convened to discuss the economic reform, Milošević gave the key speech, in which he said: 'A contemporary, efficient and self-managing socialist, and above all democratic, society can only be built on the basis of commodity production and modern market economy. The market is today the only democratic mechanism which valorizes business ideas and the activity of economic subjects. Without commodity production, self-management can only be an abstract political relationship.' As the interview with Pero Jurković published below shows, it is doubtful whether Yugoslav self-management will survive in any recognizable form.

Mirjana Kasapović, a Zagreb political scientist, has made a rare attempt to theorize certain aspects of recent developments in Serbia. This has provoked an angry response from Zagorka Golubović, an ex-editor of *Praxis* from Belgrade. What follows is an abridged account of their interesting and as yet unfinished debate.[5]

Kasapović argues that contemporary Serb nationalism is not a unified phenomenon but contains different currents, including a 'right-wing radical one'. She defines this as 'an anti-democratic political ideology and practice which, in the name of a higher right – the allegedly endangered survival of the Serb nation in Kosovo – rejects the established democratic system and democratic methods for changing it.' One component of this current's ideology is its exclusive approach to the Albanian population as an enemy. It consequently seeks a reconstruction of the Serb national state as the decisive instrument for a *violent* solution of the Albanian 'problem' in Kosovo, ranging from changing the ethnic structure of the province to placing it under a different legal system.

This 'right-wing radical' current is convinced that a precondition of its success is the introduction of a state of emergency in Yugoslavia. It argues, namely, that existing Yugoslav institutions have been constituted by a 'permanent and pragmatic anti-Serb coalition', in a manner designed to block perpetually the desired recreation of the Serb state. The 'permanent' part of the coalition is formed by Slovenia and Croatia, and sublimates the historic conflict between the European West and East. The pragmatic part is made up of the provinces of Vojvodina and Kosovo, which favour a 'totally de-subjectified and decomposed Serbia'. The coalition, therefore, must be destroyed, and this can be achieved only by an all-Serb mobilization. Hence the invitation extended to Serbs living outside Serbia proper to refuse loyalty to the federal units in which they live, in the name of the supreme Serb national interest. 'They see all relations in Yugoslavia as fundamentally derived from, and reducible to, the national dimension. One's own nation is seen as the determinant not only of its own national politics, but also of all others.'

This is essentially a totalitarian political ideology, in that it views the nation as monolithic, while all other relations within the state are viewed exclusively along the lines of an enemy–ally relationship. 'The ally, of course, is the national establishment: the national party, its leadership and leader. The enemies are as a rule to be found in the other nations. Such a structuring of the political field is a remnant of the Stalinist type of rule and a contribution to its revival: the nation turns not to the institutions of the state, but to the Party; not to the Assembly, but to the CC; not to the government, but to the party leadership.' Like Stalinism, it is also engaged 'in a terrifying reduction of all social complexity: all social relations are seen as highly transparent and society appears as a chess board upon which every move of any individual is predicted, followed and immediately judged as a move by a collectivity to which the individual belongs.' This right-wing radical nationalism could, therefore, open the door to 'a totalitarian movement based on the lower layers of the upper social class, whose aim would be to neo-Stalinize Yugoslavia.'

Golubović's response was set in the context of a more general critique of the 'unexpected turnabout in the thinking of certain intellectuals over the past few months'. Golubović wrote that many intellectuals who, in the first half of the 1980s, 'were very critical towards the existing system of government, arguing that – since it was not freely elected and since the people did not have any institutionalized possibility of expressing their will – it was of questionable legitimacy', were now defending the system and its 'legal institutions, while criticizing the mass rallies in Serbia as illegitimate.'

In her own view the mass rallies in Serbia expressed 'an elementary right of all citizens of a country which has declaratively adopted socialism and self-management – the more so as they demanded 'that irresponsible leaderships and individual functionaries account to the people for the current crisis of Yugoslav society.' Golubović therefore asked: 'What prevents those who most probably sincerely desire the democratization of Yugoslav society from recognizing, and extending their support to, these tendencies which in one way or another *are opening* the possibility for a deepening of the democratic process?' The mass rallies held in Serbia were 'undoubtedly an instrument of corrosion of this hardened bureaucratic system, which could be used to speed up democratic processes . . . a seed from which a development of democratic aspirations and processes could sprout forth.'

She, Golubović, agreed that the struggle against a 'decades-long bureaucratic system' cannot be waged on an exclusively national basis. However, can one criticize the search for support exclusively in the nation in some cases while endorsing it in others? 'It is here that I see the greatest inconsistency of Slovene intellectuals, and even of Slovene democratic and progressive politicians, whose efforts towards democratization of our society I otherwise support.'

If one accepts, Golubović went on, that the democratization of Yugoslavia will be a long-term struggle, then one should accept also that 'every effort designed to break through what has up to now been an impenetrable system can be a useful contribution to the creation of a space for the democratic process. In the conditions of "real socialism", this space has been widened precisely through extra-institutional forms of action: this was true as much in Poland as in Hungary, in Slovenia as in Serbia.' And she concluded by saying that 'the defence of non-democratic institutional forms by some intellectuals today constitutes an apologia for the existing system' and 'represents a departure from the critical stance upheld by the majority of intellectuals in the first half of this decade.'

In her reply, Kasapović pointed out that she had been dealing with only one strand of contemporary Serb nationalism, the one which works hard to create a conviction that 'justified' national interest cannot be achieved through the existing institutional channels. 'My critics do in fact exactly what they accuse me of doing, by recognizing in my analytical category of right-wing radicalism the totality of what is happening in the Socialist Republic of Serbia. This is a necessary consequence of their refusal to acknowledge the existence of different ideological positions present within "the national movement".' This refusal was politically motivated, since it allowed them to write off the right-wing radical current as so many unimportant 'excesses'.

Kasapović rejected Golubović's assertion that she equated all forms of extra-institutional protest with right-wing radicalism. To reduce all mass activity to right-radical forms of political activity would indeed be wrong in Yugoslavia today. 'Rather, it is a question of understanding concrete mass meetings and concrete attempts to use them for specific political aims. It is a question, also, whether concrete political activity could have political effects that need not correspond to the subjective intentions of the majority of participants. In Poland, the objective consequence of the mass extra-institutional movement was not the overthrow of an (illegal) order, but the introduction of an institutionalized state of exception.'

Finally, there was the question of the national background of the Serbian protest meetings, which Golubović, in Kasapović's view, dismissed too lightly. On the contrary, they could not be understood without it.

Before she excludes the national background from the discussion, the author should answer first some purely prosaic questions. How is one to explain the fact that the Polish extra-institutional movement was aimed at the (non)legitimate Polish system of government, the Hungarian at the Hungarian one, the Slovene at the Slovene (and Yugoslav) one, whereas the one thing that the Serb mass rallies do not question is the legitimacy of the republic's system of government or of its leadership? How is it that in the struggle against 'bureaucratic counter-revolution', the question of the 'national bureaucracy' itself is not being posed? How is it that the only ally of 'the people' in the struggle is its national party-state leadership? Why is it that the (unreformed) national communist party, and the type of government it is creating, are not targets of the extra-institutional rebellion against the (illegitimate) order? I am not clear why, for example, the targets of this 'extra-institutional movement' can be Vrhovec [a Croat] and Stanovnik [a Slovene], but not also Ckrebic [a Serb]?[6]

In Kasapović's view, mass action as an instrument of struggle against bureaucratic autocracy will only serve to strengthen bureaucratic reaction, unless it is a struggle for democracy with clear aims, such as 'free elections of representatives and the right spontaneously to reject those representatives' decisions.' Kasapović concluded by rejecting the suggestion that her orientation had changed. All her intervention had done was to reject 'theoretically and politically the challenge to the existing order's legitimacy from the position of right-wing radicalism, and forms of political activity consonant with this.'

Kasapović's questions are very pertinent. They point to the fact that the reason why the mass rallies did not criticise the Serbian bureaucracy was because that bureaucracy had in fact itself organized them, in order to put pressure on the Federal party. Far from being spontaneous, the recent mass rallies in Serbia were in fact little more than an instrument of inner-party struggle. Moreover, their strongly nationalist and anti-democratic charge is shown by the slogans popular on these occasions: 'Give us arms!'; 'Death to Albanians!'; 'We shall kill Vllasi!'; 'Hang Vllasi and [Fadil] Hoxha behind bars!' 'Slobodan Milošević, don't let Serbdom down!'; 'Slobodan, we will march with you to Kosovo!'; 'Kosovo is ours – don't let Enver [Hoxha] take it away!'; 'Serbia asks: when will Slobodan replace Tito?'; 'Slobodan, we are all yours – only traitors are against you!'; 'We are all Serbs!'; 'Only Unity Can Save the Serb!'; 'Montenegro is a jewel in Serbia's crown!'; 'Montenegro is a Serb land!', 'Long live King Peter!'; 'Try F. Hoxha; K. Shiroke; D. Marković; M. Bakalli; S. Kreigher; Dj. Stojsić; Dz. Nimani; J. Vrhoveć; A. Vlassi; K. Jashari; S. Dolasević; B. Krunić; P. Matić; Dj. Radosavljević; Z. Pupavci; D. Jashanci; V. Krstic; V. Marelj!'; etc. etc. Photographs show youths wearing royalist insignia on their peasant hats or bearded and dressed in black in the Chetnik style. As Kasapović indicated, the individuals whom the mass meetings denounced, and for whom trial, imprisonment, and/or death was demanded – a list of names that grew throughout the summer and autumn, and that came to include all prominent Yugoslav leaders, including Stipe Šuvar, current head of the Federal party – all came from outside Serbia proper, with the exception of Dragoslav Marković, a retired Serbian politician who had had the courage to be openly critical of the present republican leaders' nationalist course.

(c) Class Anger Explodes in Montenegro

In 1987 Montenegro, together with Macedonia and Kosovo, declared itself bankrupt. One third of its enterprises are operating at a loss; 40,000 workers, in a republic whose total population is only 600,000, are living and supporting their families on the minimum wage of 230,000 dinars (£25) per month. In the last two years 6,000 workers have lost their jobs and thousands of young people are seeking non-existent work. The social peace ended about a year ago, when the Montenegrin leadership decided to close down 'unviable' enterprises in order to save the 'healthy' sectors, but without offering any programme for dealing with the social effects of this policy. As a result, on 8 October 1988 the hungry workers staged the republic's largest postwar demonstration in the capital Titograd. The demonstration was initiated by the workers of 'Radoje Dakić', the construction machinery enterprise, and by steelworkers from 'Boris Kidrić' enterprise in Niksic.

'Radoje Dakić' occupies third place on the list of the republic's loss-makers. There is no market for its products, since the construction industry is heavily depressed. For a while the enterprise kept going by doing work in Iraq; but when the Iraq–Iran war began, the Yugoslav government was forced to accept a postponement in Iraqi payments, which led to a 13 billion dinar loss for 'Radoje Dakić'. The 1987 law on loss-making enterprises made 'Radoje Dakić' a prime target for closure, throwing its 3,000 workers into a state of complete insecurity. The Nikšić steelworks, for its part, accounted for 40 per cent of the republic's deficit in the first half of 1988, though some of this is being blamed on high electricity prices. These losses are subsidized by the combined efforts of the republic and the Federation. Closure of the steelworks, which is being proposed, would lead to a loss of 7,000 jobs.

There is also the case of the wood-pulp enterprise at Ivangrad, arguably one of the republic's greatest misinvestments. Calculations show that the factory has since its inception produced not a single unit of real value. It was closed in the summer of 1987, shedding 1,800 jobs. There are those who argue that the future of the factory lies in the production of fine newsprint, for which there is a great demand in the country, but the republic's current economic reconstruction plan does not refer to this possibility.

The textile industry too is in dire straits, and only a few days before the 8 October demonstration the 'Teteks' workers were on strike and planning a march to the republican Assembly in Titograd. Meanwhile, Montenegro's traditional sheep farming has been destroyed, as a result of the industrial push of the 1960s. And although much is being talked about the possibilities of tourist-based development, the sad truth is that the republic's rivers are polluted, its canyons filled, the remains of its Roman past buried, the tourist infrastructure dirty and inefficient.

So on 8 October 'Radoje Dakić' workers began their march in Titograd. They were joined by other workers, university and secondary school children, and by citizens from Titograd and other Montenegrin towns, including Ivangrad. Groups came from Kosovo and there was an announcement that others from Serbia and Macedonia would also be arriving. (Steelworkers, coming from Nikšić, were stopped half-way by police using batons and tear gas; turning back, the steelworkers with colleagues from other enterprises staged a mass demonstration in Nikšić.)

The Montenegrin leadership tried to address the crowd gathered in front of the state and party official buildings, but with little result. The demonstrators instead demanded their resignations. There were slogans such as: 'We want to work and earn our living!'; 'We demand bread!'; 'We have had enough of waiting!'; 'Long live the LCY!' By the evening, however, nationalist slogans became more frequent, which included: 'Long live the Serbian leadership!'; 'You have betrayed Slobodan Milošević – you have betrayed Serbdom!'; 'Who says, who lies, that Serbia is small?!'; 'Slobodan, we are your soldiers – we shall kill or we shall die!' 'Slobodan, you Serb son, when will you come to Cetinje?!' At around 6 am the following morning, the police aided by 'specials' charged the remnants of the crowd, again using batons and tear gas, and dispersed it. By now support for the Montenegrin leadership had arrived from the Slovenian and Croatian party as well as from Bosnia-Herzegovina, since it seemed that the tiny republic was about to be absorbed into Serbia. A condemnation of the demonstrators finally came from the Federal party leadership, which also condoned the use of force against the workers – an unprecedented event in post-war Yugoslavia! There were twenty-three arrests. The hospitals reported, however, only two cases of light injuries. An attempt by 'Teteks' workers to stage another demonstration that morning was prevented by the police. For a few days Montenegro was placed under a *de facto* state of emergency.

The events opened up a deep division in the Montenegrin leadership: the republic's government submitted its resignation, as did the leadership of the Titograd party. Simultaneously, an urgent meeting of the steelworks'

Workers' Council condemned the use of force, and issued a set of demands: immediate acceptance of all constitutional amendments (some of which were being resisted by Slovenia in particular); energetic suppression of 'counter-revolution' in Kosovo; speedy reform of the economy; an end to price rises and the fall in living standards; reduction of taxation on industry; the resignation of the Montenegrin leadership responsible for the crisis.

The unrest of October 1988 has brought into prominence the Socialist Youth Alliance 'alternative', supported by the current Serbian leadership. The youth organization has given its unreserved support to the workers, and had demanded a collective resignation of the Montenegrin leadership. Its president Ljubisa Stanković gave an interview to the Zagreb weekly *Danas* (22 November 1988), in which he argued that it was purely accidental that the demonstrations had started with 'Radoje Dakic' – worker dissatisfaction was bound to erupt sooner or later. But he also confirmed that the current unrest was initiated by the recent mass rallies in support of Serbs and Montenegrins in Kosovo, organized by the Kosovo Committee. The Montenegrin leadership had distanced itself from these 'solidarity' meetings, leaving, according to Stanković, 'a deep gap opened up between the people and the leadership'.

Up to now, the Montenegrin youth organisation, unlike its Slovene counterpart, had appeared faceless and passive – and hostile to the kind of initiatives coming from Ljubljana. Asked if, in the light of the October events, it would change its policy and support such initiatives as the dropping of Article 133 (defining so-called 'crimes of opinion') from the Penal Code, Stanković answered that he was not sure. In his view, what was important was the economic reform, i.e. creation of a proper market economy – and the change of leadership.

(d) Albanians March for Democracy

On 17 November 1988, a meeting of the Provincial Committee of the League of Communists of Kosovo was to be convened in the provincial capital Priština, to discuss the planned resignations of Kaqusha Jashari and Azem Vllasi, respectively the current party president and her immediate predecessor. Their resignations had been arranged as part of a deal on the constitution reached earlier between the Federal and Serbian leaderships. After years of wrangling, the Federal party leaders had under duress finally given their agreement to Serbia's recentralization, and thereby also to a significant reduction in the hard-won rights of the two-million-strong Albanian nation, thus turning the Yugoslav clock back by two decades. The Priština meeting was supposed to legitimize this. The resignations were part of a pledge that the provincial party, which had not condoned the deal, would nevertheless not resist the constitutional changes designed to increase Serbia's control over Kosovo.

That morning, miners from the 'Stari Trg' mine near Titova Mitrovica, the industrial centre of Kosovo, after completing the night shift, emerged from the 38 degrees Celsius of their pit into the freezing dawn (the first snows of winter had just fallen on Kosovo), joined forces with the day shift and began the 70-kilometre march to Priština.

Once in Priština, the miners were joined by other workers, then by students and youth, followed by secondary and primary school children – 80 per cent of the participants were below the age of 20 – and soon also by the older generation, coming from all parts of Kosovo (as well as western Macedonia) in a five-day-long demonstration of national determination. During the bitterly cold nights they camped outside the Provincial Committee headquarters, lopping the branches from the young trees planted in its forecourt to warm themselves up. The protest had two aims: to express their rejection of the proposed changes in the constitution of the Republic of Serbia; to prevent, in that context, the enforced resignation of the two provincial leaders. Although the Provincial Committee acknowledged the resignations (no vote was taken, the outcome having being determined elsewhere) and the miners thus failed to achieve their formal aims, the fact that the police did not charge – at the express order of the provincial government – suggests that they had won the battle honours, and perhaps a more lasting victory. The Kosovo working class and the local party and state leadership still have many differences to settle. But a display of unity was inevitable in the face of the anti-Albanian hysteria flowing from Belgrade: only a week earlier, a member of the Serbian Trade Union Alliance had argued publicly that 'counter-revolution' was deeply embedded in the Kosovo party and state organs and at Priština University, but above all in the Albanian working class – angering the Trepča miners and providing a stimulus for their march. After the demonstration, the Serbian party described the Priština events as the latest example of an escalating 'counter-revolution'. The Federal party came very close to agreeing with them.[7] The Kosovo leadership, however, argued that they were 'in line with the 17th Party Plenum'.[8]

This cacophony, of course, only illustrates how deeply the League of Communists of Yugoslavia is split, and how unprincipled is the politics that tries to pretend otherwise. What is clear, however, is that the dialectic of class and national liberation has in Kosovo once again proved its potent force. Even the normally hostile Belgrade reporters were impressed by the demonstrators' firmness and self-discipline. The Albanian miners had celebrated the 45th anniversary of the revolution in the best possible manner: by defending one of its fundamental achievements.[9]

The force behind the Kosovo demonstration may have been a defence of national rights; but this defence was phrased in terms not of nationalism but of democracy. In interviews freely given, the miners made it clear that if the province's status was to be changed, if its Albanian leadership was to be purged, then this must be done in an open, democratic debate and not imposed by force. The workers said what the Federal party should have said – but did not. In those freezing November days and nights, the marching workers, students and children acted as a true socialist vanguard.

(e) The End of Self-Management?

What follows is an edited extract from a recent article in the Zagreb journal *Start*, based on an interview with Pero Jurković, professor of economics at the University of Zagreb, taking up the fate of self-management under the projected economic reform.

An interesting and characteristic dialogue took place at a recent meeting of economists in Zagreb, convened to discuss the forthcoming (19th) session of the Central Committee of the League of Communists of Yugoslavia, at which the terms of the economic reform were to be established. One of the participants concluded his speech by saying that the reform needed an active social policy to ease its negative effects. This term 'negative effects' has become a ritual part of all discussion about the reform. There are many differences in regard to its meaning, but there is a common understanding that the reform has its price and somebody will have to pay this, including with the loss of their jobs. Since the professor seemed to understand what he was talking about, a member of the Yugoslav Central Committee present at the meeting asked him hopefully if he could explain what such a policy should consist of. The professor answered with full honesty: 'I don't know. That isn't my speciality.'

Whose speciality is it? Mikulić's commission for the economic reform has engaged 160 specialists to provide documentation, but the projected group for social policy never materialized. The Committee for Work and Social Policy played a game of ping-pong with the trade unions, explains Pero Jurković, but in the end both refused the responsibility. As a result there is nobody actively engaged in drafting social policy. Why? The professor says that this is because nobody wants to bite the sour apple of the class character of the reform. In the meantime, a devious game is being played between the Federation, the Republics and the Communes over who should be responsible for social policy, i.e. who should pay for it. The problem has been reduced to one of money: who will pay for the narcotic to be applied to the patient about to be subjected to a long and painful operation.

Jurković: 'No answer is being given to the question of how the reform is going to affect self-management. Instead, we hear the victorious cry *Alea iacta est!*, which means that the concepts of self-management and associated labour have been suspended. This Caesarist attitude is based in part on certain documents which in truth do not offer self-management but co-management, workers' participation. The chances are that those who think that self-management should be abolished will win. And I ask myself: Why are the Party and the trade unions doing nothing about this? If there was somebody who supported the working class in this country, they would ask the question: How is it possible that workers' wages can be allowed to fall to the level of social charity? Where are the documents on housing, on tax reform, on the effects of the planned redistribution of income? If we understand socialism as a system that reduces the difference between rich and poor, then the situation in our country is no different from the one prevailing under capitalism. In Yugoslavia, the lowest, poorest 20 per cent of households command only 6.6 per cent of total household income. In Britain it is 7 per cent, in Belgium 7.9 per cent, in Japan 8 per cent, in Sweden 7.4 per cent, in the USA 5.3 per cent. The upper 20 per cent of households dispose of 39 per cent of national income, while in the countries mentioned the range is 36–40 per cent. Finally, the richest 10 per cent of households in Yugoslavia dispose of 23 per cent of national income; in Britain the figure is 23.4 per cent, in Japan 22.4 per cent, in Sweden 28 per cent, in the USA 20 per cent. But in contrast to the capitalist countries, we have no taxation adequate to the character of our system, not even the social democratic tax policy practised in some countries.'

Jurković belongs to those economists who are in favour of a complete market, i.e. a market not just in goods but also in capital and labour. He believes that the attempt to build social relations only on labour and not on capital was historically premature. But since he is also a socialist, he does not like to see the crisis as an excuse to suspend self-management, which will mean that the workers will find themselves in a position that could be worse than that envisaged in the programmes of Western Social-Democracy.

Start: 'Is the system of self-managed labour not a utopian project?'
Jurković: 'You ask if the system of self-management is utopian. No, it is not, if one takes into account the real situation, the dialectical relationship between the development of material forces and relations of production, the state of consciousness in society. Today, however, *alea iacta est*! Laws are being introduced whose aim is clearly to do away with associated labour. History does not forgive failure. But today, when the society of labour is being suspended, it is much more difficult to find the real measure of compromise with capital. What rights will capital have over the workers?

No document is addressing this question. In fact the rights of workers are being largely disregarded. The new rules do not differentiate between the rights of the owners of the means of production and the rights of workers who do not own anything.'

Start: 'You say that for socialism to survive, social property must remain dominant. Is this not contrary to some current reform positions?'

Jurković: 'You are referring to those who argue that social property has no chance of survival, that it must be privatised. I do not agree with this. I am against the notion that individual, private ownership should become the only and absolute form of ownership. We are dealing with proposals that the whole of social ownership should be transformed into individual ownership; that workers should become shareholders in their enterprises. We must, however, protect the dominant form of social ownership, in order to protect the socialist character of society. Some will say that this will lead to inefficiency, but I disagree. That would mean that socialism as a system was impossible.'

(December 1988)

Notes

1. See interview with Miha Kovač in *New Left Review*, No. 171, 1988; also: 'Democracy and the National Question' above.
2. Latinka Perović, then head of the Serbian party, after her expulsion from the party earned a doctoral degree with a thesis entitled 'From Centralism to Federalism', in which she traces the rationale of Yugoslavia's decentralization to Lenin's policy on the national question. A fine piece of analysis, it has been treated with deafening silence thanks to the author's political 'disgrace'. See pp. 187–217 below for a discussion of Milošević's rise to power.
3. Attempts to mobilize the Serb population in other republics (Slovenia, Croatia and Bosnia-Herzegovina) failed thanks to the firm resistance of the local leaderships. Monetenegro proved to be a partial exception, due to the historic ties between Serbs and Montenegrins.
4. Just prior to the 17th Plenum, Stipe Šuvar, the head of the Federal party, accused the Serbian leadership of an uncritical attitude towards anti-communist trends bubbling up in the Serbian Academy. At the same time Belgrade workers – particularly those of the industrial Rakovica belt of Belgrade – were threatening to go on strike. This also contributed to the Serbian leadership's sudden discovery of the working-class constituency.
5. For Mirjana Kasapović's paper, see *Start*, Zagreb 19 October 1988. Zagorka Golubović's letter is in *Danas*, 15 November 1988. Kasapović's reply is in *Danas*, 22 November 1988.
6. Josip Vrhovec represents Croatia in the federal state presidency. Janez Stanovnik is the state president of Slovenia. Both were attacked at the mass rallies in Serbia for being critical of that republic's party and state leadership. Dušan Ćkrebić is a Serbian representative on the Federal party executive who failed a vote at confidence at the 17th plenary session of the party's Central Committee in October 1988. Slobodan Milošević, in an unprecedented move, refused to accept the verdict, and the Serbian press subsequently denounced the federal CC as an 'unprincipled alliance directed against Serbia'.
7. The presidency in fact took this position without consultation with the CC, breaking the party statutes in an unprecedented manner.

8. Remzi Kolgeci, current joint head of both the party and state organs, said in a recent interview: 'As long as I live I shall have before my eyes the picture of those wet and frozen children – what made them march? – and the determination of those who walked to Priština in such hostile weather' (*Danas*, Zagreb, 20 December 1988).

9. It is universally known that the Albanian population of Yugoslavia would like to see Kosovo given republican status. Yet this slogan (deemed counter-revolutionary by the officialdom) was not raised: the demonstration contained no nationalist charge.

National and ethnic distribution in Yugoslavia

2

Break-up

(a) Trepča on Strike

JELENA LOVRIĆ

Yugoslavia, February 1989. Albanian miners from the Trepča zinc and lead mine in the Yugoslav province of Kosovo are striking underground – if necessary to death – in defence of their national and political rights.

In the narrow corridors, the miners sit so closely packed that it is difficult to pass. Damp and draught. Darkness of the earth. Lead dust, so dangerous to human health, fills the air. Oxygen is scarce. The men are pale and exhausted, they lack sleep. Some are on hunger strike. Even the gravely ill are nevertheless refusing to surface, so long as they have a minimum of strength. Medical attention is offered in impossible circumstances. Their endurance sorely tried, the men's mood changes from reasoned argument to nervous passion. Thanks to the Yugoslav leadership's obduracy, the miners are clocking up a world record for staying underground.

We descend to the fifth level (out of twelve). The men tell us excitedly why they were moved to take this step. We sit on narrow planks and look into the face of an old miner, who has spent decades working in the pit. He begins to cry, bowing his head.

At the eighth level, the space is even more cramped. There is no place to sit down. We all stand. The miners ask what an Albanian has to do, in addition to hailing Yugoslavia and Tito, in order to be trusted. The younger men are well informed. Our conversation is interrupted by the loudspeaker saying that Raif Dizdarević [president of Yugoslavia] wants to meet a miners' delegation. They protest loudly. 'Let him come down!' The voice says his health is not good – a remark that is out of place among men in such a state. Later Aziz Abrashi, the mine manager, tells us that one miner's wife died two days ago, but the man refused to leave the strike to attend her funeral. Another man lost his eight-month-old baby. He also refused to leave his comrades.

We are at the ninth level. The temperature is now about 50 degrees centigrade. We step through mud and water. The miners have just heard that Rahman Morina [Kosovo party leader, whose resignation they are demanding] has just announced he has no intention of resigning. They are upset. They are at the end of their endurance. There are more of them here, and the space is even less. They beg us to leave them, saying that in their psychological state they are unable to talk. Finally they agree. A young man talks excitedly about self-immolation. His brother stands next to him, hugging him. The brother says he will follow him to death. Death seems to be all around us. Many of the miners seem to have resigned themselves to it. 'One can only die once,' says one. Uncontrolled weeping follows, of a hundred, two hundred men. Trepča is gripped by a strange epidemic of tears.

The miners say they are not nationalists, beg us to write only the truth about them, say that Tito used to come down to speak to them, so why not his heirs? They beg us also to leave them – they cannot go on, they want to spare us the collapse of their self-control. We leave them to the narrow space, the darkness, the overcrowding. They are trapped. They cannot give up. Their dignity has been trampled by the unbelievable indifference of a leadership with which socialist government has finally lost the last remnant of its already badly dented class legitimacy. We fear for them: pride is strong among the miners, it will overpower reason. Now they are left to themselves. Many are holding hands. They say there is no greater comradeship than that forged in the darkness and dangers of the earth.

(b) The Albanian Intifada

SHKELZEN MALIQI

Over the past week, Kosovo Albanians have experienced the cathartic release of long-suppressed discontent. The circumstances have been – and still are – visibly dramatic. . . .

The whole of Kosovo has risen – desperate, frightened and angry. During the last two days, its Albanian population has practically been on general strike, since only installations supporting vital systems have been working. All life has been paralysed – a kind of Albanian *intifada* has begun. Thousands of solidarity meetings are taking place, supporting and expanding the miners' demands. Schools throughout the province are not working, while in Priština students have entered their sixth day of peaceful demonstration in the '25 May' sports centre. Writers are holding daily protest meetings. All socio-political organizations are in permanent session. The strike is exclusively political and national.

The demands and positions formulated by the Trepča miners have thus spread throughout Kosovo. On Thursday 23 February, they came up with a list of ten points:

1. No retreat from fundamental principles of the 1974 constitution: any change in the constitutions of Serbia or Kosovo must be such as to allow further development of brotherhood and equality.
2. Those who proposed the law prematurely retiring teachers failing the notorious 'test of political and moral suitability' must be called to account.

3. Rahman Morina [provincial party chief], Husamedin Azemi [head of the Priština party] and Ali Shukria [member of the Federal party central committee] must submit irrevocable resignations: if they wish to know why, then they must come down the pits where the miners will tell them face to face.
4. Stipe Šuvar [head of the Federal party], Slobodan Milošević (head of the Serbian party] and a representative from each of the central committees of the socialist republics and the socialist province of Vojvodina, must come to talk to the miners.
5. The list must be published of those who organized last year's mass meetings.
6. An explanation must be given for the resignations of Azem Vllasi, Kaqusha Jashari and Svetislav Dolašević.
7. The Kosovo leadership must be elected by the Kosovo base and not by the bureaucracy of other republics.
8. The United Nations must examine the state of Kosovo Albanians.
9. The discriminatory policies of Slobodan Milošević must be condemned, since they deviate from the correct path traced by Tito.
10. The miners inform the provincial, republican and Federal leaderships, as well as the public at large, that they will not leave the *Stari Trg* pit until their demands are satisfied.

For the first three days the strike was seen as a minor local issue and — until the miners' issued their warning that they would remain underground as long as was necessary, even to the point of death — was not taken seriously. None of the invited individuals visited the mine. Only on the fourth day did Raif Dizdarević, the Federal state president, and Petar Gra-čanin, the Serbian state president, arrive. Dizdarević's talk with the miners was fruitless. On the fifth day Stipe Šuvar and Slobodan Milošević finally came to Kosovo, but only the former visited the mine. His mission, however, was unsuccessful since he did not come to meet the miners' demands but only to ask them to come out — something they firmly declined.

The miners subsequently made their emergence from the pits conditional upon the irrevocable resignations of the three 'honest' and 'Yugoslav-oriented' Albanians: Morina, Azemi and Shukria. Morina, they argued, had not been elected with the agreement of Albanian communists, had deeply offended the miners, and had not met demands formulated at a meeting in Trepča earlier in the month. Azemi had equally affronted the miners by describing their November march as nationalist in character. Shukria, finally, had betrayed not only his communist base but also his own revolutionary past — associated precisely with Titova Mitrovica and Trepča — by completely aligning himself with Milošević's anti-Albanian policies.

The miners' agony is now in its seventh day. Those whose resignations they are demanding are refusing to resign. Albanian anger and dissatisfaction have reached unimaginable levels. As a result, Morina and Azemi are today hated even by party activists and bodies who up to now have been quite compliant. Whatever the outcome of the strike, their political fate has been sealed. It will be extremely difficult in the future for Milošević to find 'honest' Albanians ready to follow his *diktat* and act as obedient instruments of Serb politics. This plebiscitary declaration shows that Milošević will have great difficulties with Albanians. The open resistance to Milošević's policy is expressed in the miners' ninth demand, and party organizations in Kosovo are now demanding that the central committees of Serbia and Yugoslavia should insist on Milošević's own resignation, since he is clearly responsible for the worsening of the situation in Kosovo and in Yugoslavia. Albanian communists say that the situation in Kosovo was improving until Milošević's arrival at the head of the Serbian party, and that a radical worsening of the situation began on 26 April when, at a meeting in Kosovo Polje, he offered his full support even to the most extreme nationalists – those who, through the activities of the Kosovo Polje Committee, set fire to Kosovo, Vojvodina and Montenegro and are now threatening Bosnia and Herzegovina too. In a recent interview given to the Split weekly *Nedjeljna Dalmacija*, Miroslav Solević, a member of the Committee, has stated: 'Revolution [as he calls it] in Bosnia and Herzegovina is inevitable: this is a sure thing, and will be implemented by the spring. The same thing will then happen to you in Croatia and Slovenia.'

On Sunday 26 February, the presidency of the provincial party finally issued a statement saying that Morina and Azemi had submitted resignations, which would be considered in due time and according to the procedure. This, naturally, did not induce the miners to leave the pits. They have asked for unconditional resignations, since they are afraid they will be cheated. The problem, however, does not lie in these individuals, who are already politically dead and can remain in power only if a totalitarian state of exception (perhaps the postponement of the resignations involves precisely such considerations?) is imposed. The problem lies in the fact that the miners' demands, and those of the Albanian people as a whole, represent the hard core of a broad front of resistance to Milošević's politics, not just in Kosovo. The Federal leadership, it seems, is not prepared to consider this option. This can be seen from Morina's statement – made to journalists the previous Saturday afternoon – according to which all provincial, republican and Federal leaderships are against his resignation (from the post of provincial party leader, which he has occupied for the past month), since this would lead to an even greater destabilization of the situation not only in Kosovo but in Yugoslavia as a whole. Yet the anti-Milošević spirit has been released from its bottle and it will be difficult to drive it back again. The destabilization of Yugoslavia is already a fact, as it is a fact that Milošević could in the end get his way only by imposing an ultimatum. But playing the card of ignoring and demeaning the Albanians was bound eventually to produce a powerful resistance.

The only question is whether the Albanian revolt was planned or not. If it was, then the whole affair is so much grist to the mill of Serb agitation, aiding Milošević in the risky game at which he has so far been a consistent winner. But if it was not, then Milošević has fallen for the old delusion of Great Serb politics, which since the second half of the nineteenth century has always refused to see Albanians as a relevant political factor, even when they were direct rivals.

Until the advent of new Yugoslavia, Albanians were seen only as agents of a foreign power – Turkey, Austria-Hungary, Italy. Today, Great Serb politics views Albanians of Albania proper – as well as Croats and Slovenes – as it had once viewed foreign powers: as people who are pitting Kosovo Albanians against Serbs so as to definitively weaken Serbia within the Federation. In 1913 the Serb politician Vladan Djordjević described Albanians as semi-civilized beings, who did not know what salt was and thought that sugar was snow; who did not possess a national consciousness or know what a fatherland was. Today too we find a similar belittling and demeaning of Albanians. Current Serbian politics does not recognize Albanians as political subjects, but sees them as a mass manipulated by some hostile anti-Serb force. . . .

The Serb press claims that the miners are being manipulated; that their strike is not a genuine expression of their will; that they have been driven underground by the same 'enemies', 'nationalists' and 'separatists' who 'forced' them to march to Priština last November. In the meantime, the men are dying. On Sunday we were told that they would carry on into the eighth day of their underground strike, since their demands had not been met. But Belgrade refuses to admit the truth. It knows it only too well, but when it suits it it prefers lies, inventions and fabrications, being simultaneously blind and merciless towards everything that stands in its way. Precisely because the Belgrade chauvinist press had called them liars and manipulated men, whose demonstration was a charade and who carried the icon of Tito's portrait only to hide the fact that they did not believe in that sacred God, the miners wished to show by way of personal sacrifice for the political cause they have embraced that nobody is directing them; that they had organized themselves; that their programme is Tito's programme.

Milošević's extreme Serb nationalism made them react not only as workers, but as Albanians, since they were being threatened and denounced as Albanians. They consequently resorted to the ancient ethos of resistance against an enemy that was attacking their national, workers' and human integrity. And the thing that gave them power, that integrated their internal strength, was their solemn vow to defend the truth. There awoke among them that supreme expression of the traditional Albanian moral code – the oath, the *besa*. For no one could take from them that which for Albanians is holy above all: the word of promise, the *besa*. By virtue of this particular *besa*, the truth will arrive on the day when they all perish in those accursed pits in which, with their hands and in the sweat of their brows, they dig for lead, zinc, silver and gold. It is necessary to unmask the lies that are being generated in such profusion by the Serb press and Serb politics. The kind which Franc Setinc–an experienced [Slovene] politician, who had endured many lies and compromises regarding Kosovo – was alluding to some months ago when he said: Thank you very much, I do not wish any longer to take part in such great lies! For he recognized that the lies about Kosovo and Albanians have gone beyond all measure, have become unbearable.

During the last few years in Kosovo, Yugoslav socialist ideology has been descending into twilight. Of an erstwhile proud structure, which until recently was hailed as an achievement of world-historic significance (the first self-managing state), not a single stone has been left today. The system has destroyed itself, leaving behind just the hollow façades of socialism, self-management, League of Communists. If Setinc – a neutral politician of Federal rank – could be subjected to a real witch-hunt and an avalanche of denunciation only because he dared to express something positive regarding the situation in Kosovo – something that departed from the official insistence that a terror and genocide was being conducted there against Serbs – then one can imagine the conditions of those who have to live daily with such lies; who in the last instance are the final target of such lies, forced to live as objects of police and other persecution; and who – when their crimes cannot be established in either a moral or a literal sense – are simply treated with contempt.

The longer the strike goes on, the more the authorities are unrelenting, the greater the miners' anger grows at the politicians who refuse to understand the point of the protest, the more uncertain is the outcome. We hear from well-informed sources that the Federal presidency has already prepared an order for the introduction of a state of emergency or military rule, to be implemented on Sunday evening – provided that the miners have left their pits. This is what the presidency expects to happen, given that conditional resignations by Morina and Azemi have been secured. The strikers, however, are demanding unconditional resignations and have refused to leave the pits until these are forthcoming.

What is tying the hands of the Federal and provincial authorities? Evidently it is Milošević's hard stand. Milošević will not give in, even at the price of a real tragedy occurring in the mines. The question is: what kind of ultimatum is Milošević using, in order to prevent the resignations of Morina and Azemi? It is now quite clear that an agreement was reached between oligarchies at the 20th party plenum of the CC LCY – an agreement that is now being endangered by the miners' action – to surrender Kosovo to Serbia: to allow its constitutional annexation. Milošević needed the powerful support of the CC LCY in order to make the constitutional changes in Serbia irreversible. He now needs people like Morina and Azemi in Kosovo in order to push through such changes, in a province which not only rejected the Serb amendments during the constitutional debate but also rose as one against them last November.

During their short visit to Kosovo, both Šuvar and Milošević demonstrated this agreement and their desire to safeguard it. Milošević did not dare to go among the miners, appearing only at a meeting of the Kosovo political *aktiv* and the party organization in *Elektrokosovo*. There he made no concessions, but insisted that it was Serbs and not Albanians who were endangered in Kosovo; that terror was being conducted not against Albanians but against Serbs. Equally unconvincingly, he argued that under the new constitution - which, according to him, had already been adopted, although the provincial assembly has not as yet given its agreement –

Albanians would not lose anything, since Kosovo would not lose any of its autonomy. According to him, the essence of the changes is to win back for Serbia those state prerogatives that it lost with the 1974 republican constitution, which allowed a separation of the provinces from the mother republic.

This argument was repeated by Šuvar, who referred to the CC LCY decision to support Serbia's re-centralization. This in turn poses the following question: Is it the LCY rather than the citizens of Yugoslavia who are sovereign? Is the LCY's sovereignty a constitutional category? Or is it not rather the case that constitutional changes can be legitimated only by a declaration of citizens, that is, those who delegate representatives to the legislative bodies? The LCY may legitimately have its own views and approach, but it does not have the right to decide alone. It is not for the CC LCY, Šuvar or Milošević to decide constitutional changes, but for citizens gathered in their assemblies and elsewhere. Any other procedure is illegitimate. The existing laws prescribe that the constitution of Serbia cannot be changed – in areas pertaining to the republic as a whole – without the agreement of the provincial assemblies. The declaration of the majority of the Albanian population against the proposed amendments to the Serbian constitution, and in favour of the existing autonomy of the provinces, is a fact. This may be against the position of the LCY, but it is neither illegal nor anti-constitutional.

Milošević – and also Šuvar – are supporting an anti-constitutional method of changing the Serbian constitution, on the basis of decisions taken at this or that meeting of the LCY. Milošević has recently shown how little he cares for legality, with his declaration that all Yugoslavia's problems will be solved by a 'policy which has been endorsed by the majority of citizens of this state, within and outside the existing institutions, within and outside of existing statutes, in the streets and at home, by populist and elitist methods, with and without argument'. In other words, it is not necessary to respect the existing constitution.

This is how we are to judge Milošević. Šuvar, for his part, pretended before the miners of Trepča to be a man dedicated to legality and principles, to an extent that was at once comic and miserable – and also, given the true situation of those miners, many of whom were fainting from exhaustion at the time, completely cynical. To men who had entered into a state of yearning for the Word, Šuvar offered empty phrases. He looked small and lost, like the meanest clerk from a novel by Gogol or Chekhov, who – entrusted with a little bit of power, the wielding of which gives him the greatest of pleasures – likes to lord it over the unfortunate and the powerless, 'supplicants' and people in general who bother him unnecessarily. His legalistic *plaidoyer* was as convincing as that of a doctor refusing to treat a victim of an accident on the grounds that his health card has not been properly stamped!

The comparison could be seen as unnecessarily cruel had not Dr Šuvar kept entangling himself precisely on the question of principles until the very end of his visit. Asked why he had bent his neck before Milošević and seemed unwilling to resist him – given that the former is beginning to cut up and reorganize Yugoslavia as he likes, holding to the principle that everything is allowed – Šuvar found it necessary to deliver a lecture to the miners on the LCY's legal procedures for replacing or removing individuals. He spoke in this manner although he knew very well how 'legal' the procedure was by which the former provincial leaders were replaced; and, equally, how 'legal' the procedure was that brought to power those whose resignations the miners were at that point demanding. He spoke of legality, knowing full well how irrelevant were the feelings of the party base compared to the will of the almighty Milošević.

The twilight of the Kosovo party, which settled in at the last session of the provincial committee, now threatens it with complete disintegration and collapse. In those days, the party experienced its final and irreversible historical demise. Many local branches are today leaving the party collectively, because of Morina's and Azemi's refusal to resign unconditionally. Before them, Serbs and Montenegrins were also collectively leaving or 'suspending' their membership. The Serbian party, on the other hand, has become a Serb national party, which cannot without conflict spread into Kosovo, since Albanians find both the party and its programme unacceptable. The Kosovo party, equally, cannot survive without excluding either the Serbs or the Albanians or both. This is what is happening, and it seems that a similar fate awaits the LCY as a whole.

Everybody carries in their mind's eye the picture of exhausted miners looking questioningly into the cameras and demanding of everybody to declare themselves one way or the other on the question of whether the truth will prevail or not and whether they will have to pay with their lives for the truth. We all, therefore, suffer from nightmares and lack of sleep, experience attacks of trembling and shivers, wring our hands in desperation. And many of us – including myself: while I write this text I wonder that I can remain sane – are discovering that we have become sleepwalkers. It seems to us that we ourselves are locked in the dark and dank underground pits, engulfed in an agony, as the 200th hour of the miners' underground ordeal approaches. It is the agony of people who have proclaimed themselves to be the torchbearers of truth in a total ideological darkness, ready to die in order to defend their own and our human dignity against the masters of that darkness. . . .

The Trepča miners may (and indeed will) enter into Albanian legend; but in reality they represent the break that establishes the Yugoslav Albanians as independent political subjects. Strictly speaking, their retreat underground cannot be called a strike, but a national rebellion that is only taking the form of a strike. And with this rebellion – whether this is recognized today or not – Albanians have made it clear to everybody in Yugoslavia that it is impossible to make decisions without them, that they are an inescapable subject of the Yugoslav political community.

(c) The Spectre of Balkanization

No amount of anti-communist propaganda can obscure the fact that, since 1945, Yugoslavia has by and large been governed with the consent of its peoples. Equally, no amount of official piety can hide the fact that the League of Communists (LCY) has held power *only* by virtue of such confidence as it has commanded in the working class and the country's constituent nations. In February 1989, an unprecedented general strike of Albanian workers in the province of Kosovo confirmed this fact in the most dramatic way possible. Since the previous November, the consolidation of an openly and indeed triumphantly nationalist leadership in Serbia had led to the banning of all public meetings and demonstrations in Kosovo. The workers therefore retreated to their strongholds – the factories and mines – in a last-ditch attempt to defend national and democratic rights. A creeping general strike of industry was by February to culminate in a near complete shutdown of the province's economic life. The vanguard was constituted by the miners of the Trepča mining–industrial complex with its headquarters in Titova Mitrovica. A historic centre of working-class activity in Kosovo, formerly owned by British capital, Trepča supplied some of the earliest members of the pre-war Communist Party. Trepča miners were also among the first to join the wartime anti-fascist resistance. Now, in the third week of February 1989, 1,300 zinc and lead miners occupied their pits 3,300 feet underground, some of them on hunger strike, for eight days. Their demands were quite simple. They called for the resignation of three provincial officials imposed on them that month at the insistence of the Serbian party.[1] They asked that any constitutional limitation of Kosovo's autonomy – something which Belgrade had been pressing for – should be subject to democratic debate. The third and most important demand was that the Albanian population should cease being treated as second-class citizens and a second-class nation in their own country. Not since the end of the war had Yugoslavia witnessed such a powerful workers' action in defence of key gains of the revolution. The issues were crystal clear, splitting the whole country into two well-defined camps and marking a watershed in its postwar history. Ranged on the side of the workers were all those forces, within and outside the League of Communists, who stand for a democratic Yugoslavia, based on full national equality. Confronting them were the forces of bureaucratic reaction, in alliance with national chauvinism, fully prepared to use violence against the working class.

The General Strike

The miners' determination and solidarity were awesome. They told journalists that they were determined to 'come out in coffins' unless their demands were met.² With them was Beqir Maliqi, the mine's chief engineer, who – though old and by the sixth day gravely ill – refused to come up. The furnacemen, also on strike, spoke of committing collective suicide if Trepča was stormed. Below the ground, a strict guard was maintained over two tonnes of dynamite, to prevent any desperate action. The sick were sent up, suffering from respiratory and stomach problems (eyes, it seems, also suffered), to be treated by doctors and either returned immediately down or – if gravely ill – transferred to a hospital in Priština, the provincial capital. By the end of the strike, 180 miners had ended there, some of them in intensive care.

Overground there was an equally tight discipline, maintained by miners wearing red armbands. Children and women waited patiently at the entrance of the pit, anxious for news. A Zagreb television crew went to visit one miner's family. They found a mother with nine children, occupying a self-made structure without windowpanes to protect them from the harsh February winds, huddled around a wood fire: despite the fact that Kosovo produces a substantial proportion of Yugoslavia's electricity, the family lived in darkness. In November 1987, the average wage in Trepča was $55 a month, barely enough to keep a family from starvation. During the strike, moreover, many of the strikers refused their wages. The family had not even a radio to stay in touch with developments at the mine.

Elsewhere in the province, everything was at a standstill. Only the electricity workers were press-ganged back to work. Students and schoolchildren were also on strike. Even privately owned shops had their doors firmly shut. The markets were empty. Yet there was no organizing committee to direct the course of events, to collect and centralize the demands, to speak on behalf of the general strike. Despite this, the people spoke with one voice, demanding national justice and democracy.

The first to send a message of support were the miners of Slovenia. The Yugoslav party leadership, meanwhile, split on how to proceed. The Slovenian party supported an appeal by the republic's Socialist Alliance that Albanian human and national rights should be respected. A similar statement was issued by the Croatian Trade Union Alliance, and the Croatian party soon followed suit. The Serbian party, on the other hand, was set against all compromise, and could count on the support of party organizations in Vojvodina, Montenegro and Macedonia. The Bosnian party maintained a prudent silence. The collective state presidency, for its part, talked of using 'all constitutional means at our disposal' to secure law and order in the province: by the time the strike reached its high point, fresh paramilitary forces had been sent in and armoured personnel carriers appeared on the outskirts of the main towns, followed by tanks and low-flying jet fighters. One might have been back in 1981, when (following mass demonstrations demanding republican status for Kosovo, which the Federal authorities dubbed an attempt at 'counter-revolution') the province was placed under a state of emergency, then an unprecedented measure in post-war Yugoslavia.[3]

The weakness of the Federal party leadership was most starkly exposed by its handling of the Kosovo strike and its aftermath. On 28 February the miners appeared to have won, with the resignation of the three hated officials. They left the pits (though the strike continued elsewhere). The following day, however, under the pressure of a party-led nationalist mass mobilization in Belgrade, the resignations were 'suspended'. By this time, it was clear that the stakes were much higher than the fate of the three men, and involved the survival of democratic gains in Yugoslavia as a whole. Under the pressure of Serbian hardiners, the LCY presidency, meeting that day, not only reaffirmed its support for the constitutional changes sought by Serbia, but also called for a ban on all new political organizations in the country. Slobodan Milošević, the Serbian party boss, promised the assembled populace 'in the name of Serbia' that the organizers of the general strike would be arrested and punished. The first arrests were made on 2 March, and on 5 March it was announced that hundred of workers faced criminal charges, as did even shopkeepers who had closed in sympathy with the strike. Kosovo is already under *de facto* military rule. At the same time Slovenia, where the process of democratization has gone furthest, is being singled out as an object of particular hatred. What is to guarantee that the practice of constitutional changes made under military duress will not be extended to the rest of the country?

'The situation is growing worse by the day and the full responsibility for it rests with the League of Communists which – instead of offering new ideas and initiatives – has become the main brake on all positive change. The complete lack of perspective in our society prevents my continuing my membership, since I do not believe that the League of Communists is capable of taking our society out of the crisis in which it finds itself. We can no longer speak of it as the vanguard', wrote a Croat Communist recently in his letter of resignation.[4]

'The Central Committee of the League of Communists has reached the bottom line of its incompetence and powerlessness, and if it had any moral dignity it would simply have dissolved itself, transferring its power to a parliament', commented the most influential Croatian weekly, after the CC plenum in January–February 1989.[5] And three weeks later, during the miners' underground strike: 'The leadership's indifference to the miners' plight has finally cost socialist government the last remnants of its already badly dented class legitimacy.'[6]

For his part, Milan Kučan, the Slovene party leader, has written: 'The key question today is: what kind of Yugoslavia? A Yugoslavia that was not socialist and democratic would not be possible.'[7] At the January–February plenum he declared: 'What is happening in the country today, and especially within the League of Communists, is simply the disintegration of Yugoslavia: its silent – and in parts of the LC conscious, or at least tolerated – transformation into another kind of Yugoslavia. Slovene Communists refuse to take any part in such activity.'[8] Thus workers, party activists and top leaders concur: what is at stake is the legitimacy of the present political order.

Contours of the Crisis

The specifically political manifestations of the current crisis can be dated with some accuracy from the demonstrations in Kosovo in the spring of 1981. This poorest region of Yugoslavia, at the centre of an unresolved national problem, registered the coming earthquake like a seismograph. By 1985, the leadership itself acknowledged that the country was facing an economic crisis, with a 5.5 per cent decline in the social product since 1979. A $20 billion foreign debt was disclosed, inflation soared (by the end of 1988 it was to pass 250 per cent), and gross fixed investment was cut sharply back. In this situation, the political consensus within the LCY – and the intricate system of checks and balances which it had hitherto underpinned – simply collapsed. The economic crisis was expressed increasingly as a political crisis, indeed as a challenge to the whole socialist project.

The crisis did not affect all social layers equally. For social differentiation in Yugoslavia was by now quite dramatic – comparable to that in major capitalist countries, according to Pero Jurković, Professor of Economics at the University of Zagreb.[9] The crisis hit the working class with special severity as industrial growth stopped or went into reverse, large-scale unemployment emerged, and personal consumption fell by 7.7 per cent between 1979 and 1985. Insecurity has grown with the Party's increasing commitment to radical liberalization of the economy – a policy which will have devastating consequences for the vast majority of workers, particularly in the underdeveloped south, without offering any clear social safeguards.[10] The Federal government, which has had no trouble in recruiting 160 of the country's most eminent economists into its commission for economic reform, has at the same time utterly failed in its attempt to establish a parallel commission for social welfare. The Federation, republics and local communes are instead trying to outwit each other at the game of who should pay the bill. Nobody is willing to take responsibility for the coming storm, least of all the leading party. The unprecedented resignation of the government under trade union pressure

Regional differentiation in Yugoslavia

	Population (1000s)	Per capita social product	Output per worker in social sector	Net personal income (1000 dinars)	Job-seekers as % of workforce in social sector
Slovenia	1,871	179	145	3140	1.7
Croatia	4,437	117	106	2208	7.7
Vojvodina	1,977	133	103	1885	15.2
Bosnia & Herzegovina	4,155	80	85	1736	23.9
Serbia*	5,574	94	93	1846	17.7
Montenegro	604	80	90	1522	24.5
Kosovo	1,760	36	69	1418	55.9
Macedonia	1,954	75	75	1399	27.0
Yugoslavia	22,334	100	100	2045	16.2

* Excluding Kosovo and Vojvodina

Source: Compiled from Tables 10.1, 10.2 and 10.3 in Harold Lydall, Yugoslavia in Crisis, Oxford 1989.

in the last days of 1988 was just one sign of the strength of current turbulence.

In addition, given the huge disparities of regional development, social differentiation has taken the form also of national inequality. This can be clearly seen from the accompanying table.

The internal balance within the Federation has also changed in a dramatic fashion. In 1987, the three southernmost Federal units – Kosovo, Macedonia and Montenegro – announced that they were bankrupt. Bosnia-Herzegovina too entered a period of political turmoil – following the collapse of its huge agro-industrial complex 'Agrokomerc'.[11] This shifted the power of decision-making into the hands of Slovenia, Croatia, Serbia and Vojvodina, and finally – after the takeover of Vojvodina by Serbia in 1988 (see below) – concentrated it in the hands of the former three. Simultaneously, the self-confidence of 'the vanguard party of the vanguard class', already badly dented, now finally evaporated, destroying in the process what remained of the authority of the Federal party centre. With workers resorting to mass strike action, the whole party–class alliance started to come apart. A powerful sense of malaise meanwhile engulfed the intelligentsia, favouring right-wing and nationalist currents.

The crisis strengthened the ever-present tendency of the republican and provincial parties to entrench themselves in local national constituencies. The outcome, however, varied considerably, given the wide economic disparities and differing national traditions. Slovenia – despite some setbacks[12] – underwent an extensive political democratization, with a host of political parties and organizations emerging by the beginning of 1989:

despite the very real differences that exist among them, they share with the ruling party a commitment to national sovereignty and further democratization. By this time Croatia too had developed a fledgling alternative political scene, although here – for ethnic and historic reasons – differences between a local–national and a Yugoslav orientation were more sharply posed. In Macedonia, on the other hand, the economic collapse encouraged the local leadership to steer working-class despair into nationalist channels, directed against the substantial (21 per cent) Albanian minority.[13]

It was in Serbia, however, that the turn to the nation took its most intense form. The formal primacy of class politics was abandoned in favour of national consolidation with the accession of Slobodan Milošević to unchallenged power in the League of Communists of Serbia at the end of 1987, after a sharp inner-party struggle. This shift within Yugoslavia's largest republic, which further altered the political balance in the country and now threatens its federal constitution, is the principal concern of this essay.

Serbia: Constitutional Revisionists

The Socialist Republic of Serbia is formally the state of the Serb nation. Yet, as will be clear from the map on page 178, it does not embrace all Serbs, a significant proportion of whom live interspersed with Croats in Croatia and with Moslems and Croats in Bosnia-Herzegovina. This has invested the Serb national question with a contradictory role in Yugoslavia. National dispersion makes the Serbs especially sensitive to any weakening of Yugoslav unity, while any mobilization of them on a nationalist basis directly threatens Yugoslavia's federal structure. The Serb national question is made more complicated by the fact that the republic of Serbia contains also the vast majority of Yugoslavia's national minorities, which is why after the war (unlike the other republics) it was not constituted as a unitary state. Apart from Serbia proper, it contains two provinces: the Socialist Autonomous Province of Vojvodina (53 per cent Serb) in the north and the Socialist Autonomous Province of Kosovo (almost 90 per cent Albanian) in the south.

The Communist Party saw the federal constitution of the postwar state as an instrument not only of individual national equality but also of Yugoslavia's unity. The Serbs (and the same could be said of Croats or Albanians) could not be united in a single republic without infringing the rights of other nationalities, so that the republics – though based on individual nationalities – had to remain ethnically mixed. The national rights of the individual nations were to be guaranteed as much by the country's federal order as by its unity.

Following the centralism of the postwar years, the 1974 constitution granted to the republics and provinces greater autonomy from the Federal centre, and to the provinces also greater independence from Belgrade. From a national and democratic point of view, this was an enormous step forward for Kosovo in particular. Self-government replaced the almost permanent state of emergency to which the Albanian population had been subject for most of the postwar period (1945–66), while the new policy of national equality opened the door for its integration into the Yugoslav political community. Government by consent in Kosovo was also a condition of greater democracy in Serbia and elsewhere in Yugoslavia, since it diminished the power of the apparatus of repression (headed until 1966 by interior minister Alexander Ranković) which had been most resistant to the political and economic reforms of the 1960s – of which the 1974 constitution was precisely the outcome. What is more, the provinces now became constitutive elements of the Federation, with direct and equitable representation in all its party and state bodies. Implicit in this reform was the view that Yugoslavia could not be regarded as an exclusively South Slav state.

The reforms, however, contained a fundamental contradiction which was to qualify this advance. In the absence of any substantial extension of popular or inner-party democracy, political power remained concentrated in the hands of the republican and provincial leaderships, making party politics a permanent hostage to state-led nationalism. This was not an inevitable outcome, so long as the new, post-Ranković generation of liberals were in power in Serbia.[14] But the purge of these in their turn in 1972, coming so soon after the removal of Ranković's administration, initiated a fragmentation of political power in Serbia. An older generation of second-ranking party leaders now came to the centre of the stage, many of whom tended to see the 1974 constitution not only as deepening the division of the Serb nation, but also as weakening Serbia's (republican) statehood. The reform gave the provinces a veto on all issues that affected them, so that the Belgrade leadership was no longer in full control over republican affairs. The presence of the provinces as independent actors at the Federal level also reduced the power and prestige of the Serbian leadership in Yugoslavia as a whole. In the mid-1970s a working commission of the Serbian party, under the guidance of Dragoslav Marković,[15] gathered arguments against this enhanced provincial autonomy in what became known as the Blue Book. This sought the return to Belgrade control of the provinces' judiciary, police (including state security service), territorial defence and economic policy. Given that acceptance of these aims would certainly have involved a new bout of repression in Kosovo – and inevitably also rehabilitation of the Ranković administration and its admirers – the document received a hostile reception from the Federal leadership. The Blue Book was never publicly discussed, but the very fact of its existence allowed the issue of provincial autonomy to smoulder beneath the surface of Serbian politics until the 1980s, when it would acquire a new and potent charge.[16]

By 1980, however, a new generation of political leaders had emerged in Serbia, grouped around Ivan Stambolić, which was successful in reunifying the republic's fractious politics. Stambolić was head of the Serbian government in 1980–82; head of the Belgrade party (with 230,000 party members the largest in the country) in 1982–84; president of the Serbian party 1984–86. In 1986 he became president of the republic of Serbia. His hand-picked collaborators followed in his footsteps: Slobodan Milošević replaced him as the head of the Belgrade party in 1984, and as party chief in 1986,[17] Dragiša Pavlović, another Stambolić protégé, took Milošević's place in Belgrade in the same year.[18]

By temperament a centralizer,[19] Stambolić was a pragmatic politician who relied on his control of key posts (and, increasingly, the press) in his efforts to provide the republic with a new role in the Federation and to rally a motley group of liberals and conservatives around the quest for constitutional revision. Marković's earlier failure had exposed the sensitivity of other republics on the issue of the constitution, so Stambolić moved slowly and cautiously to win the agreement of the Federation. If, during his time in office, nationalists were allowed access to the media, this was more to put pressure on the Federation than out of any agreement with their views. For the Serbian party was faced with a seemingly insuperable barrier, in that constitutional changes had to be sanctioned by all three assemblies – in the two provinces as well as the republic as a whole – but approval from Vojvodina and Kosovo was not forthcoming. The provinces' stand was supported by the Federal party leadership, which was concerned about the implied reduction in the rights of the national minorities – most particularly the Albanians – and did not wish to see any alteration of the national balance within the Federation, since the consequences of this would be incalculable.

Stambolić at the same time sought support from a younger generation of Albanian leaders – like Azem Vllasi.[20] These, he hoped, might accept a new compromise in the constitutional field, if Belgrade in turn backed their efforts to secure a modernization of Kosovo's political structures demanded by the enormous advance the province had made during the previous decade of self-government. However, by the time Stambolić had consolidated his position, the country had entered its current deep crisis, which strengthened conservative forces throughout Yugoslavia clamouring for an outright repression of critical voices from whatever quarter. In Croatia, under Stipe Šuvar's leadership, the party in 1984 produced a White Book on the Yugoslav intelligentsia which was clearly more of a blacklist. In Serbia, there was an attempt in the same year to organize a political show trial.[21] In Slovenia, army courts were used in 1988 against discomforting critics. All these attempts, however, were rebuffed. Only through an alliance with nationalists could the party hardliners hope to prevail. Such an alliance was to emerge precisely in Serbia, where the issue of constitutional changes, integrating national and state concerns, allowed the emergence of a powerful right-wing bloc using the potent symbol of Kosovo to legitimize its political platform.

The Anti-Albanian Campaign

Kosovo was once the geographical centre of a short-lived mediaeval Serbian Empire, whose fragments were finally destroyed in 1389 by Ottoman armies. A collective memory of the battle survived in local folksongs, and the Orthodox Church – for its own reasons – invested this defeat of a secular power with a mystical dimension. In the mid-nineteenth century, the Kosovo myth became an instrument of nation-building for the emergent Serbian principality. It was also used to justify territorial expansion to the south, aiming ultimately at Salonica, and served to mobilize the Serb peasantry for successive wars culminating in the Balkan Wars of 1912–13. Since by this time Kosovo was predominantly Albanian-inhabited, the myth also acquired racial overtones. It became a symbol of the nation at war, a central point of reference for Serb nationalists.[22] After the 1981 Albanian demonstrations, these began to complain ever more vociferously that Kosovo was becoming a purely Albanian province; that the 'cradle of the Serb nation' was becoming alienated from it. The Kosovo leadership was duly accused of encouraging Serb (and Montenegrin) emigration from the province, and the Albanian nation held to be guilty of ethnic genocide.

There is no doubt that Slavs have been emigrating from the region, but equally clearly the reasons have been mainly economic. (Already by 1970 Kosovo's unemployment reached 50 per cent of the working population, and Albanians have been leaving as well.) But Kosovo Slavs had been affected also by cultural-political factors. The rapid Albanization of the provincial administration from 1966 on was achieved by the use of national quotas, which reduced job opportunities for Slavs in the state sector where they had hitherto been privileged. In addition, thanks to the high birthrate of the Albanians, their ethnic preponderance increased steadily, transforming linguistic, educational and cultural conditions in the new democratic period. An all-Yugoslav programme of investment directed mainly at Serb-inhabited communes – in order to prevent emigration – was agreed in 1987, although it was strictly unconstitutional. But this did little to change the desperate economic state of the province, and emigration (of both nationalities) continued. Worst of all, the Federal party leadership made a cardinal mistake: it described the 1981 Albanian demonstrations for republican status as an attempt at 'counter-revolution', led by Albanian separatists. This allowed Serb nationalists to cover themselves in the robes of the revolution's guardians.

At the end of 1986, a newly formed Kosovo Committee of Serbs and Montenegrins began to send delegations to Belgrade and to organize mass protest meetings in the province itself, complaining of 'genocide' and demanding a wholesale purge of Albanian leaders and the introduction of military rule in Kosovo.[23] A powerful coalition emerged in Serbia in the late 1980s, comprising retired policemen, revanchist migrants from the province (the 1966 fall of Ranković had led to an exodus of Serb administrative cadres, creating a potential 'irredentist' constituency), the Kosovo Committee, right-wing nationalists among the traditional intelligentsia, 'disillusioned' leftists, a wing of the Orthodox Church and sections of the party and state bureaucracy. The coalition entered public life with a now notorious petition – in which the then party and state leadership was accused of high treason.[24] As a result, by the end of 1986 Stambolić's policy of seeking constitutional revision through consensus came unstuck in Serbia as much as in Kosovo.

The nationalists strove to present Kosovo as a lawless society, run by extreme nationalists and irredentists bent on 'forceful assimilation and expulsion of the non-Albanian population'.[25] The official media joined in, sparing no tactics. One of the most shameful was to invent daily stories about the rape of Serb women – despite all official statistics showing the absurdity of such racist fables. Another was to claim that the high Albanian birthrate was part of a nationalist plot and should be countered by discriminatory state measures. This hysterical campaign was effective. By 1987 Kosovo had become – in violation of both the letter and the spirit of the constitution – a legal zone *sui generis*. Factories started to be built in Kosovo for Serbs only, Albanian families were evicted from Serb villages, sale of Serb-owned land to Albanians was prohibited, rape declared a political crime. Albanians were heavily sentenced for minor and frequently invented misdemeanors. A campaign of vilification was launched in the Belgrade press against those Albanian leaders (most notoriously Fadil Hoxha, member of the party since before the war, partisan general and member of the Federal state presidency) who had fought hard to win greater autonomy for Kosovo in the constitutional debates of 1966–73. Racial slurs in the media were tolerated. This anti-Albanian campaign in Serbia in turn encouraged the leadership of Macedonia to begin a policy of (unconstitutionally) restricting educational opportunities for Albanian children, limiting welfare benefits, at times even destroying Albanian houses, and generally discriminating against this part of the republic's population.

Not surprisingly, relations between the Kosovo and Serbian leaderships grew distinctly cool. The anti-Albanian campaign in Serbia was mounting so fast that the implications of any surrender of provincial autonomy for the preservation of basic national rights became quite stark. The newly emergent critical intelligentsia, which just like their counterparts in the rest of Yugoslavia chafed at bureaucratic rule, and the working class, which suffered still more from the high-handedness of the local Albanian bureaucracy, were inevitably drawn behind the latter into a struggle for defence of national rights. The process of democratization in Kosovo came to an abrupt end, under the mounting pressure from Serbia. The Albanian nation closed ranks.

Stambolić, who had made tactical accommodations to the Serbian nationalists, now discovered that they were emerging as a political force out of party control and were legitimizing a view of the history of Serbia and Yugoslavia which was not just anti-communist but viscerally reactionary. Under their pressure Serbia was moving in the direction of an open confrontation with the Federation. Serbian nationalists were joining forces with party hardliners, and indeed with all those who did not like growing political liberties.

The Split

Two clearly defined poles – one more liberal, the other nationalist-conservative, led respectively by Stambolić and Milošević – thus emerged in the Serbian party in early 1987.[26] Although the main line of differentiation was the attitude to growing Serb nationalism, the fundamental divide was really over the character and role of the party. The liberals were against party arbitration in the ideological field; they argued that a concept of party unity which outlawed the articulation of different opinions during formulation of the party line, on pain of expulsion, was contrary to party statutes. Milošević, on the other hand, pushed for a top-down monolithic party in complete control of the state and, increasingly, also one with a national vocation. Vigorous support for this orientation came from the party *aktiv* in the University of Belgrade, which had been captured by hardliners.[27] What was to cement Milošević's victory, however – against a background of economic crisis, working-class unrest and nationalist agitation – was the growing sense of insecurity throughout the Serbian party apparatus: the appeal to unity behind a strong leader proved irresistible for the majority of top and middle-rank cadres.

By 1987 the cause of inner-party democracy and the struggle against nationalism could no longer be differentiated. Milošević now began systemically to break collective discipline, refusing to speak against Serb nationalism at consecutive party plenums. Faced with the mounting nationalist counter-revolution, the liberals demanded that the party should go onto the offensive. The struggle between the two wings emerged into the open in April 1987; by September, at the 8th Central Committee Plenum, the liberals had been thoroughly defeated. Pavlović and Stambolić were voted off the party presidency, removed from the Central Committee and finally expelled from the party together with their supporters and co-thinkers. Their departure marks also the date of the Serbian party's open endorsement of nationalism.[28]

This brutal purge, together with the nationalist overtones of the televised 8th Plenum debate, shocked the country. That the victory had not come easily, however, was proved by the viciousness of the subsequent campaign against the defeated party faction, and by the scale of the purge of key party and state organs. Particular attention was paid to the media. In a manner that combined the techniques of traditional Stalinism and the Western gutter press, all real and potential critics were characterized as 'anti-people' – that is, anti-Serb – and 'anti-party'. At the same time, a prompt expression of *total* loyalty to the new leadership – including the obligatory attack on its opponents – was made a condition of political survival and/or continued employment. After Kosovo, democracy was also snuffed out in Serbia.

In his letter of resignation from the central committee, Pavlović warned that 'the public denunciation and humiliation of people because, at a single meeting and on a single issue, they had a different position from the majority opens the way to a monolithic, Stalinist type of party, and the infallibility of the party leadership'.[29] Milošević – as the infallible leader of a monolithic Serbian party – is today able to disperse an emotional mass of hundreds of thousands (as he did in Belgrade on 28 February 1989) with a single sentence promising the arrest of counter-revoluntionaries.

The Resurgence of Reaction

The ideological basis of Milošević's victory was a coalescence of state-led nationalism and a neo-Stalinist concept of the Party and its role in society. Their fusion into a coherent political project was made possible by the drive to restore the unity of the republican state – now reinterpreted as the state exclusively of the Serb nation. Belgrade's traditional hegemony over Serbia's cultural and political life gave its intelligentsia a decisive role in Milošević's rise to power, while the Serbian conservatives used the growing power of nationalism to deliver a mortal blow to their liberal opponents in the party.

There is no space here to survey the origins and progress of the momentous shift to the right that took place in Belgrade intellectual life in the course of the 1980s. In Serbia – and not only there – integration of the various trends of artistic and political thought increasingly took place on a uni-national plane, leading to different and indeed conflicting views of Yugoslavia's past and future. Yet it was in Serbia, above all, that the scope of intellectual critique changed dramatically, in that it reached beyond the usual complaints about the suppression of political and artistic liberties to challenge the Party's entire historic legitimacy – and, in the process, also the revolution itself. This right-wing challenge, articulated above all in the language of virulent nationalism, returned to pre-war traditions.[30] Indeed, one of its ingredients was an effort to rehabilitate the Chetniks, as defenders of the nation against its 'historic' enemies – counterposing their 'prudent' wartime conduct to the alleged unnecessary sacrifice of Serb lives by the Communists.[31] The history of pre-war Yugoslavia was rewritten in a manner designed to evoke sympathy for Serbian bourgeois politicians, especially in the military or state-building roles. Almost imperceptibly, a revision of the past merged with a reinterpretation of contemporary Yugoslavia, its character and problems, to produce a whole new world-view radically different from, and hostile to, the postwar political consensus.

While the Writers' Association of Serbia became at this time a bastion of populist nationalism, at times coloured with religious bigotry, nationalism in its state-centred form took root in the Serbian Academy of Arts and Sciences, which in 1986 produced a document called the Memorandum. Involving the efforts of some of the best-known Serbian intellectuals, it represented the most sustained and coherent piece of revisionism of anti-communist orientation to appear legally in Yugoslavia in the postwar period.[32]

The Memorandum argued that, after the Liberation, an 'alien' (i.e. federated) model of Yugoslavia was imposed on the Serb nation. The main culprit was the CPY, which had blindly followed the Comintern's anti-Serb 'policy of revanchism including genocide' during the war and, by endorsing the federal structure, exposed the Serbs after the war to discrimination. The second culprit was the Slovenes and Croats (represented by the Slovene Edvard Kardelj and the Croat Josip Broz Tito), who 'created a social and economic order in accordance with their needs and interests' that was fundamentally inimical to the Serbs. The 1974 Constitution then deprived the Serbs of the right to their own (integral) state. The third culprit was domestic quislings: 'the hardened opportunism of generations of Serb politicians after the war'.[33]

The situation in Kosovo, the Memorandum stated, was 'Serbia's biggest defeat since 1804' (the date of the first Serb uprising against the Ottoman state). 'In 1981 a war – a truly special, open and total war – was declared against the Serb nation ... with active and open support of certain political centres in the country: a war far more devastating than that coming from across the border.' In this war, the Serb nation remained alone: the LCY avoided 'a real showdown with the neo-fascist aggression', while the leadership in Serbia 'seem[ed] unwilling to respond to this open war in the only appropriate manner: a resolute defence of the nation and its territory.'

But if the Communists had deserted the nation, why did it not rise to defend itself? This was because the nation was the victim of a cruel ideological trick perpetrated by the LCY, with its endorsement of the Comintern thesis that the Serbs had oppressed other nations in pre-war Yugoslavia. The resulting 'guilt complex' or 'state of depression in the Serb nation' was 'fateful for its spirit and morale'. Its intellectual and spiritual leaders must carry out 'a total re-examination of all social relations', beginning with 'a total re-examination of the constitution', in order to restore the 'vitality' of the nation. A resurrection of its democratic past was also required: 'Because of the narrow-mindedness and lack of objectivity of official historiography, the democratic tradition which bourgeois Serbia fought for and won in the nineteenth century has remained until now completely overshadowed by the Serb socialist and workers' movement.'[34]

The Memorandum's xenophobic nationalism and Chetnik echoes would earlier have elicited a swift condemnation from the Serbian party. This time, however, the counter-attack was never mounted, since the leadership was split over how to deal with domestic nationalism. Stambolić, president of the republic, and Pavlović, head of the Belgrade party, condemned the Memorandum in public soon after its publication. But although the Serbian party presidency and central committee also formally condemned it, this fact was – at Milošević's insistence – kept secret from the public. The silence of the highest political authority, naturally, spoke louder than words. For not only did it suggest tacit support, it also inhibited public discussion of the Memorandum at the time when it was most needed.

Nationalism Triumphant

The battle which the Serbian liberals joined in 1987 was by this time being fought throughout Yugoslavia. In 1986, Milan Kučan – after a period of work in Federal organs – returned to take over the party leadership in Slovenia. Kučan knew well that a powerful conservative bloc was emerging within the party, ready to play the card of social insecurity to block the necessary economic and political reforms; that the ruling party's decline in numbers and prestige limited, in any case, its ability to go it alone; and that, therefore, an alliance with progressive forces outside the party was imperative. But whereas the political mood in Slovenia (and, to a lesser extent, in Croatia) supported such a course, the unresolved constitutional problem favoured the nationalists and party hardliners in Serbia. The latter openly argued that enemies of the system were to be found in the highest political positions – on the editorial boards of student and youth magazines; in the republican Assembly; in the League of Communists and its central committee; even in the party presidency – at the same time that the nationalist intelligentsia accused the party liberals of being 'soft' on Kosovo. By playing the Kosovo card, Milošević was able to place himself at the head of the emergent nationalist-conservative coalition, crush the liberal opposition and – by forging 'unity' within the party – satisfy also the morbid fear of the central apparatus that the party was losing control over political life in the republic. From now on, all criticism of the party leadership was presented as an attack on Serb national interests.

It was with his speech of 27 April 1987 at Kosovo Polje – the organizing centre of Serb and Montenegrin nationalists in Kosovo – that Milošević broke collective party discipline in the most spectacular fashion and inaugurated his bid for power in the League of Communists of Serbia. In his address to the assembled Slavs, he spoke of the injustice and humiliation they were suffering; of their ancestral land; of the proud warrior spirit of their forefathers; of their duty to their descendants. The speech was aimed at the people's emotions: listening to the speech, Pavlović saw 'an idea turned into a dogma, the Kosovo myth becoming a reality'. Milošević spoke like a general addressing his troops before a decisive battle. 'It was here that the orientation towards war-like measures for the solution of the Serb and Montenegrin problems in Kosovo started', Pavlović writes.[35]

Milošević endorsed the view that the Serb nation was at war, and offered the nationalists the support of the party. He thereby, in effect, removed Kosovo Serbs (and Montenegrins) from the jurisdiction of the provincial authorities, tearing up in the process the existing constitution. The head of the League of Communists of Serbia was speaking not on behalf of the party (which, of course, includes also Albanians and other non-Serbs), not on behalf of the republic's (ethnically heterogeneous) working class, but on behalf of the Serb nation – anywhere in Yugoslavia. In a direct challenge to the fundamental principle of the Yugoslav federation, he was thus endorsing the bourgeois nationalism recently reformulated by the Memorandum: 'The establishment of the full national and cultural integrity of the Serb nation, irrespective of the republic and province in which it finds itself, is its historic and democratic right.' The leadership of Croatia, this implied, legitimately represented only Croats, that of Slovenia only Slovenes, and so on. In Kosovo Polje, Milošević conjured up the spectre of Yugoslavia's Balkanization.

On his return from Kosovo Polje, the party president – now acclaimed as national *vozhd* – called a meeting of the party executive. His report was delivered in a manner designed to create an emotional impact within this body – for Milošević was seeking *post facto* authorization for his speech. 'What we are discussing here can no longer be called politics – it is a question of our fatherland.' It was important that the party base should understand this: 'It is when we begin to speak at party meetings in this manner that the party will be able to take things into its hands.' And he reminded the meeting that he was not only president of the Central Committee but also the head of security and territorial forces in the republic.[36]

The Serbian party now found itself in the embarrassing position of being openly hailed by people whom not long before it had customarily denounced as hardened nationalists. Yet Serbia has an old socialist tradition: when Milošević addressed party members and the nation with the words 'Only determination and belief in the future could have transformed the defeat of a nation such as happened at Kosovo into a brilliant clasp linking all future generations of Serbs – an eternal symbol of its national essence', a hundred years earlier the Serb socialist Svetozar Marković had already given the answer: 'Serbia does not depend on the revival of the dead, on rotten material, for erecting the foundation of its future. Other ideals must be provided for its future.' And when the party leader went to address meeting after meeting to press the message that recentralization of the republican state was Serbia's 'historic task', and the Belgrade press wrote about 'the third Serbian uprising', he was answered by another Serb socialist, Dimitrije Tucović, who in 1912 had denounced the bourgeois warmongers preparing for the Balkan Wars: 'The historic task of Serbia is a big lie.'

The resurgence of Serb nationalism was instilling fear not just in the rest of Yugoslavia but also in the head of the Belgrade party, who during that spring and summer watched the media's assiduous fostering of an image of Albanians as dangerous, primitive and anti-Yugoslav.[37] They spoke of the Albanian people in the language of blood, rape and murder, while passing in silence over the welling violence of Serb nationalist meetings in Kosovo, with their slogans; 'Kill Fadil [Hoxha]!', 'An eye for an eye!', 'Brothers do not be afraid; the time has come for a final showdown!', 'The Serb nation has always shed blood for its freedom!', 'Let us go, brothers and sisters, to attack Kosovo!'. The media were doctoring facts, inciting to revenge, publishing with approval pictures of raised fists and of Serbs arming themselves in Kosovo 'for defence of their homes'. The Serb population was being moulded into an angry mass, 'aiming for a national catharsis that can only end in tragedy'. As Pavlović was to write about the principal Belgrade daily *Politika*, it was 'dynamite under Serbia'.

This had very practical consequences, since it was creating a security problem in the capital city. Pavlović told the Belgrade party that its task was to fight not irredentism in Kosovo but Serb nationalism at home. He complained at meetings of the party presidency that at Serb nationalist rallies the word 'comrade' was replaced by 'brother' and 'working class' by 'nation'. The press, radio and television were increasingly becoming an instrument of the power struggle within the party leadership. Pavlović warned that the forces of the Ranković era were being rehabilitated; and that, in effect, 'Tito, Kardelj and the policy of the LCY were being put on trial'. Milošević was sowing the illusion that the Kosovo problem was a matter of subjective determination, while the nationalists saw its solution in terms of national confrontation. Their continual rallies (both in Kosovo and in Belgrade) were increasingly dangerous: 'A political climate is being prepared in Belgrade that seeks a state of emergency, a firm hand in Kosovo.' Yet 'without the participation of the Albanian masses there can be no real or lasting results. And how can we win and mobilize them if we continually sow doubt in their Yugoslav patriotism?' Pavlović denounced the press for talking about Kosovo 'in words reeking of lead and gunpowder, revenge and revanchism, the renewal of the suicidal Vidovdan [Kosovo] myth.' And, on an ominous note, he added: 'If a nation adopts the right to be angry, how can it deny the same to another? A confrontation of two nations leads to a war. Instead of redirecting anger towards a rational understanding of problems and their solutions, the appeal to anger serves to strengthen the authority of the speaker.'

Neo-Stalinism

The conflict within the Serbian party was not just about Kosovo, but also about 'the place and role of the party in overcoming the crisis, and in the struggle against nationalist counter-revolution. Kosovo was intentionally being substituted for something deeper and more serious.' When he heard Milošević remind the party presidency that he, as head of the Serbian party, was also in charge of the republic's territorial army, Pavlović realized that the split in the party was inevitable. 'After these words, our ways parted: I began to run away from the tragedy, while he started to run towards it. An angry mass disposes of a tremendous striking power. And who will be its target?' Ultimately the federation, since 'the drive to unite the Serbs into a single state would inevitably bring them into conflict with other nations in Yugoslavia'.

At the height of the inner-party struggle, in September 1987, Pavlović urgently called a press conference to denounce the nationalist paroxysm in Serbia.[38] He was armed with the Federal state presidency's recommendation that the Serbian central committee, and especially the Belgrade party, should 'paralyse the nationalist and anti-Albanian activities of the bourgeois Right and all other anti-socialist forces present in the Writers' Association, certain sections of the Academy and other associations, publishing houses, institutions and public forums.' The Federal state presidency had further demanded 'a sharp differentiation' in order to 'prevent publishing and editorial policy being used to spread anti-Albanian sentiments'. Pavlović stated that those who did not struggle against Serb nationalism were in the business of fanning nationalist hatred. Those who did so were 'defending the honour of the Serb nation, of their profession and of socialist Yugoslavia'. Pavlović warned his audience that in Serbia – as elsewhere – the nation was made up of at least two camps, and that party members should state clearly which one they belonged to. In a scarcely veiled reference to Milošević, he criticized those who 'irresponsibly promise speed' in solving the Kosovo problem. This speech was promptly denounced by the Belgrade dailies as 'anti-party' and 'anti-Serb'. At a hurriedly convened meeting of the Serbian party presidency, Milošević accused Stambolić and Pavlović of bringing disunity into the Serbian party, and called for 'differentiation' on the issue of support for 'the party line' in relation to Kosovo. At this fateful meeting, which started the process of his political demise, Pavlović argued that 'nationalism is the final instrument, the last defence of dogmatism. In my opinion the key problem lies in the unwillingness to confront Serb nationalism.'[39]

For most of 1987 a momentous battle was being waged between liberals and hardliners for the soul of the Serbian party. It was a battle between 'democracy and authoritarianism, self-management and bureaucratic etatism, national equality and nationalism, federation and unitarism, freedom and fear'.[40] The liberals were defeated in the end not by force of argument, but by a party machinery based on Stalinist conceptions of unity and democratic centralism. When Milošević called at the September 1987 plenum for Pavlović's removal, he won by emphasizing the need for party unity. Without it, he claimed, no problem – including notably that of Kosovo – could be tackled. It was the unchallengeable power of the executive over the central committee that ensured him the overwhelming majority on the latter body. In his letter of resignation from the central committee, Pavlović wrote: 'The machine of democratic centralism – that is, of centralism – grinds down, in the name of a single, self-confident egocentric and imposed opinion, those who are sincerely convinced as well as those who are not; breaks down the wise and the honest along with the careerists and lackeys; levels the sceptics and the gullible, naive and uninformed. It transforms them all into subjugated individuals.'[41]

Pavlović's letter of resignation was the swansong of opposition to resurgent Stalinism in the Serbian party. It echoes with resonances of the Soviet opposition's struggle against Stalin himself. In a situation where authority of the party or party leader replaces internal dialogue, where instruction from above substitutes for the initiative of party members, 'does this not lead to a situation in which the party is reduced to one individual who speaks eternal truth? Following the "top down" principle, the CC is today being asked to give full support to the line of the 8th plenum, that is, to Milošević. Since when do the views of one man represent the sum total of the party's position on Kosovo? The impression is given that he is the only one in the leadership who wants to – and can – solve the Kosovo problem and that, therefore, he is able also to solve quickly all other social problems. Those who do not agree are being purged and purges are being treated as the supreme example of democratic centralism in action – but what will happen when it turns out that purges only postpone the necessary solutions?'[42]

In his book, Pavlović recalls Trotsky's early warning against an authoritarian understanding of democratic centralism, and contrasts the conceptions of Lenin or Trotsky with that of Stalin. Lenin woke up too late to the danger which Stalin represented for the Soviet party, possibly because 'under Lenin's control, democratic centralism was an instrument of the revolution's achievements. But in Stalin's hands it became a kind of private guillotine cutting off the heads of all those who thought differently.' Pavlović thus calls for the legitimation of differences within the party and the right of tendencies to exist within it. And, indeed, only a concept of democratic centralism in which the tension between 'democratic' and 'centralism' was maintained could offer a real future to the LCY.

Whereas, in Kosovo Polje, Miloševic offered himself as a liberator of the Serb nation, Pavlović argued that liberty cannot be treated as an exclusively national category. 'I have never fought for Serbs to be freed, but for them to be free in relation to one another.' For otherwise they are faced with the far greater problem of having to free themselves from their liberator. 'It is here that Slobodan and myself differ. Only socialist democracy can unite and stabilize Yugoslavia, and only a democratic Serbia can be a strong factor of Yugoslav cohesion. Any other Serbia can attract only fear and suspicion.'[43] If nationalism can be defeated only from within the nation, and if the League of Communists of Serbia – which has the monopoly of political power – has abandoned internationalism, then who is going to lead the struggle against nationalist counter-revolution in Serbia? Pavlović sought the answer once more in the Serbian socialist tradition: 'With the same energy with which we are ready to protest against the foreign tyrant, let us also protest against the tyrants at home, those whose alleged love of the people allows them to be the greatest reactionaries and whose patriotism does not prevent them from being the greatest black marketeers.' A bureaucracy aligned to nationalism can be defeated only by a re-statement of the Yugoslav socialist project, based on the power of the working class. For this Serb, Yugoslav and Communist, no call to arms to defend national rights within socialist Yugoslavia was legitimate: such a call could justifiably be issued only to defend the socialist foundation of the Yugoslav Federal state.

A Nation at War

Having crushed the opposition in the Serbian party, the Milošević faction now turned to the business of unifying the nation, in order to prepare for a final onslaught on the two barriers to constitutional revision: the leaderships of Vojvodina and Kosovo, and the Federal party leadership itself. Serbia, which only a few years earlier had been a lively centre of activity and debate, suddenly succumbed to a numbing 'unity'. The capital of Yugoslavia became the headquarters of an embattled Serb nation. The media were used, as in wartime, to attack the enemy; punish traitors; report on the situation at the front (drawn against practically all other republics[44] and the two provinces); raise the national spirit; recall past victories; commemorate the wounded and dead in past battles going back to the fourteenth century. The message was that of a heroic nation, surrounded by perfidious enemies. The military prowess of the defunct bourgeoisie was honoured by erecting statues of its generals. Serbian peasant dress, especially hats, became a sudden fashion. This orgy of national self-pity and exhilaration was – and is – at times interrupted only by reports of marching workers, coming from Serbia and beyond to Belgrade to protest against low wages or the real or threatened bankruptcy of their enterprises and to demand the resignation of managers and functionaries.

An extremely important role in this orchestrated process of national homogenization has been played by mass rallies in solidarity with Serbs and Montenegrins in Kosovo. Ostensibly spontaneous, they have been carefully organized and financed by the party-state machine.[45] During 1988 such rallies – tens of thousands strong – took place in practically every major city or village in Serbia. At these – as well as at party plenums, republican assembly sessions, trade union conferences and meetings of the party base; in universities, factories and schools; at suitable state occasions – one message was constantly hammered home: the Serb nation is fragmented because its state is divided into three pieces. Milošević spoke of the historic hour: 'Serbia will be united or it will not exist.' The Belgrade press wrote about 'the third Serbian uprising'.

The disinclination of the Serbian party to submit itself to the Federal party's authority simultaneously grew. Nationals mobilization in Serbia and the aggressive tone of its press resulted in rising tensions throughout the country, and in the summer of 1988 the Federal party presidency demanded of Belgrade that nationalist demonstrations be stopped. The republican leadership refused. Its representatives simply declined to attend meetings of the presidency until its demands were met. The frequency of the rallies if anything increased throughout the autumn, their mood growing more militant. Slogans demanding arms and the criminal prosecution of other Yugoslav leaders (in the case of Albanian leaders also their execution) became frequent. No party or state leader – be they from another republic or province or from the Federation, and irrespective of his or her status – who appeared not to harbour 100 per cent support for the 'new course' in Serbia was exempt from the hate campaign.[46]

Nationalist rallies now spread into Vojvodina and Montenegro, demanding the local leaderships' resignation. These rallies were by now seriously destabilizing the country, opening the possibility that – in a repetition of the Polish 1981 – the army might have to take over. In October, Yugoslav state president Raif Dizdarević warned – without mentioning the culprit by name – that the country might have to be placed under a state of emergency. Faced with the readiness of the Serbian leadership to use the card of civil war to settle inner-party differences (what the Bolshevik party's left wing described as 'Bonapartism' during its struggle with Stalin), the Federal party finally gave its assent to Serbia's recentralization, and thereby to a significant reduction in the hard-won national rights of the two million Albanians. This policy of appeasement was, however, rejected by the Serbian party, which now simply informed the Federation that the internal affairs of the republic of Serbia were its *exclusive* prerogative. In early October the *party* leadership of the province of Vojvodina was overthrown by a carefully planned and orchestrated mass action. It was replaced by Milošević's appointees, ready to enact the desired constitutional changes.

The Federal party leadership took the next fatal step by legitimizing *post facto* this undemocratic and illegal method of changing not just the republic's constitution, but also the character of the Yugoslav federation.[47] What is more, in accepting the Vojvodina party leaders' resignations, it also broke its own party statutes.[48] The Vojvodina *putsch* was organized by local power groups, not all of whom were party members. By sanctioning their act, the Federal party allowed alien bodies to intervene in its internal life, to the point of removing topmost party leaders. Where this practice could lead was illustrated dramatically only a day after the Vojvodina events, when a demonstration of angry Montenegrin workers in Titograd was exploited as the backdrop to a determined attempt to replace the local republican leadership with Milošević's men. The possibility that Yugoslavia's whole Federal structure might collapse now prompted the Slovenian, Croatian and Bosnian leaders to act. Under their

pressure, the Federal party leadership condemned the Titograd demonstrations and gave the local party the green light for a show of force – in
another sorry precedent. The Montenegrin leadership, however, survived
for only two months: January 1989 it was finally overthrown by an
organized mass action, leaving Montenegro in a state of political chaos
and its relations with the Federation in Milošević's hands.

Milošević was now ready to round on the Federal party leadership itself.
The Belgrade press launched a well-rehearsed campaign, demanding the
resignation of the Federal party presidency and its current head Stipe
Šuvar. The televised 17th plenum of the CC LCY – held on 17–20 October
1988 – exposed the open breach to the gaze of the whole country. In an
unprecedented move, the Federal party presidency asked the CC for a vote
of confidence: when the vote was counted, Dušan Ckrebić, a close
collaborator of Milošević, alone had been voted down.[49] Milošević then
refused to accept the vote, and the Belgrade press denounced the
all-Yugoslav Central Committee as an 'unprincipled alliance' directed
against Serbia! A month after the plenum, the Serbian leadership
organized a 350,000-strong public meeting in Belgrade, at which the
'fighting spirit of the Serb nation' was once again hailed, other Yugoslav
leaders attacked and a 'united' (as opposed to federal) Yugoslavia
proclaimed. 'No force can now stop Serbia's unification!' screamed the
front-page headlines.[50] They were not counting with the Albanian
working class.

Wedding without Meat

On 17 November 1988, the day before the Belgrade rally, a meeting of the
Provincial Committee of the League of Communists of Kosovo was to be
convened in Priština to discuss the resignation of Kaqusha Jashari and
Azem Vllasi, respectively the current party President and her immediate
predecessor, which had been arranged as part of the deal on the
constitution between the Federal and Serbian leaderships. That morning,
miners from the Trepča 'Stari Trg' mine, after completing the night shift,
emerged from the 38 degrees Celsius of their pit into the freezing dawn,
joined forces with the day shift and began the 70-kilometre march to
Priština. They were the vanguard of what turned out to be the largest
Albanian demonstration since the war: half a million participants over the
next five days.

Journalists met them half-way. 'They were wearing their shabby miners'
outfits and looked quite exhausted. The front row carried a picture of Tito,
two miners' flags, the party flag, Yugoslav, Albanian and Turkish flags.
Their slogans: "Tito–Party!"; "Jashari–Vllasi!" "Tito–Kardelj",[51] "We
will not surrender our cadres!" '. A correspondent from the daily Borba,

one of the rare journalists able to speak the Albanian language (only three out of thirty Yugoslav journalists then accredited to Priština were in possession of this essential tool of their trade!), asked a miner if they were going to Priština to complain about their wages. 'Everybody gathered around to listen. The miner answered that this was a day for politics, not for tears. The journalist said that politics was a dangerous business – the "specials" were ahead and there might be trouble. The grim-faced man responded angrily: "Journalist, have you ever seen a wedding without meat?".'[52]

Once in Priština, the miners were joined by other workers, then by students and youth, followed by secondary and primary schoolchildren – 80 per cent of the participants were below the age of twenty – and soon also by the older generation, coming from all parts of Kosovo (as well as western Macedonia). The aims of this highly disciplined protest were to express their rejection of the proposed changes in the constitution of the Republic of Serbia; to prevent, in that context, the enforced resignation of the two provincial leaders.[53] This defence of national rights was phrased in the immaculate language of democracy. In interviews freely given, the miners made it clear that if the province's status was to be changed, if its leadership was to be purged, then this must be done in an open, democratic debate and not imposed by force. The workers said what the Federal party should have said – but did not. In those freezing November days and nights, the marching workers, students and children acted as a true socialist vanguard. That November Yugoslavia was celebrating the 45th anniversary of the revolutionary state's foundation and the Albanian workers paid its homage in the best possible manner: by defending one of its fundamental achievements.

Although the Provincial Committee acknowledged the resignations (no vote was taken, the outcome having been determined elsewhere) and the miners thus failed to achieve their formal aims, they did give advance warning that they were prepared to organize a general strike if the proposed changes were carried out. After the demonstration, the Serbian party predictably described the Priština events as the latest example of an escalating 'counter-revolution'. The Federal party came very close to agreeing with them.[54] The Kosovo leadership, however, argued that they were 'in line with the 17th Party Plenum'.

The intensifying battle with the country's leadership meanwhile went through another futile round at the 20th Plenum of the Central Committee of the LCY. By now it was quite clear that the Party was split from top to bottom into two opposed coalitions. The Plenum was nevertheless united in confirming once again its support for Serbia's constitutional demands: Albanian national rights were treated as small coin in a much vaster exchange. Azem Vllasi was removed from the central committee and three highly disliked officials placed in charge of the Kosovo party. Their sole task was to ram the required constitutional changes through the Kosovo assembly. The Albanian working class responded by organizing a general strike. The federal state answered with military force and mass arrests. The stakes were getting higher at each round, and they concern not just Kosovo but Yugoslavia as a whole.

Whither Yugoslavia?

In Kosovo, the Yugoslav leadership is faced with two options: the democratic one, which means recognizing the legitimate aspirations of the Albanian population, or permanent military occupation, which will lead to democracy being extinguished throughout Yugoslavia. This is the central message of the Ljubljana Declaration of 1 March 1989 against the state of emergency in Kosovo. Supported by all political and social organizations in Slovenia as well as the Helsinki Federation groups in Zagreb and Belgrade, the Declaration has been signed by a million people in Slovenia – out of a total population of two million.[55]

Balkanization of Yugoslavia has never been inscribed either in its multinational composition or in its federal structure. The unity of the country rests on a recognition of its ethnic plurality. However, the rise of state-led nationalism in Serbia is threatening to break Yugoslavia into a force-field of warring nationalities, pushing the country back into the past. Since the current party leadership in Serbia can survive only by constant invention of enemies, any suppression of Yugoslav democracy will be carried out in the name of a South Slav 'national' unity. But which people's rights can ever be safeguarded by the denial of similar rights to another? How could the federal structure survive such a triumph of Yugoslav unitarism?[56] Any suppression of democracy will likewise be carried out in the name of party unity. The balance between the hardliners and their opponents has shifted in favour of the former and, at the extraordinary party congress due in December 1989, they will try to impose a Stalinist monolithicity on the rest of the LCY. However, far from uniting it, this would lead only to the Party's disintegration – to a mass exodus of its members. Since Yugoslavia is a party state, moreover, this would cripple all state institutions, making military intervention ultimately inevitable.

The two coalitions within the Party are well aware of what is at stake. Yet, with the partial exception of Kučan in Slovenia, nobody in power has addressed these fateful questions openly and directly. The democratic camp has been muted and ineffective, reluctant from the start to confront Milošević. The Croatian and Slovenian party leaders have failed to protest at the illegal methods of changing the country's constitution, at the Stalinist methods used to remove Milošević's opponents in the Serbian party, at his constant infringement of party statutes, at the Serbian party's condoning of ever more frequent calls to violence against party and state officials or even whole nations.[57] While the current leaders in Serbia have trampled the Party's statutes and the country's constitution underfoot, their Croatian and Slovenian counterparts have responded by backing Serbia's constitutional demands without expressing the least doubt as to their democratic nature – albeit protesting when the inevitably undemocratic enforcement of them has led to workers being victimized. Like Belgrade, they too apparently reckoned without the Albanian workers' determination – which has, indeed, been most inconvenient for their politics of appeasement. Their passivity has derived from a fundamental delusion that the political field in Yugoslavia can be isolated into so many watertight (republican) compartments. Federal bodies, meanwhile, have been used to give the semblance of unity to an increasingly divided Party, thus making more difficult an all-Yugoslav counter-offensive against the mounting reaction.

Clearly, the formulation of an alternative to Milošević must rupture the façade of so-called democratic centralism. Readiness to break the collective discipline of the League of Communists has become the hallmark of the Serbian party under Milošević. Why then is the other side so scrupulous in its adherence to collective decisions? Kučan has already talked of the right of minorities in the party to hold different views. But are such minorities to be constituted only on a single-republic basis? Has not this concept led Slovene and other members of the LCY central committee repeatedly to vote for measures in Kosovo that had no support in the Albanian population.[58] The current crisis has manifestly led to strong internal differentiation within the LCY, and the time has come to recognize this openly. The debate on a comprehensive political reform is already under way in Yugoslavia: central to it will be democratization of the internal life of the LCY, which can have a meaning only if it includes recognition of the right of tendencies to cross republican and provincial borders.

The Ljubljana Declaration emphasizes the need for Yugoslavia to become a 'legal state': that is, a state that respects human rights and recognizes political differences as legitimate. It calls for affirmation of the political, economic and cultural autonomy and equality of all nationalities living in Yugoslavia. It demands that legal institutions and existing laws be altered only by democratic means, with the full agreement of all those concerned. In this it must command the wholehearted support of all socialist and democratic forces. Democracy in Yugoslavia, though, cannot be contained within the terms of nationhood and citizenship. Only a democracy that is socialist in character can preserve and build on the gains of the revolution, withstanding nationalism within and capitalist rapacity without. The *common* interests of the Yugoslav working class have been the foundation of the postwar state, and the only guarantee of national equality within it.

Why, therefore, should anyone assume that Milošević represents the interests of Serbia's workers? Why should one assume that the nationalist gamble in Serbia has paid off in its intention to divert class dissatisfaction into more obedient channels? In Serbia, as elsewhere in Yugoslavia, the working class is in fact engaged in increasingly coordinated strike action. The number of strikes is rising, the number of participants is growing, the actions last longer and are better organized. Although they above all seek economic justice, political demands too are increasingly being articulated. 'We are entering the period of organized class struggle. The working class is beginning to build up its own cadre, which does not belong to the bureaucracy, speaks the workers' language and learns quickly from the experience of other workers.'[59] Will it not also learn from the recent action of the Kosovo workers?

Of course, when – in Serbia today as much as in Romania, or in the Soviet Union under Stalin – there is no democratic possibility for the expression of political views different from official ones, gauging political consciousness accurately is impossible. We may be pretty sure that the Ceauşescu régime is highly unpopular among Romanian workers; or that Stalin's in the period between, say, 1927 and 1935 enjoyed a not negligible degree of working-class support in parts of the country; or that some Chinese workers were enthused by the Cultural Revolution, while others were repelled. But these are all hypotheses and socialists have to judge the régimes in question by quite other criteria. There seems little doubt, from the tenor of the rallies organized by the Serbian party in the last two years, that many workers have indeed been mobilized behind the nationalist banner. And many workers in Vojvodina and Montenegro have certainly been ready, for their own reasons, to demonstrate against their local bureaucrats – thus serving Milošević's very different ends. But what does this prove?

The incidence of strikes in Serbia shows that the Serb nation is by no means as homogeneous as nationalists claim and that, unlike in Stalin's Soviet Union or Ceauşescu's Romania, there are still social constraints on the authoritarian project of the central party leader. After all, it is against Serbian workers that Milošević's strong state must eventually be used, after the Albanian workers or Slovene democrats who should be their best allies against neo-Stalinism have been crushed. Milošević, it is true, has sometimes struck a demagogically anti-bureaucratic note – but only to incite the replacement of one group of leaders by another, more compliant. The essential logic of his project is the construction in Yugoslavia of a bureaucratic dictatorship under a single leader.

There are some signs that the liberal wings of the Party and the intelligentsia are finally making efforts to come together on an all-Yugoslav basis to resist the neo-Stalinist resurgence.[60] Nationalist mobilization divides the Serbian working class from workers and progressive forces in other parts of the country, leaving them to confront alone the growing social misery[61] and the enhanced power of the local bureaucracy. Yugoslavia's leaders, though bitterly divided on many issues, share a commitment to a market economy that will above all hit workers in the underdeveloped south. Whereas a democratically planned economy is not achievable within the existing socio-political order, it is equally evident that without a Federal plan to check the destructive effects of the market the national and class compact that gave birth to the postwar state will simply collapse. Such a Federal plan is a condition of Yugoslav unity – no successful challenge to bureaucratic-nationalist reaction can be mounted unless it speaks on behalf of Yugoslavia as a whole.

The imposition of an undemocratic constitution on the Albanian population in March 1989 could, in the end, be effected only by a recourse to force which – despite the eventual coerced acquiescence of the provincial assembly – denies all legitimacy to the act, while simultaneously threatening the national and democratic rights of all Yugoslavs. Albanian workers and intellectuals have done all they could to avoid violence and bloodshed – the former by sticking to peaceful methods of struggle, the latter by their last-minute desperate appeals to reason and justice.[62] Responsibility for the loss of at least twenty-nine lives within days of this act thus rests exclusively with the federal leadership. Equally, the edict issued to Albanian workers to return to work on pain of dismissal and imprisonment recalls Reaganite methods of dealing with recalcitrant workers; it represents a direct attack on the all-Yugoslav working class, which is soon to be called upon to bear the burden of the restructuring of the economy. The legitimacy of the post-war state, however, was built at once upon national equality and working-class sovereignty: no programme of recovery can avoid addressing itself to both national and class constituencies. The existing institutions are proving increasingly incapable of expressing and resolving the contradictions of the established order. The battle has already been joined for their transformation; its outcome will be determined by the strength of the contending social forces and their allies, both within and outside Yugoslavia's borders.

(March 1989)

Notes

1. One of these, new party leader Rahman Morina, was also – tellingly – the province's police chief.
2. *The Guardian*, London, 25 February 1989.

3. For an extensive discussion of these events, and of their historical background, see 'Kosovo between Yugoslavia and Albania', Part I, Chapter 2, this volume.

4. Published in *Nedjeljna Dalmacija*, Split, 22 January 1989.

5. Jelena Lovrić, *Danas*, Zagreb, 7 February 1989.

6. Lovrić, *Danas*, 28 February 1989.

7. Milan Kučan answers Janez Janša in *Delo*, Ljubljana, 5 November 1988; for a summary of the exchange, see 'Will the Centre Hold?', Part III, Chapter 1, this volume.

8. *Oslobodjenje*, Sarajevo, 5 February 1989.

9. *Start*, Zagreb, 10 December 1988.

10. The party leaderships of Slovenia, Croatia and Serbia, though deeply divided on key political issues, share nevertheless this economic orientation. In a recent speech to the republican assembly, for example, Milošević stated that the market was the essence of democracy.

11. Miha Kovač, 'The Slovene Spring', *New Left Review* 171, September–October 1988.

12. Ibid.

13. Darko Hudelist, *Start*, Zagreb, April 1988, gives an extraordinary portrayal of the popular mood in Macedonia, among both ethnic communities.

14. The best known were Marko Nikezić and Latinka Perović. The term 'liberal' is customarily used to describe these reformers. Given their role in the suppression of the student movement in the late sixties, their democratic inclinations should not be overestimated.

15. Marković was a wartime partisan leader and one of the most influential Serbian politicians in the second half of the 1970s. In 1980 he was head of the Federal Party.

16. Dragoslav Marković, *Život i politika 1967–76*, Belgrade 1987. It was the principles of equality of the South Slav nations with the national minorities that Marković in particular found difficult to accept, although in the end he submitted himself to party discipline and, it seems, also accepted the argument. In 1988 Marković publicly dissociated himself from the current Serbian leadership and was reviled as traitor to the nation in the Belgrade press.

17. Stambolić came from a peasant family – his father and uncle joined the partisans in 1941. (The uncle, Petar Stambolić, occupied the highest positions in Serbia and Yugoslavia in the late 1970s.) Initially a youth activist, he became a factory worker by choice and studied law as an extra-mural student at Belgrade University, where he met Slobodan Milošević – an Orthodox priest's son. Stambolić soon became manager of his enterprise, and brought in Milošević as his deputy.

18. Pavlović, who comes from a family of intellectuals, acquired degrees in engineering and economics at the University of Kragujevac, and finally a doctorate in politics at Belgrade University. As an intellectual with a propensity for hard work and an austere lifestyle, he was not much liked by the party apparatus.

19. For example, Stambolić wished to strengthen presidential power by having republican presidents elected by popular referenda, but this met with resistance even in his home state.

20. Vllasi headed the Socialist Youth Alliance of Yugoslavia in the last years of Tito's life. After a long spell in the Federal centre, he returned to Kosovo to head the local Socialist Alliance. Among the first in Kosovo to call the Albanian 1981 demonstrations a 'counter-revolution', he became Kosovo party leader in 1986, at the head of a younger team, following a party purge. Two years later, however, after a vociferous campaign in the Belgrade press, he was replaced in 1988 by Kaqusha Jashari. In February 1989, he was removed from the CC LCY. Today he sits in a Priština prison, charged himself with fomenting 'counter-revolution'.

21. Milan Nikolić, a well-known socialist and a 1968 student leader who was one of the defendants in the now famous trial of the Belgrade Six, warned in his last defence speech of the growing danger of Stalinism in Yugoslavia and argued passionately the cause of socialism and democracy. *New Left Review* 150, March–April 1985.

22. For Chetniks, Kosovo ws 'the holy place of Serbs'. More recently, at a meeting of the Association of Serb Writers, called for the purpose of severing all relations with the

Association of Writers of Slovenia, its head, a well-known nationalist Matija Becković, stated that Kosovo would be Serb even if not a single Serb lived there.

23. These visits created a tense emotional charge in the capital. 'From the first visits of Kosovo Serbs and Montenegrins to Belgrade, reality began to be dangerously mixed with imagination and myth. Emotionally, people started to feel as if they themselves were living in Kosovo.' Dragiša Pavlović, *Olako obećana brzina*, Ljubljana–Zagreb 1988, p. 90. This book is the most systematic critique of resurgent Serbian nationalism to have appeared to date. It belongs to the best traditions of that Serbian socialism which has provided such a central component of Yugoslav revolutionary thought.

24. For this petition and the subsequent debate between 'Michele Lee' and Mihailo Marković et al., see Part I, Chapter 3, this volume.

25. Zagorka Golubović, Mihailo Marković and Ljubomir Tadić, Part I, Chapter 3(c), this volume.

26. An account of this split is to found in Pavlović, op. cit.

27. Indeed, the liberals lost the first public duel fought over *Student*, the journal of Belgrade undergraduates. In April 1987, *Student* carried a text arguing the existence of a Stalinist group in the University party *aktiv*, naming several of Milošević's close supporters. The *aktiv* replied by launching a public denunciation of *Student* as 'anti-Tito'. Pavlović, head of the Belgrade party, and Branislav Milošević, then Minister of Culture, came in to defend *Student*. The University *aktiv*, supported by *Politika*, under Slobodan Milošević's control, responded by extending the anti-Tito charge to them both.

28. Pavlović recounts how, on joining the Party in 1963, he had to state that he was not religious. 'It took another quarter of a century', he writes, 'for me to have to state that Serbdom was not not my religion either – but this time round I was on the way to being expelled from the Central Committee, from the Belgrade party committee and from the League of Communists of Serbia itself.'

29. Op. cit., p. 36.

30. Its central aspiration is to re-establish the political hegemony Serbia enjoyed in pre-war Yugoslavia, before its cancellation by the revolution.

31. A typical example of the genre is Dragoljub Živojinović and Dejan Lučić, *Barbarizam u ime Krista*, Belgrade 1988. This book accuses the Vatican, the Comintern and the CPY of a joint historic conspiracy ('clerocommunism'), including genocide, against the Serb nation.

32. This judgement, fully shared by the present author, is argued out by Pavlović, op. cit., pp. 280–92. Extracts from the document were published in *Večernje Novosti*, Belgrade, 24–25 September 1986.

33. Similar views were held by the wartime Chetniks and Royal government-in-exile, who insisted that the federal conception of the future state was directed against Serb national interests. See memorandum by Constantin Fotić. Yugoslav Royalist ambassador to the United States, submitted to the founding conference of the United Nations. *Danas*, Zagreb, 28 February 1989.

34. Pavlović condemned the Memorandum for seeing Yugoslavia as an extended Serbia or, alternatively, placing Serbia outside Yugoslavia altogether. The document, he wrote, is the product of 'a primitive, anachronistic and sick Serb consciousness, ignorant and intolerant of Serb diversity. Its understanding of national equality betrays a bureaucratic mentality – it is a moral negation of any true democracy in Yugoslavia' (op. cit., p. 331).

35. Op. cit., p. 312. Pavlović adds: 'If I experienced the speech in this manner, then I can only imagine how this recall of the "fighting spirit" of the Serb and Montenegrin nations must have been experienced by Albanians. After all, Albanians also have ancestors and could also recall their "fighting spirit". They also have a collective consciousness, they also are a warrior nation with their own heroes and a fighting tradition.'

36. Pavlović, op. cit., p. 318. In April of 1986 Stambolić had given quite a different speech at Kosovo Polje: 'Do not allow yourself to be provoked either by the [Albanian] irredentists or by Serb nationalists. People like that are the greatest enemies of our

country. They do not act because they like you – they are playing their own game. They wish to divide and rule. The Serb nationalists in Belgrade are not working so as to make life better for you. Their motto is: the worse off you are, the better it is for their nationalist aims.' *Danas* 8 November 1988.

37. Indeed, non-Yugoslav: claiming that 400,000 immigrants from Albania settled in Kosovo during and after the war, the nationalists have been demanding in effect a large-scale expulsion of Yugoslav Albanians from Yugoslavia.

38. A shortened version of his speech is in *Labour Focus on Eastern Europe*, vol. 9, no. 3, November 1987–February 1988.

39. Ibid., p. 139.

40. Ibid., p. 226.

41. Ibid., p. 228.

42. Ibid., pp. 223–9. Pavlović admits his own responsibility for helping to create an authoritarian atmosphere in the party and republic by not speaking up earlier. Before his expulsion, he was offered a good job if he would resign; but he refused and thus became an object of universal bureaucratic hate in his own republic. Unemployable in Serbia, he finally moved to Slovenia, proving that a Yugoslav can live in exile in his own country.

43. Ibid., pp. 223–9.

44. With the exception of Macedonian: the Macedonian party's anti-Albanian policy has made it the Serbian leadership's natural ally, despite the fact that Serb nationalism also has an anti-Macedonian edge. (Macedonia was once included in the mediaeval Serbian empire, and Macedonians were classified as 'South Serbs' in pre-war Yugoslavia.)

45. As a result, and this must be stressed, these rallies never led to violence.

46. In a recent interview Dušan Dragosavac, a former partisan and member of the political leadership in Croatia, who had been targeted in this way, summed up the situation as follows: 'This is nothing but an anti-communist strategy, the creation of hatred among the nationalities, the creation of discord in the League of Communists. It is a permanent witch-hunt, anti-statutory and lawless.' *Danas*, 13 December 1988. Dragosavac's 'crime' lies in his open hostility to nationalism – compounded by the fact that he is ethnically a Serb.

47. It must have known what was going to happen, for – breaking with normal practice – it failed to send any representative to the meeting of the Vojvodina party committee scheduled for the day of the resignations, thus leaving it to face the demonstrators' wrath alone.

48. The impression was given that it was not worth defending an unpopular leadership. Why then did the party not argue in favour of new elections, in accordance with its statutes?

49. This rare recourse to democracy proved that a considerable number of Serbian members must have voted against him in the secret ballot.

50. *Politika*, Belgrade, 20 November 1988.

51. The late Edvard Kardelj, one of Tito's closest collaborators, was the chief architect of the 1974 constitution.

52. *NIN*, Belgrade, 10 November 1988.

53. The workers were particularly angry at the charge made a few days earlier by the president of the Serbian Trade Union Alliance that 'counter-revolution' was deeply embedded in the Kosovo party and state organs and at Priština University, but above all in the Albanian working class!

54. Its presidency did in fact endorse this view, without consultation with the CC – breaking the party statutes in the process.

55. *Delo*, Ljubljana, 2 March 1989.

56. In a prescient passage Pavlović wrote: 'It is not the aggressive character of Albanian nationalism, nor the appearance of Serb revanchism, nor indeed the emergence of separatist Serb nationalism, that is potentially the most dangerous form of nationalism in Yugoslavia today. It is Serb chauvinist *unitarism* (op. cit., p. 335; my emphasis).

57. The arrests of Azem Vllasi, the managers of the Trepča metallurgical complex, the managers of the Elektrokosovo power plant, the provincial president of the Socialist Youth Alliance and other political and economic leaders of the province on trumped up charges are without precedent in post-war Yugoslavia.

58. To break with this practice would require rejection of the official line that counter-revolution is taking place in Kosovo and lead to a sober and principled re-examination of the status of the Albanian nation in Yugoslavia, of the kind attempted by Branko Horvat in *Kosovo pitanje*, Zagreb 1988.

59. Mladen Zuvela, member of the Croatian party leadership, *NIN*, Belgrade, 25 December 1989.

60. This growing body ranges from people like Koča Popović – a leading partisan general and poet, once Yugoslavia's Foreign Minister, who has publicly condemned nationalism and anti-Albanian revanchism in Serbia – to the recently formed Association for a Yugoslav Democratic Initiative, which has called for Kosovo's status to be determined by a referendum of its inhabitants.

61. It is estimated that 58 per cent of workers in Serbia proper do not earn enough to satisfy their basic needs. *NIN*, Belgrad, 25 December 1988.

62. For the appeal, signed by 215 Kosovo intellectuals, see *Borba*, 23 February 1989.

3

Civil War in Yugoslavia?

The first show trial of a major political figure since that of Milovan Djilas thirty-odd years ago is about to open in Yugoslavia. Driven by its desire to criminalize the Albanian aspiration for national equality in Yugoslavia, but unable to put a whole people on trial, the Serbian bureaucracy – with Federal consent – is instead charging Azem Vllasi, together with several Kosovo workers and managers, with counter-revolution. If condemned, they could face a firing squad. Anything short of their unconditional release will strengthen tendencies towards the country's disintegration.

For about forty years after World War Two, the political consensus in Yugoslavia in regard to the national question was broadly speaking Leninist. It was understood that the state created in 1918 had not been the product of a bourgeois revolution and that the Yugoslav bourgeoisie had been incapable of establishing a parliamentary democracy. The reason for this was sought mainly, though not exclusively, in its inability to solve the national question. The pre-war state had been built on national oppression and could not be maintained without it. Consequently, the revolution that took place in 1941–45 was seen as a fusion of socialist and national-democratic programmes. The new state was organized on a federal basis, with republics acting as the national states of individual South Slav nations, while two autonomous provinces were established to take care of national minorities. This arrangement was the necessary basis for the industrialization of an essentially peasant society and for inaugurating a socialist democratic order.

Whereas the pre-war state never knew a moment of national peace, the postwar federation, and the socialist premise of the new order, stabilized national relations to such an extent that the revolutionary character of the Communists' solution could before long be eased out of the collective memory. The existence of the republics and provinces came to be seen as 'natural' and 'obvious'. Today, a new Right has emerged in Yugoslavia which, because of its commitment to restore capitalism, finds it necessary to uncouple the national question from its socialist content. These critics of Yugoslav socialism argue that the above solution of the national question in Yugoslavia could have been reached through a 'natural' evolution of the bourgeois order. It neither required in the past, nor implies in principle, any commitment to socialism. Whereas before the war a progressive evolution was suspended by the economic and political convulsions in Europe, today it could be safeguarded by Yugoslavia joining the European Community.

The imagined benefits of such membership depend to a large extent on the ideologues' national location. They all hope that the West, by means of direct economic aid or investment, would help to quell potential working-class resistance to capitalist restoration. But whereas the non-Serbs hope that Western love of democracy will prevent a takeover of the Federation by Serbia, their Serbian counterparts are convinced that the West will place its bets on the largest nation, since only Serbia's hegemony in Yugoslavia can guarantee the strong state necessary to keep the workers down.

At the same time, the nationality policy of the LCY is in total disarray, which is not surprising since national equality in Yugoslavia has always depended on the success of the socialist project. These days, however, party officials themselves are declaring that the project has always been a 'utopian' one. The political infrastructure of the country has over the past two years undergone a vast transformation, which, however, remains hidden from the untutored eye, since the outward appearances of the past architecture have been kept in place. Just as the Slav newcomers to Dalmatia used the masonry of Emperor Diocletian's palace to build their own houses, adapting the temple of Jupiter to the new Christian rites, so today also the structures and symbols of socialism are used for wholly different purposes. A formal, that is legislated, return to a full market economy has not stopped vibrant speeches about the central role of the working class; although federalism has gone out of the window, federal party and state organs are still in place; party and state functionaries swear by national equality while openly subverting it; autonomous provinces exist on paper, but function as mere departments of a centralized Serbian state. The survival of these outward shells testifies to the tenacity of the past; but today they serve to uphold an increasingly uneven and contradictory political development which bodes ill for the country's future.

In June 1989 on behalf of *Labour Focus* I talked to two members of the newly established Association for a Yugoslav Democratic Initiative. The text below incorporates substantial parts of that conversation. Pavluško Imširović, a Serb socialist living in Belgrade, was a student leader in 1968, and was subsequently sentenced to two years in prison. In 1982, he was imprisoned once again, this time for two months, for organizing a demonstration against martial law in Poland. In 1985, he was charged, together with five other Belgrade intellectuals, for 'counter-revolutionary activity'. *Labour Focus* took an active part in the ultimately successful international campaign for the release of the Belgrade Six. Shkelzen Maliqi, an Albanian socialist from Priština, was with Imširović in the 1968 student occupation of the University of Belgrade (then renamed 'Karl Marx Red University'). In recent years, more through force of circumstances than from any particular ambition, he has become a prominent spokesman for the Albanian community in Yugoslavia. As a result, he finds himself today on the political blacklist and could easily end up behind bars.

The Pandora's box of the national question in Yugoslavia was opened in 1987 by Slobodan Milošević, then party head of Serbia and today its state president. He was the first to break with the previous rule that political differences must be solved through official channels, i.e. on the basis of an inter-bureaucratic consensus. Milošević's plan to change the country's internal balance of power in favour of Serbia led to the abolition, first *de facto* and then *de jure*, of the constitutional arrangement that granted Yugoslavia's substantial national minorities equal status with the dominant South Slav nations. From now on it will be the Serb majority, vested in the People's Assembly of the Socialist Republic of Serbia, that will decide the exact measure of national rights to be enjoyed by Albanians, Magyars, and others.

This is how Pavluško Imširović summarizes Milošević's grand design. 'At the famous 8th plenum of the Serbian party's central committee, held in November 1987, party leader Slobodan Milošević's militant line won against the more moderate one of the republican president Ivan Stambolić. Milošević summed up his strategic aims in the slogan that Serbia should be constituted like all other republics – a position which would logically entail that the provinces be separated from Serbia and constituted as independent Federal units but which he interpreted in the exactly opposite sense of complete centralization. The winning faction was pressing for a homogenization and consolidation of the apparatus, on the territory of the republic as a whole. The idea was to gain control over the provinces, but to keep their separate representation in the Federation, gaining in that way three automatic votes out of eight at the Federal level. And if Serbia could also win control over Montenegro and bend Macedonia to its will, it would then be in a position to suspend consensual decision-making at the Federal level. This would allow the Serbian bureaucracy to remake the Federation – that is, the apparatus of power at the Federal level – according to its needs and desires.' The maintenance of appearances was thus functional to the changing of reality.

Serbia's unification was ensured in April 1989, when dozens of men, women and children were killed by the Federal police sent into Kosovo to end Albanian national resistance to the removal of the Province's autonomy. The unification was achieved, in fact, through a small-scale civil war, which could be kept small because the Federation had officially sanctioned the change. Milošević achieved Federal compliance by mass mobilization on a nationalist basis. Imsirović describes how this was done: 'For two years mass rallies have been instigated, and usually organized, by the Serbian party and state apparatus. They were well-organized and financed. The participants were given free transport, technical services and even money. Those who appeared as direct organizers – i.e. the members of the Committee for Protest Rallies from Kosovo Polje – were all party members. Some of them are retired high functionaries of the police, pushed into the background and pensioned off after the fall of Ranković. These ex-policemen have apparently become an exceptional pool of cadres for Milošević.'

The provinces were stripped of their reality by an effective coup d'état staged by the Federal apparatus against the Federation, which thereby turned into its opposite, a non-federation, in accordance with the same logic that made provinces non-provinces. According to Imširović, 'the decision made at the Federal level for an armed intervention in Kosovo, which took place with the declaration of a state of emergency last April, was the apparatus's answer to the general strike in Kosovo. With this general strike led by Kosovo miners, the most combative layer of the Albanian working class, this nation tried to defend the modicum of autonomy which it had enjoyed until then. And with this application of military and police force against the general strike in Kosovo, we saw something truly paradoxical. Namely, the armed forces of the state were used against people demonstrating in defence of the existing constitution, the existing state order. In other words, the state broke up demonstrations in defence of the existing, valid constitution. It thus brought down a constitution which inhibited its plans, by using state violence against it.'

The Federal blessing for the violent suspension of the existing constitution was due partly to bureaucratic miscalculation and partly to fear, induced by the Serbian leadership's readiness to resort to civil war. It is worth examining in some detail the process by which reality was turned into appearance, if we are to grasp the danger that the crisis of the bureaucratic order poses today for Yugoslavia's internal peace and stability.

Maliqi describes how the deal between the Serbian and Kosovar bureaucracies was bungled. 'In 1987, the provincial leaderships in Vojvodina and Kosovo found themselves in a dilemma over which current within the Serbian party they should support, particularly as there was no obvious difference between the two in regard to the push for Serbia's unification. They feared Stambolić more than Milošević, since they considered him a more capable and competent politician. Milošević was an unknown individual widely perceived as simply a careerist. The Stambolić–Milošević split was seen basically as a battle for power within Serbia proper. Miloševic also let it be known that he was ready to reach a compromise with the provinces and the Federation. However, in the course of the summer of 1987, when the Serb nationalist movement in Kosovo and Serbia became more radical and Milošević threw his weight behind it, Azem Vllasi, the head of the Kosovo party, started to move closer to Stambolić. Although at the 8th Plenum of the Serbian CC he did not speak publicly and the Kosovo representatives abstained from voting, Vllasi did speak at the closed session in defence of Pavlović and his view that Serb nationalism was becoming dangerous. The trouble was that even at this time the Kosovo leadership did not take the differences between Stambolić and Milošević very seriously. They supported the positions of Stambolić and Pavlović, but did nothing to save them, because they thought they would be able to handle Milošević more easily than Stambolić.'

The brutal purge of Stambolić and his supporters following this plenum provoked considerable consternation among reform-minded members of the Federal CC, the one body with the authority to intervene in the affairs of the Serbian party. But, according to Maliqi, 'it actually seems to have been the provincial leaderships who blocked an attempt in the Federal CC to investigate the manner in which the Stambolić forces had been routed in Serbia. The Slovene party leadership raised this question, but the provinces – who at that time still believed in their deal with Milošević – said that this was unnecessary. At this point in time the official procedures for changing the Serbian constitution had just begun and it seemed that concessions were going to be made to the provinces. It was believed that a behind-the-scenes compromise would be stuck to, whereby the Republic would be more closely involved in provincial politics, but the provinces would retain the lion's share of their autonomy. This was their big mistake.'

The Serbian leaders kept up the momentum. At the end of October 1988, the Vojvodina leadership was overthrown by a Belgrade-inspired mobilization of ethnic Serbs and Montenegrins living there. This was done in order to put pressure on the Federal party, which was due to meet that month. Maliqi again: 'Soon after the fall of the Vojvodina leadership, the 17th session of the CC LCY took place, at which the Federal party and state leaderships lined up behind Serbia. The nationalist movement in Serbia had by then grown so strong that it was impossible for the Federal leaders to influence it by recourse to their party authority. They therefore sanctioned Serbia's proposed constitutional changes. Although they were aware of the possibility of mass resistance in Kosovo, they were much more frightened by what was already happening in Serbia. They gave their agreement under the influence of the Serbian mass movement, which involved hundreds of thousands of people. Kosovo, after all, is far weaker and easier to control. Serbs are more numerous and their distribution across Yugoslavia means that the country could not withstand a mass Serb revolt. The Kosovo Albanians, on the other hand, live in a province whose powers are limited, and which can put forward its demands only at the Federal level. The Serbian leadership immediately demanded Vllasi's political elimination, because he was seen as a dangerous individual, as somebody who now symbolized Kosovo autonomy. There was no longer any place for Vllasi on the CC LCY and he was soon forced to resign.'

By resorting to mass mobilization, the Serbian party leadership got its way, wiping out in the process the remnants of the authority of the Federal party, which had provided the political backbone of the Yugoslav state since 1945. The CC of the League of Communists made one last attempt to act as an all-Yugoslav authority. In Maliqi's words: 'After the session, the Federal party leadership got in touch with the Kosovo leadership and the head of the Federal party, Stipe Šuvar (a cadre from Croatia), arranged for a common meeting of the Provincial and Federal central committees. Šuvar thought that the Federation should have the final say. This was the Croatian idea – that the Federation not Serbia should decide what should happen in Kosovo. Šuvar's plan was that some of the Kosovo leaders should resign in return for Federal intercession, but the Kosovo leadership refused to comply.'

What were the reasons behind this apparently suicidal intransigence on the part of the Provincial leadership? The plain truth is that they did not trust the head of the Federal party. Šuvar had gained his leading position with Serbia's support and the Federal party under his direction had sanctioned the illegal overthrow of the Vojvodina leadership. What is more, 'at its 17th session the CC had directed a public warning to the Kosovo party – an unprecedented act – criticizing it for having conducted a wrong policy in Kosovo. The Albanian leadership was offered no concrete alternative by the Federal leadership. The meeting of the Federal and Provincial leaderships was in any case aborted, since Milošević refused to come. He refused to accept Federal involvement, taking the position that Kosovo was an internal Serbian affair. The Federal CC's open condemnation of its Kosovo members strengthened Serbia's hand, giving it the opportunity to insist on what amounted to a total purge of the Kosovo party. Serbia demanded the resignations of Vllasi, the new provincial party chief Kaqusha Jashari, and some others. In fact, they sought as many resignations as possible.' The last vestige of the Federal party's authority collapsed finally when, a few months later and against its will, the Montenegrin leadership was overthrown with Serbia's support by a younger generation of functionaries. The new Montenegrin leadership has pinned its hopes on becoming a junior partner to the Serbian 'big brother' in Milošević's New Order. Since the Montenegrin economy is in a state of total collapse and the new leadership has few ideas on what remedy to apply, its plan is to integrate Montenegro's economy with Serbia's. On Federal issues, also, Montenegro has lost its previous independence. Thus by the beginning of 1989 Serbia had acquired control of four votes in the Federation. What is more, the party purges which followed in Vojvodina, Kosovo and Montenegro changed the composition of the Federal CC in Serbia's favour, choking off all possibility of an effective challenge being mounted from within the Federal party. The Federal party ceased to exist in anything but name. The outward shell was there, but the substance had gone. This success could only embolden the Serbian bureaucracy to further action. Although it controlled only four out of eight votes, it felt confident that on certain issues it could also count on Macedonia.

The Flight to Nationalism

This tectonic shift within Yugoslav politics encouraged the local bureaucracies to embed themselves even deeper into their national constituencies and in general fanned nationalism throughout the country. In June 1989 Macedonia followed in the footsteps of Serbia by voting to remove from its constitution any mention of its Albanian and Turkish minorities. Such a Macedonia is ready to support fully Serbia's policy with regard to the provinces and also with regard to internal democratization, against Croatia and Slovenia, since these latter two republics have been highly critical of certain aspects of Macedonian internal policy. The sorry state of Macedonia's economy, however, is likely to result in the replacement of the current leadership by a younger and more impatient generation, coming from the youth organization. (A challenge from the party organization within the ministry of the interior was defeated only last September.) The Macedonian Young Turks have as few ideas as their elders about how to achieve the miracle of an economic turnabout; but they see the removal of the current office holders as the necessary precondition. What is more, the Macedonians harbour bitter experience of pre-war attempts to turn them into Serbs, and the new leaders are likely to be far less supportive of Milošević than the current ones.

Slovenia has responded to this danger 'from the East' by increasing as much as possible the distance between itself and the Federation. Throughout 1988 Serbia, aided by conservative forces within the Federal leadership, invested considerable energy in an attempt to discredit and ultimately unseat the liberal Slovene leadership. Its strategy, pivoted on encouraging a conflict between Slovenia and the Army, culminated in the trial of the Ljubljana Four; this, however, backfired since the trial provided the occasion for the Slovene people as a whole to rally behind the Republican leadership in defence of Slovene sovereignty. This national mobilization set off the process which, in September 1989, led the Slovene Assembly to adopt a constitution affirming the Republic's right to secession and establishing the local state as fully sovereign. The new constitution explicitly denies the right of the Federation to impose a state of emergency without the approval of the local Assembly. At Serbia's insistence, this move was condemned by the Federal Presidency as 'unconstitutional' and 'separatist'. The Federal bureaucracy also voiced its concern at the more liberal provisions in the Slovene constitution for individual citizen's rights, at the removal from it of the leading role of the party, and at the acceptance in principle that Slovenia's small but numerous political parties and groupings would be allowed to contest the forthcoming elections (spring 1990). Its gradual but constant broadening of internal democracy and its resolute stand on the question of national sovereignty have given the Slovene party a mass support without which it would not be able to stand up to Federal interference.

Understandable as the Slovene move may be, it remains wholly within the logic of the fragmentation of the Yugoslav federation. The Slovene leadership has argued that Serbia's criticism is wholly unwarranted, since Slovenia had not interfered in Serbia's own constitutional labours. Defending the slogan of 'All power to the republics!', in the spring of 1989 the Slovene party leaders invited their Serbian counterparts to discuss points of difference. This initiative failed, since Belgrade imposed conditions so stiff that they would have amounted to Slovene surrender. What was demanded was full support for Serbia's policy in Kosovo. And although the Slovene leadership had already in effect provided a great deal of support by voting in favour of a host of Federal party and state measures (including the introduction of the state of emergency into Kosovo without which Serbia's unification would not have been possible), it could not publicly agree to this demand. For Kosovo was by now no longer, so to speak, a foreign policy issue, but had become a crucial dimension of Slovenia's internal politics. When, in March 1989, troops were sent to Kosovo in response to the Trepča miners' strike, the Slovene party was moved (under pressure from its own miners among others) to sign the so-called Ljubljana Declaration, together with all other, official and oppositional, political organizations in Slovenia, protesting against the state of emergency in the name of national equality. It was repudiation of this act that Belgrade was demanding, knowing full well that the Slovene party could not comply without isolating itself from its popular base.

Mass mobilizations in Kosovo and Slovenia proved to be an effective instrument for narrowing the space for bureaucratic manoeuvre and thus limiting the damage caused by bureaucratic *Realpolitik*. It is obvious, nevertheless, that the same process which led to the loss of Kosovo's autonomy has resulted in the enhanced autonomy of Slovenia. How is this to be explained? One part of the explanation lies in a tacit agreement by the republican leaderships, reached at the end of last year, to uncouple the question of the status of Yugoslavia's national minorities (in effect, the provinces) from that of the South Slav nations (i.e. the republics). This measure was justified on the grounds that Serbia should have control over its own republican state machine in the same measure as such control was exercised by Slovenia, Macedonia, Croatia, etc. But the idea that strong national republics would guarantee national equality has, in reality, turned into its opposite. By conceding Serbia's right to swallow the provinces, the republican leaderships have dealt the Federation what may prove to be the terminal blow. The weakening of Federal authority has in turn increased national insecurity.

Today all Yugoslavia's nationalities, Slav and non-Slav alike, have grown more insecure and civil war has become more likely rather than less. Slovenia's erection of constitutional barriers may prevent Federal (i.e. Serbian) interference, but is no substitute for a positive programme for the republic's role in the Federation. The Montenegrin nationality feels itself today in acute danger from Serbianization (the recent grotesque spectacle involving the return of the bones of Montenegro's last king and queen for reburial in 'the homeland' will not assuage it!). The same can be said for the Macedonian. At the same time, nationalist mobilization in Serbia has exposed Serbs living in other republics (not to speak of Kosovo!) to national revanchist reactions from the locally preponderant nations.

Bosnia-Herzegovina – the land that plays the thankless role of a buffer zone between Croatia and Serbia – has been a state of turmoil for the last three years. This republic, with its mixed population (45 per cent Moslem, 31 per cent Serb, 17 per Croat), was immobilized by the great 'Agro-komerc' scandal of 1987, partly instigated from Belgrade, which in the space of a few months removed its long-standing leadership without replacing it with any durable new combination. The stability of this republic has rested traditionally on its strict 'Yugoslav' orientation, which today – in the massive restructuring of the international balance of power – is ceasing to provide a firm foundation. In an attempt to alter its neutral stance, Belgrade has been encouraging Serb-inhabited communes to reject the authority of Sarajevo and proclaim their loyalty to Serbia. There are signs that Belgrade is also planning a campaign to revive memories of the ancient Christian–Moslem conflict, in which the struggle against an alleged 'Moslem fundamentalism' supposedly at work in Bosnia would play a central role. Bosnia-Herzegovina, however, will not bend so easily:

the departure of the old leadership has opened the door to a crop of younger and better educated politicians, many of them of Moslem origin, who are determined to maintain the national status quo in Bosnia and Yugoslavia. Moreover, if republican politics were to split along national-religious lines, it is likely that the traditional coalition of Moslems and Catholic Croats would again spring into being, isolating the Orthodox Serbs.

This is why the Serbian leadership is now turning its attention to Croatia, the republic which has always held the balance of power in Yugoslavia. The target is its supposed soft underbelly, the Serb population of Croatia (11 per cent of the republican total), which — as in Bosnia-Herzegovina — is being pushed into the unhappy role of champions of the New Order. This role Croatian Serbs seem not at all keen to assume, since they are well integrated into the Republic's political and economic life. The attack 'from the East' on Croatia has been two-pronged: in addition to raising the Serb question in Croatia, the validity of Croatia's borders — both internal and with regard to Italy — are currently being contested by reference to the London Treaty of 1915! Croatia's lacklustre and divided leadership, constituted after the great 1972 purge of the Croatian party on the grounds of nationalism, has shown itself neither able nor willing to play the national and democratic card on the Slovene model. It has tried to avoid taking sides, preferring instead to speak of a 'Yugoslav synthesis'. Serbia's recent offensive in Croatia, however, has raised the national temperature. More out of fear than desire, Croat politicians appear increasingly ready to fight the mounting menace to the Republic's national sovereignty and territorial integrity. An inner-party struggle has been unleashed whose outcome will determine also just how fast Croat nationalism will grow in the forthcoming period. The signs of its revival are already there, so that Serbs in Croatia might all too easily become an embattled nationality in turn.

Once Federal support was withdrawn, Albanian national and democratic rights could be curtailed. Yet the withdrawal of this support need not have provoked quite such an outcome in Kosovo — nothing like that happened, after all, in Slovenia — had not another factor come into play: namely, Kosovo's great poverty.

In this respect, Kosovo occupies a unique place in the Federation. Nowhere else are the economy, the administration and the welfare state so heavily subsidized by the Federation. This relation of dependence has limited the standing of the Kosovo bureaucracy in the eyes of the Albanian masses, and blocked progress towards the modicum of democracy achieved elsewhere in Yugoslavia. The local bureaucracy, in its efforts to safeguard Albanian national rights in Yugoslavia, has been reduced to playing on differences between the republics, or on tensions between the

Federal party and its Serbian wing. Jealous of its privileges, within Kosovo itself it imposed strict limits on all autonomous thought and action. Only when it realized, in late 1988, that Serbia had succeeded in removing its Federal protection, did the Albanian bureaucracy turn for support to the people which it claimed to represent. But Vllasi's hurried attempts to fill the local party-state with his own people had hardly got off the ground before the Federal army and police moved in.

By this time the Albanian population, under working-class leadership, was already on the move. The local bureaucracy responded by opening the mass media, but this gesture was too little and too late. This is how Maliqi explains what happened: 'The mobilization of the Albanian masses started before the 17th session of the Federal CC. It coincided with the public debate about the constitution. The debate in Kosovo started on 10 October 1988 – in fact very late (i.e. after it became clear that Belgrade would not respect the deal it had made). The public was presented with drafts of the proposed Federal, Republican and Provincial constitutional amendments. It was then that the Albanian people spoke up. It became clear that the Albanian nation was against the constitutional changes proposed by Serbia. By this time the government in Vojvodina had already fallen and there was this terrific pressure coming from Serbia. This broke the psychological barrier of silence. People up to then had said little, but now a space appeared. The media were now quite open (which does not mean that one could say whatever one wished), because Vllasi and Jashari realized that this was their only line of defence. Two sets of constitutional amendments were debated: one proposed by Serbia and one by Kosovo. (Vojvodina too had had amendments which were practically identical to the Kosovo ones, but after the fall its government it renounced this earlier stance.) The two sets differed on issues relating to the key institutions of the state – such as the judiciary, the police, territorial defence, international relations and planning. The Serbian party had criticized its Kosovo counterpart for not declaring itself in favour of the Serbian constitutional amendments, which it said the Kosovo party should have done in accordance with democratic centralism. Vllasi's (new) position was that this was a matter for the people and not for the party. He insisted on observing the constitutional rule that changes in the constitution are decided by the will of the citizens. The debate in Kosovo was public. It was organized at the level of the communes by the competent body, the Socialist Alliance. Each socio-political organization, each professional organization (such as the Association of Writers, or of Philosophers, etc.), had also to take a position. In other words, the correct constitutional procedure was honoured. And the Socialist Alliance had to report that practically every commune was against the constitutional changes demanded by Serbia. The people gave its support to the Provincial amendments. Serbia at this point instigated a terrific pressure for the leading Kosovo representatives to resign. This provoked tremendous resistance in the Provincial party committee, so that its meeting – which was to decide on the purges – was postponed several times. Some people resigned in advance.'

What emerges from this account is that the political institutions provided by the existing constitution were perfectly able to express the popular will. The Serbian leadership's challenge to the constitutional procedure on the grounds of 'democratic centralism' – the Kosovo party being an integral part of the Serbian LC – was a wholly cynical exercise, since the Serbian party is itself an integral part of the all-Yugoslav party, which up to that point had not supported Serbia's amendments. However, as we have seen from the above account of the 17th session of the CC, the Federal party leadership had no stomach to defend the existing constitution. The time for bureaucratic manoeuvres was up, but manoeuvring was all that this leadership was capable of. Yet the Federal leadership includes Slovene, Croatian and Bosnian representatives, i.e. representatives from the three Yugoslav republics which do not approve anti-Albanian politics. How is one to explain their going along with the Serbian constitutional changes? An answer that relies solely on the fear induced by Serbia's mass mobilization is by no means sufficient. An explanation must be sought also in the economic domain: to endorse Albanian mass resistance would have involved taking responsibility for Kosovo's economic problems. Slovenia and Croatia were not willing to do that, Bosnia could not. The understanding that it would not be possible to sustain Yugoslavia's federal order without a consistent commitment to more even economic development – a position from which the Federal party has been retreating throughout the 1980s – proved to be accurate. Kosovo's economic weakness (and a similar logic can be seen at work also in Montenegro and Macedonia) has played a crucial role in Yugoslavia's growing instability. The chain of national equality snapped at its weakest link, endangering the democratic prospects for each and every Yugoslav nationality. The iron rule (that one finds operating already in the Habsburg Monarchy) which ordains that the national question in a multinational state can be solved only in a comprehensive manner – socially, economically and politically – in the late 1980s came into operation in Yugoslavia in all its destructiveness.

The positive side of this regressive movement was the emergence of autonomous popular action. According to Maliqi: 'When it became clear that the Serbian leadership was going ahead brazenly and without any scruple, and that its aim was to eliminate Vllasi, the day that the meeting was finally scheduled the miners of Trepča met and said that enough was enough. Saying that they should be consulted as well, they made a protest march to Priština. They were followed by others. That evening there was a meeting of the Provincial party committee, attended by representatives of Serbia who insisted that Vllasi, Jashari and others had to go. This caused an explosion the following day. Several hundred thousand men, women and children marched from different parts of Kosovo to Priština, braving snow and sleet, some marching for more than ten hours. The demonstrations lasted 4–5 days. They were completely peaceful. The basic rule of behaviour was imposed by the miners of Trepča, who came out with clear slogans. They hailed Tito, the party and the Federal party leader Šuvar, and refused to surrender Vllasi and Jashari. And when these people did resign, the miners demanded that the resignations be revoked. One of their key demands was that the 1974 constitution be left in place, at least as far as its basic principles were concerned.'

It is worth recalling at this point that Trepča miners had always formed the backbone of the working-class membership of the Communist Party in Kosovo. They continued to support traditional party policy on the national question, even after the party had abandoned it. Such was the strength of this idea that action could be mounted without any formal organization, and with a force that delivered a deadly blow to Milošević's plan for a peaceful imposition of Serbian 'unity'. Maliqi confirms that 'there were no formal autonomous organizations of the miners or the working class. No special committees. It was a question of the general mood. It was enough for someone to make a move and everybody would follow. The first to move were the workers and they were later joined by the [Kosovo] leadership. The November demonstrations had a big impact, undermining Milošević's whole project. His demands for constitutional changes became illegitimate in Kosovo. The Serbian leadership immediately proclaimed the demonstrations to be an act hostile to Yugoslavia – a counter-revolution – and tried to impose this view upon the Provincial party committee. The idea was to criminalize the workers' action. However, this did not go through. For two months a battle was waged around the assessment of the November demonstrations. A veritable underground struggle was also taking place within the all-Yugoslav leadership. Here again, Serbia insisted that its position should become the official position of the Federal party. In the meantime the Serbian party tried to bring its own people – people who did not even stand publicly as candidates – onto the Kosovo leadership. In this way Rahman Morina emerged as the Provincial party secretary. Serbia insisted that Vllasi be expelled from the CC LCY, and this indeed happened at the CC meeting held at the end of January 1989. This provoked an immediate revolt in Trepča. In other factories protest meetings also took place, to cancel the imposed resignations and reject the Serbian assessment of the character of the November demonstrations. The miners demanded that Šuvar and

Milošević come to talk to them, which both refused to do. The new, imposed leadership of the Province then produced its own position, which was even more condemnatory than the Serbian one. It was this, in particular, that enraged the miners. They now had no legitimate means to express their disagreement. The drive for adoption of the constitutional changes reached its peak at this time, which further electrified the atmosphere. This is why the miners decided to go down into the pits and not come out until their demands were met. The bottom line was that the three Serbian-imposed officials – Morina, Azemi and Shukria – should resign.'

The decision of Vllasi and his supporters to open up the media was of decisive importance. 'The Trepča miners formulated ten demands and the others simply solidarised with them. The miners' demands were transmitted through the media, which now became completely open. The local press also reported support from other parts of the country, from Croatia and Slovenia. In fact, this time workers in other factories started to move a week before the miners began their underground strike. In some factories, in the middle of February the workers started to reject lunch – they would come into the canteen, walk through and throw down their empty trays as a sign of their dissatisfaction. This kind of action spread and culminated in a general strike. The central demand was the three resignations, but some worker party members also condemned Milošević's policies and demanded his resignation.' Mass action pulled in the local party organizations. According to Maliqi, 'they were instructed to oppose the workers' action but as a rule refused to obey. After a few days, some party secretaries solidarized with the miners and demanded that at least the three should resign. The first step was made by the youth organization, then others followed. Factory party organizations, in particular, threatened collective resignations from the LC.' The Kosovo party split along national lines, with Serbs and Montenegrins insisting that Serbian demands should be unconditionally accepted, while 99 per cent of Albanians were against this. It was, in fact, a total collapse of the party in Kosovo.

The Yugoslav leadership was faced with a clear choice. One response, as the Ljubljana Declaration argued, would have been to respect legal norms and, with them, the will of the Albanian people. The other choice, supported by Milošević, was to change the constitution by force. Having accepted Serbian constitutional amendments, however, the Federal leadership could not but opt for the latter. It decided to put down the general strike by force but, to minimize bloodshed, only after the miners had come out. To get them out, the Federal party got the three Kosovo officials to resign. Maliqi describes what happened next: 'A big protest rally was immediately organized in Belgrade, which became a kind of occupation of the Federal Assembly. The Federal leaders, it seems, feared that the situation in Serbia would get out of control and provoke a civil war. The rally in Belgrade came up with quite radical demands, including the wholesale resignation of the Federal leadership and in particular the party leader Šuvar. This was rejected, but in return the decision to impose a state of emergency in Kosovo was announced. When, at about 10 o'clock in the evening, Milošević appeared before the crowd, there was little he could throw to them. So, when a group at the front started to chant: "Arrest Vllasi!", he gave his word that there would be arrests. The following day Vllasi was arrested, on the pretext that he had visited the striking miners in Trepča.'

The state of emergency imposed in Kosovo broke the back of the workers' action. This opened the way for legalization of the constitutional *coup d'état*. In Maliqi's opinion, 'Vllasi's arrest was linked to the impending vote in the Kosovo assembly. The idea was to intimidate the Kosovo leadership and the assembly delegates. For, along with Vllasi, the managers of all the larger enterprises were arrested, including those of Trepča and other mines, and in this way an atmosphere of fear was created. The army moved in and occupied all strategic points and special police units were also sent in. The constitution was to be voted in at the end of March, so at first a state of emergency was not formally proclaimed, but instead something called a "state of exception", in order to avoid the situation in which a new constitution would be adopted under military rule. All the same, in the Province expectations were high that the assembly would vote against the changes, all the more since only a short while before it had voted in favour of Kosovo's own, quite different amendments. These hopes were disappointed. As soon as the Serbian constitution had been formally voted in, the state of emergency was announced and mass arrests began.'

This action by the Federal state removal the last vestiges of the legitimacy of the postwar order. Never before had the constitution been violated so fully, national rights taken away so brazenly, the working class repressed so openly. The Federal state invoked wartime measures. According to Maliqi, 'there were several attempts in Trepča to continue the struggle, but then the militarization of labour was introduced – i.e. workers were obliged to return to work as if it were a war situation. Each worker was sent an order to report to work, and anyone who refused to obey was either sacked or arrested. This is how the general strike was broken. Immediately after the Serbian constitution was adopted by the Provincial assembly, students and other citizens started to protest. Four days later, the Serbian assembly voted in the new constitution in a celebratory mood. In Kosovo this caused demonstrations in several places. But whereas before it had been workers who gave the lead, the workers were now silenced and as a result the revolt was more disorganized.

Demonstrators were drawn in the main from the poor quarters of the cities, from the shanty districts of Priština and from towns like Podujevo and Suva Reka, where there is a lot of poverty. The demonstrations involved the poorer section of the population and the educated layers did not join them, which is why they took a more extreme form. The conviction grew that the intelligentsia had betrayed the people. It was an act of desperation. And it must be remembered that the repression this time round was quite severe. There was shooting. Although a few of the demonstrators were armed, the majority just used stones. The police used firepower and many people died, many of whom were not even on the demonstrations. Some were shot down at bus stations, others on the road.'

The League of Communists had sanctioned what amounted to a fratricidal war. As Maliqi says, 'the units sent to Kosovo were not prepared for what happened. Some of them, especially the reservists from Serbia, were quite scared. At times they fired uncontrollably. It is said, but I have no means of knowing for sure, that units from Slovenia and Croatia refused to shoot. There were also clashes between local Albanian police and units from outside: in Uroševac, where the first mass demonstrations took place, women with children marched first and when a unit from Macedonia started to club them, it seems the Albanian police intervened to protect them.'

An ugly new Yugoslavia was born from the Kosovo bloodshed. The Federal state's show of force sent a clear warning to all nationalities. In Slovenia, as we have seen, the result was a constitution giving the Republic virtual independence. Everywhere the lines of national divide were now drawn more sharply. The state of emergency in Kosovo has not yet been lifted and is likely to become permanent, since the Serbian bureaucracy has in fact lost any political instruments for controlling Kosovo.

In Kosovo, for the first time since the war we have seen Yugoslav workers lead a popular movement on a democratic programme. The collapse of the Kosovo party-state – the structure which was meant to safeguard Albanian national rights – did not prevent an organized resistance to the bureaucratic *putsch*. Yugoslavia's revolutionary legacy was simply repossessed by the workers. The survival of the country today, as in the past, depends not so much on the existing state institutions as on popular democratic action. Maliqi and Imširović are both convinced of this. In Maliqi's words, 'the workers were the vanguard of the national-democratic movement in Kosovo and the factories will once again become centres of resistance – if not open, then at least passive resistance. They will wait for the moment to organize themselves, perhaps by forming independent trade unions or some parallel secret organization. The workers have this self-discipline, they are an organized force and one conscious of its power, and they will not undertake adventurist steps of a kind that will only provoke repression. They, and a section of the intelligentsia, place their hope in the process of democratization in Yugoslavia; in that context, they will seek legal channels to achieve the return of a normal situation in Kosovo.'

The main opposition to the process of democratization lies in the coalition between the new right and sections of the party-state apparatus. Such coalitions are emerging in all the republics and express local specificities. The Milošević phenomenon may seem extreme and untypical but in reality it is paradigmatic of the new order now emerging in Yugoslavia. This is Imširović's assessment: 'Milošević emerged as a man who allowed national self-expression, who cancelled certain taboos, who related favourably to Orthodoxy and its institutions. All that noisy clamour about the 1389 Battle of Kosovo, about the role of the Orthodox religion in preserving Serb cultural traditions, represents not just Milošević's flirtation but his open alliance with the Orthodox church, Serb nationalism and Serb chauvinism. For since his arrival in power there is no longer any mention of Serb chauvinism Since the 8th Plenum Serb nationalism has been promoted to a state-building Yugoslav force; to a mild, harmless phenomenon which can only be positive. But this is a nationalism summoned up to help preserve the power of one fraction of the Yugoslav apparatus, which as a whole is riven by fractional struggles.'

'Milošević's social basis – the forces on which he relied to get rid of Stambolić's fraction and repressively consolidate the apparatus of power – are provincial party functionaries, in other words, the middle and lower ranks of the party apparatus. Milošević was able first to win over regional party committees and then to make an assault on the Belgrade party, the largest party organization in the country, which under Dragiša Pavlović was a Stambolić bastion. After Pavlović's departure, the Belgrade party was thoroughly purged. The purge was made easier, given a certain cadre basis which Milošević had established during his own time at the head of the Belgrade party, and which he used in his onslaught. Milošević, after his victory, replaced those purged with a group of *arrivistes*, primitive careerists, who have no moral or political scruples and who are highly unpopular. The other important layer of support for Milošević is the rising entrepreneurial class in Serbia. We are told daily that the Albanian people's desire for autonomy or a republic is counter-revolutionary, yet at the same time you can see people on Belgrade television arguing openly in favour of capitalist restoration in Yugoslavia. The demands raised by the Albanian masses have never questioned the social character of ownership or the achievements of the revolution – such socialist achievements as have survived over the past forty-odd years. We have never heard from the Albanians a demand for the re-privatization of social ownership. But we have heard such demands come from precisely those social layers and political groupings that support Milošević. At the time of the military intervention in Kosovo, in March 1989, there was an interview with a well-known entrepreneur from Kosovo, one of the Karić [ethnically Serb] brothers, who – as a successful businessman – spoke warmly, indeed passionately, in favour of reprivatization of the means of production in Yugoslavia. And nobody dreamed of stopping him or calling this by its right name: the programme of counter-revolutionary restoration of capitalism.'

Imširović, however, does not think that Milošević's support in the Serbian masses is very solid: 'His influence on the Serbian masses is highly overestimated. This is proved by the fact that the first thing he did was to purge all the media, placing them under tight party control. In Serbia today, there is practically no organ that can write critically. All editorial boards have been purged and critical journalists sacked. He has made the press speak with one voice. A person confident of his legitimacy could have allowed at least a mildly critical paper, such as a student paper with its small print-run. But Milošević is well aware that the appearance of any other political alternative would soon bring him into question, since it would expose how weak his influence in the masses really is. Observers from outside frequently identify his influence in the masses with his control of the media. And when one reads the Belgrade press, one gets the impression that Milošević is a charismatic personality. Posters bearing his face are printed in large numbers, there is no illustrated journal without his photograph. We can speak of a kind of renaissance of the cult of personality.'

This is not to say that the nationalist appeal of Milošević's project has not found a resonance in the Serbian masses. 'With his chauvinist hullabaloo, Milošević has succeeded in temporarily slowing down political mobilization in Serbia, in confusing the masses and in exporting their dissatisfaction, by turning the existing social tensions against an imaginary outside enemy. Today his enemy is the Albanians, tomorrow it will be the Slovenes, the Croats, the Moslems, etc. – indeed anybody who resists him. The rapid growth in the number of strikes and the broadening of workers' demands suggest that he does not have much time to implement his programme of gaining power at the all-Yugoslav level and consolidating the Yugoslav bureaucracy; that he must move very fast, conquering one Federal unit after another, in order to confront the masses with a strong apparatus of repression. All the individual republican and provincial apparatuses are in crisis. Milošević's aim is to consolidate the bureaucratic structure of power. And the final aim is a confrontation with the masses, to put a stop to their political development. This is why he and his supporters have fought so hard over the last year for the convocation of an extraordinary party congress, which will now take place in January 1990. The idea is to achieve a numerical majority there and then proceed to a wide purge of the party apparatus in the other Federal units. Whether he will succeed remains to be seen. But if he does, then we can expect a rapid purge of the party apparatuses in Slovenia and Croatia and their "normalization" around the programme of the Serbian bureaucracy. This means purges, the consolidation of power by purely repressive measures, the shutting up of intellectuals and workers. Re-centralization would consolidate the power of the Yugoslav bureaucracy as a whole.'

Milošević's success involves the return of a state based on national repression, albeit in the guise of Yugoslav unity. How easy will it be to reconcile this with the emergence of the local parties as national champions? According to Imširović, 'we are witnessing a notable confusion in the Yugoslav bureaucracy. At times they resist Milošević, while simultaneously they seem to be retreating step by step. We are dealing with a struggle between several factions. There are differences between them, but also a readiness to capitulate. Fractions are formed on the principle of loyalty to the local apparatus – or the dominant current within it – not to the people, to the class, to the achievements of the revolution. This can best be illustrated by the case of Šuvar. Šuvar stood up to Milošević at the 17th Party Plenum and defended a Yugoslavia based on national equality in the same way that Chamberlain stood up to Hitler and defended Europe in 1938 – retreating step by step and encouraging his adversary's appetite. Šuvar is evidently more afraid of mass mobilization in Croatia than he is of Milošević. With Milošević he will always find a common language. It is true that his faction is the bearer of an alternative strategic option. But at the moment when he had a chance to gain undoubted support in Croatia, at the moment when a mass wave of solidarity with the Kosovo miners welled up in Croatia, Šuvar retreated cravenly, because he was frightened of this quite different but far more effective kind of resistance to Milošević. Instead, together with other Yugoslav functionaries, he gave his blessing to military rule in Kosovo.'

'One cannot have much hope that this or that part of the apparatus, this or that local bureaucracy, will put up a decisive resistance to Milošević. Although the Slovene party signed the Ljubljana Declaration, it has done so little to realize its political programme that one wonders whether this is indeed the line of the Slovene party. The signature of the liberal wing of the Slovene party was a means to legitimize it in the eyes of the Slovene masses, nothing more. All these years, the Slovene liberals have failed to take their programme for a democratic transformation to the masses in other republics, to look for allies or mobilize outside Slovenia. This is the best proof of how seriously they take their programme. It seems they are hesitating between the hope that they may yet find a common ground with Milošević and the fear that the latter will purge them all and replace them with what the Slovene youth press ironically describes as 'healthy forces', i.e. orthodox Stalinists.'

In Imširović's view, 'the fateful and decisive force in Yugoslavia has not yet made its will known, has not mounted the political stage in all its power. The working class is still searching for adequate forms of struggle, its own form of intervention in the conflict of the various factions. It is ready, as has been shown in Kosovo, to give support to its own national bureaucracy at a time when the latter is defending what is in its interest. But it is not willing to play the role of cannon fodder in inter-bureaucratic quarrels. Šuvar is aware of this, which is why he was not brave enough to mobilize Croatian workers to resist Milošević. The wave of solidarity in Croatia and Slovenia was a real blow at the foundations of the anti-Albanian South Slav coalition and an inspiration for the development of a democratic federation based on national equality. Such a federation, naturally, must be based on self-determination, including the right to secession. Without voluntary adhesion to the federal community, there is no equality in decision-making within it.'

Since this conversation took place, Slovenia has adopted a constitution which should lead to relatively free elections in the republic in the coming spring and possible loss of power by the local party. The Federal party and state bodies have condemned this act, but – short of the Yugoslav army taking direct power in the country as a whole – they no longer have the authority or the means to reverse it. The outcome of the struggle at the Federal level will have fateful implications for all Yugoslavs. According to Maliqi, 'in Kosovo, the people are ready to act, but right now everybody is waiting for the outcome of the struggle for power in Yugoslavia as a whole. Slovenia, and to some extent Croatia, have a quite different concept of how the Federation should work from the one held by the current leadership in Serbia. The difference is of a principled nature, the two concepts are mutually exclusive and cannot coexist. The Albanians support the former model, because it allows for a democratic expression of popular will. In the Albanian masses, as I have said, there is a general will to resist, but at present there is no means of coordinating this. They are ready to intervene massively on the key questions regarding the constitution of the Federation. But if such a struggle were to fail, then we would face a permanent and violent repression. There is a plan for a fresh colonization of Kosovo, to "correct" the ethnic structure in favour of Serbs. That such a plan exists is only confirmed by all the talk in Serbia today about the "genocide" against Serbs which has allegedly been conducted by Albanians over the past 300-odd years! In fact, when Kosovo was incorporated into Serbia at the end of the Balkan Wars, already three-quarters if not more of its population was Albanian. Since then, there have been three attempts to "correct" this percentage, but they have all failed to a greater or lesser degree. Today, it is even more difficult to imagine how this would work. But it is nevertheless being proposed. The idea is that Serbs would be brought in, while Albanians would be resettled throughout Yugoslavia – and some encouraged to leave the country altogether. There is an even more radical plan, which relies on an eventual civil war in Yugoslavia to expel as many Albanians as possible to Albania. There is also a third option, according to which the Albanians would be forced to accept a redrawing of frontiers. Kosovo would be divided: Kosovo proper would be joined to Serbia, while Metohija would go to Albania. The majority of Albanians would then be expelled to Albania. A substantial part of the remaining population would be resettled. Naturally, this is all speculation, but such intentions do exist and are expressed today. The most radical are the Chetnik elements, who are ready for a massacre of Albanians, for a true genocide. Currently all this looks most unreal; but it is possible to imagine a situation in which Yugoslavia would enter a whirlpool of national strife, and various nationalist forces would seize the opportunity to create what would amount to a regional crisis. And while the attention of the world was focused on larger countries like China, the Soviet Union or Poland, they would try to press forward to a "final solution".'

Maliqi's argument is that 'we are dealing with a crisis of state socialism which has used up its historical credit. Everywhere the party-state is falling apart. In Yugoslavia there are forces which seek more democratic channels of state legitimation. Yugoslavia is a multinational state and any attempt to impose a single national will would provoke the country's break-up. In which case the question of Kosovo would still be open, since Yugoslavia's disintegration would not only lead to an intervention of big powers, but also open up a regional conflict in which Bulgaria and Albania would be bound to get involved. There is no doubt that a democratic transformation of Yugoslavia demands a democratic transformation of Serbia. The current leadership is obsessed by the idea of a Greater Serbia, but I do not believe that it will remain in power for any period of time, since I do not believe that it is able to bring any read advance or benefit to the people of Serbia. In Serbia, also, there are forces capable of offering another vision of Serbia and of Yugoslavia: that is, of Yugoslavia as a democratic community of all its peoples. Such forces are to be found in a section of the intelligentsia and also in the working class. For although the Serbian working class may appear momentarily blinded by the nationalist project, its future lies in cooperation with the working class in other parts of the country.'

(October 1989)

PART FOUR

Systemic Collapse (1990–91)

Introduction

In the summer of 1989, Milošević's nationalist campaign reached its peak with the celebrations for the 600th anniversary of the Battle of Kosovo. The Croatian leadership was increasingly being targeted as 'anti-Serb', despite its efforts to come up with a new 'Yugoslav synthesis'. Ivica Račan, leader of the League of Communists of Croatia, was by now habitually described as an 'Ustasha' in Serbia's official press, despite the fact that his family had been murdered during World War Two by the Ustashe. In the Knin area of Croatia (now described in the Serbian press for the first time as 'Krajina'), politicians from Serbia and retired Army generals were fomenting armed rebellion against the Croatian party and state authorities. Faced with the danger of being forcibly removed from power by this 'anti-bureaucratic revolution' – which had already toppled the established authorities in Vojvodina, Montenegro and Kosovo – the Croatian party leadership at its December 1989 congress followed its Slovene counterpart in opting for multi-party elections the following spring.

At the end of January 1990, the Yugoslav Communist Party held its 14th – and, as it turned out, last – congress. A central pillar of Yugoslav unity disappeared practically overnight. In the country at the time, I saw people weep in the streets. There was much fear. By the end of 1990 multi-party elections had taken place throughout Yugoslavia albeit only in the individual republics. In Bosnia-Herzegovina, Croatia, Macedonia and Slovenia the Communist Parties lost. In Serbia (under their new name) and in Montenegro they won. Deprived of their assembly, the Kosovo Albanians boycotted the elections. The whole year was spent by the republics in either preparing themselves for elections or digesting their results. At the end of December 1990, the Army announced the formation of a new communist party: the League of Communists – Movement for Yugoslavia. An attempt by Ante Marković, Yugoslavia's Prime Minister, to forge a federalist alliance of 'forces of reform' had proved ineffectual at the polls (apart from in Macedonia).

All eyes were now directed towards the Army, which made clear its intention to be an equal partner in all negotiations regarding Yugoslavia's future. Although the Army maintained formally a position of equidistance from the six republics, its sympathy with the Serbian régime was unmistakeable. Indeed, it took some time before recognizing the new governments in Slovenia and Croatia as legitimate. At the beginning of January 1991, it actually became involved in planning military intervention in Croatia, whose territorial defence forces had been conveniently disarmed following the elections.[1] In response, Slovenia and Croatia declared themselves wholly sovereign states, offering the other republics a blueprint – based on the model of the European Community – for a confederal Yugoslavia. This was accepted by Macedonia and Bosnia-Herzegovina, albeit with some amendments, but Serbia and its Montenegrin satellite insisted on a tight federation. For good measure, Serbia declared that if the latter option were rejected, it would seek the creation of a Greater Serbia: it now described Yugoslavia's internal borders as merely 'administrative'.

The United States and the Soviet Union declared themselves at this juncture in favour of Yugoslav unity. The European Community started to debate the Yugoslav crisis. All three proclaimed their full support for Prime Minister Marković. In March 1991 huge demonstrations against the Milošević regime erupted in Serbia, and it seemed the whole country would be placed under martial law. In a draft resolution, offered for consideration by the socialist group in the European Parliament, I called for recognition of the sovereignty of the six republics and two provinces. In May, the country was plunged into another crisis by Serbia's refusal to allow Croatian representative Stipe Mesić to take his turn at the head of the Yugoslav presidency. Slovenia and Croatia responded by holding a plebiscite on total independence.[2] I wrote in early June: 'Time is running out for Yugoslavia. Only a miracle – in the shape of a democratic alternative emerging in Serbia – could save it now.' Within days, Slovenia and Croatia declared their full independence. On 27 June the Army began a full-scale invasion of Slovenia. In Belgrade, the news was announced by General Marko Negovanović, head of military Counter-Intelligence. In a letter to the London *Guardian* I wrote that a military coup had taken place in Yugoslavia and warned that it must not pass, for 'if in Yugoslavia today, why not in the Soviet Union tomorrow?'

Notes

1. The generals' manifesto reproduced pp. 270–74 below makes clear the Army's links with the August coup plotters in the USSR.
2. For a full account of this episode, see my survey of Yugoslav politics in the eighties in *Eastern Europe and the Commonwealth of Independent States*, London 1992.

1

The League of Communists Breaks Up

The 14th Congress of the League of Communists of Yugoslavia is very likely to be its last. It took place only to end in complete disarray with the walkout of the entire Slovene delegation. Despite the fact that this was widely expected, the break-up of an organization as old as Yugoslavia itself and one with which the country has been strongly identified for almost half a century has produced a grave sense of foreboding in the population. Indeed, the most striking aspect of the Congress was not what happened at its sessions, but the gulf that existed between its preoccupations and the needs and aspirations of the popular masses. No resolution, from whatever side, managed to transcend this gulf. The departure of the Slovene delegation was made inevitable by the political primitiveness of the Milošević cadre, who came to the Congress with the sole intention of defeating each and every Slovene proposal in the name of 'unity', 'democratic centralism' and an 'integral Yugoslavia'. Having won several important votes by large majorities, Milošević claimed that the Slovene delegation represented an unimportant minority. This shows the extent to which his growing megalomania has deformed the Serbian party's sense of reality. Milošević's proposal that the Congress continue without the Slovenes was rejected by the delegates from Croatia, Bosnia-Herzegovina, Macedonia and the Army.

The individual republican parties had prepared themselves for the eventuality of a split and came to the congress with the sole wish to avoid being blamed for this. A proposal made by several Bosnian and Croatian delegates — that the Party should formally separate into a socialist and a communist wing — would have resulted in a horizontal split, allowing the reformists to keep an all-Yugoslav organization. This, however, was rejected. Instead, the Party split vertically, into republican, i.e. national, organizations. This is virtually bound to split the republican parties themselves into national components, wherever the conditions exist for this. A deepening polarization of the country's political life along national lines is thus to be expected.

Such an option, naturally, is denied to the Army. The disintegration of the LCY has led to a crisis of identity in an institution that, more than any other, is rooted in the state created in the war of 1941–45. The Army, it seems, is staking its hopes on prime minister Ante Marković's reforms, which if successful would lead to a re-centralization of political power in the hands of the Yugoslav government and the all-Yugoslav assembly (in that order). This would allow the Army to keep its all-Yugoslav profile. Yet Marković's reforms have no hope of being implemented, in the absence of a consensus within the present political establishment. The Party's accelerated fragmentation over the past two years has inhibited the central institutions – the Federal state presidency, government and assembly – from guiding the country towards peace. The fact that despite its popularity the Federal government was unable to insist on a negotiated settlement in Kosovo bodes ill for the country's future. Everything thus depends on the nature and tempo of decomposition of the existing power bloc in Serbia. This decomposition has already begun. Over the past few months, several new parties have been formed in this republic, the most important of which so far is the Democratic Party, assembling as it does Serbia's most prominent intellectuals, including Milovan Djilas.

To maintain its control, the Serbian ruling party is ready to play over and over again the Kosovo card. Each time it does so, the political spectrum not just in Serbia but throughout the country shifts perceptibly to the right. The interview below with Veton Surroi, a prominent member of the democratic opposition in Kosovo, shows that in the province we are dealing not with an ethnic conflict but with a struggle between the forces of democracy and the forces of reaction.

In a recent interview published in the Zagreb daily *Večernji list*, Zdravko Grebo, a member of the Bosnian party's central committee and one of those who at the Congress argued in favour of a formal split into two currents, described accurately what is at stake. 'The kind of unity which disappeared at the 14th Congress (excluding the fact that the Party had already split into republican–national fractions, since this was never officially recognized) could be maintained only within a single-party system when membership of the Party provided the only channel for political activity. It is not surprising that as a result, the League of Communists came to incorporate a multiplicity of mutually exclusive political options. But since at the Congress the League declared itself against its monopoly of political power, sooner or later these will split up into different organizations. To demand democratization of the Party's internal life is to overlook this fact. People who at the 14th Congress called for unity do not wish to acknowledge this painful truth. Such calls are motivated by the fear which the loss of political monopoly has induced, not only in certain party leaders but also in the vast nomenklatura, which is perfectly aware that only thanks to this monopoly were they able to become deputies, enterprise managers, directors, officers, ambassadors, representatives, secretaries or university professors. These are weighty political factors – we know what happens when "consciousness becomes a material force".'

If the League of Communists has become incapable of keeping the country together, then new political organizations are required to reconstruct its fractured unity. There is little doubt that most crucial in this regard will be the emergence of parties on the political Left, whose programme of economic and political reform will incorporate the socialist values now being thrown into the gutter, including scrupulous adherence to the principle of national equality. Much hope will rest in this respect with the newly founded Social-Democratic Alliance of Yugoslavia.

Yugoslavia's contemporary political spectrum can be divided into approximately five groups. First, there is the 'official bloc', made up of the republican Leagues of Communists, Alliances of Socialist Youth and Socialist Alliances of Working People. These days, the latter are busily transforming themselves into autonomous organizations, at least in Slovenia and Croatia, with their counterparts in other republics likely to follow suit. Second and most numerous are the new national parties, which include, among others, the Peasant Alliance, Democratic Alliance and Christian Democrats in Slovenia; the Peasant Party, Democratic Union and Christian Democrats in Croatia; the Radical, Liberal and Democratic parties in Serbia proper; the Democratic Alliance in Kosovo; the All-Macedonian Action in Macedonia; the Hungarian League in Vojvodina. Thirdly, there are parties like the Croatian Social Liberals, the Croatian and Slovene Social Democrats, the Montenegrin Liberals, the Macedonian Socialists and the Social-Democratic Alliance of Yugoslavia, all of whom aspire to partnership with similar Western European formations. (It is difficult to tell as yet whether these names in all cases accurately reflect party policies.) The fourth category is made up of a host of non-party 'citizens' initiatives', such as Greens, Helsinki Watch Committees and Committees for Human Rights. Here belongs also the Yugoslav Democratic Initiative, first swallow of the democratic spring. Last but by no means least are the sprouting independent trade unions, whose muscle was displayed in mid-January when an engine-drivers' strike in Croatia cut the interior of the country off from the coast for two days and a night. Elections to the communal and republican assemblies, and perhaps also to the Federal one, are due in April in some parts of the country and are bound to reshuffle the political pack of cards.

The following interview with Veton Surroi, a leading member of the

Yugoslav Democratic Initiative and of the Social-Democratic Party of Kosovo, was conducted in February 1990.

(March 1990)

Kosovo and the Struggle for Democracy in Yugoslavia: Interview with Veton Surroi

Is there a direct link between the failure of the 14th Congress of the League of Communists of Yugoslavia and the subsequent events in Kosovo?

At the Congress, a unity that had existed only on paper broke up for good and with it the very structure of the LCY. The Albanians of Kosovo understood this as the beginning of the end of a policy from which they have suffered for the past nine years. So they demonstrated to mark the end of the old policy and to express a hope that the coming multi-party system would make possible also the articulation of their national demands. You should understand that the situation in which Kosovo lives – a state of isolation maintained by police terror – simply generates demonstrations. The violent anti-Albanian campaign has excluded Albanians from all political life, so that national frustration takes precedence over all other concerns. At the same time, however, there are those who believe – and there is evidence for this – that initially spontaneous demonstrations were in fact fanned by provocateurs.

The spark that set aflame the deep anger existing in the population was the death of an Albanian man in a village near Skopje in neighbouring Macedonia. He died as a result of the local authorities' decision to demolish – in the name of brotherhood and unity! – the traditional high wall surrounding his house. He was killed by a bulldozer when he tried to take down his front gate to save it from destruction. The result was an immediate popular protest in Kosovo, despite the fact that all public gatherings are illegal there. The first demonstration was held in Priština on 23 January: it lasted for two or three hours and passed off peacefully. The protest continued on the second day, when political demands were also raised, ranging from lifting the state of emergency to a referendum on the status of Kosovo. This time the police intervened in a very brutal manner, using water cannon, teargas, truncheons and boots. As in the occupied West Bank, the police used the tactic of singling out individuals for very heavy beatings as a warning to others. Not even children were spared this treatment. Protests consequently spread, especially to places that are traditionally restless and outside effective control, such as the small town of Podujevo, where 20–30,000 people can gather within a very short time. Podujevo, because of its proximity to the Serbian border, is usually the first to suffer military or police action. It is very poor, and has an educated but largely unemployed young population. The protest spread initially because there was no possibility of dialogue about the people's grievances. After the killings, things became quite different.

The first deaths occurred on the third day, in Orahovac. That day the police opened fire without warning at mourners returning home after attending the funeral of a person who had died of natural causes. They killed three people and wounded about twenty. Such incidents were repeated in the following days, which suggests that there was a conscious policy of trying to provoke a national uprising. In Malishevo, for example, fire was opened from a convoy of armoured personnel carriers without any reason – even the local police station was sprayed with bullets. Three people were killed and a dozen wounded. This daily carnage made the revolt grow until at some point it began to involve the villages, a development unprecedented since the war. When the Albanian villages rise, then one really is dealing with a national uprising.

People went to the demonstrations unarmed. This must be true, since otherwise many people would have been killed, including policemen and non-Albanians. One would have had a general bloodletting, a general civil war. But this did not happen – the only deaths were on the Albanian side. The police were in fact conducting a massacre. Our information, based on hospital records, speaks of 35 dead and 139 wounded, but it is very likely that the number is larger, since many probably did not go to hospital. Every wounded demonstrator is considered a criminal and is liable to at least 60 days in prison. So it is better to be treated at home. As far as we can establish, the vast majority of the dead were killed without any provocation.

The intentions of the authorities are indicated by the fact that the Kosovo party committee had sent a warning to the hospitals, even before the demonstrations began, that they should prepare themselves for a lot of casualties. These days, hospitals in Priština regularly lack such basic medicaments as penicillin – but now fresh supplies were rushed in. A shortage of blood soon developed, however, and when the chief surgeon asked for fresh blood supplies – we were also involved in asking for blood donors – we were accused by the mass media of preparing an all-Albanian uprising. Serb and Montenegrin doctors refused to operate on 'terrorists'. There were many other examples of actions that would be considered criminal even in wartime. For example, people coming out of a bus at a bus station were fired at and those who tried to help the wounded were severely beaten. On another occasion, some passers-by who had taken a wounded man into their car to drive him to hospital were stopped and beaten up. A man coming to the aid of his wounded brother was beaten unconscious and the wounded man was then shot dead at point blank range. In Kačanik, a small boy was shot by a sniper outside his house though there were no demonstrations then taking place. He is right now on a life-support system. A 17-year-old girl was killed when a policeman stopped his car, saw a crowd of people in the distance and opened fire. A secondary school teacher was arrested and died in custody. Workers going to work were fired on. All this done by Serbian 'specials' and reservists.

What is the reason for the police brutality?

Over the last few months Milošević has been losing ground in Yugoslavia, thanks to a visible shift of power from the party to the state: in the first instance, to the Federal government and prime minister Ante Markovic. Marković's economic programme needs a different political framework, a dispersion of political decision-making. This amounts to a direct attack on Milošević's power base: party monopoly combined with nationalism. And the only way that he can preserve the status quo is to play the Kosovo card, to present himself as a defender of the territorial integrity and sovereignty of Yugoslavia. This trick always works, not because there is any real danger of Albanian secession, but because Albanians can be presented as a foreign body within a Slav state and society. Albanian political demands can, therefore, always be treated as suspect. Even demands for a multi-party system and free elections can be interpreted as 'separatism', etc.

A new category – that of 'terrorism' – is being used today to describe their actions. In the past, Albanians were accused of 'counter-revolution', 'nationalism' and 'irredentism'. The charge of 'irredentism', with its implication that the territory is ethnically Albanian, has now been replaced by 'separatism'. After Tiananmen Square, and also because the communist régimes in Eastern Europe had used it against their political opponents, the term 'counter-revolution' was no longer found suitable. 'Terrorism' has been chosen instead, partly because it justifies the use of the repressive apparatus and partly to combat growing Western protests against the evident violation of the human and civic rights of the Albanian population.

From Milošević's point of view, the demonstrations could be used to postpone free elections in Kosovo and maybe also in Serbia. For in his speeches he has argued that parliamentary democracy is impossible until the rights of the Serb and Montenegrin minority in Kosovo are safeguarded. But since these rights are an infinitely flexible category, it will never be possible to prove that this has been achieved. The practical consequence is a spiralling repression that has no obvious cut-off point. Also, and this is very important, Milošević has used the demonstrations in Kosovo to argue that the suspension of the 14th Congress has itself led to a further destabilization of Yugoslavia. This, then, is the interrelation between the failure of the Congress and the demonstrations: while Albanians saw it as the incipient disintegration of a nine-year-long repression, Milošević argued that the break-up of party unity amounted to Yugoslavia's own disintegration. In the short term, moreover, he has been successful. He managed to get the Federal Assembly to insert the term 'terrorism' in its resolution on Kosovo. This will oblige the executive to use 'anti-terrorist' methods of policing – which, as we have seen, are very draconian.

But in the long run?

Only two outcomes are possible: either this reactionary policy will fail, due to eternal and external pressure – i.e. from within Serbia and/or from other parts of Yugoslavia – or it will lead to a generalized conflict throughout the country. A middle solution is impossible.

What has been the reaction in other republics and from the Federal party and state authorities?

Slovenian and Croatian leaders have made it clear that Serbia's repressive policy leads nowhere and should be replaced by a dialogue with the opposition. We in the opposition were the first to suggest – with our declaration 'For Democracy – Against Violence' – that the opening of a dialogue is a precondition for ending the vicious circle of violence in Kosovo. The dialogue should take place at all levels, but must include the Federal one, since the provincial authorities are a direct party to the conflict. The response of the Federal government and presidency was to endorse such a dialogue, but only after the demonstrations have ended. The demonstrations, however, will not stop unless the dialogue begins. The real relationship of forces at the Federal level was shown by the fact that the Federal Assembly adopted the resolution in which the demonstrators were called 'terrorists', which puts the whole situation into a completely new context.

How do you explain the adoption of such a resolution, when the Assembly is made up of delegates from all over the country, many of whom do not approve of the repression in Kosovo?

My guess is that the Assembly simply expressed the balance of forces within the Party. The Federal leadership is split down the middle, and this makes all forward action difficult. From Marković's point of view, Serbia is a strong political factor which can endanger his political reform. He therefore chose to appease it on the issue of Kosovo. But this is very short-term thinking, since instability in any part of the country brings the reform into danger.

What was the effect of your Declaration in Kosovo itself?

One of our wishes was to canalize the protest around five rational demands, which is why we offered the Declaration for the public to sign. We have had more than 400,000 signatures so far! The very act of signing, with full name and address, concretizes the individual political demand and provides a solid basis for collective negotiation. The people placed their trust in the opposition, which in turn did something that had never been done before: to make each death a public fact. This allowed everybody, even those who had not attended the demonstrations or signed the Declaration, to participate in actions that we subsequently organized – such as the two 'days of mourning', with the sounding of factory whistles and car horns at a specific hour one day to commemorate the dead, etc. In fact, we did not call them 'days of mourning' but 'days of sorrow', since public mourning is normally an act of state, but we have a state that is killing its people and that is ready to arrest all who wish to express public grief in its place.

Who forms the Kosovo opposition?

The day before the demonstrations began, the Kosovo branch of the Association for a Yugoslav Democratic Initiative (UJDI), the Association of Philosophers and Sociologists of Kosovo, and the local Committee for Human Rights, appealed to the public not to go onto the streets. It was clear to us that such an act would only feed the repressive regime and would in any case endanger human lives. After the bloodshed began, we offered the Declaration for people to sign. The Democratic Alliance of Kosovo came out at this point in support of our action. We have now formed a Coordinating Committee of the signatories of the Declaration, which is headed by three people: myself for UJDI, Adriz Ajeti for the Committee of Human Rights and Isuf Berisha for the Philosophers' and Sociologists' Association. We hold press conferences and initiate other actions – such as the appeal for the re-start of the school term to be postponed because of inadequate public security. In addition to the four organizations I have mentioned, others have now joined: the Initiative Committee for a Social-Democratic Party, one of whose founders is Shkelzen Maliqi; and the Initiative Committee for a Youth Parliament, whose president is Blerim Shala, a journalist on the local youth paper *Zeri e Rinis* (it is significant that the Initiative Committee for a Youth Parliament was founded in Vranjevac, the shanty suburb of Priština.) We expect these days also the formation of a Liberal Party and a Green Party.

What do the Democratic Alliance and Liberal Party stand for?

The former has about 200,000 members. It calls for parliamentary democracy, free market and – something specific to them – a 'constitutional emancipation of the Albanian people'. The Democratic Alliance, in other words, aspires to be a kind of national movement. It is not so much a party as a product of the popular response to so many years of repression. In my opinion, however, political pluralism cannot be subsumed within a national movement, but must be the articulation and crystallisation of all the different and antagonistic social interests present within Kosovo society. The Liberal Party is being formed by Albanian graduates of the University of Zagreb, who are on the same wavelength as the Croatian Social-Liberals.

A further important component of the pluralistic scene will be independent trade unions, which are in the process of formation. In contrast to Slovenia, where the new unions are being formed from above by simple transformation of the official trade unions, in Kosovo they will be formed from below at the level of individual enterprises, schools, etc. and will later join up. Already, journalists, doctors, historians and others are forming their own professional organizations.

These are all city-based organizations. What about the peasantry?

There is a problem here, in that the Kosovo village is backward and unproductive. Because it exists at a subsistence level, it has no distinct awareness of its own specific interest and is not the bearer of a new agrarian development. The strong trends of emigration into the cities and abroad also militate against this. The peasant himself does not know what to do with his land and there are no models elsewhere in Yugoslavia that he can follow. The Peasant Party in Slovenia, for example, is a political party which will fight for agricultural interests, for example over the price of fertilizers or milk. The Kosovo peasant, who does not produce for the market, cannot follow the Slovene example.

Kosovo is specific in that, unlike the situation in the rest of Yugoslavia where villages are faced with a labour shortage, the land is overpopulated.

Indeed, Kosovo as a whole is overpopulated. The density of population is in fact the greatest in the country. Yet right now we are expecting new settlers!

Where will they go?

Before the war, Kosovo was settled by several waves of Serb and Montenegrin colonists, who were given land taken away from Albanian peasants. This will happen again, since land transactions very often take place without official registration, so that many owners do not have any proof of legal purchase. Also, state land amounting to 40,000 hectares is envisaged for distribution to the colonists. The trouble is that, even if this could be achieved without a massive social upheaval, it would merely bring new problems. For example, a settlement of some 20,000 people is planned in Glogovac, where there is already a population of that size without the conditions for a decent life. It is a kind of madness, characteristic of this regime! A popular slogan in Serbia and Montengro right now is: 'Just give us the order, Slobodan [Milošević], and we'll march to Tirana!'

The settlement proposal is in fact intended for its psychological effect. Milošević's politics are based on launching the most impossible ideas, which then serve as points of conflict. The first intention is to provoke Albanians into further action. And the Croats and Slovenes, if they react, will be accused of wishing to see a purely Albanian Kosovo. This is a politics of conflict-making. The aim is to gain time.

There is an emerging opposition today also in Serbia too, isn't there? Can one realistically expect some positive gesture from it in regard to Kosovo?

The very emergence of opposition to Milošević is a positive development. But one should not expect any early differentiation on the Kosovo issue. Serb national hysteria has been nurtured for so many years that it will take time before it calms down. I do not think that the Serbian opposition is strong enough to choose Kosovo as a point of confrontation with Milošević. In any case, some of the new parties, such Vuk Drašković's Party of Serb National Renewal or the Radical Party, are even more hysterical on the issue of Kosovo than the Serbian League of Communists under Milošević.

In Serbia, as in large parts of Yugoslavia, frustration with the existing system is producing not only an anti-communist but also an anti-socialist mood. In Serbia, however, we have in addition an extreme nationalism centred on the issue of Kosovo. It is, moreover, spilling today beyond the ethnic into the religious sphere: Yugoslav Moslems (the main national group in Bosnia-Herzegovia) will be the next to suffer the accusation of being an 'alien' – non-Christian, non-European – element in Yugoslavia. The reactionary stance of the Serbian party is tending to produce a right rather than a left opposition. Milošević himself, moreover, is still moving to the right. The key ideas found in 'Peace in Kosovo', a document recently adopted by the Central Committee of the Serbian League of Communists (this name has become a pure joke!), have been taken directly from the programme of the extreme chauvinist Party of Serb National Renewal. And one still has to ask: is this right-wing enough for contemporary Serbia? My impression is that the Serbian party leadership simply does not comprehend that the world has changed. Milošević and his henchmen place their hopes in the trilogy of nationalism, the police and the army, all under the control of the nomenklatura. Confronted with the tangible popularity of the communist parties in Slovenia and Croatia and, to an extent, also in Macedonia and Bosnia, the Serbian party can only play the Kosovo card. This it does, gaining each time a few months of respite.

Finally, if free elections were held in Kosovo today, who would win?

Those individuals who have actively resisted repression. And in this regard, we are all different. There are democrats, but also old village chiefs. The provincial assembly is very large and it is possible that we will see elected to it quite a few village characters who have made their name by being more Albanian than the next man. These people would not concern themselves too much with the content of new laws, but would shout about Albanianism just like those who today swear by Serbianism. This is a real danger. A six-month armistice on the issue of Kosovo would make their neutralization easier. The left democrats, who have been formed in contact with others in Yugoslavia, need the time to define their political profile within the Albanian national discourse. I myself, for example, have considerable differences with certain people from the Democratic Alliance; but I am unable to formulate them openly, for fear that this would be misused by the current regime. We are, therefore, engaged in a desperate race not only against Milošević's policy of constantly raising the stakes, but also against sheer time in our efforts to create an organizational basis for the genuine pluralization of Albanian political life. We do not wish to see a party-based monism replaced by one based on nationalism.

We operate today under the tremendous pressure of a national uprising that draws its inspiration also from the fact that Ceauşescú's regime was overthrown precisely by a popular uprising. After nine years of repression and a year of martial law, after so many have died, the people are no longer afraid. However, despite the obvious parallels between Kosovo and Romania, we know that the situation in Yugoslavia is different; that direct confrontation will not work; that Kosovo's problems go beyond the immediate problem of national oppression and can be tackled only on the basis of a transformation that would allow free expression of all the different national, social and group interests throughout Yugoslavia. We intend to make our own contribution to this process.

2

Yugoslavia Goes into a
Penalty Shoot-Out

The demise of communist rule in Yugoslavia has opened up the possibility of the country's disappearance as a single state. As the contradictions of the new politics unfold, it is clear that – far from solving any problems – such an outcome would be a disaster for all its nations and citizens. Not only would Yugoslavia's break-up make national issues still harder to resolve, it would also put an end to the newly emerging system of parliamentary democracy.

The March–April 1990 elections in Slovenia and Croatia have brought to power right-of-centre nationalist governments. (It should be borne in mind that the Federal government itself is committed to the introduction of fully-fledged capitalism.) In Slovenia, the old ruling party – the League of Communists of Slovenia: Party of Democratic Renewal – opted for a proportional system and direct election of the republican president. DEMOS – a coalition comprising National Alliance, Peasant Alliance, Social Democrats, Christian Democrats and Greens – won 55 per cent of the votes (126 seats out of 240); the Communists 17 per cent (38 seats); the Liberals (former Social Youth Alliance) 14 per cent (38 seats). 16 seats went to the Socialists (former Socialist Alliance of Working People), two each to the Italian and Hungarian national minorities, and the rest to independent candidates. The Communist Party leader, Milan Kučan, was elected president of the republic with a relative majority (44 per cent) of the vote, thus sealing the new national compact.

Socialist insignia have been removed from the state's name, emblem and flag. Anti-communist hysteria (as opposed to rhetoric) has been kept in check, but all key government posts have gone to DEMOS, a purge of the media and key economic and cultural institutions is proceeding, and philosophy students wishing to study Hegel, Marx or Freud are being tacitly encouraged to think again. The ruling coalition has declared itself the guardian of national interests (its motto being 'Who is not with us is against the nation!') and has suspended secret voting in parliament itself. While refusing to sanction salaries for deputies (allegedly to save money), the ruling coalition has been busy employing its own MPs in the state apparatus, thus transforming people's representatives into servants of the state executive.

The proportional system, nevertheless, has led to an equitable distribution of parliamentary seats, and Kučan's election to a degree of power-sharing. The expected weakness of a coalition government has been mitigated by several factors. A 'fair' distribution of the spoils of office, made more attractive by the new entrepreneurial climate, has helped to keep the different parties together. Externally, the coalition has been aided by a consensus on economic priorities and a common fear of Serbia under Milošević. These two concerns led to the June declaration of Slovenia's full sovereignty within Yugoslavia (not secession) signed by all parliamentary parties and groups. The transition to a post-communist order has been facilitated also by the disarray of the Communists, consequent upon the loss of forty years of state power: financial problems, a vertiginous drop in membership, and an as yet unsuccessful search for a new political identity. Judging by their behaviour in the Slovene parliament, Communists, Socialists and Liberals have *de facto* united to form a viable, if limited, opposition (one recent success was to stop a ban, advocated by a government minister, on Serbo-Croat being spoken in the republic's parliament).

In Croatia, the Communists – in the mistaken belief that this would return them to power – opted instead for a first-past-the-post electoral system and election of the president by the national assembly. In the event, a single party – the Croatian Democratic Union (CDU) – won 41.5 per cent of votes (69 per cent of seats). The Coalition of National Agreement (a mixed bag of Liberals, Christian Democrats, and ex-Communists – some of whom had occupied leading positions in 1968–71) gained 15 per cent of votes (4 per cent of seats); the League of Communists of Croatia: Party of Democratic Change (including a number of candidates shared with the Socialists) won 28 per cent of votes (21 per cent of seats); while the Socialists (ex-Socialist Alliance) on their own gained 6.5 per cent of votes (2.5 per cent of seats). The rest was divided between Serb Democrats and independents, including a Green (elected with Communist support). The system, in other words, gave a two-thirds parliamentary majority to a party that had gained just over 41 per cent of the popular vote. Such a parliament naturally elected Franjo Tudjman, president of the CDU, as the republic's head of state. The CDU has since made conciliatory gestures towards Croatia's Serbs, including offering one of the five vice-presidential posts to Jovan Rašković, leader of the Serb Democrats; but such overtures have been rejected, on advice coming from Belgrade.

The Croatian Communists, too, are in disarray, for very much the same reasons as those operating in Slovenia. Their predicament, however, has been made worse by several additional factors. First, they won a majority of Serb votes (Serbs form just under 12 per cent of the total population in Croatia), but now these supporters have either become disillusioned or are switching to the Serb Democratic Party. Secondly, the inner-party struggle between reformers and conservatives was never decisively won by the former, and this is impeding the party's efforts to acquire a new political profile. Furthermore, since conservatives tend to be Serb and re-formers Croat (for reasons that go back to the extensive purge of 1971), the Party faces further splits along national lines. The Croat majority, moreover, has responded – like its Slovene counterpart – to the threat emanating from Serbia by closing ranks with the CDU in defence of national sovereignty. This process has been facilitated by the support Belgrade has extended to open, organized Serb rebellion against the new government – including calls for armed struggle – in parts of Croatia. Finally, the CDU's political hegemony is encouraging defections from the Communist ranks, the most spectacular being that of Bernard Jurlina, former head of the Croatian Trade Unions and a member of the Party's Central Committee, who was rewarded by a vice-presidential post (a new term – 'jurlinism' – has entered the Croatian vocabulary to denote this novel kind of opportunism).

The voting system has had a negative effect on Croatia's newfangled democracy. CDU control of parliament – combined with the Communists' collapse – has strengthened the Party's authoritarian tendencies, already visible in the election campaign. Pretending that its victory was 'plebisci-tary', the CDU – like its counterpart in Slovenia – has been busy purging the media, and cultural and educational institutions. The new government has been paying particular attention to 'purification' of the official language, removing all 'foreign' (i.e. Serb) 'imports', frequently with comic results – a measure designed to intimidate in particular its Croat opponents. The CDU party flag has become the official flag (of Croatia) and, as in Slovenia, all socialist insignia have been removed from the name and emblem of the state.

Nevertheless, the CDU is not so much a party as a coalition of moderate and extreme nationalists and anti-communists. Tudjman, occupying a centre position, has been trying to keep his 'hawks' in check, mainly by letting them loose in the cultural sphere; but this has been a difficult task in the face of the extreme 'hawkishness' of official Serbia and the Serbian opposition alike. The CDU, moreover, faces a specific problem: a lack of intelligentsia. Unlike in Slovenia, where DEMOS emerged out of the traditional intelligentsia, the Croat intelligentsia voted almost *en bloc* for non-CDU parties. Without intellectuals, the transition to post-communism will be difficult (who, for example, among the CDU veterans is capable of writing the new constitution?), and the CDU's need for their

cooperation will work to moderate this resurgent national fundamentalism.

Multi-party elections are due to take place before the end of the year also
in Bosnia-Herzegovina (where the newly formed Party of Democratic
Action, based on the Moslem population, is likely to emerge the winner),
in Montenegro (whose political life remains split between pro-Milošević
factions, which include the ruling Communist Party, and various Montenegrin nationalist and democratic groupings), and in Macedonia (where
no obvious winner has come to the fore, although the nationalist VMRO –
Internal Macedonian Revolutionary Organization – is emerging as a likely
leader). Yugoslavia's disintegration threatens the survival of these three
republics and the national existence of the population inhabiting them.
Macedonia, in particular, is vulnerable because its immediate neighbours,
Bulgaria and Greece (as well as extreme Serb nationalists in Yugoslavia),
do not recognize the existence of the Macedonian nation. In August 1990,
also, Prime Minister Ante Marković announced the formation of a
government party – Alliance of Forces of Reform – which could do well in
ethnically mixed areas.

In Serbia, elections have been postponed till December – or, equally
likely, to the Greek calends, given the regime's determination to rule
Kosovo against the will of its population. The opposition parties –
predominantly nationalist, chauvinist and anti-communist – share with
the ruling party the desire to 'save' Kosovo for Serbia, even at the risk of a
generalized civil war. This unity of purpose has provided the League of
Communists of Serbia with sufficient breathing space to carry through
unification with the Socialist Alliance (thus strengthening its grip on the
infrastructure of state power) and to conduct a referendum in early July
stripping the two provinces – Kosovo and Vojvodina – of the last vestiges
of their autonomy. The referendum, moreover, has conferred advance
approval upon a new constitution which will severely limit the prerogatives of the republican legislature in favour of the executive. Yet elections
must come – as the West never tires of reminding Communists in power.

Following the referendum, Serbia has indeed entered into a *de facto*
pre-election campaign, which is likely further to destabilize Yugoslavia,
given that strident nationalism will provide the exclusive terrain for
political infighting. Wholesale expulsion of the Albanian population from
Yugoslavia might only too easily become a popular election slogan. The
ruling party, moreover, is these days seeking a pretext for a massive show
of force in Kosovo as a card with which to trump its 'patriotic' opposition.
This could easily lead to a civil war in Serbia, which is likely to spread to
the rest of Yugoslavia.

The only check on Serbia's ruling mafia and its equally unpalatable
opposition has so far come from the two provinces. The Kosovo

government and parliament, with the support of the local opposition, announced on 2 July (the day of the referendum) Kosovo's effective independence from Serbia. The declaration proclaimed the equality of Kosovo with other federal units; the equality of all citizens and nationalities in Kosovo; the status of Albanians as a fully-fledged nation within Yugoslavia; and respect henceforth only for the Federal (rather than the Serbian) constitution. This amounts to Kosovo becoming a constituent republic of Yugoslavia or, as the declaration states: 'an equal and independent unit, within the Yugoslav federation or confederation'.

The Serbian régime has responded by suspending all government bodies in the province and dissolving the Kosovo parliament – in defiance of the Federal constitution, which denies even the all-Yugoslav assembly the right to dissolve national assemblies in the individual federal units. The province has become an occupied territory. Its Albanian population has turned to civil disobedience. Serbia has been playing a zero-sum game with Kosovo, constantly raising the stakes. According to the current constitution of Serbia, forced upon Kosovo and Vojvodina last year, provincial assemblies have the right to seek postponement of all constitutional changes for six months. If they continue to withhold agreement, then the changes must be submitted to an all-Serbian referendum. By dissolving the provincial assembly just before the referendum, Serbia has not only acted illegally but has also made sure that a new constitution – denying the provinces all say in constitutional matters – will be adopted by the end of the year. (Regrettably, Mihailo Marković, once a member of the *Praxis* group of intellectuals but now a close adviser of Milošević, played a prominent role in these anti-democratic moves.)

The Yugoslav presidency has given cover to Serbia's anti-Albanian measures, although the Slovenian and Croatian representatives voted against it. Slovenia was alone in publicly condemning the dissolution of the Kosovo parliament and the use of force to resolve differences between Yugoslav nationalities. In doing so it proved that it understands the essence of the Yugoslav state community far better than the latter's constitutional guardians. For the first time since World War Two, the Albanian population is being forced to choose between staying in Yugoslavia – with the loss of all political rights – and unification with Albania. Given the extraordinary commitment of the Albanian people to the preservation of their national and civil liberties, and the presence of a highly articulate and politically capable Albanian intelligentsia, Serbia will find it difficult to crush Kosovo. In the province the parties of the opposition, locked-out state officials and parliamentarians, academic bodies, dismissed enterprise managers, purged journalists and teachers, etc. have now formed a united Democratic Forum, commanding the seemingly total support of the population. An even more telling sign of the strength of this Albanian national accord has been the ending of all blood feuds, thus closing a thousand-year-old chapter in Albanian history. Kosovo's eventual location will be decided, of course, also by the post-communist evolution of Albania itself.

Milošević is raising the stakes not only in regard to Kosovo, but also in regard to Yugoslavia as a whole. The latest threat is that, if the other republics do not accept Serbia's vision of Yugoslavia, then Serbia will seek annexation of territories belonging to other republics and indeed in some cases whole republics. This used to be a demand of the extreme wing of the Serb nationalist movement; its adoption by Milošević testifies to the continued right-wing slide of the Serbian ex-Communists.

Vojvodina, with its 53 per cent Serb majority, is unlikely to follow Kosovo on its collision course with Belgrade. To be sure, its Hungarian, Croat, Romanian and Ruthenian minorities are busy these days organizing national parties, in reaction to the severe reduction of their cultural rights and their elimination from the provincial parliament and government. Growing nationalism in their motherlands has made its own contribution to this resurgence of national agitation. And Serbia also faces problems in its dealings with Serb and Montenegrin national groups in Vojvodina. The cadres appointed by Belgrade after the overthrow of the old leadership in 1988 have proved to be incompetent and corrupt. Removal of provincial autonomy has also led to an economic pillage of the province, and a grave decline in the living standards of the population in what used to be Yugoslavia's second-richest federal unit. A sign of the new times is also Belgrade's intention to close down the provincial Academy. Thus, although Vojvodina is not going to declare its independence from Serbia, it will fight to restore its autonomy and cultural and economic – hence also political – life. Unlike in Serbia proper, its opposition parties – most notably the League of Social Democrats – called for an outright boycott of the referendum.

(September 1990)

3

The Slide towards Civil War

The federal organization of the Yugoslav state has made the transition to post-communist rule particularly chaotic. Some republics have already had multi-party elections, others not. Over the past three years, a muffled conflict within the Communist Party leadership over the desirability and terms of a radical change has been transformed into an open conflict between the federal units – or rather, between Serbia and all the others. Most worrying for the future of the country is the burgeoning violence in the ethnically mixed areas of Yugoslavia's central regions.

The unknown factor in the current power struggle is the Yugoslav People's Army. Its birth and development took place first as a part of the revolution and anti-fascist national liberation war, and then as a part of the emergence and consolidation of the communist system. The relative autonomy of the armed forces, and their role in policing internal dissent, increased substantially as a result of extensive party purges in the early 1970s, at precisely the time when a major devolution of state power to the republics and provinces was initiated. The collapse of Communist Party rule has left the armed forces without a political master.

The representatives of the chief republics – Slovenia, Croatia and Serbia – have become in their different ways the spokespersons for a new post-communist order. The effects of this turn, combined with professional self-interest, political conservatism and Serb preponderance in the officer ranks, have produced an unstable and potentially danger-ous force. As the Army seeks a new role, it is possible that sections could emerge as a serious threat to the new parliamentary-democratic system, using as a pretext the need to defend Yugoslavia's territorial integrity.

In 1981 the Army could still be found grumbling over the politicians' incompetence, which had required it to intervene in the majority-Albanian Kosovo province of Serbia. Such qualms seem to have diminished with the crumbling of unity within the party-state leadership. Two years ago the Army was involved in trying to inhibit political democratization in

Slovenia. Last year it participated in dismantling the political and cultural autonomy of Kosovo – a move both violent and unconstitutional. This summer it staged military manoeuvres in Bosnia, in which Slovenia and Croatia were designated as the 'enemy' (coloured blue). Within weeks of this exercise it intervened in the internal affairs of Croatia, by sending two of its MIGs to turn back police helicopters despatched by the Croatian authorities to recapture the town of Knin from a group of armed Serb insurgents, who had cut off road and rail links between Zagreb and Split.

These actions amount to little more than occasional harassment – as yet. Indeed it is difficult to ascertain whether they commanded the full support of the Minister of Defence and the Chiefs of Staff. If some generals harbour political ambitions, they are at present kept in check by the multinational character of the conscript army, by the legitimacy of the new governments in Slovenia and Croatia, and – last but not least – by fear of possible Western reaction. Yet a military *putsch* cannot be altogether excluded. Much will depend on the outcome of forthcoming elections in the republic of Serbia.

In the Spring of 1990, the Communist Parties of Slovenia and Croatia, bowing before the inevitable, organized free and fair elections, in which they lost power, but gained around 20 per cent of the popular vote (less in Slovenia, more in Croatia). Despite the fact that the CPs emerged as a re-spectable parliamentary opposition – with no single party winning an ab-solute majority of the popular vote – they are faced today with a drastically declining membership and severe political disorientation. What is more, the constant pressure from Serbia is forcing them into a coalition with domestic parties to their right, in defence of national and republican state sovereignty. This autumn, it will be the turn of the other republics to go through the electoral process, in which ethnically-based parties are likely to win the lion's share of the vote in individual national constituences.

It is unlikely that the Serbian elections will be as equitably organized, or proceed as peacefully, as was the case in Croatia and Slovenia. In Kosovo itself, it is practically certain that the Albanian parties will be banned. Kosovo's provincial assembly was in any case dissolved in July by a unilateral decision of Belgrade and will not be reconvened. The locked-out deputies, the Kosovo opposition parties, and the newly formed Alliance of Independent Trade Unions, have signed a declaration proclaiming the complete independence of Kosovo from Serbia. This will be used as the pretext for not holding elections in the province.

The future of Yugoslavia will be decided in Serbia. Serbia's ruling party – a party whose ideology and practice are taking on fascist tones – has adopted a twin-track strategy whose ultimate aim is to dismantle Yugoslavia and replace it with Greater Serbia. One track of this policy looks on the Serb diaspora as the chief (though not the only) instrument of destabilization of the other republics. This summer – after Kosovo, Vojvodina and Montenegro – it was Croatia's turn for the treatment. Bosnia-Herzegovina – with elections scheduled for 18 November 1990 – is coming next. The Belgrade media were engaged in a vicious propaganda campaign against Croatia well before its new government was in place. Since then, they have been fanning fear among the Serb population in Croatia, by alleging that the new authorities there are planning to massacre them *en masse*.

Belgrade has been organizing and even arming local militants with a view to provoking civil war in Croatia – in which Belgrade would intervene as protector of the Serbs. The Serbian régime has at its disposal thousands of 'volunteers' ready to march anywhere in Yugoslavia, and can also rely on full support from most of the Serbian opposition parties for such action. A current joke – which is not really a joke – is that Serbian leader Milošević's power rests on four pillars: the daily *Politika*, the Army, the Serbian Orthodox Church and the Serbian Academy of Arts and Sciences. In Serbia, in other words, forces with the politics of the right-wing Russian nationalist Pamyat movement both hold power and provide the chief opposition.

The other track is directed towards winning the elections, scheduled for later this year. There is a theoretical possibility that the coming elections in Serbia will break the back of the ruling party, and open the door to a new intra-national settlement in Yugoslavia. The chances of this happening, however, are remote. For one thing, there is the Kosovo myth. Over the past three years, the Serbian Communist Party has built up national hysteria around the issue of Kosovo, creating a right-wing emotional and political climate in the Republic. Whenever the party's influence has appeared to be in decline – as in the immediate aftermath of the elections in Slovenia and Croatia – the party has used the Kosovo card to cow its opposition.

The July decision to dissolve the Kosovo assembly and take over all the economic, political and cultural institutions in the province was announced simultaneously with the decision to fuse the Communist Party with the Socialist Alliance of Working People of Serbia – the organization which, according to the current constitution, organizes elections. The ruling party, now named the Socialist Party of Serbia (SPS), has thus killed two birds with one stone. It has gained control over the vast infrastructure of this para-state organization (financed by deductions at source from each and every wage packet) and over the mechanism of the electoral process.

At the same time, it has pushed through a new draft constitution by means of a fraudulent referendum, which imposed stiff conditions for the registration and activity of the opposition parties. The muted and incoherent response of these parties proved their essential impotence – not a single one in Serbia felt strong enough to call for a boycott, despite the obvious adverse effects the new regulations would have on their electoral chances. This was in sharp contrast to Kosovo and Vojvodina, where the referendum elicited a far sturdier response. In Vojvodina, the Social Democratic League under Nenad Čanak has been particularly outspoken.

The undemocratic character of the whole process has encouraged the Serbian Academy of Arts and Sciences to proclaim SPS leader Slobodan Milošević the greatest personality in Serbian history. Mihailo Marković, the ex-*Praxis* editor and one time critic of the Yugoslav Communist Party from the standpoint of 'humanist Marxism', sits today on the SPS Central Committee together with the writer Dobrica Ćosić (removed from the Serbian party central committee for her nationalism in 1968) and a host of corrupt nonentities elevated to power by Milošević. Unlike in Croatia and Slovenia, where the opposition gained reasonable access to the state-run media prior to the elections, in Serbia the media remain the exclusive property of the ruling party.

In Kosovo, the Albanian-language radio and television have been closed down, prompting an Albanian deputy to declare at a recent session of the Federal Assembly that Kosovo finds itself today back in the Middle Ages. The Belgrade press, on the other hand, maintains an output of unrelenting abuse that would put to shame the most notorious of British tabloids. Over the past eighteen months, for example, *NIN* – Serbia's most prominent weekly, once noted for its liberal political and cultural orientation – has published a respectful interview with Israel's Ariel Sharon, a sympathetic account of General Franco's Spain, a paeon of praise for Oswald Spengler's *Decline of the West* (as an example of 'post-modernist vitality') and a warm appreciation of the 'iconoclasm' of Gabriele D'Annunzio, without mentioning the poet's role in the annexation of the Croatian and Yugoslav port of Rijeka to Italy on the eve of Mussolini's coming to power.

A new stock in trade of the government-controlled Belgrade press is the charge that Yugoslav Communists came to power in 1945 as a result of a Vatican–Comintern conspiracy directed against Serbia. All other Yugoslav nationalities – Albanian, Croat, Slovene, Moslem, Macedonian, Montenegrin – are regularly depicted as racial enemies of the Serbs. In these conditions it is hard to describe Serbia as a bastion of communist conservatism – it might indeed be shaping up as the vanguard of a fascist counter-revolution in Yugoslavia.

The coming elections in Serbia will thus be state-managed. Unlike in Slovenia and Croatia, the opposition parties will not sit on the electoral commissions, whose members will be appointed by the state. Yet the plight of the Serbian economy and the desperate condition of the Serbian working class are making the regime nervous. Despite all the preparations, the ruling party is not certain of victory. A public opinion poll conducted in August in Serbia proper (that is, Serbia without Vojvodina and Kosovo) suggested that the SPS would gain one third of the vote. Vuk Drašković's Serb National Renewal party was trailing far behind with around 10 per cent. The largest proportion of those questioned, however, were undecided.

To help them make up their mind, the SPS will move at an appropriate moment – most likely in Kosovo, but it could be anywhere – to create a civil war situation and present itself as the only force capable of saving the Serbs from national extinction. The Knin incident in Croatia is only a dress rehearsal for future action in Bosnia-Herzegovina and Montenegro. There are historic precedents for this tactic – the most sinister being Hitler's use of the German question in Czechoslovakia and Poland on the eve of World War Two.

The régime's most tempting option, however, is to provoke the Kosovo Albanians into an uprising. Belgrade has spent the summer months busily sacking Albanians from all positions of responsibility in Kosovo and replacing them with Serbs, some of them well known for their anti-Albanian fanaticism. Kosovo workers, the majority of whom have not been paid since April, are also being summarily dismissed and replaced where possible by Serb workers. The Serbian police has subjected the population to systematic harassment and is increasingly trigger-happy. A chemical war of a kind is being conducted against the local population as hospitals and clinics are closed to Albanians seeking medical help.

In Belgrade, officials of the ruling party and the opposition speak openly and calmly of the coming war in Kosovo and the desirability of killing tens of thousands of Albanians. The idea is that Albanians, once brought to their senses, will meekly accept either a reduction in their status to that of second-class citizens or the partitioning of Kosovo between Serbia and Albania. In the Serbian half, containing at least half-a-million Albanians, the 'alien' population would either be expelled or assimilated by force.

The Albanian democratic opposition is well aware of these scenarios. Its adoption of the Gandhian tactic of peaceful civil resistance has earned it much respect in the country and abroad. In July the European Community and the US House of Representatives passed resolutions severely criticizing the conduct of the Serbian and Yugoslav governments in Kosovo.

The Croatian and Slovenian parliaments, especially the latter, have condemned the dissolution of the Kosovo assembly. In Kosovo itself, the growing lawlessness of the occupying power, the deliberate engineering of the economy's collapse and pressure from angry workers have pushed the Kosovo Alliance of Independent Trade Unions into calling a general strike from 3 September 1990.

Despite the fact that they face a state armed with the most sophisticated weapons of 'riot control', the Kosovo Albanians have, it seems, taken up the challenge. They have accepted that they may have to die for their freedom, if necessary, while hoping that domestic and foreign pressure will combine to prevent such a bloody outcome. The Kosovo Albanians cannot stop the growing counter-revolution in Serbia on their own. To be sure, as in the past, the defence of national rights and sovereignty will play a crucial role in the struggle for democracy in Yugoslavia.

Non-Serb nationalities are today erecting a defensive ring around Belgrade which, in the last instance, only a military *putsch* can dismantle. Belgrade's intervention in Croatia misfired, however, precisely because the army drew back from starting a civil war.

The relatively moderate response of the Croatian government to the Knin incident, directed partly by wisdom and partly by necessity, has raised both its own standing and that of the republic's president Franjo Tudjman in the eyes of the Croatian population. The previously suspicious opposition – in particular the left-leaning Croat intelligentsia – rallied to the government. Serb deputies in the Croatian parliament elected on the Communist Party ticket also stood by the Zagreb government. Sympathy for Croatia's Serb minority grew as a result, preventing a complete Croat–Serb split. Responses of this kind, however important they are in keeping the danger of civil war at bay, will however be of limited import only, since national homogenization in other parts of Yugoslavia will feed the idea that the Serbs are a beleaguered nation. This could deliver them straight into the hands of Milošević and his gang. What is needed is a breach in Serbia itself. This is why – despite the intended electoral machinations of the SPS – the coming elections in Serbia will mark a crucial political date in Yugoslav history.

In the absence of an alternative, the Yugoslav Prime Minister Ante Marković's newly formed Union of Reform Forces could emerge as a major challenger to Milošević's SPS – provided that Belgrade can be prevented from unleashing civil war in the meantime. It is becoming clear that an outline of a new Yugoslav settlement scrupulously respectful of national equality should be offered by anti-Milošević forces in advance of the Serbian elections. Their ability to do so will provide a critical test of Yugoslavia's emerging democracy. The alternatives are too dreadful to contemplate.

(October 1990)

4

The Generals' Manifesto

The document published below was leaked initially to the Slovene press. It was soon published in Croatia, where it appeared in *Vjesnik*, Zagreb (31 January 1991), from which this translation is taken. Issued by the Federal Council of National Defence, it was read to Army commanders throughout Yugoslavia on 25 January 1991. The FCND is a purely military body, whose sole purpose is to advise the Yugoslav presidency – Commander-in-Chief of the federal armed forces – on military matters. In issuing this document, the FCND breached the country's constitution and laws.

To understand the significance of the document, one must recall the nature of the Communist Party organization – the League of Communists – in Yugoslavia. Until March 1990, the Party was made up of the Leagues of Communists of Yugoslavia's six republics and two provinces, together with the party organization in the Army. This provided the Yugoslav Army with direct access to political decision-making. At its 14th Congress in March 1990, however, the all-Yugoslav Communist Party broke up. The republican (though not provincial) parties survived, albeit under different names. In the multi-party elections that followed, Communists lost power in Slovenia, Croatia, Macedonia and Bosnia-Herzegovina, but not in Serbia and Montenegro. The party organization in the Army was formally disbanded, by an act of the Yugoslav Federal Assembly banning all political organizations in the Army.

The disbanded party organization in the Army decided to organize itself as a party in its own right. At the end of that year several active and retired generals, including the current Federal Ministers of Defence and the Interior (both generals) and the current Chief of Staff, came together to form a new Communist party: the League of Communists – Movement for Yugoslavia. As the document says 'the Army . . . cannot solve the question of Yugoslavia. This can only be achieved by a strong political organization.' The LC-MY proclaimed itself the heir of the now defunct League of Communists of Yugoslavia, and took over the party building in Belgrade. Its adherents among the civilian population, however, remained few in number. Unlike the old LCY, the LC-MY is not organized on a federal basis. The reason for this can be gleaned from the reference in the document to 'mistakes of the League of Communists of Yugoslavia'. The LC-MY has expressly condemned the Slovene and Croatian Communists for organizing elections in the first place, and for accepting defeat when it came. Hence the reference in the document to 'those who wish to destroy [the party] from within' and the need to 'liquidate the fifth column among us'.

It is doubtful that the LC-MY expresses the view of all Army officers. There are many indications suggesting that the officer corps is politically divided. Conscripts, who form the bulk of the armed forces, are drawn from all the Yugoslav nationalities and can be assumed to be loyal to their national governments. It is significant that the document refers to reallocation of Slovene and Croat conscripts away from their home republics even before 25 January 1991.

The Army's attitude to the non-communist governments in the four republics has remained ambiguous. While not openly rebelling against them, it has refused to treat them as legitimate. In Slovenia and Croatia, in particular, the Army immediately after the elections confiscated the weapons held by the local Territorial Defence units – despite the fact that these weapons are the legal property of the republics concerned. It also stopped all delivery of weapons to them from the usual domestic suppliers (located mainly in Serbia). The republican governments, partly out of need and partly from a desire to enhance their sovereignty, began to import weapons from abroad. Croatia, we now know, imported some arms through Hungary. Hence the reference in the document to Hungary being implicated in 'Western designs' against Yugoslavia. These weapons were used not only for ordinary police work, but also to arm incipient republican armies – what the document calls 'illegal paramilitary organizations'. By now, however, the difference between legal and illegal has become moot, given that republican and Federal authorities (both government and presidency) are all openly violating the country's constitution. Nevertheless, in January 1991 the Yugoslav presidency, threatened by a military coup, ordered the disbanding of 'illegal armed units'. This is the 'Order' to which the document refers. It was not clear, however, whether the presidential Order referred to republican paramilitary forces (made legal, incidentally, by acts of their assemblies), or to armed bands of Serb civilians in Croatia, illegal under both republican and Federal laws.

It is the new Croatian government in particular which has become the prime target of the Army's anger. The reason for this lies in the pivotal role played by Croatia in Yugoslavia. On the evening of 25 January, the FCND showed a film on Belgrade television (which is under tight control of the

Serbian authorities) purporting to show Croatian ministers planning actions which the document describes as 'attacks on the garrisons, warehouses and other military objects, as well as sabotage and terrorist attacks, like organizing assassinations, liquidating family members and so on'. The film was made by KOS, the powerful Army counter-intelligence service. The film, naturally, caused much panic among the Serbs and much resentment among the Croats.

On the night of 25–26 January, the Army was put on full alert. Tanks appeared in several Croatian towns and troop movements were reported in several others. Croatia appeared on the brink of a full-scale invasion. In the event, nothing happened. Croatia refused to disband its forces, and the Yugoslav presidency did not react. Troops withdrew to barracks, but the Army issued a warrant for the arrest of the Croatian Ministers of the Interior and Defence – hence the reference in the document to 'legal' acts to be undertaken against 'the perpetrators of these great crimes'. According to Federal law, the Army has the right to try civilians in its own courts on all matters affecting its own and national security. The Croatian government, however, has refused to hand over its ministers. Their trial continues in their absence. It is worth noting that General Martin Špegelj, the Croatian Defence Minister in question, joined the Partisans as a young teenager in 1941; has ever since been a member of the (now reformed) Croatian Communist Party; was at one time in charge of Army cadre policy; and until a few months ago was commanding officer of the Fifth Army District, which covers Slovenia and much of Croatia. This, then, is a member of the 'fifth column'. At the height of the scare, Croatian president Franjo Tudjman (another retired general with Partisan credentials) wrote a letter to US President George Bush pleading for his support in defence of the 'young democracies' in Croatia and Slovenia. In March 1991, the Federal public prosecutor charged Tudjman with high treason, arguing that the letter amounted to inviting a foreign state to intervene in Yugoslavia.

The main thing that bothers the Army is its uncertain future, especially in regard to financing. Army funding has become the victim not only of the economic crisis, but also of the conflict between the republics. This conflict takes many forms, including economic warfare. In the summer of 1990, for example, the Serbian government introduced tariffs on goods imported from Slovenia and Croatia. It also first imposed additional taxes on Croatian and Slovenian firms operating in Serbia and subsequently confiscated them outright. All this was quite illegal, but neither the presidency nor the Federal government did, or could do, anything. Slovenia and Croatia retaliated by withholding part of their dues to the Federal state, thus directly affecting the military budget. Given the atmosphere of general economic and political uncertainty, the Federal budget is no longer set annually, but quarterly. At the time when the document was issued, the Army did not know what would happen to its money after March 1991. This could not but increase the sense of anxiety felt by its commanding officers.

The Yugoslav Army is faced with a great but probably insoluble problem in that, having lost its political master, it is now in the process of losing also its civilian commander. In March 1991, faced with mass demonstrations at home, the Serbian régime asked the presidency to impose a state of emergency throughout Yugoslavia. When the presidency refused, Serbia withdrew its three representatives (Serbia plus the two provinces). Montenegro followed suit. Although within days all these resignations were rescinded, the presidency has never recovered. It has become a body without any authority. The Army has been left to fend for itself, and is now placing its hopes in Federal Prime Minister Ante Marković. The LC-MY is a non-starter, and many Army top commanders do not take it seriously. But the Army, while formally declining to take the side of any republic, remains committed to the defence of Yugoslavia's — and its own – integrity. The main question which it will have to face sooner or later is whether its hostility to non- and anti-Communist governments justifies an alliance with Serb nationalists.

The Serbian–Army alliance is a potent generator of Yugoslavia's current political crisis. Were it not in place, the Yugoslav republics could solve the problem of transition in the armed forces, and also the inter-state conflict, with relative ease. As it is, Serbia feels sufficiently strong to wage a *de facto* war against its neighbours, most notably against Croatia and Bosnia-Herzegovina, using the Serb diaspora. The aim is to force these two (others would follow) to accept Serbia's hegemony within a new Federation; alternatively, if they persist in seeking independence, to annex large parts of their territory. Neither option, of course, is acceptable to Yugoslavia's non-Serb nations, who need only look at Kosovo to know what awaits them in a Yugoslavia dominated by Serbia. This means that, unless Milošević is toppled by his own hungry workers, the country is set for a full-scale civil war.

On the path to this war, two dates are of significance: 15 May and 30 June 1991. On the first, Stipe Mesić, Croatia's representative on the Yugoslav presidency, is due to replace Serbia's Borisav Jović at the top of the Federal hierarchy. If the changeover at the head of the Federation can be peacefully accomplished, peace may prevail and a new compromise among the Yugoslav states be forged. Otherwise the country will be plunged into war. 30 June is the final date set by Slovenia for an all-Yugoslav agreement, after which it will leave the Federation unilaterally. Croatia has said it will then follow suit. Kiro Gligorov, once Prime Minister of Yugoslavia and now Macedonia's president, has recently stated that if Slovenia and Croatia go, so will Macedonia. This is also the position of the Moslems of Bosnia-Herzegovina, who together with the Croats living there form two-thirds of the republic's population. Kosovo has already declared itself separate from Serbia. Montenegro is split into pro-Serbian and pro-independence camps. Serbia, for its part, is bent on grabbing other people's territories. Given all this, the Army will disintegrate into its national components.

Despite its socialist and anti-imperialist rhetoric, the Army document is inspired by the simple material interests, collective and personal, of what used to be one of the most powerful departments of the ancien régime. Thus Branko Mamula, once Federal Minister of Defence and now an active spokesman for the LC-MY, on retirement in 1987 built himself a villa on the Croatian coast using conscript labour (as was revealed by the Slovene journal *Mladina*). Another active member of the LC-MY is Nikola Ljubičić, likewise a retired minister of defence, who was saved from a corruption scandal by Milošević. Yet another is Lazar Mojsov, once Yugoslavia's head of state, who pushed for the introduction of martial law in Kosovo on the grounds (false, of course) that the Albanians were contemplating an armed uprising. (He is now employed by the Serbian bank Beobanka.) And so on.

It would be absurd, of course, to argue that all Yugoslav Army officers are corrupt. There are those who seem to be quite simply Yugoslav patriots. Nevertheless, a 'Movement for Yugoslavia' which is willing to tolerate a situation in which some Yugoslavs are denied all political rights, while others (Serbs and Montenegrins) are allowed to arm themselves and engage in open terrorism – and a 'League of Communists' which shuts its eyes to the revival of the Chetnik cult, the abuse of Tito and the Yugoslav revolution, and the growing calls for restoration of the monarchy (all this in Serbia), while waging struggle against anti-communism only in Slovenia and Croatia – is a party that can be explained only by the Army's interest in the continuation of its pay, its property and its power.

(March 1991)

Report Concerning the Actual Situation in the World and Yugoslavia, and Immediate Tasks of the Yugoslav People's Army

In this Report we wish to draw your attention to the more important features of the latest developments in the world and our country, and to the fundamental tasks of the Yugoslav People's Army (YPA) in 1991, especially the most immediate ones.

Our basic conclusion and current estimate is that one phase of development of both Yugoslav society and relations in the international community has been completed. The end of the 1980s marks the beginning of a new phase, which will be essentially different from the previous one. . . .

Though future developments in the USSR cannot be predicted with any certainty, one can confidently state at this moment that the process of disintegration of this great country has slowed down. The Soviets have started to regain their nerve and to realize that the path which they had chosen does not lead to a successful reform, but to disaster. Forces favouring the maintenance of the Soviet state and its institutions have grown and reaffirmed themselves. These days, they are taking decisive measures to arrest separatist tendencies in individual parts of the country. This is being done in ways that, in places, are highly problematic, facing great resistance in the country and outside pressures. The Soviet Army is also being mobilized. This development of the situation in the USSR, irrespective of where it may lead, limits the West's freedom of action and scope for influencing world events.

In Yugoslavia too, socialism has not yet been finished off, brought to its knees. Yugoslavia has managed to withstand, albeit at a high cost, the first attack and wave of anti-communist hysteria. Real prospects of maintaining the country as a federative and socialist community have been preserved. . . .

Western planners have achieved considerable success in the realization of their basic strategic orientation – the destruction of communism and the socialist option – but not of their ultimate aim. They have not succeeded in overthrowing communism in any country where the revolution had been authentic. This is why the strategists of the anti-socialist crusades have been forced to regroup their forces and to look for new aims and modalities of attack. In regard to their main competitor, the Soviet Union, they are likely to continue supporting the disintegrative tendencies. . . .

As far as our own country is concerned, the West has realized that the Yugoslav idea and socialist option have much deeper roots than they had envisaged, so that the overthrow of socialism in Yugoslavia is not the same thing as in other countries. This is why we can expect that they will modify the method of their action and move to an even stronger attack. It would be very important for them to achieve complete success in Yugoslavia. For they would be cutting into a country where revolution had been authentic.

Their further activity is likely to develop on two fronts, with two different aims. On the one hand, they will try to overthrow those Communists who have retained power, either in individual republics or at the Federal level. They will try to impede the execution of the economic reforms, or influence their actual implementation in order to cause social unrest. Then, following the same recipe as in Bulgaria or Romania, they will cause constant repetition of elections until their protégés take power. The other front is the break-up of Yugoslavia, accompanied by vilification of Communists. This strategy has been confirmed by several explicit actions. This is shown also by the well-known prognosis of the CIA that 'Yugoslavia will fall apart within eighteen months'. We know with what intentions such statements are given, and that they always have a clear function. The same is true of the State Department declaration of 25 December 1990, which contains a threat that the USA will 'strongly resist all use of force or pressures aimed at arresting the democratic processes or establishing a non-democratic unity of Yugoslavia'. The essence of the message is quite clear: they will overthrow socialism in Yugoslavia even at the price of its disintegration. At the same time, this is a warning to the Army not to prevent this process.

The support for democracy expressed in certain circles in the West is a transparent demagogy, because for them democracy is only that which corresponds to their aims and interests. For them, democracy in our conditions is primarily one that is anti-socialist.

The main activity against our country will continue to be directed through Hungary, because Hungary is in many ways already implicated in the game against Yugoslavia.

Last year was truly dramatic for our country. Anti-Yugoslavism and anti-socialism were proceeding apace. Everything looked bleak. This year will be even more difficult, but unlike in the previous one a way out is becoming visible. It has become clearer what needs to be done. This will depend first of all upon the engagement of social forces in the execution of three most important tasks.

First, it is necessary to ensure a complete fulfilment of the economic reform, in such a way as to prevent economic collapse and uncontrolled behaviour. In this regard, it is necessary to find safe, stable Federal solutions, especially in regard to the YPA. It is important to achieve this also because there exists a concept for destroying the Federation by starving it of funds, thus making its work impossible. Continuing the reform implies changing everything that was not good. This must be achieved gradually, rather than through upheavals.

Secondly, the functioning of the Federal state must be secured, as a precondition for agreement regarding the future organization of Yugo-slavia. If the policy of *fait accompli* continues, then it will be very difficult to avoid bloodshed, something that must be prevented at all cost. . . .

It is necessary that the existing Army bodies – both as institutions and as made up of citizens of this country – participate in all discussion regarding Yugoslavia's future. Speaking of this, all our experience suggests that Yugoslavia can exist only as a state. If it is not a state, then it is not Yugoslavia but something else. That which some in Yugoslavia offer as a confederation is factually not a state, nor can it be. The state can be unitary or federal. A unitary state has no chance in Yugoslavia and will not be accepted, because it failed its historic test. Yugoslavia can only be a federal community, with certain original prerogatives and federal functions. It is possible and necessary to discuss the kind and scope of these prerogatives. In doing so, it would be good to take into account the solutions adopted by many other unions of the federal type.

Thirdly, everything must be done to make sure that in the next five or six months the League of Communists – Movement for Yugoslavia becomes the main political force in the Yugoslav space, and the bastion of all left-oriented political parties, associations and organizations. At this moment, it is the only all-Yugoslav political force. It would be an excellent thing to have several parties of pan-Yugoslav orientation on the political scene. . . .

Our basic task must be the creation of conditions for the functioning of the Federal state. This means, first of all, the liquidation of all breaches made in the field of unity of the armed forces: i.e. disarming and liquidating all paramilitary organizations in Yugoslavia. Implementation of this task will create the basic conditions for a peaceful resolution of the crisis and a democratic transformation of Yugoslavia. At the same time, it will inflict a powerful defeat upon nationalist-separatist politics and practice, while encouraging forces working for the preservation and development of Yugoslavia on socialist foundations.

With the issuing of the Order of the Presidency of the SFRY the execution of this task has begun in favourable conditions, especially in regard to the affirmation of the YPA's standing in society. The public is becoming acquainted in the most concrete way with our firm decision to ensure that the Order is implemented. The adopted Order confirms also our commitment to work strictly within the Constitution and the Law, which in the given conditions is also politically the most acceptable way. If the Order is not executed as it stands, then legal and other organs — with all the consequences that inevitably follow their action — will be brought into play. The relevant organs are in possession of indisputable proofs concerning the completely illegal formation and arming of paramilitary units, and their preparation for conducting sabotage as well as other terrorist and violent actions. If the Order of the Presidency of the SFRY is not implemented, these ruinous facts will be publicized, within the context of actions undertaken against the perpetrators of these great crimes. Everybody to whom the Order refers should bear in mind that the illegal armed units will be dissolved and disarmed, in the manner and time prescribed by the Order or sanctioned by law.

It is necessary right now to ensure a high level of combat readiness of our units, and the functioning and security of our system of leadership and command. It is particularly important to establish a maximum degree of security in the units, because those whose heads will roll are ready to undertake desperate steps such as attacks on garrisons, warehouses and other military objects, as well as sabotage and terrorist attacks like organizing assassinations, liquidating family members, and so on. In the previous Report, we paid attention to facts indicating quite concrete preparations for such actions. For this reason, the protection of people, objects and units has never been so important as now.

We shall ensure full implementation of the decision regarding the Territorial Defence of Slovenia and the delivery of recruits for military service. These two tasks have not hitherto been in the foreground, because our main efforts have been focused on disarming paramilitary organizations. In regard to the recruits, some measures that come under their own jurisdiction will immediately be implemented. A part of the recruits from Slovenia and Croatia, now serving in the Fifth Military District, will be transferred to other Military Districts, and to Air Force and Anti-Aircraft

Defence. Responsibility for illegitimate changes in the plans drawn up by the Chief-of-Staff regarding the allocation and distribution of recruits will be established, and measures undertaken that will ensure a more effective implementation of this task. A procedure has been initiated for changing the law, with the aim of returning to the YPA this prerogative for the whole territory of the SFRY.

It is well known that we find ourselves in a very difficult financial situation. We must, therefore, use our financial resources with great care and probity. The order concerning the priority of payment must be understood with great seriousness and executed most faithfully. The Federal government has already discussed this, and some solutions have been reached. By the end of this month it will be necessary to find a solution for the stable functioning of the YPA. . . .

In parallel with this, we must dedicate ourselves to the constitution and well-being of the League of Communists – Movement for Yugoslavia. The existence of such a party of socialist orientation is a condition for the survival of our Army's unity and integrity. Hence, the great importance of the tasks under discussion.

Based on the ideas of Yugoslavism, national equality, brotherhood and unity, freedom and social justice, the [Communist] Party [of Yugoslavia] achieved victory in the war of 1941–45.

These are the same ideas that will bring victory to the League of Communists – Movement for Yugoslavia. The Army can ensure the conditions for a peaceful resolution of the crisis, but it cannot solve the question of Yugoslavia. This can be achieved only by a strong political organization, whose programme will be accepted and supported by the broadest social layers. All those who work against our country know that this is so. This is why they have attacked the League of Communists – Movement for Yugoslavia. They would even like to ban it, fearing its growing strength and influence in society. If communism is dead, as they say, why are they frightened by this organization?

We must patiently explain to the people the meaning and significance of the League of Communists – Movement for Yugoslavia. In the LC-MY, there should also be people who think differently. They are always welcome. But we cannot allow ourselves to repeat the mistakes made by the League of Communists of Yugoslavia. There is no place in this organization for those who wish to destroy it from within.

The most important thing for our party is to turn to the youth. Not only because the youth won the war and revolution and represents the future of any society; but because the fundamental ideas of the League of Communists – Movement for Yugoslavia are familiar to young people. Patriotism and the socialist idea has the greatest support in the young generation.

The Undoing of Yugoslavia

One year after the break-up of the League of Communists of Yugoslavia (LCY), the federal Yugoslav state itself seems set for dissolution. Despite its federalist rhetoric, Serbia, under nationalist demagogue Slobodan Milošević, began the process last November when it adopted a new constitution. It was followed this February by Slovenia and Croatia. Macedonia is expected to do the same. Montenegro has vowed to stick with Serbia come what may. In Bosnia-Herzegovina, the Moslem and Croat nationalities would like this republic also to declare itself a sovereign state, but this option has so far been rejected by the Bosnian Serbs. The two remaining federal units, Vojvodina and Kosovo, have meanwhile been swallowed up by Serbia (many Montenegrins fear that their republic will suffer the same fate). At the same time the demonstrations over the weekend of March 9–10 in Belgrade raising democratic demands offer a hope for the destabilization of Milošević on his home ground. Given the fact that Milošević's Greater Serbia plan is doomed to failure simply by weight of numbers (Serbs make up just 36 per cent of the Yugoslav population) nothing more than short-term solutions to the crisis are in sight.

Serbia's iron-fisted policy in Kosovo, where Albanians are in the majority, has led the province to secede from Serbia and declare itself a fully sovereign republic within Yugoslavia. However, the Yugoslav option is being denied to it. Slovenia, Croatia, Macedonia and to an extent also Bosnia-Herzegovina take the position that the subjects of current negotiations must be the six existing republics, thereby excluding the two provinces, Kosovo and Vojvodina, from the discussion regarding Yugoslavia's future and encouraging the feeling among Kosovo Albanians that they would do best to seek unification with Albania.

Serbia, meanwhile, has revised the Federal constitution not just by annexing the two provinces, but also by adopting the position that the proper subjects of any new political settlement are not the republics/provinces at all, but the South Slav nations. In its view, Yugoslavia's internal borders are administrative, not political; hence Serbia has the right to represent all Serbs, irrespective of where they live. Official Serbia has publicly committed itself to annex parts of Croatia and Bosnia-Herzegovina – eventually also of Macedonia – in the event of the federation being replaced by a looser state structure.[1] Arguing that all Serbs wish to live in a single state, it has been encouraging secessionist movements among Serbs living in these republics. In Croatia, this has taken the form of armed struggle: attacking local police stations, blockading roads and railways, forming armed guards, disseminating strident anti-Croat propaganda, and so on.

Thus civil war is no longer merely a distant prospect: already initiated in Kosovo, it is now spreading into Croatia. In Bosnia-Herzegovina, too, Serb nationalists have set up institutions of power parallel to the republican assembly and government. The motto 'One Serb nation, one Serb state' runs counter, of course, to similar rights for the other nationalities, which is why Serbia's policy is pushing the country in the direction of civil war.

Apart from the six republics, two other agents have emerged as subjects in their own right: the Yugoslav Army and the Federal government headed by Ante Marković. The Federal Ministers of Defence and the Interior, the army chief of staff and several other active and retired generals have recently formed a new party, the League of Communists – Movement for Yugoslavia, whose backbone is the 'Yugoslav Army and its commanding officers, as an institution and as citizens.'

This party is intended 'within the next five or six months to become the strongest political force'. The Army top brass has experienced the communist loss of power in parts of the country as a betrayal: 'In some of the Yugoslav republics, anti-communist "democracies" won their elections, in part because of the traitors within their local communist leaderships. It is especially important to liquidate such people from our party, the party that is led by our commanding officers. We should not repeat the errors made in the recent past; we should liquidate the fifth column among us . . .'

At home, the Army has formed an alliance with Serbia while in the longer run it counts on conservative forces in the Soviet Union (and the Soviet Army in particular) to save 'Communism and socialist society' and thus solve that other paramount issue – 'the continued financing of the Yugoslav army, [which] the hostile forces have discontinued or threatened to discontinue.' Serbia's current intransigence is a direct result of the Yugoslav military's support.

Prime Minister Marković, on the other hand, enjoys the support of the West, which is awed by the prospect of Yugoslavia's complete break-up. The West's strong card is the International Monetary Fund, without whose goodwill Yugoslavia faces an imminent economic collapse. Marko-vić's position is that the country must choose between him and the generals. But his plan of uniting Yugoslavia around a common economic reform has foundered as much on the stubbornness of the republics as on the rapidly growing incoherence of the Yugoslav economic space. He has thus been left with the ungrateful role of Yugoslavia's undertaker – a task which, nevertheless, he has performed with some honour. It was above all Marković, who, on the night of 25–26 January, helped to avert a military intervention in Croatia which, had it been successful, would have led to the introduction of military rule in the rest of Yugoslavia, setting off in all probability a generalized civil war.

The pre-eminence of national politics in Yugoslav internal life is nothing new. The recently published stenographic account of a February 1991 meeting of republican and federal leaders called to discuss Yugoslavia's future shows an uncanny resemblance to the last congress of the LCY in January 1990.

There is Milošević's Serbia (flanked by an impotent Montenegro), hoping to decide by sheer force of Serb numbers the fate of the Federation, ready to start civil war if defeated at the conference table. Lined up with Serbia is the Army, which fears not just anti-communist retribution but also the loss of its material privileges – in budgetary terms, and through the dismantling of the military-industrial complex, which only a centralized state can prevent. On the other side are Slovenia and Croatia, convinced that they stand a better chance of navigating the transition in a looser association, which they also perceive as an indispensable protection against Serbian aggression. Bosnia-Herzegovina and Macedonia occupy a middle position, torn between the twin fears of a Serb-dominated Yugoslavia and Yugoslavia's dissolution. The February meeting of the country's state leaders ended exactly like the 14th Congress of the LCY: Croatia and Slovenia walked out, Serbia pushed for the meeting to continue without them, Macedonia and Bosnia-Herzegovina voted to postpone the meeting to a more opportune moment.

Several subsequent meetings of the presidency were also sabotaged by the Serbian side. However, it is easier to dissolve a party than a state. The republican assemblies may vote themselves full sovereignty, but nobody wants to be the first to leave. The crafty Slovenes have invented a new term – dissociation – to describe what they wish to see happen. The existing Yugoslav association should be dissolved and replaced by a new one.

Two dates are seen as crucial: 15 May and 30 June 1991. On the first, Croatia's representative on the Federal presidency is due to replace Serbia's as the country's head of state for a year. If the Army and Serbia allow this to happen – that is, if they agree to respect the Federal constitution – then the prospect of a peaceful settlement of the Yugoslav conflict will be much enhanced. 30 June, on the other hand, is the final date set by Slovenia for a negotiated inter-Yugoslav agreement. If no agreement is reached, then Slovenia, followed by Croatia, will secede unilaterally.

Contemporary Yugoslav politics contains novel features, but bears also the marks of the old. The disappearance of the LCY has undoubtedly removed the minimal protection from the ravages of international capitalism which the working class had enjoyed after 1945. Nevertheless this protection had already worn thin, becoming little more than one by-product of an inert and increasingly conservative system – which, moreover, was showing signs of morbidity by the early 1980s. The introduction of martial rule in Kosovo in 1981 was followed, in succession, by an attempt to reintroduce strict censorship; the failure of an initiative to open up debate among party members; the trial of six Belgrade intellectuals on trumped-up charges; the legitimation of an aggressive Serb nationalism in Serbia; official tolerance (again in Serbia) of crude attacks on the LCY's nationality policy; the trial of four Slovene intellectuals in military courts; *putsches* in Vojvodina, Kosovo and Montenegro; and the bloodshed in Kosovo.

The industrial working class and public sector workers responded to the leadership's impotence in the face of the growing economic crisis with strikes: between 1980 and 1985 their number doubled (from 235 to 696); it then rose to 851 in 1986 and to 1,685 in 1987. In that year, Milošević came to power in Serbia and the Army became restless. Meanwhile, a democratic alternative was offered by the western republics: in 1988, Slovenia quietly legalized opposition; in 1989 the Slovenian and Croatian Leagues of Communists opted for multi-party elections. The military party has described this as an act of betrayal. Yet in the words of Ivica Račan, leader of the League of Communists of Croatia (now the Party of Democratic Change), all the party did was to return its mandate to the people.

The multi-party elections of 1990 did not lead to a sharp break with the past. In Serbia and Montenegro, the ruling Communist parties won overwhelming majorities. In Slovenia, a non-communist coalition, DEMOS, won the elections but the leader of the Slovenian Communists (now Party of Democratic Change) Milan Kučan became the republic's president. In Macedonia, no party gained an absolute majority; despite the strong showing of the nationalist VMRO, the Macedonian assembly elected Kliro Gligorov, an old Communist, as its president. In Croatia, the main Croat nationalist party – the Croatian Democratic Union (HDZ) – won almost two-thirds of the seats, but key positions – including that of the president – went to ex-Communists. Croatia's president Franjo Tudjman was thus able to say recently that there are more people sitting in the Croatian parliament with Partisan war documents dating back to 1941 than in any other such body in the country. Only in Bosnia-Herzegovina did the nationalist parties win outright: the joke goes that the elections were in effect a census, since Croats voted for the Croat national party, Serbs for the Serb one (Serb Democratic Party) and Moslems for the SDA. In Kosovo, Albanians refused to take part in the elections, having declared themselves independent from Serbia last November; their demand was for democratic elections to their own institutions.

Despite elements of continuity, the sense of political dislocation is great, due to the combined effects of the change of administration, the dismantling of the previous socio-economic system and the depth of the economic recession. Whatever happens to Yugoslavia, there is little doubt that its heirs will continue to be unstable for some time to come. This is primarily because a power vacuum has been created at the very base of Yugoslav society, with the near-complete absence of parties representing the working class. The dismantling of the system based on social property and the vertiginous rise in industrial unemployment has dramatically weakened this class, which is only beginning to organize itself at the trade union level. Its resistance is at present obfuscated by the siren calls of the various national flags, just when the state of permanent tension is aiding authoritarian tendencies which will sooner or later be targeted against it. This is why a speedy and democratic political settlement at the all-Yugoslav level is of the greatest interest to the country's working population.

The greatest obstacle to such a settlement has been Slobodan Milošević's régime. This is how a Belgrade independent weekly *Vreme* (4 March 1991) describes its tactics:

> Slobodan Milošević is undoubtedly the central figure in Yugoslav negotiations, not because of his contribution or initiatives, but because of his hostile stance to all dialogue – his evident desire to make any agreement seem impossible. Thus, for example, he used the [anti-Croat] demonstration of women [held in Belgrade at the end of February] to make it difficult for Tudjman and Mesić to come [to a scheduled meeting of the Federal presidency]; then, when they did not come, he pressed for negotiations to take place without them.
>
> Milošević agreed to join the [inter-Yugoslav] talks unwillingly and only under pressure from domestic and foreign public opinion, but he clearly believes that his aims cannot be achieved that way. Recent events have strengthened the sovereignty of the republics as well as the legitimacy of their borders, while republican presidents are increasingly behaving as his equals.
>
> Milošević, who lacks all diplomatic and negotiating skills, is also harvesting the bitter fruits of a politics which, over three years, has made Serbia the least desirable partner in Yugoslavia. Apart from [Montenegrin president] Momir Bulatović, he cannot convince anybody that he does not wish to dominate. He is

also burdened by the dead weight of the Communist ideology, rejected in four of the six republics. . . .

The link between the two parties [the Socialist Party of Serbia and the League of Communists – Movement for Yugoslavia] is evident. The LC-MY relies on the Army, whose help Milošević is increasingly seeking – despite the fact that this is undermining his position as Serb national leader. The LC-MY, on the other hand, cannot count on winning elections anywhere in Yugoslavia, not even in Serbia. This party and its leaders probably harbour no illusions in this regard, but this does not prevent them from acting ever more aggressively and with open ambitions.

Their only chance lies in the Army taking power, following which the LC-MY would take the place once occupied by the LCY. This project of renewal of Communist power is, of course, hopeless. Yet Serbia's conduct in the negotiations suggests that it is counting on this option. The fact that it is not taking them seriously argues that it is relying on the power of the Army. In its attempt to renew socialist Yugoslavia, the Army would ensure that all Serbs live within the same state, which is what Milošević says he wants. Yet a military *coup d'état* would spell the end of Milošević and of the dream of an all-Serb state.

(March 1991)

Note

1. Serbia's eventual encroachment into Macedonia will be contested by Bulgaria. The Bulgarian government has recently published a statement in which it commits itself to recognizing a sovereign Macedonia, if and when this is adopted by the Macedonian parliament, and abandoning all claims on its territory.

6

Youth Rebel against Milošević

Mounting gloom about the ability of Yugoslavia to survive as an integral state was suddenly pierced by a ray of light in March 1991, with massive demonstrations against the hardline régime in Serbia, Yugoslavia's largest republic. Called originally by opposition parties to protest against the ruling party's iron control over the local mass media, the first demonstration on 9 March was met with the full array of instruments of riot control: water cannon, tear gas, mounted police, dogs, rubber bullets and finally live ammunition. By the end of the day, two people had been killed and Army tanks made their appearance on Belgrade's streets. The following day, tens of thousands of young people demonstrated in Serbia's key towns, leading to a four-day occupation of the main square in Belgrade. The targets of their anger were the government and republican president, Slobodan Milošević, whom the crowd likened to Saddam Hussein. One hundred days after its overwhelming victory in the first multi-party elections since the war, the legitimacy of the ruling party – the Socialist Party (formerly League of Communists) of Serbia (SPS) – was thus dramatically brought into question.

Involving a multitude of young people and several university centres, the demonstrations expressed the clear repudiation by Serbia's younger generation of the policies of national hatred pursued by Milošević over the past four years. The spontaneous eruption of Serbia's youth into national politics has put paid to Milošević's claim to speak for Serbia far more effectively than all the combined efforts of the opposition parties. The appearance of the army on Belgrade streets said it all: Milošević is the first republican leader in Yugoslavia's postwar history to have requested military intervention in defence of domestic 'law and order'.

The ground for the March events was prepared by a widespread sense of disappointment with Milošević's betrayal of his electoral promises, chief among them a commitment to protect the population's living standards and work for a peaceful resolution of the Yugoslav crisis. Three months after the elections, half of Serbia's workforce remains unpaid; old-age pensioners and workplace invalids have not received their pensions; and Milošević's hardline stance in negotiations with the other republics has brought the country to the brink of civil war. As a student delegate told Milošević: 'Never before has Serbia been so isolated, so much hated, its international prestige so low.'

The March demonstrations mark a watershed in Yugoslav politics, giving rise to fresh hope that differences regarding the country's future will be resolved by negotiations rather than force. For this to happen, though, Milošević must go. This can only be achieved by the citizens of Serbia themselves.

A petition demanding his resignation has been circulated in Serbia, and it is highly significant that the Serbian intelligentsia, which contributed so much to Milošević's rise to power and only months, indeed weeks, ago was still hailing him as the saviour of the Serb nation, should now have sided overwhelmingly with the young demonstrators and trodden the path to its Canossa in Belgrade's Republic Square.

The parties of the opposition have hitherto shied away from challenging Milošević's aggressive and ultimately unrealistic national programme, thereby contributing to their own political (and electoral) marginalization. Now, however, in the words of a Serbian human rights activist: 'the students have proved that it is not freedom (*sloboda* in Serbian) and Serbia which are mutually exclusive, but rather freedom and Slobodan.'

On hearing the students declare the Serbian emperor naked, the rest of Yugoslavia heaved a sigh of relief. It will be difficult for the Belgrade media to argue henceforth that Milošević's opponents are automatically enemies of Serbia. By rejecting the identification between Milošević and the Serb nation, the students have raised the hope in other parts of Yugoslavia that their representatives can negotiate with Serbia without being constantly subjected to ultimata, demands for unconditional surrender, and threats of civil war or military intervention.

The immediate condemnation by most of the other republics of the use of violence against demonstrators, and especially of the army's involvement, gave the lie to Milošević's favourite demagogic device: the claim that all other Yugoslavs – and much of the world besides – are joined in an anti-Serb plot. The chief plotter against the nation's freedom turned out to be none other than the republic's own president! Serbia's young have thus emerged as a key protagonist of Yugoslavia's unity.

The way forward must lie in fresh elections in Serbia. Milošević's charisma as an undisputed national leader, created and maintained by his control over the mass media, has been a key instrument of his party's electoral victory. Thanks to the students' action, this control is now weakening. Nor will Milošević be able in future to rely on the Federal Army, for the Army has vowed to remain henceforth outside the political fracas. This does not mean that Milošević's régime will give up without a fight. It will create its own military forces and continue to play the nationalist card. It will also seek to dismantle the remaining Federal institutions – the collective presidency, the government and the Army – threatening to bring Yugoslavia down with itself.

The young demonstrators, on the other hand, have given a mandate to the Serbian opposition parties to articulate a programme based not on confrontation, but on cooperation with Yugoslavia's other nationalities. It remains to be seen whether the opposition is capable of assuming this historic responsibility. Much will depend also on whether the political parties in the rest of Yugoslavia are able to grasp the importance of what happened in Serbia during the March days, and make an adequate response.

'Civil war? We leave that to the older generation,' one Belgrade student told a German television crew. He was speaking at that moment for all the young people of Yugoslavia – politically marginalized, largely unemployed and overwhelmingly dissatisfied with the options on offer from their elders. His words hold a particular poignancy for the Albanians of Kosovo, who, thanks to Milošević, have for two years now been having a taste of something very close to civil war.

In the mass media of Western Europe, the potential for civil war in Yugoslavia is ascribed variously to its multi-ethnic makeup; to the differing cultural traditions of 'Mitteleuropa' and the Ottoman Empire; to memories of the atrocities committed by local Nazi collaborators during World War Two; to a struggle between the remnants of Communism and a new anti-Communist majority. All these factors are present, but they do not play more than a marginal role.

If civil war does come to Yugoslavia, it will be through attempts to alter existing borders by force. Milošević has made it absolutely clear (as recently as 28 March at a meeting of republican heads of state) that if the other republics persist in their plans for a confederal Yugoslavia, he will seek the creation of a Greater Serbia – that is, a state embracing all Serbs living in Yugoslavia.

This implies the disappearance of Montenegro and Bosnia-Herzegovina and the amputation of a substantial part of Croatia. It is likely that Macedonia also would be a victim. From the national point of view, such a state would be an absurdity, since within it Serbs would not even command a numerical majority. This has not prevented Milošević from encouraging militant Serb nationalists in Croatia and Bosnia-Herzegovina to form National Councils with the aim of annexing these territories to Serbia. At the end of March, such a Council in Croatia announced the secession of a self-proclaimed 'Autonomous Province of Krajina' (an area embracing only a minority of Serbs in Croatia, along with a considerable number of Croats) and its adhesion to Serbia.

It is worth spelling out why such acts can lead only to war. During World War Two, Yugoslav Communists were able to organize a mass anti-Nazi resistance, and also win the civil war, primarily because they understood that the aspirations of the country's diverse nationalities could be satisfied only by their acquiring their own states within the new Yugoslavia. This was the basis for the federal organization of the postwar state: six republics and two provinces.

The formula ensured national peace for almost half a century. The borders of these federal units are thus not administrative, but deeply national and political. They do not coincide with ethnic borders, nor could they do so; they separate many Croats, Serbs, Moslems and Albanians from their mother republic/province. But international borders too in many parts of Europe do not follow ethnic boundaries. The key point is that these frontiers – and this holds equally for Yugoslavia – cannot be changed except by agreement or war.

The first attempt to alter Yugoslavia's internal frontiers came in 1988–89, when Serbia incorporated by force two federal units, Kosovo and Vojvodina, and imposed a puppet administration upon a third, Montenegro. Yugoslavia has not yet recovered from the shock of this aggression, nor will it be able to regain any stability until it has been rolled back. The secession of the so-called Krajina – only one day after a conference of republican presidents in the Croatian town of Split – is a fresh attempt to use this method to destroy Yugoslavia from within. Milošević, by supporting the Krajina leaders, has in effect declared war on Yugoslavia.

Milošević has never been interested in a collective agreement. In the past he has managed to torpedo all efforts to resolve the political crisis by peaceful means, each time upping the stakes in this deadly game with Yugoslavia's future. Now, with time running against him, he is becoming even more dangerous. The adventurist character of his policy was illustrated clearly by the farce – a farce that could easily have turned into tragedy – surrounding the resignation, on 15 March, of Borisav Jović, chairman of the Yugoslav state presidency, from that body.

With demonstrators' shouts still ringing in his ears, Milošević tried to push the presidency into allowing the introduction of a state of emergency throughout Yugoslavia. When he failed to win a majority for this, he engineered Jović's resignation, as well as that of the representatives of Vojvodina and Montenegro. The Kosovo representative, having sided with the majority, was promptly (and unconstitutionally) dismissed by the Serbian Assembly. The elimination of four out of eight members of the Federal presidency not only made the collective head of state impotent, it also left the Army without a functioning commander-in-chief.

Jović's act was unprecedented in Yugoslavia's modern history, causing a severe constitutional crisis. Neither the Federal presidency, nor the Serbian Assembly, nor the relevant bodies in other republics and provinces, were informed of this decision before it was made public. He subsequently justified his resignation on the grounds that the current relationship of forces on the presidency 'supports the break up of the country', taking the opportunity also to launch a violent attack on Ante Marković, the Federal prime minister, whom he accused of being an agent of foreign governments.

In a dramatic address to the nation following Jović's resignation, Milošević announced that Serbia would no longer obey the Federal presidency; that he himself, as president of Serbia, would have nothing to do with it; and that he was organizing police reservists to prevent alleged rebellions in Kosovo and the Moslem-inhabited south-west of Serbia. He concluded his speech by calling upon the 'imperilled Serb nation' to unite behind him. The Serbian prime minister brought up the rear by informing the Serbian Assembly of an impending attack by the Croatian and Bosnian authorities on Serb-inhabited towns – a piece of misinformation which he subsequently had to retract.

Milošević's attempt to undermine collective Federal bodies did not, however, succeed. Five days later, on 21 March, Jović simply rescinded his resignation and returned to his presidential post without any explanation; the vassal provinces and Montenegro trailed behind. Nevertheless, the eruption of this unforeseen constitutional crisis had been sufficient to shift public attention away from the demonstrations that had taken place in Serbia, and to the even more urgent issue of who – if anybody – rules Yugoslavia.

The secession of the so-called Krajina from Croatia is intended to serve the same purpose: to provide Milošević with extra time – even at the price of civil war. It has already cost three lives; traffic between the coast and the interior has again been interrupted; tourism – on which Yugoslavia vitally depends for its foreign currency – has been dealt a mortal blow. By deploying its tanks in a part of the disputed area – Plitvice National Park – the Army is back on the streets again. Given Milošević's warlike stance, and Croatian determination to prevent the break-up of their republic, it is difficult to see how it will be able to return to barracks in the foreseeable future.

These events prove once again that Yugoslavia has no future unless democracy wins in Serbia. This is why the demonstrating Serbian youth gave rise to such hopes that peace would prevail. In the last two weeks of March, thousands of Serbian citizens signed the petition below demanding Milošević's resignation. The main message of the March demonstrations was: give peace a chance. The Serb youth, however, in its majority, owes loyalty to no particular party in Serbia. The vast majority of the opposition parties have been so complicit with Milošević's nationalist programme that it is difficult to see how they can offer the youth the positive alternative it seeks. Until such an alternative is articulated, Serbia will remain a menace to the rest of the country. Yugoslavia as a political, economic and cultural space will continue to crumble, tottering between hope and the threat of civil war.

(April 1991)

The Serbian Intellectuals' Appeal

Only three months after his election to the post of president of the republic, Slobodan Milošević has lost the confidence of the people.

The whole world, all the Yugoslav republics and peoples (with the exception of the puppet régime in Montenegro) and finally now also Serbia and its youth have come out against Milošević's Serbia. His skill in acquiring enemies has brought Serbia to the very brink of civil war.

The crude and violent manipulation of Serbian public opinion could no longer cover up these facts. The arrogance and scorn with which Slobodan Milošević has treated everyone, including his own people, reached their peak on 9 March when he ordered an attack on Serb people, when human lives were lost, and when torture was used against imprisoned Serb youth.

Having failed to persuade the army to introduce a state of emergency in Yugoslavia, the purpose of which could only be the preservation of his personal rule, Milošević went on to destroy the presidency of Yugoslavia, thus foreclosing the last possibility of a peaceful resolution to the crisis.

The President of Serbia has chosen the politics of war. The bringing of tanks into the streets and the undermining of any agreement about the future of Yugoslavia testify to an adventurism and selfish egotism which the Serb people can no longer tolerate.

Milošević cannot implicate the whole of the Serb nation in the creation of enemies for which his despotism has been responsible.

The Serb people is no longer willing to allow Slobodan Milošević to keep it in isolation, to feed it with lies, to beat it and burden it with historic mortgages.

Speaking in the interest of all citizens of Serbia, we demand of Slobodan Milošević that he immediately resign his post.

(*This public appeal is dated 17 March 1991. It was published in the independent Belgrade weekly,* Vreme, *on 25 March 1991)*

7

Yugoslavia in Trouble

(a) Will Yugoslavia Survive?

This is the question preoccupying the Yugoslavs, worrying their neighbours, and giving a headache to the European Community. The United States and the Soviet Union have likewise felt the need to come out publicly in favour of Yugoslavia's unity. Since the end of the Cold War the strategic significance of Yugoslavia may have faded, but its future has become linked to that of another multinational state: the Soviet Union. Neither Europe nor the wider world is ready for a major reorganization of the continent's borders.

The very fact that a state's existence is being questioned suggests that its problems are not superficial, but fundamental. What, then, has gone wrong with Yugoslavia? Any answer to this question must include three components: the fate of the Communist Party, the relationship between the constituent nationalities, and the economy.

Up to the mid-1980s, everything that happened was the exclusive concern of the Communist Party, which not only represented the country's unity but also channelled its differences. In the second half of the 1980s, the arrival of a sharp economic crisis, which the country's leaders were unable to resolve, set off a chain reaction. Workers began to strike; the poorer republics and provinces went bankrupt; and the ruling party started to split along national lines. By 1990, two camps broadly speaking emerged: one seeking democratic, the other repressive solutions. The first camp was led by the republics of Slovenia and Croatia, the second by Serbia, Yugoslavia's largest republic. Political differences now fused openly with national differences. In early March 1990 this polarization broke up the all-Yugoslav Communist Party into its national components. A central pillar of Yugoslav unity disappeared in a matter of days.

Later that year, multi-party elections were held throughout Yugoslavia. In four republics (Slovenia, Croatia, Macedonia and Bosnia-Herzegovina) the Communists were defeated, while in the remaining two (Serbia, Montenegro) they retained power. By now, however, the word 'Communist' meant very little. The Serbian Communist Party had already become the party of aggressive Serb nationalism. Its quest for dominance within the Federation – cloaked in a pan-Yugoslav rhetoric – provoked most of the other republics to demand a loosening of the state structures: i.e. transformation of the federation into a confederation of fully sovereign republics. The exception was Montenegro, which had in the meantime become little more than a vassal state of Serbia. Serbia also managed to swallow up Yugoslavia's two provinces (Vojvodina, Kosovo) just prior to the elections. Its expansionism frightened the rest of Yugoslavia.

The elections took place only in the individual republics but not at the all-Yugoslav level. This enhanced republican independence with respect to the Federal centre. As the battle for power between the republics grew in intensity, the initial division – federal *v.* confederal – became sharper. Slovenia, Croatia, and to a lesser extent Macedonia and Bosnia-Herzegovina, began to contemplate Yugoslavia's complete dissolution. Serbia announced its intention, in that event, of annexing parts of Croatia, Bosnia-Herzegovina, Montenegro and eventually also Macedonia. The ethnically Albanian population of Kosovo – though now denied legitimate representation – sided openly with Serbia's opponents. As the country became engulfed in a constitutional crisis, its violent disintegration emerged as a possible outcome – and the Army as a possible arbiter.

The apex of the Yugoslav state is the Federal presidency, which has eight members, one each from the six republics and two provinces. Its importance lies in the fact that it commands the Army. One of the aims behind Serbia's expansionism was to win a majority on the presidency, thus gaining control of the Army. But it did not succeed: despite all its efforts, it could muster no more than four of the eight votes. Serbia, however, was counting on Army support in any clash with the other republics. The preponderance of Serb and Montenegrin nationals among the officers, and the strong commitment to Yugoslav unity animating the top brass, appeared to lend this strategy credibility. The moment of truth, however, came in March 1991, when huge anti-government demonstrations, made up mainly of students and young people, erupted throughout Serbia. Its peak was a three-day occupation of the centre of Belgrade, capital of both Serbia and Yugoslavia. In Vojvodina and Montenegro too students took to the streets. Serbia demanded that the whole of Yugoslavia be placed under military rule, but the Army declined. Its decision to stay out of inter-republican disputes has weakened not just Serbia's hand, but also the importance of the Federal presidency. The result was to strengthen the confederal tendency.

The last remaining Federal body of any importance is the Federal government, headed by Ante Marković. The government, formally appointed by the presidency, is in theory responsible to the Federal Assembly. This Assembly, however, is the old one, elected under the previous system. Its mandate ran out a year ago, but has been periodically extended until such time as Federal elections can be organized; if the confederal solution prevails, such elections will become redundant. The Federal government has thus survived only by the good grace of the republics: it has no autonomous source of authority. Despite this, Markovič has remained an influential figure in Yugoslav politics, since he commands the confidence not only of the Army, but also of the West, i.e. of Yugoslavia's creditors. Their support for Marković is support for Yugoslav unity.

The array of forces, then, is as follows. Effective power lies with the six republics, whose heads have been meeting on a weekly basis over the past month, with little result. In addition to the republican presidents, there is Prime Minister Marković, arguing that Federal elections are a necessary condition for successful economic reform and continued Western aid. There is also the restless two-million-strong Albanian population: they have recently been deprived of all national rights; they remain excluded from inter-Yugoslav talks; and they live under harsh Serbian occupation – but no lasting solution can ignore their needs and aspirations. And finally, there is the economic crisis – a political player in its own right – whose avenging angel will be the working class. During the election year Yugoslav workers were largely inactive, not least because the republican governments made sure they were paid. Now, however, strikes are being resumed and on a much larger scale than before. In April 1991, 700,000 Serbian workers struck for two days – and promised to do so again. Tens of thousands of workers in other parts of the country have been striking on and off during the past few months. More than half of the Yugoslav workforce does not receive wages with any regularity, while the other half lives on or below the minimum guaranteed wage. The country's economy meanwhile continues its nose-dive, threatening millions of them with the dole.

Yugoslavia today resembles a vast network of trenches, behind which lie encamped conflicting interests spawned by developmental problems, but also by the heady ambitions of competing national leaders. In this war of attrition, each side is counting on rebellion erupting in the enemy's interior, and with some luck also among its front-line troops. In the Great War of 1914–18 in Europe the outcome was decided by a combination of factors: outside (American) intervention; military mutinies; civilian hunger marches; national revolts; revolutionary upheavals; and general war-weariness. Something like this could also happen in Yugoslavia. Let us hope only that the peace settlement, when it comes, will not repeat the mistakes of Versailles.

(April 1991)

(b) Draft Resolution on Yugoslavia to be Put before the European Parliament

1. In the view of this Parliament, the only legitimate subjects in deciding Yugoslavia's future are the freely elected assemblies of the constitutive members of the Yugoslav Federation: the six republics and two provinces. It therefore calls upon the Yugoslav Federal government immediately to organize free elections to the assembly of the Province of Kosovo, in order to enable the Province to elect its representatives to the Yugoslav Federal bodies.

2. The Parliament considers Yugoslavia's internal borders – the borders of the six republics and two provinces, as prescribed by the last Federal Constitution (of 1974) – to be inviolable. It will not recognize any changes made to these borders, unless they are achieved by mutual consent: i.e. by the express will of the elected assemblies of the Federal members concerned.

3. Whereas the Parliament wishes to see the preservation of Yugoslavia's integrity, it considers that violent means of maintaining inherited structures are both unacceptable and doomed to failure. In response to such attempts, it is willing to recognize, at their request, the existing Federal members as fully sovereign states provided that: (a) they guarantee full rights to the national minorities; (b) they guarantee full discharge of the Yugoslav Federation's international obligations.

4. With this in mind, the Parliament calls upon the Yugoslav republics and provinces (in the case of Kosovo, assuming free election of its assembly) to establish the necessary instruments for an orderly transition towards a new, democratically agreed, form of association, either by investing the present Federal government with the necessary powers, or by constituting – through some other democratic process – another, equally empowered, collective body.

(April 1991)

8

The Kosovo Boomerang

Yugoslavia's latest crisis erupted on 15 May, when Serbia and its satellites flouted the Yugoslav constitution by blocking Stipe Mesić, Croatia's representative on the Federal presidency (Yugoslavia's collective head of state), from taking his turn as president for the coming year. The voting confirmed the basic line of division within Yugoslavia: the representatives of Macedonia, Bosnia-Herzegovina, Slovenia and Croatia voted for Mesić; Serbia, Vojvodina, Kosovo and Montenegro voted against. But the men who cast the votes for Vojvodina and Kosovo had no legal or political right to be there in the first place.

According to the Yugoslav constitution, the eight-man presidency is made up of representatives from each of the six republics and two provinces. Each of these representatives is elected by secret vote in the appropriate republican or provincial assembly and remains responsible to that assembly. On 15 May each year, the presidency elects a new president in accordance with a strict rota. Thus on 15 May 1989 the post went to Slovenia (Janez Drnovšek), on 15 May 1990 to Serbia (Borisav Jović) and on 15 May 1991 it was due to go to Croatia (Stipe Mesić). The system of rotation was established in the early 1970s, to express the equal status of members of the Yugoslav Federation.

This constitution was drawn up when Yugoslavia was still a federation of equal nations. But only a year after his rise to power in Serbia, Milošević began to dismantle it. In 1988, the Serbian Assembly adopted an amendment to the republican constitution cancelling Vojvodina's and Kosovo's political autonomy. Nationalist mobilizations were also organized to bring down the governments in Vojvodina and Montenegro and replace them by Serbian stooges. Kosovo, though abandoned by the rest of Yugoslavia, resisted. There were mass demonstrations of Albanian citizens and, in February 1989, a general strike led by Kosovo miners. The province was then placed under military occupation. The following month, with tanks ringing the assembly building and military jets flying overhead, Kosovo deputies voted in the required constitutional amendment. In July 1990, however – following the break-up of the League of Communists of Yugoslavia, multi-party elections in Slovenia and Croatia, and (most important) the establishment of a state of terror in Kosovo – the provincial Assembly declared Kosovo's independence from Serbia. Serbia responded by dissolving the provincial Assembly and government, and its own assembly voted in a new republican constitution which reduced the provinces to a status lower than that of a municipality.

With the adoption of the new Serbian constitution, the federation as defined by the Yugoslav constitution ceased to exist. Without a functioning assembly, Kosovo representatives in the Federal Assembly and on the Federal presidency became illegitimate, and with them also the work of these bodies. The other republics, pursuing their own selfish interests, connived at this illegal state of affairs until 15 May 1991, when it was no longer possible to avoid the issue. For if Serbia could get away with vetoing Croatia's representative, then it rather than Yugoslavia would decide the country's future. The Federal presidency consequently fell apart. As this author predicted at the time, the boomerang released in Kosovo in 1988 returned three years later to deliver a mortal blow to Yugoslavia. The decision by the Serbian régime to bring down the Yugoslav presidency proves conclusively that it sees Federal organs outside its control as an impediment to its own survival.

At the beginning of 1991, Milošević appeared at the height of his powers. Although the dissolution of the Yugoslav Communist Party had scuppered his earlier plan to use the party machine to win for Serbia the hegemony it had enjoyed in pre-war Yugoslavia, the illusion that this could be achieved persisted, because of the Army's evident hostility to the new régimes in Slovenia and Croatia. With control over four Federal units, Serbia now enjoyed disproportionate influence within the Federal institutions. On the presidency, which is commander-in-chief of the Army, Milošević now wielded four of the eight votes. Furthermore, egged on by renegades such as Mihailo Marković of *Praxis* fame, he encouraged armed rebellion among Serbs in parts of Croatia (the so-called Krajina) and Bosnia-Herzegovina, in order to undermine these republics' ability to resist. Last but not least, by winning a huge majority in the Serbian elections of 1990 he marginalized the domestic opposition.

The March demonstrations in Serbia, however, provided a moment of truth for Milošević. He entered Yugoslav history as the first republican head of state to ask the Army to intervene in a domestic dispute. Indeed, Milošević pressed the Army to introduce a state of emergency throughout Yugoslavia. But the Army – keen in principle, but fearing a possible breakdown of discipline in its own ranks – would not comply without the authority of the presidency. The latter, supported by Federal Prime Minister Marković, refused the request. Kosovo's representative broke ranks to vote with the independent republics. The Army high command, shaken by the Serbian demonstrations, now rallied behind Marković (though not all of them unequivocally).

Milošević, defeated in the presidency and challenged at home, now opted for a strategy of making the Federal institutions unworkable. His immediate response was to denounce the Federal presidency as an agent of Yugoslavia's destruction, and Marković as a Western stooge. On 16 March, the representatives of Serbia, Montenegro and Vojvodina resigned from the presidency. Milošević declared that the presidency no longer existed and (somewhat inconsistently) that Serbia no longer recognized its authority. At a hastily convened secret meeting, he told local government heads that Serbia was *de facto* in a state of war. Milošević's bluff was called, however, and two days later it was back to business as usual on the presidency – but only for the time being. The Kosovo representative was placed summarily under house arrest and replaced by a man appointed by the Serbian assembly. The new man, Sejdo Bajramović, is an oddity even for recent Serbian politics: elected by 0.03 per cent of votes in his Kosovo constituency (Albanians had unanimously boycotted the Serbian elections), this retired army sergeant is renowned only for his addiction to tombola. Vojvodina and Montenegro also came up with new presidential representatives.

Between mid-March and mid-May Yugoslavia lived a charmed life as a country teetering on the brink of civil war and/or military coup, while its 'high politics' became more and more of a charade. For several weeks during March and April republican heads met in conference at different luxurious locations, accompanied by a swarm of journalists, in order supposedly to forge a new consensus. These meetings, all of which ended in failure, served only to shore up Milošević's position in Serbia. His strategy of destabilization, if anything, gained a new lease of life. The following brief survey of some of the key events in the period between the end of March and the middle of May give an idea of how this strategy works.

- On 31 March, an armed unit from 'Krajina' (part of Croatia in which Serbs form a majority) tried to occupy the Plitvice National Park in Croatia, and were repulsed by the Croatian police. At Jović's request, but over Slovene and Croatian protests, the Federal presidency met in emergency session and ordered the Army to occupy the park.
- On 16 April, 750,000 Serbian workers declared a general strike and the republican government quickly met their terms 'for the sake of Serb national unity'.
- On 2 May, in Borovo Selo in eastern Croatia, Serb militants ambushed a bus carrying Croatian police and killed twelve of them. Serb Chetniks –

a proto-fascist nationalist formation – publicly boasted of having taken part in the massacre. The fact that some of the victims had been severely tortured added credence to their claim. There followed another emergency session of the Federal presidency, another threat of military takeover – and another part of Croatia occupied by the Army.

- In Bosnia-Herzegovina, Serb followers of Milošević set up three new 'Krajinas' as a future part of Serbia, and refused to recognize henceforth the authority of the republican government.

- By now, an anti-Army mood had become entrenched in Croatia, reaching a high point on 6 May in Split, when 30,000 workers massed outside the Navy command centre demanding an end to the blockading of Croatian villages by the 'Krajina' militia (with Army complicity). A soldier's death led to yet another emergency session of the Federal presidency, at which the Army was given additional policing powers in Croatia.

- Fearing that a military occupation of Croatia was imminent, the population of several ethnically Croat villages and towns in Bosnia-Herzegovina took to the streets to block Army tanks moving towards Croatia. The Army sent in a parachute unit to 'liberate' its troops. Thanks to the combined efforts of the Croatian and Bosnian presidents, this particular conflict was defused.

- In the Dalmatian ports of Zadar and Šibenik, however, anti-Serb riots and destruction of Serb property erupted, after a local man was killed by a 'Krajina' activist. Anti-Croat riots and destruction of Croat property followed in 'Krajina'.

- Since the soldier killed in Split was a Macedonian, demonstrations followed in Macedonia, at which Milošević and Croatian president Tudjman were denounced as warmongers.

- Slovenia's response to this turbulence was to speed up legislative procedures preparing independence.

- In the Serbian Assembly, demands were voiced that Serbia should raise an army for a war against its enemies. Though this was rejected (albeit only formally, for in reality Serbia already has a well-armed paramilitary force), a Serb National Council, involving the ruling party and the main parties of the opposition, was established, its chief aim being to create 'one state for all Serbs' – the slogan of the Serbian extreme Right.

- Political ferment was in evidence also in Montenegro, where the opposition left the republican assembly for good.

- In the Serbian part of the Sandjak, which is largely Moslem in ethnic terms, a Moslem National Council was set up aimed at winning local autonomy.

- Also in May, the Serbian authorities distributed firearms to all Serb nationals in Kosovo, who proceeded to practise by shooting unarmed Albanian civilians.

In mid-May, a constitutional crisis was added to this inflammable mixture. On 10 May, a Federal Assembly session broke up in confusion, when delegates from Croatia, Slovenia and Kosovo refused to recognize Bajramović as Kosovo's representative on the Federal presidency. Vojvodina and Montenegro then withdrew their own candidates. On 15 May they, together with Serbia and Kosovo (represented temporarily by the vice-president of the Serbian Assembly!), cast their votes against Mesić. The country was suddenly left without a head of state. Federal Premier Marković, supported by the Army, proposed a compromise: Slovenia and Croatia should accept Bajramović in return for Serbia voting for Mesić. Slovenia refused this shabby deal, but the desperate Croatia agreed – and was tricked. Another victim of the trick was the US Ambassador to Belgrade, assured personally by Milošević that Serbia would vote for Mesić, provided Bajramović was confirmed in the Federal Assembly. In the Assembly, Kosovo delegates protested against their rights being traded in such a cynical manner – Serb delegates responded by questioning their very right to sit in the Federal Assembly. Eventually, although the Slovene and Albanian delegates accompanied by many Croats and Moslems voted against Bajramović, his confirmation went through. But the farce reached its climax when, at a renewed meeting of the presidency, Serbia, Montenegro, Vojvodina and Kosovo solemnly proceeded once again to vote against Mesić. The Slovenian, Croatian and Macedonian representatives then packed their bags and went home. Milošević's second attempt to destroy the Federal presidency had succeeded. His next target will be the Federal government.

The logic behind this combination of crisis at the top and seething chaos below was spelt out by the Serbian branch of the Alliance of Forces of Reform (which supports Ante Marković):

By obstructing the election to the post of President of the member from Croatia, Milošević's personal regime has completely revealed its real intentions in regard to the future of Yugoslavia. We are witnessing the final act in the destruction of Yugoslavia, which has been pursued over the last few years in accordance with a clear plan: to force Slovenia to leave the country; to cause chaos within, and the territorial disintegration of, Croatia and Bosnia-Herzegovina; to transform Macedonia into a southern province of Serbia; to provoke a military intervention in the name of protecting Yugoslavia – understood as Serb property; to stop all reforms and prevent all economic and political changes that could bring Milošević's personal regime into question. By their refusal to accept the constitutionally prescribed procedure for electing the President, the representatives of so-called 'unified' Serbia, acting as Milošević's personal executives, have shown that they do not recognize the equality and sovereignty of the other republics, or accept the basic rules of democratic procedure. They have shown, in other words, that they no longer recognize Yugoslavia.

If so, then war remains the only option. Ever since the March demon-strations, Milošević's regime has been sliding fast to the right, embracing cooperation with the Chetniks. His followers elsewhere – Milan Babić in the Croatian 'Krajina', and Radovan Karadžić, his counterpart in Bosnia-Herzegovina – are openly collaborating with the Chetnik leader Vojislav Šešelj. Judging by the growing occupation of Croatia, the disintegrating authority of the government of Bosnia-Herzegovina, the growing number of incidents involving armed civilians, and the rising number of dead, it would be fair to say that civil war in Yugoslavia has already begun.

The destruction of the Yugoslav presidency, on the other hand, has left the Yugoslav Army without its civilian commander-in-chief, strengthen-ing the hand of putschist currents within it. There is little doubt, however, that a military coup would only hasten the disintegration of the Army. This is why the Army leaders, working with Marković, expressed their support for Mesić's election. But time is running out for Yugoslavia. Only a miracle – in the shape of a democratic alternative emerging in Serbia, strong enough to remove Milošević – could save it now. Such a miracle almost materialized at the beginning of March, when Serbian democracy suddenly displayed its tremendous potential. Then the youth of Serbia demanded an alternative to Milošević's politics of war. It was cast aside, however, by the main parties of the opposition, eager to join Milošević in his megalomanic quest for a Greater Serbia ('one state for all Serbs').

Herein lies Serbia's tragedy. The so-called democratic opposition seems to be unaware that Milošević is grooming the Chetniks not simply as a striking force against the Croat, Moslem, Albanian, Slovene, Macedonian, Hungarian, etc. 'national enemy', but also as his personal insurance against any 'velvet revolution' happening in Serbia. It was only in the aftermath of the March demonstrations that the régime decided to legalize Šešelj's Serb Radical Party. Serbian Democrats would be wise to heed the words of Ibrahim Rugova, leader of the Albanian Democratic Party, addressed to his Slav countrymen: 'You are all potential Albanians.'

(June 1991)

Letter to *The Guardian* on the Coup

2 July 1991

Dear Sir,

There is now little doubt that a military coup has taken place in Yugoslavia – the first in Europe since the Greek colonels' coup of 1967. Acting outside all constitutional provisions and in defiance of the civilian authorities, the so-called Yugoslav People's Army has declared an all-out war on one part of Yugoslavia, treating it as a foreign enemy. Europe, East and West, should search its conscience and its common sense to decide whether allowing a military junta to take power anywhere in Europe augurs well for the continent's future. If in Yugoslavia today, why not in the Soviet Union tomorrow?

In pursuing their holy war against Slovenia and Croatia – a war planned ever since multi-party elections took place in these two republics – the so-called Yugoslav General Staff are in fact waging war on Yugoslavia as a whole. Who or what has given these generals and colonels the right to decide for themselves how the Yugoslavs should arrange their future? And what kind of Yugoslavia could emerge out of their victory? Only a prison-house of its nations and citizens (occupied Kosovo has stood as the model for two years now). Indeed, this very day (Tuesday) in Belgrade, as the so-called Yugoslav Chief of Staff is offered the hospitality of Serbia's state-controlled media to proclaim a war to the finish against the Slovene people, Serb mothers are protesting in the Serbian assembly against their sons' lives being used as small change in this grim adventure of the generals.

In what sense, therefore, can we speak of this army, deployed to bring down the democratically elected government of Slovenia, as a Yugoslav Army? It is Yugoslav only in that it has compelled thousands of Slovene, Croat, Serb, Albanian, Macedonian, Moslem, Montenegrin, etc. conscripts to kill and maim each other, while offering them no future other than that of prolonged and bloody civil strife. What a tragedy for a country born out of a national liberation war! Whatever mistakes the governments of Slovenia and Croatia have made in their pursuit of independence, they all pale into insignificance before the military's brutal pursuit of power for its own sake. The war now taking place in Yugoslavia is not a war of the Yugoslav Federation against rebel republics, nor is it a war between Yugoslavia's constituent nations. It is a war designed to defend a bankrupt parasitic regime in Serbia and a deeply undemocratic concept of Yugoslavia. The so-called Yugoslav generals would be well advised to consult their history textbooks to learn what happened to that other multinational state Austria-Hungary, which in 1914 also embarked upon the path of war to defend its territorial integrity against the aspirations of its population and the call of liberty and democracy.

Yours sincerely,

Branka Magaš

PART FIVE

War
(June–December 1991)

Introduction

The Federal Army's attack on Slovenia wiped out all hope that Yugoslavia could be reconstituted in any form. The Slovenian campaign was over in under two weeks, the number of casualties and scale of destruction remaining relatively small. The Army lost this war and withdrew – Slovenia was free to go. It was different with Croatia. Low-intensity warfare was initiated in the so-called Krajina part of Croatia by small units armed and trained by the Army. This grew in scope and by August had turned into a full-scale war. It was a war fought by unequal contestants: a lightly armed and recently formed Croatian National Guard faced one of the most powerful armies in Europe, across a front stretching in an arc from the River Danube in the east to the Bay of Kotor in the south. By the end of 1991, one third of Croatia was under occupation. Scores of its towns and villages and much of its communication network had been damaged or destroyed. Several thousands of its citizens had been killed and over half a million made to flee their homes. Threats of bombing Croatia back to the Stone Age appeared in the Serbian press, which now habitually described all Croats as Fascists.

Although bloodied, Croatia never contemplated surrender. As for Slovenia, the war was one of self-defence. By contrast the opposing side – Serbia and the Serbian-dominated Army – never managed to define any coherent set of war aims. Belgrade talked at different times of keeping Yugoslavia together, of protecting the Serb minority in Croatia, of defending Serbia from a 'Fourth Reich', of protecting military property and personnel from Croatian aggression, of creating a single state for all Serbs. With most non-Serb officers and conscripts – and, as the war grew in intensity, also many ethnic Serbs – defecting or refusing to be drafted, the Army had to rely increasingly on unwilling reservists and so-called volunteers from Serbia. In large parts of the war zone, the result was a complete breakdown of military discipline. A situation in which one side was so overwhelmingly superior in military hardware was conducive to large-scale massacres of the civilian population.

The war in Yugoslavia caught the British media unawares. Squeezed between their own ignorance and Foreign Office inertia, they resorted to simplistic stereotypes. On the eve of the Army's full-scale attack on Croatia I wrote a memorandum designed to inform editors and journalists of the true nature of the conflict, which I termed a Third Balkan War designed to give Serbia access to the Adriatic Sea. I was reassured to see this view confirmed by prominent domestic opponents of Milošević like Bogdan Bogdanović, or the Serbian democratic resistance gathered around the weekly *Vreme*. Watching the growth of an anti-war movement in Serbia, at a time when Vukovar was being systematically destroyed and Dubrovnik shelled from both land and sea, I felt that my original thesis – that the war would not be popular in Serbia – was being vindicated.

If the war in Croatia has proved anything, it is that the project of a Greater Serbia cannot be realized. To be sure, Serbia and its Army lost this war first and foremost because of the Croatian people's will to resist. Had Croatia surrendered, the West would have accepted a Serbian-dominated Yugoslavia. But Serbia lost the war also because it found insufficient support for it in Serbia itself. However much this war has embittered relations among the nationalities that inhabit the Yugoslav area, hopes for future cooperation will build upon this fact.

Yugoslavia was created in 1918 and recreated in 1941–45 in order to solve certain specific and related tasks: national emancipation, creation of a stable and democratic order, economic and social modernization of one of the most backward parts of Europe. The first Yugoslavia, created from above, fell apart because it could not carry them out. The second Yugoslavia, created from below, was far more successful in forging a federation of free nations, in transforming an agrarian into an industrial society, and in educating the population. At the point at which regress overwhelmed progress – in the sphere of national rights, economic advance and social justice alike – that second Yugoslavia too began to disintegrate. Its disappearance, however, does not erase the problems which it tried to solve. The ethnic configuration of the area, the similarity of its languages, the ties created by its common history, and above all its high degree of economic interdependence, will surely produce new forms of cooperation. But if any future is likely to work, this must be based on the free consent of the nations concerned.

1

A Requiem for Yugoslavia

I

As with any bereavement, the hardest thing for those left behind is accepting the fact of death. But now even I, after years spent keeping the log – with an ever more horrified fascination – of Yugoslavia's march towards the point of no return, am forced to admit defeat. It is merely a sign of my own irresponsible faith in some last-minute miracle that it should have taken nothing less than a full-scale Federal Army attack on one of Yugoslavia's constituent republics to force me to accept that the past must be buried. Over the past four years or so I had become increasingly convinced that Yugoslavia was indeed dying. That it was just a matter of time. That its death actually made sense and should be welcomed. Yet even now, as I insist that the last rites be performed and the international community recognize the reality of Yugoslavia's collapse, the appropriate response to death eludes me.

I, a Yugoslav, think of the country in all its magical, seductive variety of landscapes, nationalities, languages, religions, histories and regional identities. Bosnia, northernmost outpost of European Islam, its minarets cheek-by-jowl with Christian-Orthodox and Catholic steeples, has ever since Roman times firmly resisted the encroachment of the Mediterranean world – my own world – into the Balkan core. This is where the bell began to toll for Austria-Hungary, another multinational state which failed its peoples. Gavrilo Princip has entered the history textbooks, but few would recall that he was just one of a whole generation of Croat, Slovene, Serb and indeed Moslem and Montenegrin plotters against an Empire already dead in all but name.

I, a Croat, think of my Serb friends in Belgrade and our friendship born in the bright light of 1968. In the mid-1980s, we fought a stubborn battle together against an earlier attempt to stem the tide of democratization in Yugoslavia. Macedonia, with its extraordinary ability decade after decade to produce some of Yugoslavia's finest poets, I know less well; but the row of books behind my desk contains histories of Macedonia and a soon-to-be-used Macedonian–Croat dictionary. The many jokes I, a Dalmatian, have shared with my Albanian compatriots about our common Illyrian origins cannot have been entirely jokes, for how otherwise do you explain why I felt so much at home with these people? And what should one make of the fact that it took a decade of pedantic examination by experts, not to speak of passionate quarrels, to distinguish the poetry and language of *Mountain Wreath* – one of the masterpieces of Balkan literature, written by Montenegrin Bishop-Prince Njegoš in the middle of the last century – from those of a similar work written by Ivan Mazuranić, first commoner Ban of Croatia, in the purest literary Croat? For Slovenia my affection has if anything blossomed during the last five years in the heat of obsessive arguments and counter-arguments about the future of socialism in Yugoslavia, compelling me to acquire a working knowledge of Slovene. This, not the formal state structures, was what made us Yugoslavs. Yet when I called a Slovene friend a week or so ago – it already seems like years – Yugoslav Army MIGs were flying over Ljubljana and she was rushing off with her small children to an air-raid shelter. As I write these lines, the radio reports MIGs in action over Osijek, a city in north-eastern Croatia which -- nationally mixed already then – participated in the Croatian national revolution of 1848: the first such movement to speak also in the name of South Slav unity.

Hard as I try, I am not yet ready to accept the break-up of Yugoslavia. Yes, the red star adorning the Federal Army uniform and the country's flag is now a cruel deception. But I think of my uncle, still in his teens, dying in 1943 in Šumadija, the heartland of Serbia and one of the most beautiful parts of Yugoslavia. A partisan fighting side by side with his Serb comrades, he too wore a red star on his cap. When this Croat 'National Hero of Serbia' was commemorated just a year ago in Kruševac, the old capital of Serbian kings, which in the 1930s became a communist stronghold, the occasion was packed by Serb war veterans. Many of the young workers also present must by now have been recruited into the Federal Army, and sent to fight against Croatia. That the Kruševac ceremony was a requiem not only for the partisan dead, but also for Yugoslavia, was in fact already clear. For at the very time the Croat visitors (my mother among them) were being welcomed by their hosts, other Serb war veterans and active Army officers were busy training terrorist groups in Croatia's mountains for a war to the finish against the republic's democratically elected government, then barely four months old.

II

I think of Slovenia and Croatia and recall the last – indeed the only other –

time in postwar history when Yugoslav MIGs were used to intimidate a Yugoslav people. A year before the Kruševac event, in March 1989, the assembly of the 'Socialist Autonomous Province' of Kosovo was convened to consider amendments to the constitution of the 'Socialist Republic' of Serbia designed to strip the Albanian nation of its political rights. The Yugoslav People's Army aided the deliberations by encircling the assembly building with tanks, while MIGs swooped low to remind the people's deputies that power comes out of the barrel of an air-to-surface rocket launcher rather than popular suffrage or socialist constitutional niceties. Kosovo's forced subjugation ended the Yugoslav Federation in all but name, and proved beyond any doubt that Great Serbian nationalism – that old enemy of Yugoslavia, which the partisans thought they had slain on countless battlefields across Yugoslavia – was once again on the march.

Yugoslavia was not, as so many claim today, an artificial state. But its viability always depended upon political commitment to, and institutional arrangements for, the full equality of its constituent nationalities. After 1945, the federal framework was frequently adapted to the country's growing diversity until 1974, when the new federal constitution acknowledged the effective sovereignty of the six republics. The two provinces acquired similar constitutions and became equal partners with the republics at the federal level. In 1987, however, an assortment of Serb generals and party or state functionaries carried out a coup within the League of Communists of Serbia. Adopting a plan drafted by the Serbian Academy of Arts and Sciences, aimed at making Serbia once again – as in pre-war days – hegemonic, they set the republic on a collision course with the rest of Yugoslavia.

Until as late as 1989, the project seemed to be successful. The governments of Vojvodina, Montenegro and Kosovo were toppled one after another, and replaced by men (and two, maybe three, women) whose only virtue was absolute loyalty to the Serbian régime. In Kosovo resistance was fierce, including mass demonstrations and two general strikes. I recall the nine-day hunger strike of Kosovo miners – traditionally the backbone of the local Communist Party – conducted deep down in the shafts of the old zinc and lead mine of Trepča. It was lifted only when the President of the League of Communists of Yugoslavia promised them restoration of Kosovo autonomy – a promise he and his companions had no intention of keeping. Instead, the province was occupied and 'pacified' by state terror.

The Serbian campaign had by then grown in scope, targeting Croats ('Ustashe'), Moslems ('Fundamentalists' or 'Islamicized Serbs'), Macedonians ('Southern Serbs'), Slovenes ('selfish exploiters of the Yugoslav South'). In reaction, first the Slovene then the Croat Communists took the historic decision to institute multi-party democracy in their republics. It was this decision that, in March 1990, finally put an end to the League of Communists of Yugoslavia – the party that created the present-day federation out of the ashes of a bloody war, and then ruled it for the next forty years, growing more conservative and corrupt in the process, and eventually ditching its last ties to the working class. Serbia's formal incorporation of Kosovo and Vojvodina, and its *de facto* rule over Montenegro, meanwhile redistributed legislative and executive power in the country to its advantage, destroying a balance maintained ever since the war. As a result, the federal structure began to keel over – to crash down once and for all on 26 June 1991. By now all that was left of Yugoslavia was an empty shell: the institutions remained in place – there were things you could call the Yugoslav presidency, the Yugoslav assembly, the Yugoslav government, Yugoslav foreign affairs, Yugoslav economic policy, and so on – but these were mere forms, devoid of all substance.

In so far as Serbia did succeed, it was because of the support it found in the Army. The symbiosis between the Army and the Serbian régime, resting upon the solid foundation of growing Serb dominance within the officer corps, was reinforced after the Communist parties were removed from power in all the republics except Serbia and Montenegro. As first tank units, then the airforce, went into action against Slovenia – and as the same threat hung over Croatia – the Army spoke of its constitutional duty to defend Yugoslavia's territorial integrity. But what kind of unity could the generals have been thinking of when waging war against two of the nations that had created Yugoslavia in the first place? The Yugoslav presidency, the Army's supreme commander-in-chief – which in principle, though not in reality (since Croatia and Slovenia would have vetoed it), could alone have authorized this war – was no longer in existence, victim of yet another act of wanton destruction by the Serbian state leadership of all that went by the name of Yugoslavia. The path of its hegemonic drive is littered with many such casualties. But worst of all has been the former trust and solidarity among the Yugoslav nations, derived from their common struggle against fascism and for national and social liberation.

III

Imagine Belgrade during these days. In one of its central streets, the staff at the Ministry of Defence is working late into the night, planning further military operations in a war that has not been formally declared and for which everybody disclaims responsibility. In the nearby square, the Federal assembly and government carry on with their meetings, unable or unwilling to stop the generals. Slovenes and Croats have departed, Macedonians are demanding the recall of their conscripts, Moslem and

Albanian deputies condemn the aggression. At the same time, in the Serbian assembly a few doors away, MPs talk of a Serbian army under Serbian control – as if it did not already exist! – interrupting their work only to face Serbian mothers demanding the return of their sons from war. Further to the west, Slovene and Croatian populations are being mobilized into self-defence units, listening to radio reports of troop movements, and dying in growing numbers – together with young Army conscripts from all parts of the country. And all the time the supposed Yugoslav capital remains calm. The military may have taken direction of the country's politics into their own hands, but there is no general state of emergency, there are no tanks guarding key buildings and crossroads in Belgrade, no martial music broadcast on the radio. Peace in Belgrade while war invests Ljubljana and Zagreb shows how deeply implicated official Serbia is in the military's enterprise. This is its war.

The failure of the military to impose its *diktat* on Slovenia and Croatia, however, has forced the Serbian régime finally to unveil its Plan Number Two: the carving of a Greater Serbia out of prostrate Yugoslavia. It was indeed inevitable that the Socialist Party (ex-League of Communists) of Serbia would sooner or later take up the Chetnik banner. But this project has been attempted before and failed, and it will fail again. Serbia is economically too backward and Serbs numerically too weak for Yugoslavia to be turned into a Greater Serbia. The trouble is that Milošević's régime has long ago burnt its boats and, faced with a choice between its own collapse and continuation of the war by other means – i.e. stripping the Army of its Yugoslav name and turning as much as possible of it into its own armed force – it has chosen the latter. Unless . . . As the mind sifts through various possible ways in which the catastrophe might perhaps still be averted, the only hope that keeps returning is that the two republics can resist long enough for popular resistance to war to emerge in Serbia itself. It was, therefore, with great excitement that I read how the people of Loznica, a small place quite near Kruševac, had interposed a human barrier to stop the transport of Army reservists being sent against Croatia – on the very day that General Njegovanović appeared on Belgrade TV to hurl yet another military imprecation in the direction of the two western republics.

The Serbs – pushed into the role of aggressors – are, of course, victims of this policy equally with the rest. In Serbia, as in other parts of Yugoslavia, right-wing nationalism threatens the home nation as much as it does the alleged national enemy. Over the past year, much of the Yugoslav population has indeed been supplied with weapons, or armed itself on the black market. Yet despite this militarization reaching into the very roots of Yugoslav society, and despite the heady rhetoric of state-sponsored nationalism, the Yugoslav peoples have in fact so far shown little desire for waging an all-out civil war. But Milošević and the generals are allowing them no choice. However hard one scrutinizes the words and actions of the various parties in power across the country, one will find that only Milošević's régime depends for its survival on the pursuit of war. Yet if we look at the population of Serbia – burdened with huge unemployment, irregular payment of wages barely sufficient to keep body and soul together, and collapsing social services which endanger their sick, young and old; persistently cheated by promises never delivered – why should they wish to wage war on other Yugoslavs, equally imperilled? One had a glimpse into the tremendous democratic potential of Serbia in March this year, when hundreds of thousands of young women and men demonstrated for three days and nights against Milošević's aggressive policies. Milošević – that great scourge of Serbia's enemies – was forced to invite the Army to defend him against: the Serbs! Just a week after these demonstrations, 750,000 metal, leather and textile workers came out on strike across Serbia, and only two days before the military attack on Slovenia the Serbian trade unions threatened a general strike, to force the republican legislature to throw out a trade union bill that would effectively have removed the right to strike. But who will give voice to this great craving for peace and democracy? Serbian opposition MPs speak in unison with the ruling party about a Greater Serbia: a state in which all Serbs would live together at the expense of all other Yugoslav nations. But the young recruits and fathers with small children now being drafted, will they really fight for the politicians' imperial ambitions?

IV

War is the supreme test of any political formation. This one will show how deeply the positive achievements of postwar Yugoslavia are rooted in the hearts and minds of its peoples. If one surveys the extraordinary events of the last few weeks, one is struck by the fact that hostilities have remained localized, erupting only at Belgrade's instructions. One can also see resistance to domination and aggression coalescing around key points of the Yugoslav Communists' historic legacy, not least in the application of partisan tactics, which the Slovenes have used with such dazzling success. The federal organization of the state – the solidity of the nation-states created by postwar Yugoslavia – has provided all the structures needed in order to defend national and democratic rights. And if the stubborn determination of Slovenia and Croatia proves anything, it is that Yugoslavia has been an association of equal and sovereign nations. They – and not they alone – will fight hard to prevent the borders of Yugoslavia's six republics and two provinces being redrawn in order to bring a Greater

Serbia into being. They must be supported. Of all the various under-pinnings for a lasting peace in the Balkans, two are crucial: the rights of national minorities, and the inviolability of these borders (unless, of course, changed by express will of the freely elected assemblies of the eight federal units).

What, then, about the future? I was certainly not alone in feeling pain as, on 25 June, I watched frontier posts being erected between Croatia and Slovenia for the first time since 1527. Vojvodina and Croatia were joined within a single state back in 1700, while the border between Croatia and Bosnia-Herzegovina became an internal one *de facto* in 1878. The ceaseless shifting of international borders in the Balkans throughout the nineteenth and early twentieth centuries provided also a basis for the area's integration. It has become clear, however, that unions in the old mould must be dissolved to allow the birth of new forms in which cooperation between the peoples in this region of Europe, and of the region with Europe as a whole, can take place. As old structures break down, new ways will be found to build upon these natural and historic ties that once used to be summed up by the name of Yugoslavia.

(June 1991)

Memorandum for the British Media

I. Serbia's challenge to the post-war settlement in Yugoslavia

1. According to the Federal constitution, Yugoslavia's constituent re-publics (Bosnia-Herzegovina, Croatia, Macedonia, Montenegro, Slovenia and Serbia) are not administrative units but national states (*države*).

2. Their borders – like those of the borders of the two autonomous provinces (Kosovo and Vojvodina) – are specified by the Federal constitution.

3. These borders, drawn in the aftermath of World War Two, were not chosen *ad hoc*, but on the basis of weighty ethnic, historical and economic considerations. They have remained unchanged ever since.

4. They were drawn in full awareness of the multinational nature of all but one of the republics.

5. All Yugoslav constitutions since the war have specified that no border can be changed except by agreement with the Federal member(s) concerned.

6. The sanctity of Yugoslavia's internal borders is part of the post-war settlement between the nations of Yugoslavia.

7. This constitutional settlement – articulating the principle of full equality of Yugoslavia's nations (since 1974 also of national minorities with the majority nations) – was approved by the assemblies of all the Federal units, thus establishing its full legal validity.

8. This settlement has been challenged *for the first time* since the war by Milošević's régime, thereby leading the country to the brink of an international war.

9. Milošević's régime has sought a *revision* of the post-war settlement at two levels: political and territorial.

10. Serbia's expansion began in 1989–90, with the incorporation of Kosovo and Vojvodina, and the cancellation of their political autonomy (albeit retaining their votes in Federal bodies!).

11. This act was unilateral and, since it was approved neither by the

Kosovo Assembly nor by the Yugoslav Federation, was also illegitimate and illegal.

12. In the case of Vojvodina, its Assembly's approval came only *after* the previous government had been toppled by extra-institutional (i.e. illegal) means (the so-called 'anti-bureaucratic revolution').

13. Milošević's Serbia has since then challenged the political and territorial integrity of two further republics: Croatia and Bosnia-Herzegovina.

14. In the case of Croatia, it has actively supported the creation – in August 1990 – of the so-called Autonomous Region of Krajina (ARK) on its territory. This entity – which does not recognize the authority of the government in Croatia – is illegal and illegitimate.

15. Over the last year, ARK militias have been waging an open war against the Croatian state and people.

16. The creation of an illegal armed force in the ARK has been actively supported also by the Yugoslav Army.

17. By preventing the Croatian state from exercising its authority over the whole territory of the republic, the Army too has been in flagrant breach of the Yugoslav constitution.

18. Serbia's new (1990) republican constitution asserts the right to intervene in all Yugoslav republics and provinces containing Serb minorities. This is contrary to the letter and spirit of the postwar settlement.

19. Serbia's President Milošević has openly and repeatedly endorsed non-institutional (i.e. violent) forms of political change within Yugoslavia.

20. In the case of Bosnia-Herzegovina, Serbia (aided by the Army) has actively supported the creation of two additional 'Krajinas': one in the north-west and the other in the south-east of the republic. As a result, the latter's central authorities (assembly and government) have effectively collapsed.

21. The northwest Bosnian 'Krajina' has since united with the 'Krajina' in Croatia, while the southeastern one has proclaimed its adherence to Montenegro, Serbia's satellite state. These moves are a direct attack on the territorial integrity of both Croatia and Bosnia-Herzegovina.

22. Serbia (supported by the Army) has armed and trained Chetnik and other paramilitary units in the Croatian area of eastern Slavonia, and these are now engaged in an open war against the republic of Croatia, leading to considerable loss of life and destruction of property.

23. It is *only in Serbia* that we find political parties represented in parliament – i.e. not marginal – formally committed to revision of the post-war internal borders – in accordance with the axiom: 'All Serbs must live in the same state'. This means the creation of a Greater Serbia.

24. *Serbia alone* among the six Yugoslav republics is engaged in promoting armed action on the territory of another republic (Croatia).

25. Although five of Yugoslavia's six republics are multinational, *only*

Serbia has claimed the right to gather all its nationals within the borders of a single state.

26. A Greater Serbia could be created only at the expense of other Yugoslav nations.

27. The creation of a Greater Serbia would thus inevitably lead to a generalized inter-national war in Yugoslavia.

28. A Greater Serbia would be an absurdity from the Serb national viewpoint itself, since within it Serbs would constitute an absolute national minority (as the Hungarians were before 1914 in the Hungarian half of Austria-Hungary).

29. Serbia's expansion would open the door also to an international conflict in the Balkans and East Central Europe.

II. The border dispute between Croatia and Serbia

1. In Croatia today, we can see the beginning of such a generalized war.

2. This is why Croatia's territorial integrity (like that of other threatened Federal units) must be supported by the international community, especially Europe.

3. Croatia has no territorial claims on Serbia. The Croatian–Serbian border is disputed only by Serbia.

4. Through its political and/or military activity, Serbia has in effect laid claim to Croatian territory both in eastern Slavonia and in the so-called Autonomous Region of Krajina (ARK).

5. Out of around 550,000 Serbs who live in Croatia, only a minority (44.3 per cent) live in these two areas. Annexation of these Croatian territories would thus leave behind the majority of Serbs living in Croatia, and could in no sense be presented as solving any 'Serb problem' in that republic.

6. Serbia's Claim on Eastern Slavonia.

(a) This claim is not justified on ethnic grounds. Eastern Slavonia contains nine municipalities, with a total population of 647,853. In eight of these municipalities, Croats form an outright majority. In the case of the ninth (Beli Manastir) where they are a minority, Serbs form a still smaller minority (35 per cent and 24 per cent respectively of the total). The ethnic picture of eastern Slavonia is as follows: 66 per cent Croat, 14.4 per cent Serb, and 19.6 per cent others (mainly Hungarians). The 93,120 Serbs who live in eastern Slavonia form 17.52 per cent of the total Serb population in Croatia.

(b) Serbia's claim to eastern Slavonia cannot be justified on historical grounds either, since this territory has never been part of the Serbian state.

(c) It cannot be justified on economic or geographical grounds either: the area is separated from Serbia by the River Danube, and forms an economic unity with the rest of Slavonia.

7. Serbia's claim to the so-called ARK.

(a) In the case of ARK (total population 206,896), the ethnic claim is stronger, since a majority (68.9 per cent) of the population involved is Serb. However:

(b) The eleven municipalities claimed by ARK contain only 26.7 per cent of the total Serb population in Croatia.

(c) They contain also a substantial Croat minority (21.9 per cent) – a larger proportion than that represented by the Serb minority in eastern Slavonia.

(d) ARK *does not border Serbia*. Thus any Serbian annexation of this territory would necessarily imply also annexing a large part of another republic, i.e. Bosnia-Herzegovina.

(e) Serbia cannot claim ARK on historical grounds either, since this territory has never been part of the state of Serbia.

(f) Such a claim cannot be justified on economic grounds either, since the area's economic prosperity has always depended on its direct links with the coastal cities of Dalmatia, integrated economically in turn with northern Croatia.

(g) Separation of the ARK from Croatia would cut the republic in two and make it unviable as a state. Underpopulated as the ARK territory is, it forms the natural (geographic) link between the Croatian ports of Dalmatia and the industrial centres in the Croatian north.

(h) If the ARK were to be amputated from Croatia, these links would be cut, damaging permanently and inexcusably the economic well-being of the population of the 'Krajina' itself as well as that of the rest of Croatia.

(i) To sum up: ARK does not contain the majority of Serbs in Croatia. It has no common border with Serbia. It is geographically, historically and economically an integral part of Croatia.

III. War in Yugoslavia

The military attack on Slovenia on 27 June was a relatively straight-forward event: on the one hand, Slovenia (its government and people), on the other, the Army (acting outside any constitutional framework). In the case of Croatia, however, the situation is complicated by the fact that the war being waged against this republic is of a guerrilla type (constant raids from a territory protected by the Army), and that it involves part of the republic's Serb population. But however 'low-intensity' this war may appear, it is nevertheless a war conducted by one Federal state against another, the aim of which is expansion towards the Adriatic Sea. Serbia's current war against Croatia is, in fact, a Third Balkan War, being very similar in nature to the two earlier Balkan Wars of 1912 and 1913. If one accepts that peace in Europe depends on the maintenance of national-state borders – or their alteration only by consensual *and* peaceful means – then the democratic media in a democratic country cannot stay neutral, but must condemn Serbia's aggression against Croatia.

IV. The Serb Question in Croatia

Since the beginning of their respective national movements, the relationship between Croats and Serbs in Croatia has gone through several phases, some harmonious and some conflictual. The Second World War witnessed simultaneously mass killings of innocent Serb civilians by the Nazis' Ustasha puppet state (NDH), Chetnik massacres of innocent Croat and Moslem civilians, and a high degree of cooperation between the two nationalities within the Communist-led Partisan movement.

Over the past few years, the Serbian propaganda machine has been trying to create the impression that Serbs were the chief victims of the war, and that 700,000 of them were killed in the Ustasha concentration camp at Jasenovac (Croatia) alone. According to the best recent authority – Bogoljub Kočević (Veritas Foundation Press, London 1985), who is an ethnic Serb – the actual wartime losses suffered by the main Yugoslav nationalities were as follows (in thousands):

Serbs	487	Moslems	86
Croats	207	Macedonians	7
Slovenes	32	Albanians	6
Montenegrins	50	(Jews	60)

These figures should be correlated, of course, to the absolute size of the nations concerned. If one translates actual losses into demographic losses, then the Moslem nation suffered a higher loss (8.1 per cent) than the Serb (7.3 per cent) or Croat (5.0 per cent).

Of the total number who perished in the war (947,000), 216,000 died in concentration camps. The majority of camp deaths occurred in Bosnia-Herzegovina (85,000), Serbia (79,000) and Croatia (48,000). It should be recalled here that the NDH state included Bosnia-Herzegovina, but also that those killed in its concentration camps included not only Serbs but also Jews, Roma, Croat Communists and democrats, etc.

Serbian propaganda habitually suggests that anti-Jewish pogroms occurred only on the territory of the NDH. Yet the figures tell a different story. At the start of the war, the Jewish community in Yugoslavia numbered 76,654 members, of whom 32,000 found themselves included in the NDH, 30,000 in the part of Serbia (without Kosovo and Vojvodina) established as a German protectorate under the Serb general Nedić. By the end of the war, 23,000 had been killed in the NDH (18,000 of them in Jasenovac) and 24,000 in Nedić's Serbia (12,000 on the outskirts of Belgrade, in trucks fitted with gas outlets). In Zagreb, the pre-war home of 12,000 Jews, 3,500 were saved through civilian action; in Belgrade, 1,115 out of a total of 11,870.

The blame for all these crimes rests, of course, primarily with the Nazi state. The NDH state and the Serbian protectorate alike were part and parcel of the Nazi occupation policy. Its victims came from all national groups, with Jews suffering by far the most: 60,000 out of 76,654. One should not forget, of course, the contribution which the civil war made to the figures quoted above, amounting to almost half the total figure: 237,000 Partisan dead and 209,000 killed on the other side. The Partisan army was drawn from all the Yugoslav nationalities, as were its Chetnik, Ustasha, etc. opponents. These casualties were built into the foundation of the postwar political-constitutional settlement.

The transformation of Yugoslavia into a Federal state at the end of the war was beneficial also to the Serb population in Croatia, who became fully integrated into the political and economic life of the republic. A new division along Croat–Serb lines began to appear, however, with Miloše-vić's accession to power in Serbia, and was consolidated by the uneven and disorderly disintegration of the Yugoslav communist system. In the Croatian elections of 1990, the majority of Serbs in Croatia voted for the League of Communists of Croatia, only a minority for the nationalist Serb Democratic Party. However, the victory in the republican elections of the Croatian Democratic Union, running on a Croat nationalist programme, created a strong sense of unease among Croatia's Serbs, which escalated further when the new administration showed itself frequently insensitive in its approach to this minority. By this time, moreover, the Croat majority too had become fearful of Serbia's aggressive expansionism. Its worst fears were confirmed when Serbia started to build the 'Krajina' (ARK) into a bastion of its hostile presence at this (for Croatia) vital communications point, and when the Army came in to assist the ARK's secession from Croatia. In Knin, which during World War Two had been a Chetnik stronghold and which now became the centre of the ARK, the fortunes of the Serb Democratic Party were revived by an influx of Communist-elected councillors into its ranks. Though the Croatian government subsequently made considerable efforts to win the confidence of the Serb minority, war had by then arrived with its inevitable negative effect on good relations between Croats and Serbs in Croatia.

Whatever criticisms can be made of the Croatian government's treatment of the Serb minority, there have been few signs of systematic persecution, certainly not of the kind suffered by the national minorities in Milošević's Serbia. In the light of the figures quoted above, the charge propagated by the Serbian media that the Croatian government is 'Ustasha' is thus quite false. Indeed, Croatia's new constitution gives full rights to the Serb minority, including the right to appeal to all relevant international bodies.

However, as long as Serbia (backed by the Army) continues to use the Serb-inhabited areas in parts of Croatia to pursue its war of attrition against the Croatian government and people (the great majority of those killed in Croatia since August 1990 have been ethnic Croats), Croat–Serb relations in the republic will inevitably continue to deteriorate. Indeed, one of the worst aspects of this Contra-style war in Croatia is its effect on the civilian population, as testified by the increasing number of refugees of both nationalities. The longer the war continues, the more bitter Croat–Serb relations will become and the more difficult it will be to envisage a peaceful future for this part of the Balkans. This is why it is imperative that the European Community and the nations comprising the ECSC intervene to put an end to the aggression of Serbia and its allies against Croatia, before the war spills across Yugoslavia and over its international borders.

(July 1991)

3

A Country Unravels

Despite warning signals apparent since 1987, Europe was caught unprepared by the war in Yugoslavia. As its media then attempted to make sense of this (to its eyes) sudden disintegration, the temptation to seek an explanation in the country's multinational make-up proved too great to resist. Once the war was thus classified as an 'ethnic' conflict, 'age-old' intolerance between the national groups involved – especially Croats and Serbs – became the new paradigm, disregarding long periods of peaceful coexistence and the joint struggle against the Nazis. Astonishingly, the press began to resuscitate disputes once confined to tiny emigré groups or area specialists. The Theodosian line between the Eastern and Western Churches, the Ottoman invasion, the Habsburg Empire, the Military Border. Yugoslav Royalty, Chetniks and Ustasha – and much more besides – became the stuff of journalistic lucubration.

Yet this war – in whose current phase one Yugoslav republic is being pulverized by the might of the Federal Army, acting outside civilian control and backed by just two other Yugoslav republics – is not about what happened in the distant past. The war in Croatia has its direct predecessor in the war in Slovenia, just as the Federal Army's attack on Slovenia has its own antecedents – all causally linked – that go back to Tito's death in 1980. The chain of events that led directly to the war involves Milošević's coup in Serbia and the fanning of state-sponsored nationalism that followed it; the forced incorporation of Vojvodina and Kosovo into Serbia, and their effective removal from the Federal institutions while leaving their votes in Serbia's pocket; the overthrow of the Montenegrin government and its replacement by Milošević's men; the break-up of the League of Communists of Yugoslavia; the multi-party elections which returned non-Communist governments in all but two republics (Serbia and Montenegro); the creation of the armed Krajina in Croatia; the Army's attempt to bring down the Croatian government; successive attempts by hardliners to put the country under a state of emergency; the blocking of proposals for a Yugoslav confederation by

Slovenia, Croatia, Bosnia-Herzegovina and Macedonia; the effective marginalization of the Federal presidency and government.

All this amounts to a plot against Yugoslavia, conceived since 1943 as a state of equal and sovereign nations. The federal structure inaugurated after the war amounted to a comprehensive settlement of the national question in Yugoslavia – a feat that had eluded the pre-war state, which paid for its failure by disintegration and the civil war of 1941–45. Once in place, this federal structure could not be unravelled – whether in favour of a recentralized Yugoslav state (as the Army once dreamed) or to the benefit of a Greater Serbia (as Milošević and part of the Army believe today) – without civil war erupting once again. A national state once acquired – in its concreteness of borders, parliaments, courts, schools, police forces, etc. – is never surrendered without a fight. Successive Yugoslav constitutions all refer to the internal borders of Yugoslavia as *state* borders, unchangeable without the agreement of the parties concerned. Moreover, the existing borders already respect as much as possible the ethnic principle. Postwar Yugoslavia, after all, did not emerge as the result of any particular Yugoslav nation winning the war, but as the result of a war of national liberation fought by all.

Milošević is saluted these days, by supporters and many opponents alike, as the first man to realize that Tito was dead – 'Tito' being the code word not just for communist rule, but also for the postwar international settlement. Donning the mantle of Nikola Pašić (the man who led Serbia into the Balkan Wars of 1912–13, in which it took what are now Kosovo and Macedonia), Milošević has sought to implement Pašić's dream of a Greater Serbia stretching also to the Adriatic Sea. The Army has increasingly gone along, mainly because many of its Serb officers never thought of Yugoslavia as anything else but an expanded Serbia. In a recent book Latinka Perović, a major Serbian political leader purged in 1972, speaks urgently of the permanent danger that the symbiosis between Yugoslav unitarism (blindness to the country's multinational constitution) and Great Serb nationalism represents for all Yugoslavs.

Belgrade speaks these days of 'those who wish to stay in Yugoslavia', as if Yugoslavia could exist without Slovenia, Croatia or Macedonia. Yugoslavia in fact entered its death throes with the Federal Army's attack on Slovenia. Today, every shell that hits a Croatian village or town, every tank that attacks a Croatian hospital, every plane that strafes a Croatian church and every ship that blockades a Croatian port marks a progression of its agony, just as Kosovo's loss of autonomy was a blow at the heart of the Yugoslav Federation. The Foreign Office and the Quai d'Orsay, fascinated by the good idea that Yugoslavia once was and by their country's contribution to its birth, seem unable to grasp this fact. Seventy-odd years ago Croats, Slovenes and Serbs thronged their antechambers, seeking to persuade them that Austria-Hungary was dead and they should support the creation of Yugoslavia. It took the terrible carnage of World War One for them to agree. Today, Slovenes, Croats and Albanians – soon to be joined by Macedonians and Bosnian Moslems – address their petitions for recognition and/or protection to Hurd, Major and now also Carrington. One wonders how many of Croatia's citizens have to die, and how many of Croatia's villages and towns have to be destroyed, before these mandarins accept that the right of national survival ranks far higher than the exigencies of *Realpolitik*.

(September 1991)

4

The Spread of War

(a) The Vampire of Greater Serbia

On 28 August 1991 the village of Kijevo (population 1,000) – a Croat enclave in the middle of the so-called Serb Autonomous Region of Krajina – ceased to exist, having been literally razed to the ground by the so-called Yugoslav People's Army deploying aircraft, tanks and howitzers. Following a 12-hour bombardment the population fled to the nearby mountain of Kozjak, pursued by the vengeful aircraft. The village was then looted and set on fire. A British TV cameraman filmed an army officer tearing up the board with the village's name, and stamping on it with his boots to the great cheering of the men around him – men under the command of Martić, once a local police chief and member of the League of Communists and now the Krajina strongman. Characteristically, the destruction of Kijevo had been promised two days earlier in the Belgrade press. The village's only 'crime' was that – like so many other villages and towns – it spoiled the image of a Serb-only 'Krajina'.

As in any war, there comes a point when its nature becomes so blindingly clear that only those complicit with the aggressor can henceforth deny it. This point was reached in Kijevo. Kijevo proved beyond all doubt that the war raging on the territory of Croatia is not an inter-ethnic conflict, pitting the rights of the Serb minority against the hegemonic aspirations of the Croat majority, but a war of conquest designed to create a Greater Serbia extending over parts of Croatia, Bosnia-Herzegovina, Vojvodina, Kosovo, Montenegro and northern (at least) Macedonia.

Croatia has become the target of an all-out war of a kind not seen in Europe since 1945, not because it contains a Serb minority, but because it is the biggest obstacle to the plan hatched by the Serb-dominated chiefs of staff and the leaders of Serbia. If Croatia falls, then the war will spread into the rest of Yugoslavia. Indeed, as I write these lines reports are coming in of the war being extended into Bosnia-Herzegovina. The generals are in a hurry. The EC-sponsored peace conference is due to take place on 7 September and the Serbian régime wants to be in a position to back up its territorial claims by a military *fait accompli*.

Having failed to re-centralize Yugoslavia under Serbian hegemony, Milošević's régime, aided by the chiefs of staff, has opted for a Greater Serbia. It welcomed the coup in the Soviet Union, not just for ideological reasons, but above all because it feared that the new Union treaty transforming the Soviet federation into a confederation of sovereign states would be used as a model for Yugoslavia as well, since it was more or less exactly what Bosnia-Herzegovina, Croatia, Macedonia and Slovenia had been advocating for a year. This was openly stated on Belgrade TV by Mihailo Marković, Milošević's chief *porte-parole*. The Serbian régime does not wish to be part of any structure which it cannot dominate. Milošević has justified the annexation and wholesale incorporation of other republics and provinces by his concern for the fate of Serb minorities. This is how Hitler once justified the annexation of Austria, the partition and occupation of Czechoslovakia and the attack on Poland. Like Milošević, Hitler also spoke of the need for all Germans to live within a single state. The methods used to destabilize these countries prior to attacking them were the same: official protests, mobilization of a section of the minority, blocking of any alternative to war – and assurances to the European powers that this was the way to a lasting peace. To be sure, Serbia does not have the clout of Hitler's Germany and its victims are 'only' small local states. Yet, unless the Serbian régime is stopped and stopped soon, the war will engulf the whole of Yugoslavia and spill beyond its borders. Why should Serbia, its neighbours will ask themselves, be the only one allowed to expand? 600,000 Serbs living in Croatia form a much smaller percentage of the national total than 2,500,000 Albanians living in what used to be Yugoslavia, or 2,000,000 Hungarians living in Romania. Pressure on the Hungarian government to protect the Hungarian minority in Yugoslavia (thousands of whom have already fled into Hungary) is growing by the day. The Albanian intellectuals in Kosovo speak of a Serbian–Albanian war in 1992 as inevitable. There are many such potential claims throughout Central and East Europe. If Serbia is allowed to expand by force of arms, then an arms race in the region as a whole will become inevitable, destabilizing much of Europe for the foreseeable future.

Milošević's régime came into being in 1987, following a coup within the then ruling party, the League of Communists of Serbia. A purge of thousands of party and state functionaries, liberal intellectuals and independently minded enterprise managers was conducted in close synchronization with the overthrow of the governments in Vojvodina and Montenegro (then similarly purged) and a military occupation of Kosovo, whose assembly and government were simply eradicated. The ideological argument for this entire aggressive strategy was provided by the Serbian Academy of Arts and Sciences, which insisted that Serbs were threatened by their neighbours and that the postwar federal system was inimical to Serb national interests. Ever since then, the Serb population has been exposed to a morbid propaganda in which the allegedly 'tragic' Serb history and Serb war graves are chief ingredients. The Ottoman invasion, the Balkan Wars, the First and the Second World Wars – all are presented as little more than a plot against the Serb nation. Dobrica Ćosić, a writer of turgid historical 'epics', often proclaimed as the spiritual 'father of the nation', announced to all Serbs that now their last chance had come, and missing it would lead to their obliteration as a nation for ever. Thus does the régime, in vampire-like fashion, feed off blood spilt in the past, while proceeding to spill fresh blood in Kosovo, in Slovenia, and now, with particular ferocity, in Croatia. Bosnia-Herzegovina will be next. Never mind the fact that 90 per cent of the Kosovo population is Albanian, or that only 17 per cent of the population in the Croatian province of eastern Slavonia – scene of the most intense fighting over the past month – is Serb. It makes little difference that 'Krajina' is an ethnically mixed area, which does not even border Serbia; that Bosnia-Herzegovina is in majority non-Serb; that 91 per cent of the inhabitants of Montenegro declared themselves non-Serb at the last (April 1991) census; that northern Macedonia contains only a handful of Serbs. In the eyes of the Belgrade vampires, these are all 'ethnic and historic' Serb lands. This, of course, means war now and war in the future. But then the régime's life (like that of the Nazi Party) depends on the continuation and further escalation of bloodshed.

In those parts of other republics earmarked for inclusion in Greater Serbia, the conflict cannot but escalate into total war, targeted directly and in the main against the local population. As I write these lines, I listen to a BBC World Service direct report from the Slavonian town of Osijek. Although the reporter is an experienced journalist, who has covered wars in Asia and Africa, he talks emotionally of the devastation which the incessant bombardment from heavy artillery and the airforce has brought to this city of 150,000. The city is being systematically destroyed, and civilian casualties are great. The targets are all civilian: hospitals, schools, ambulances trying to reach the wounded and the dead. The war now being waged by Serbia and the Serbian-dominated army against Croatia is a classic 'dirty war' of the kind practised by CIA-funded armies in the Third World. Its aim is twofold: to expel from the designated area the 'wrong' (i.e. Croat) population, and to break the will of the population as a whole to resist, thus enabling Serbia to establish its 'peace'. Milošević's strategy is unlikely to work, since it offers nothing but slavery to at least two-thirds of the Yugoslav population. Indeed, to all of them, since such a 'peace' could be maintained only by a military dictatorship.

What is unique about this régime – at least as far as Europe is concerned – is its particular combination of strident nationalism with a recidivist Stalinist ideology, embedded above all in the only structures of the Yugoslav Communist state that managed to escape the process of democratization: the Serbian Communist Party and the Army High Command. The Serbian party had escaped the modest democratization undertaken from 1986 on in Slovenia and Croatia, where the principle of multi-candidacy for all party posts was introduced. It is this unreconstructed party-state machine that was used by Serb generals to engineer the 1987 coup within the party, with the inevitable consequence of a large purge of all political opponents to the hardline elements. The possibility of any liberal comeback was cut off by the great nationalist surge after 1987, which the party-controlled media instigated and kept going. The Stalinists' victory in Serbia was then used to marginalize and replace all liberal officers of whatever nationality in the Yugoslav army. It is this nationalist backup which the Soviet plotters lacked. In Yugoslavia, however, the special relationship between Serb nationalism and political reaction was sufficiently strong to challenge the post-war political settlement. But a price was also paid: first the Yugoslav Communist Party, then the Yugoslav state were torn apart, opening the door to outright military aggression. Serbia has been using the Army to expand its borders, but it is the generals who will inherit Greater Serbia.

It is important to stress that the 'Serb question' in Croatia was opened not with the victory of Tudjman's party – the Croatian Democratic Union – in April 1990, or even four months earlier with the Croatian Communists' decision to institute a multi-party system. It was exploited for the first time in the summer of 1989, as a crucial component of the Stalinist mafia's plot to bring down the liberal wing in the Croatian party. Had this plot succeeded, a wide purge of Croatian party and state institutions would have followed, which would have aligned Croatia with Serbia, thus ensuring a Stalinist triumph throughout Yugoslavia. It was in order to avert this threat that the liberals in the Croatian party presidency conducted their own minor coup in the republican party, leading it to accept the electoral reform. The liberals' victory in Croatia ensured that the Stalinists would not win by political means alone. The seeds of the current war were thus sown in December 1989, when the League of Communists of Croatia followed the Slovene example and decided to hold multi-party elections in the republic – a decision which, in turn, led to multi-party elections elsewhere in Yugoslavia.

Unable to prevent multi-party elections, the Stalinist mafia opted for a different strategy. In Serb-inhabited areas of Croatia an immediate local rebellion against the new government was organized by local communist structures aided by the Army, which supplied them with weapons. This gave birth to the Knin 'Krajina', whose territory was then extended step by step using threats and manipulation of the population's fear of the unknown. Something similar happened also in Bosnia-Herzegovina, where in every municipality with a Serb majority – be it relative or absolute – political control was established by strong-arm action. This was then used as the basis to create two further Krajinas, which immediately declared themselves independent of the Bosnian government. As in the case of the Croatian Krajina, these new structures were immediately militarized, preventing any possible challenge to the new régime either by the non-Serb minorities or by Serb opponents. The same pattern has since been applied to areas of eastern Slavonia controlled by the Army and local Chetnik units. It is significant that foreign journalists are not allowed to visit these areas, and that the reason for the failure of the EC 'trojka' mission in late August was Serbia's unwillingness to allow foreign observers into the so-called 'liberated territories'.

It is now clear beyond any doubt that the war taking place in Yugoslavia is not an ethnic war, but a war of territorial conquest – the first in Europe since 1945. As far as the Army operations are concerned, it has been a classical land war (so far) in which certain Yugoslav republics – first Slovenia, now Croatia – are treated as hostile countries and their population as the enemy. What has been surprising has been the lukewarm response by the rest of Europe to the agony of the Croatian population. Serbia has been relying on divisions within the EC, while its propaganda machine busily foments the image of Germany and Austria bent on recreating a kind of Fourth Reich, or at least a new Habsburg Empire. Milošević is thus counting on European political confusion and inertia to implement the Chetnik plan forged in World War Two to establish a Greater Serbia (possibly under a Yugoslav name) shorn of all undesirable nationalities – Albanians, Croats, Hungarians, Macedonians, Montenegrins, Moslems – in accordance with the old recipe: kill one third, expel one third and assimilate one third. Every attempt by other Yugoslav leaders to form an alternative model for Yugoslavia – a confederation of sovereign states – has been sabotaged by Milošević's Serbia. This is why no peace conference, whether held in Yugoslavia or The Hague, will succeed unless and until this régime has been defeated. Its downfall can be envisaged only as the result of a combination of efforts: an economic and political isolation of the régime in Belgrade by Europe as a whole, which would aim to underpin and support resistance by the threatened republics and provinces in Yugoslavia itself and, equally important, the growing rejection of war in Serbia itself – whose potential was shown in the massive March 1991 demonstrations throughout Serbia. The issue of whether a considerable part of Europe can look forward to war as its future is being decided in Croatia today. The recognition of every one of Yugoslavia's federal members as a sovereign state in its own right, and within its borders as defined by the last (1974) Yugoslav constitution, and safeguards for the rights of national minorities living within them, form the sole basis for a lasting peace. It is also a precondition for any new, voluntary association of the peoples of Yugoslavia.

(September 1991)

(b) Letter to the British Government in the Name of the Croatian Peace Forum[1]

What the EC can and should do NOW about Yugoslavia.

Following on from positions it has already adopted – no alteration of internal borders by force; full rights for minorities – the EC should take the following steps:

1. It should immediately recognize Yugoslavia's eight federal members as sovereign (not necessarily independent) states/entities. The fact that the Peace Conference involves the presidents of Yugoslavia's six republics suggests that the EC already treats these as *de facto* sovereign subjects. The above act of recognition would not, of course, change Yugoslavia's external borders.

2. Since only the Yugoslav presidency can order the Army back to barracks, and since the representative for Kosovo was not elected in accordance with the Yugoslav constitution – thus making the presidency inoperable – the EC should demand that the Province's assembly be immediately recalled (or freshly elected) in order to elect Kosovo's representative to the presidency.

3. Since the war is about to spread to Bosnia-Herzegovina; since this would lead to a generalized war throughout Yugoslavia, and beyond; and since Bosnia-Herzegovina cannot be divided between Croatia and Serbia without inflicting a great injury upon the Moslem nation (including the part of it living in the Sandjak), it is important that, in addition to recognizing Bosnia-Herzegovina as a sovereign state, the EC should call for: (a) immediate extension of the monitoring force into the republic, as a preventive act; and (b) demilitarization of Bosnia-Herzegovina.

The EC should at all times bear in mind that any imposed alteration of the existing internal borders would not only sanction the use of force in European international affairs, but also lead to generalized warfare throughout the region, which could easily become endemic.

Note

1. This letter was handed in at 10 Downing Street following a demonstration against aggression in Yugoslavia in September 1991.

Lessons of History:
War Returns to Yugoslavia

One can state the precise time when the Socialist Federative Republic of Yugoslavia came to an end: 5 am on 27 June 1991 – when the Federal Army launched a frontal attack on Slovenia. This action was taken without authorization from the Yugoslav presidency, the Army's commander-in-chief. It is inconceivable that such authorization would have been forthcoming in any case, since the Federal constitution expressly forbids Federal troop movements in any Yugoslav republic or province without its formal consent. This provision of the constitution, moreover, merely reflects the fact that the Yugoslav Federation was structured as a union of equal and sovereign republics (with provinces having *de facto* identical rights, and *de jure* too so far as military intervention is concerned). The Army's attack was thus unconstitutional – an act of high treason, a *coup d'état*. Why did it happen?

Such a decision could not have been taken on the spur of the moment. On the contrary, it is clear that this momentous step by the Chiefs of Staff was simply the final twist in an evolution of Yugoslav politics that had already long been heading towards disintegration. At which point in time did this fissiparous tendency first become manifest and what were its generators? 1867, the year of the Austro-Hungarian Compromise, marks the point at which the dissolution of the Habsburg Monarchy became inevitable: after that year, the unity of the Empire was ensured only by internal repression and the needs of the European balance of power. The Yugoslav equivalent of 1867 came 120 years later in 1987, when a party coup made Slobodan Milošević president of the League of Communists of Serbia, and thus undisputed leader of the largest Yugoslav republic, on a platform that was manifestly nationalist and anti-constitutional. His victory over his constitutionalist opponents in the party and their liberal allies – followed by massive purges throughout Serbia's political and state life, and notably in the media – delivered the first blow to Yugoslavia's political unity, and ultimately also to its territorial integrity.

How could this come about? Why did Serbia in particular become the bastion of political reaction, and why did the other republics and provinces passively accept Milošević's drastic restructuring of the republic's internal politics – despite all the evidence pointing to its disastrous ultimate outcome? For an answer one must go back in time another decade and a half, to the equally massive 1971–72 countrywide purge of reformers in the League of Communists of Yugoslavia (LCY). All the republican parties were affected by this purge, but especially those of Serbia and Croatia. A whole generation of capable young leaders was suddenly removed from political life and replaced by older party cadres committed to the status quo. In its effects, the purge – sanctioned by Tito – amounted to a Yugoslav equivalent of the Warsaw Pact invasion of Czechoslovakia three years earlier. A new emphasis on ideological purity now went together with a re-concentration of power in the hands of Tito and his immediate circle. The effects of the purge differed from one republic to another. In Croatia, where it was carried out in the name of a struggle against Croat nationalism, it led to a potentially dangerous re-drawing of the ethnic balance in favour of Serb cadres. In Serbia, where it was presented as an offensive against technocrats and liberals, the party was flooded with small-time apparatchiks (something similar happening also in Macedonia).

Only after Tito's death, in 1980, was it possible to begin the painful, and at times seemingly hopeless, process of rebuilding the liberal-reforming current within the individual parties. But by this time the cards were heavily stacked against it (except in Slovenia, where the purge had been less drastic). For one thing, the purge had produced a new pattern of relationships between the republics and provinces. The position of the southern republics, and especially Bosnia-Herzegovina, was enhanced, while Croatia's capacity for autonomous action at the Federal level was significantly reduced. Serbia emerged as the bastion of a new wave of Yugoslav unitarism, strengthening thereby its traditional ideological ally: Great Serb nationalism. Superimposed on this realignment, however, was a counter-current – symbolized by the adoption of the 1974 constitution – that was a fruit of the liberating 1960s. The 1974 constitution emphasized the statehood of the six republics, and also gave Serbia's two autonomous provinces direct representation at the Federal level. There was now, therefore, a blatant contradiction between state-political decentralization and party-ideological re-centralization. In the 1980s, a decade of growing economic crisis, this was to produce an explosive situation.

The 1971–72 party purge had, in the long run, an even more dramatic consequence in that it brought the Army to the very centre of political life, even giving it an *ex officio* place on the Federal party presidency. Never before had a purge involved a simultaneous replacement of the political and state leaderships of the two largest and most powerful republics –

Serbia and Croatia – and it had been possible to conceive and conduct it only with the help of the Army. The Army, of course, has always held a special place within Yugoslavia's political life, partly because of its Partisan origins and partly because of the country's sense of insecurity during the years of the Cold War. Unlike the Federal Ministry of the Interior, which was purged and decentralized in the mid-1960s, the Army was left untouched. It is true that in 1968 there was a possibility of it too being brought more firmly under state-civilian control. For a review of Yugoslavia's defence capabilities in the wake of the invasion of Czechoslovakia revealed serious weaknesses, and led to a decision to organize, Partisan-style, popular forms of self-defence. This decision gave birth to Territorial Defence (TD) forces, funded and controlled by individual republics and provinces, but linked to the Army. Arguments over the relationship between the TD and the Army soon produced a division within the military establishment similar to that in the party at large, with liberal minded generals wanting greater independence for the TD while conservatives complained that this would produce republican armies and encourage separatism. But the 1971–72 purge of the reformers within the Party, conducted with the Army's backing, tilted the balance firmly in favour of the military hardliners. Thereafter, the autonomy of the Army from civilian institutions grew during the last few years of Tito's life, and strengthened considerably after his death. Many generals, on retirement, sought for themselves a civilian role within the Federal and republican party leaderships.

For all these reasons, Tito's death represented a turning point in the life of the country. As head of state and commander-in-chief of the Army, he was replaced by an eight-man collective presidency, made up of representatives of the republics and provinces. The party presidency was similarly constituted, with the difference that here the Army contributed a ninth member. Both these bodies operated formally on a consensual basis; within a few years, however, the suppressed contradictions of the previous decade came to the fore, placing them under intolerable strain. A struggle between hardliners and liberals opened up on several fronts. In this struggle, Great Serb nationalism was from the outset to find itself firmly aligned with Stalinist hardliners.

The first front was opened up in Kosovo, where large-scale demonstrations in March–April 1981 were suppressed by military intervention, leading to considerable loss of life and the imposition of a state of emergency in the province – the first time such a measure had been applied in any part of Yugoslavia since World War Two. Since then, not just the province's Albanian leaders of the day, but also independent intellectuals, have argued that the demonstrations got out of hand thanks to *agents provocateurs* planted by the Serbian police – a thesis that acquires plausibility in the light of subsequent events. For the Kosovo demonstrations allowed a re-opening of the whole question of this overwhelmingly Albanian province's status within Serbia, uniting nationalists inside and outside the Serbian party on a platform of reintegrating both provinces into Serbia and reducing Albanian national rights. The result of this was a growing campaign for revision of the Serbian constitution, which soon acquired a strident anti-Albanian tone. The leaders of Vojvodina too, and anybody else supporting the position that Kosovo and Vojvodina should remain autonomous, were denounced as corrupt bureaucrats putting their office before the sacred cause of national unity.

The second front was opened up on the issue of Federalism, as defined by the 1974 constitution. Great Serb nationalists and Yugoslav unitarists alike argued that the constitution had destroyed the unity of the country as a whole, and of Serbia in particular, by giving too many powers to the republics and provinces. This first push towards a re-centralization of Yugoslavia came in the mid-1980s and took an 'educational' form. Its main thrust was that, in order to strengthen the country's unity, control over school curricula should be given to the Federation. It quickly became clear, however, that this concern for unity was little more than an attempt to Serbianize school textbooks, particularly in regard to the interpretation of history and to language. Complaints that Slovenes, Macedonians and Albanians did not know Serbo-Croat, that Croats were unnecessarily calling their language Croat, and that the Cyrillic script in Serbia was under threat of extinction, grew in volume. This educational offensive in the event came to nothing, but it did send a warning signal to all the non-Serb nationalities. A vigorous counterattack was led by the writers' associations in the other republics and Kosovo. In Slovenia, indeed, it was this writers' revolt against the proposed educational reform which was to produce, a few years later, one of the first non-Communist parties in Yugoslavia – the Slovene Democratic Alliance – which then won the 1990 elections as part of a wider coalition. (The Great Serb ideologues, however, backed by the Army, did win one victory – over a new national anthem: a nineteenth century Pan-slav song was adopted in the mid-1980s, despite strong protests from the non-Slav nationalities.)

The third front was opened up on the issue of civil liberties, especially freedom of the press and association. This was an issue on which the Army held very strong views, and the only one which caused an initial – albeit temporary – difference between it and the Serb nationalists. The initiative on this occasion came from the hardline Croatian party leadership, which in 1984 published a notorious 'White Book', listing several hundred intellectuals from all over Yugoslavia as counter-revolutionaries of different hues. Also in 1984, six Belgrade intellectuals were arrested and charged with counter-revolutionary activity. This anti-democratic offensive, however, turned out to be counterproductive, given the West's increased emphasis at the time on human rights in Eastern Europe, and Yugoslavia's growing dependence on Western aid. It became even more untenable with Gorbachev's arrival in the Kremlin. The White Book was accordingly set aside, and only one of the Belgrade Six was imprisoned, and then for a relatively short time. It was precisely at this point that Slovenia emerged as the vanguard of democratic change in Yugoslavia, involving both active and tacit cooperation between spontaneous grass-roots, 'alternative' politics and culture, the official youth organization, and the reforming wing inside the Slovenian party (strengthened by Milan Kučan's election as the Slovene party president). In Croatia too, the hardline wing associated with Stipe Šuvar – a man close to the Army and the instigator of the 'White Book' – lost out to a more moderate grouping inside the party.

A fourth – and as it turned out decisive – front was opened up in Serbia, where in 1987 key Serbian generals backed Slobodan Milošević in his bid for power. The hardliners' coup inside the Serbian party was quickly consolidated using state-sponsored nationalism. Hundreds of meetings were organized throughout Serbia, demanding removal of the provinces' autonomous status, the re-centralization of Serbia, and the re-centralization of Yugoslavia. These meetings – reminiscent of China's Cultural Revolution, and dubbed the 'anti-bureaucratic revolution' – also demanded the resignation of all liberal politicians throughout the country. The 600th anniversary of the battle of Kosovo (in which Ottoman armies had scored a decisive victory over the remnants of a short-lived Serbian empire) was used to issue a call to all Serbs to close ranks behind Milošević. A march through the institutions by all means necessary to create a Serb-dominated Yugoslavia was also announced. The Vojvodina and Kosovo governments were toppled by carefully orchestrated mass mobilizations. The rest of Yugoslavia watched in silence these first acts of destruction of the Federal order, in the mistaken belief that Milošević's *blitzkrieg* would end at the borders of Serbia. But then Bosnia-Herzegovina too was severely destabilized, by means of an all-too-convenient alleged corruption scandal involving its Moslem leaders; and a successful coup was organized in Montenegro, bringing down its government and replacing it with one loyal to Milošević. In the provinces and Montenegro, party and state administrations were purged and filled with men loyal to Milošević. In Kosovo the resistance was fierce, involving several mass demonstrations and two general strikes, but eventually the province was subjugated by the Army.

These changes completely altered the national and political balance in Yugoslavia. Milošević and his military backers could now count on four out of eight votes on the presidency, which commanded the Army. Serbia looked poised to win control over the whole country. The political war now extended to new fronts, with Serbia and the Army effecting a division of labour. In Croatia, Serbia raised the issue of the Serb minority (just as it had done earlier in Kosovo), alleging that it was being mistreated and demanding intervention by the Federal party and state. It began to organize mass rallies in Croatian areas populated by Serbs, at which Croatian party leaders were roundly denounced as anti-Serb and anti-Yugoslav. In Slovenia (where there is no settled Serb population), meanwhile, the Army exerted tremendous pressure on the party leadership to muzzle the increasingly free press, threatening direct intervention if it were not obeyed. In 1988 the Army arrested three journalists working for the Slovene youth paper *Mladina* and an Army sergeant, accusing them of stealing military secrets. (This had more than a whiff of personal vengeance about it, since *Mladina* had spearheaded criticism of the Yugoslav Army and revealed corruption involving some powerful generals.) As all this was going on, Serbia called for an extraordinary congress of the LCY, at which a new centralizing party constitution was to be adopted.

It is now becoming increasingly clear (through interviews recently published by high-ranking Slovene and Croat generals and backed by documentation) that the Army chiefs of staff were already preparing a military takeover, for which Serbia – where all Federal institutions are located – would be used as a safe house. It seems the Army was convinced it could win by primarily political means, backed up by a token show of force. It seems also that the West, fearing Yugoslavia's break-up, was inclined to back the generals provided that some sort of civilian façade could be preserved. (The powerless Federal government, headed by Ante Marković, was an obvious candidate to play this role.) The link with Milošević's Serbia thus worked to the Army's advantage. However, at a more fundamental level, it has turned out also to be its undoing. For the rise of Serb nationalism, and Serbia's quest for hegemony in Yugoslavia, could not fail to provoke a strong sense of fear among the non-Serb nationalities who comprise two-thirds of the country's population. Macedonia, which had formerly tended to ally itself with Serbia on the Albanian question, now became increasingly restive. So too did Bosnia-Herzegovina, despite sympathies for Milošević among the Serb third of its population. In Slovenia, new political parties made their appearance and the assembly began legislative preparations for multi-party elections. In Croatia, the party came under strong popular pressure to stand up to Serbia and the Army; here too new political parties started to be formed and, fearing an imminent 'fraternal' intervention, the Croatian party (headed coincidentally at the time by a Serb president) opted likewise in

December 1989 for multi-party elections. By now, of course, communist régimes were being swept aside in much of Eastern Europe. Croatia's decision to hold multi-party elections at the same time as Slovenia (April 1990) meant that the conservative alliance had lost the political war and the process of democratic change in Yugoslavia as a whole would now be unstoppable. The all-Yugoslav party congress, held in late February 1990, proved to be the last. By the end of 1990, multi-party elections were held throughout Yugoslavia – with the exception of Kosovo. Only in Serbia and Montenegro was the Communist Party (under a new name) returned to power.

Preparation by the Army and Serbia for an outright war took several forms. In Croatia, Bosnia-Herzegovina, Macedonia and partially also Slovenia, TD forces were disarmed. In Croatia and Bosnia-Herzegovina, Serb municipalities were armed. In both republics, but especially in Croatia, majority Serb areas were encouraged to declare themselves independent from the central republican authorities. In the armed forces, unreliable officers holding important posts – especially those of Slovene and Croat origin – were retired and replaced by Serb officers. In their preparations for war, the chiefs of staff also reorganized military regions in such a way as to minimize local republican or civilian influence. New corps, under the direct command of the Ministry of Defence, were installed in certain sensitive areas such as the Croatian city of Knin – centre of what, in August 1990, was to become the 'Autonomous Region of Krajina'. In the course of 1991, such Krajinas were formed also in eastern Croatia, as well as in northern and southern Bosnia-Herzegovina. In the first half of 1991, several attempts were made to bring down the new government in Croatia and/or place the country as a whole under military rule. The 'Autonomous Region of Krajina', and then other Serb-inhabited parts of Croatia, were encouraged to wage an open armed struggle against the Croatian government. All attempts by the new governments in Bosnia-Herzegovina, Croatia, Macedonia and Slovenia to negotiate a looser form of Yugoslav association – a confederation of sovereign states of the kind recently agreed in the Soviet Union – were firmly rebuffed, leading Croatia, Macedonia and Slovenia increasingly towards independence. Under the impact of such developments, the Federal institutions – the presidency, the government and the Assembly – became marginalized and impotent.

When, in late June 1991, Slovenia and Croatia formally declared their independence (as they had announced six months earlier that they would, if no political agreement could be reached), the Army responded by an outright attack on Slovenia. It is as yet uncertain whether this attack was intended to keep Slovenia in Yugoslavia, or to drive it out altogether. What is certain is that the Army's defeat in Slovenia quickly led to an open change of course, in that the Chiefs of Staff no longer made any pretence of seeking to hold Yugoslavia together, but lined up instead behind the project of Greater Serbia. As I write these lines, Croatian territory is being parcelled up by an intensive attack of combined Serbian and Army forces, intent on drawing up new borders that would force much of the present Yugoslavia into a Greater Serbia (a state where Serbs would still be a minority, and which could be held together only by force). The Army is turning Bosnia-Herzegovina into a bastion of its armed might, despite the evident resistance of its Moslem and Croat populations. Macedonia in the south has in the meantime declared itself an independent state, Kosovo is on the verge of open rebellion, as is the Moslem population of the historic Sandjak province divided between Serbia and Montenegro. Having destroyed the first Yugoslavia, Great Serb nationalism has finally managed to destroy the second Yugoslavia as well.

If one looks for the lessons of history, then the following seem to hold for Yugoslavia. (1) Yugoslavia as a state is not viable unless it grants equal rights to all its national groups. (2) Centralism in Yugoslavia has always ended in Serbian domination of the state, which means that unitarism embedded in the apparatus of the central state feeds off and encourages Great Serb nationalism. (3) Great Serb aspirations come to the fore when democracy is suppressed in Serbia, which means that a democratic Serbia is a precondition for any kind of Yugoslavia. (4) Serb nationalism , like all others in Yugoslavia, grows as a result of uneven economic development.

This last 'lesson' has not been covered in this essay, yet there is little doubt that uneven economic development has been the main motor of Yugoslavia's political disintegration. Throughout the country's history, Serbia has tried to compensate for its relative economic weakness by attempts (usually successful) to dominate the central state apparatus. In pre-war Yugoslavia, there were no barriers to its political domination, but Communist Yugoslavia erected the Federal structure to act as a bar to any such hegemonic aspirations. The Serbian liberal leaders purged in 1971–72 understood that any true future for Serbia must lie not in attempts to dominate others, but in acquiring the ability to tackle the problems of its own development in cooperation with others. The sovereignty of the other republics, as well as the national affirmation of the Albanian population within Yugoslavia, were seen by them to be also preconditions for a democratic constitution of Serbia itself, without which Serbia could not properly attend to its own problem of transition from an agrarian to an industrial and modern society. Serbia was not itself responsible for the purge of that generation of capable political leaders. They were sacrificed on the altar of a false all-Yugoslav party unity, i.e. the maintenance of an undemocratic system of government. A tragic outcome was thus built into the core of the Yugoslav revolution of 1941–45 – in the

Stalinist formation and mentality of the party which organized and led it – producing ultimately not only the war-devastated Croatia of today, but also a Serbia gripped by the ruthless tyranny of destructive nationalism. The Serb nation is today feared and disliked by its neighbours, yet the past tells of its ability to speak the language of freedom and national tolerance. As recently as March 1991, hundreds of thousands of young Serb men and women came out onto the streets to express their aspirations for democracy and their abhorrence of the Milošević régime, only for their protests to be sidetracked by equally nationalist opposition politicians. Peace in the Balkans will return when Serbia recovers its democratic and socialist tradition.

(October 1991)

6

The War in Yugoslavia

The 1991 war waged by Serbia against Croatia has rightly been described as the first classical war in Europe since 1945. It has involved the destruction of cities, villages and economic infrastructure by heavy artillery, mortar, rocket, tank and aircraft fire; the seizure of territory and expulsion of population; the blockading and bombardment of ports and their immediate hinterland; the call-up of tens of thousands of reservists; a death toll running into thousands. The twin aims of the war are to re-draw well-established borders, and to create a new hegemonic power in the region. If the first affects directly only Serbia's neighbours within the former Yugoslavia, the second contains implications that go well beyond the country's international frontiers.

The war erupted as a result of the inability of Yugoslavia's constituent parts to resolve their differences by purely political means. Over the past four years all common political institutions – the League of Communists of Yugoslavia, and the Federal Assembly, presidency and government – have collapsed one after another, without being replaced by alternative structures. The Federal Army has been turned into a Serbian army. The Federal constitution and common legal code have also been among the casualties: electoral systems and constitutional provisions now differ widely from republic to republic, following the elections of 1990. Of the eight Federal units, five – Bosnia-Herzegovina, Croatia, Kosovo, Macedonia and Slovenia – have either declared themselves wholly sovereign or intend to do so imminently, the decision in most cases being backed by a plebiscite. Yugoslavia exists today *only* in the sense that the international community has not shown itself ready to acknowledge its demise.

The British Foreign Office, in particular, must find this prospect discomforting, given the long-standing relationship between Great Britain and Yugoslavia. Between 1915 and 1918, London acted as host to the Yugoslav Committee, as it sought the support of the Allied and Associated Powers for the creation of Yugoslavia. The idea of a common South Slav state was welcomed on the grounds that it would meet Serb, Croat and

Slovene national aspirations, and also provide the region with stability – expectations that in the event, however, were only partially borne out.[1] Again, in 1941, it was to London that the Yugoslav government and Royal family withdrew, while the British decision in early 1943 to rely on Tito's partisan forces contributed vitally to the post-war legitimation of the communist-led newly constituted Yugoslav Federation. There is little doubt that on both these occasions – in 1918 and in 1943–45 – British policy swam with the forward tide of history in the Balkans, a tide in which Yugoslavia occupied a rightful place. Today, however, the tide is evidently flowing through different channels. The British government finds itself the reluctant recipient of numerous pleas to admit the collapse of Yugoslavia and recognize the independence of its republics (as well as the right of Kosovo Albanians to determine their own fate). But the belief that Yugoslavia in some form is necessary persists. For the peacemakers at The Hague, the bottom line seems to be that if the individual republics must eventually part, then they must do so consensually. The maintenance of some common framework, on the other hand, would be to their benefit.

However reasonable this position may appear, the fact of war suggests that a stable consensus will not easily be found. Europe shows little appreciation of the depth of the Yugoslav crisis, or the real dynamic of the country's disintegration. This was already clear in April 1991, when the Croato-Slovene confederal proposal was finally rejected out of hand by Serbia. Europe was caught off balance when the Serb-dominated Army responded to the subsequent declarations of independence from Ljubljana and Zagreb by a declaration of war – in the case of Croatia a total war. The ramifications of this violence are by now being felt throughout the region: never before has the Balkans seemed so unstable as it is today. The Serbo-Croat war has confirmed, in the most brutal and uncompromising manner, the close relationship between a just international settlement and regional stability.

For a country to disintegrate in this particular manner, something must have gone very badly wrong. To seek the guilty party in the various nationalisms that legitimized themselves through the ballot box during 1990 is to beg the question of why politics should have taken this form. On the other hand, any temptation to seek deeper causes by going back in time as far, for example, as Emperor Diocletian's division of the Roman Empire should be avoided, since it does not help us understand at all why *this* war should be being waged at the present time. It is true that fissiparous tendencies, rooted in Yugoslavia's historic, religious, national, economic, etc. diversity, have long been at work. Yet integrative trends have also been in play over the past two centuries. What needs to be explained is why the former have now prevailed, at least for the time being. Of the many causes of Yugoslavia's destabilization, there is one which is of particular salience:

the decision of the League of Communists of Serbia to challenge the postwar national settlement. This decision can be dated to the famous Eighth Plenum of November 1987, when Milošević and his supporters purged the Serbian party of all its moderate elements. Serbia, for reasons that demand an in-depth study not possible here,[2] thus became the first revisionist state in post-Communist Europe. Its challenge was experienced by other Yugoslav member states as a direct threat to their fundamental national interests. This basic division between Serbia (and eventually also Montenegro) and the rest was subsequently reproduced each time the country faced a major decision. It was also reproduced at the Yugoslav Peace Conference in The Hague.

Yugoslavia emerged out of the Second World War as a Federal republic, replacing the earlier Serbian-dominated and highly centralized monarchy. The postwar settlement, written into successive constitutions, was based on the understanding that Yugoslavia is a multinational state; that the union of its peoples was freely willed (the much-quoted right to national self-determination, including secession); that the principle of absolute national equality must govern all internal relations; that the republics are nearly-sovereign national states, with well-defined borders; that their borders (as well as those of the two provinces) cannot be changed without the consent of the parties concerned. Whereas up to 1974 the constitution specified full equality only of the six South Slav nations (Croat, Macedonian, Montenegrin, Moslem,[3] Serb and Slovene), in 1974 national minorities too were granted equal rights with these nations: as a result, Kosovo and Vojvodina acquired para-state attributes and became Federal members in their own right alongside the republics. This settlement, it must be stressed, was accepted in full awareness of the multinational nature of all Yugoslav republics and provinces. The Yugoslav Communists, in other words, opted – like their Soviet counterparts – for a territorial-political solution of the national question. A different principle was meanwhile applied to national minorities living *within* the eight Federal units. Here they enjoyed full cultural and political rights (use of their national language in state affairs; proportional representation at municipal and higher levels), but no more. No provision was made for the formation of new political territorial entities within individual Federal units.

Under Milošević, Serbia has challenged successively all the basic tenets of this comprehensive settlement of the national question in Yugoslavia. To begin with, it posed the demand that Serbia should be 'like other republics', by which it meant complete removal of the autonomy of the two provinces – a step so radical in its implications that the other republics declined their official support. The incorporation of the provinces into Serbia had to be achieved, therefore, by resort to extra-parliamentary means: by mobilization of hundreds of thousands of Serbia's Serb citizens on an openly nationalist platform. Although the League of Communists at the all-Yugoslav level did eventually sanction Serbia's 're-centralization', the Federal constitution affirming the near-equality of republics and provinces remained unaltered. Serbia's campaign to become 'like other republics' thus had several fateful consequences. First, it legitimized Serb nationalism and extra-institutional forms of political activity in pursuit of national claims. Secondly, since the Albanian population's resistance to Kosovo's loss of self-government was fierce, the Army was sent in to occupy the Province, thus introducing the country to the idea that the Army could be used against a Federal member. Thirdly, Serbia kept the provinces' votes at the level of the Federal presidency, thus increasing its share of votes from one to three (an interesting outcome of the quest for 'equality'). Finally, by dismissing the Kosovo Assembly and its executive, Serbia destroyed the legitimacy of the Kosovo representation in all Federal bodies, and with it the legal validity of the latter's decisions. This undermined their authority at the very time when the economy was showing acute signs of structural crisis.

Serbia, however, was not satisfied with becoming 'like other republics'. It managed to alter further the internal political balance in its own favour by organizing a 'spontaneous' overthrow of the Montenegrin government, which it replaced with men loyal to Milošević. This brought the number of Serbian-controlled votes on the Federal presidency to four. The republic was now in a position to block all decisions on this body – which was constitutionally also the commander-in-chief of the Yugoslav Army.

The scope and speed of Milošević's success was truly astonishing. Within the space of two years, he managed to rid himself of his rivals in Serbia, and become the arbiter of the country's future. The Yugoslav Army (but not only the Army) began to treat Milošević as a new Tito: i.e. as a strong man able to keep the country together – on what could not but be an anti-democratic course – by the application of brute force if necessary. The violent re-centralization of Serbia was indeed accompanied by calls for re-centralization of the Federal state and the League of Communists of Yugoslavia. Milošević's propaganda machine, inspired by the Serbian Academy of Arts and Sciences, placed into circulation a whole gamut of slogans that came to dominate internal political debate. The semi-confederal Yugoslav framework, based on the 1974 constitution, was criticized as the primary cause of the economic decline of the country as a whole and especially of Serbia; it was to be replaced by a 'flexible and modern federation'. The League of Communists was criticized for being an anarchic, corrupt and undemocratic body; a new organizational model based on one-member-one-vote, tighter internal discipline, and much reduced power of the Party's republican branches, was called for.

Throughout 1989 the Serbian party pressed for the convocation of an emergency congress of the League of Communists of Yugoslavia, at which such a structure would be ratified. The newly legitimized Serb nationalist constituency, in addition, launched an attack on the Federal structure as such, on the grounds that it had divided the Serb nation. It insisted that Yugoslavia's internal borders were purely administrative – and artificial. This amounted to an attack not just on republican territorial integrity, but also on the right of the local Communist parties and governments to represent Serb minorities at all – either at home or on the Federal level.

In a recently published volume, Latinka Perović[4] calls attention to the danger which the combination of Great Serb nationalism and conservative centralism has always posed for Yugoslav democracy. Indeed, Milošević's success could not be explained by sole reference to events in Serbia itself. Already by the mid-1980s a hardline current – strong especially in the party organization in the Army – was in the ascendant in the League of Communists of Yugoslavia. It was to be tempered, ultimately, by Gorbachev's reforming zeal and by the collapse of Communism in East Central Europe, but in 1987 its hand was dramatically strengthened by the events in Serbia. Against these radical conservatives stood a reforming wing, concentrated mostly in Slovenia and Croatia; this not only resisted the push for re-centralization, but also wished to strengthen political pluralism and civil liberties throughout the country. After 1987 the split between the two blocs could only grow, with each twist in the increasingly heated political atmosphere upping the stakes. The unilateral decision – in the autumn of 1989 – by the Slovene party to institute multi-party elections the following spring, and Croatia's decision – in the winter of the same year – to follow suit, were seen by the other side as little more than a declaration of war. The final outcome of this polarization was the collapse of the League of Communists of Yugoslavia at its 14th Congress, held at the end of February 1990.

The immediate effects of this momentous event were cushioned temporarily by the fact that the Federal government, headed by Ante Marković, was itself committed to a full market economy and multi-party political system. But the disintegration of the all-Yugoslav party organization left the Army without its traditional political master, at the same time as the civilian authority was badly shaken by Milošević's march through the institutions of the system. The elections held during 1990 in all Yugoslav regions (with the exception of Kosovo where, under military occupation, they were inevitably boycotted by the Albanian majority) served only to confirm the fundamental division between Serbia and Montenegro, on the one hand, and the rest of the country on the other. Whereas in these two republics the Communist parties won with huge

majorities, in the others nationalist governments were formed (in Macedonia, a nationalist/reform-Communist coalition). The subsequent decision
by the Army High Command (in December 1990) to form its own party
(the League of Communists – Movement for Yugoslavia) reflected its
determination not merely to play an independent role in the country's
politics, but also to turn the clock back. War was now only six months
away.

This (as any) war developed as the result of a clash of political wills. The
focus here will be on the Serbian–Army coalition, because this was the side
that willed and initiated it. It could be argued that the war has had three
phases, at the end of each of which the war aims of the Serbian–Army
coalition were reformulated (without necessarily abandoning the earlier
aims). In the first phase, Serbia (with the Army's support) created an armed
base in the so-called 'Krajina' region of Croatia, from which it could
challenge the Croatian government's authority. Although the Krajina was
consolidated as a distinct unit only after the election of Franjo Tudjman's
Croatian Democratic Union (HDZ) in April 1990, the project was in fact
initiated in the summer of 1989, with the aim of toppling Croatia's
moderate communist leadership and replacing it by a hardline current
centered on Stipe Šuvar (scourge of 'dissident' intellectuals and former
president of the League of Communists of Yugoslavia). The instrumentalization of Serb minorities gathered pace after the elections, so that by the
middle of 1991 six Krajinas had been established: two in Croatia and four
in Bosnia-Herzegovina.[5] This amounted to a *de facto* partitioning of these
two republics. The Krajinas – whose loyalty was not to their indigenous
republics but to Serbia – were used to put pressure on the two republics to
accept the Serbian concept of a 'flexible and modern federation' (i.e. a
Serbian-dominated Yugoslavia). If they would not submit, moreover, the
Krajinas would be a key instrument for demarcating new borders – the
borders of a Greater Serbia. The Greater Serbian alternative was
confirmed by the adoption of a new republican constitution, which gave
Serbia the right to determine the future of Serb minorities outside Serbia.
The ruling party (now renamed the Socialist Party of Serbia), backed by
the opposition parties represented in parliament, simultaneously adopted
the position that, in the event of other republics seeking confederation or
secession, Serbia would claim its 'historic and ethnic territories'. Between
August 1990 and the time of writing of this article (November 1991), the
six Krajinas have all been pressed into the war against Croatia.

In its second phase, initiated by the Army attack on Slovenia on 27 June,
the war was fought in the name of Yugoslav unity. The 'Yugoslavia' in
question was at first conceived in its territorial entirety. Following the
Army's defeat in Slovenia, however, the label 'Yugoslavia' was attached to
an increasingly diminished territory, until it was reduced to the future

Greater Serbia: Serbia proper; parts of Croatia (with or without a Serb majority); the whole of Bosnia-Herzegovina, Kosovo and Vojvodina; Montenegro; and eventually also part of Macedonia. Serbia now counter-posed the right of 'those who wish to remain in Yugoslavia' to the claims of Slovenia, Croatia, etc. to independence.

The third, and decisive, phase opened up with the Army's frontal attack on Croatia. In this phase, the war became a full-scale war to the finish. Croatia was rightly perceived as the pivotal republic, whose fate would also decide the fate of the Serbian–Army project. If Croatia were defeated, then the warring alliance's recovery of the whole of Yugoslav territory (including the reconquest of Slovenia) would become viable. If not, there was always the alternative of Greater Serbia, which could call itself Yugoslavia in order to claim the property and international legitimacy of the now defunct Yugoslav Federation. Indeed, in October 1991 four Serbian-dominated members of the Yugoslav Federal presidency simply declared themselves to *be* the Federal presidency – and proclaimed the country to be at war.

Serbia and the Army have been ready to throw into the war against Croatia not only all their men and armour, but also the full blast of a propaganda based on the concept of racial enemies. Indeed, ever since Milošević's rise to power, the Serb population has been told day in and day out that its neighbours – Albanians, Slovenes, Croats, Moslems, Macedo-nians, etc. – harbour the worst intentions towards it, and that only military victory can ensure its physical survival outside Serbia proper. It was not enough to claim that Tito's Yugoslavia had always been directed against the historic interests of the Serb nation. In order to mobilize the populace for a total war against Croatia, it was necessary to seek a 'proof' that Serb minorities were endangered; this was found in the civil war of 1941–45, when hundreds of thousands of Serbs (though not they alone) had perished, many of them at the hands of the Ustasha quisling state. This is why the Croatian government, its armed forces, the young Croat volunteers – and indeed all Croats – came to be habitually described as 'Ustashe' in mass circulation papers such as the daily *Politika Ekspres* (favourite of the Army officers). The war to 'save Yugoslavia' was thus transformed into a Third Balkan War: one last attempt to 'solve' the Serb national question by creating a Greater Serbia. It is telling, however, that the political authorities in Serbia have been unable to defend their project before their own population. If one examines their war propaganda (which naturally targets its own citizens as a priority), it becomes clear that the constraining factor upon their actions is precisely the mood of the population in Serbia proper. The propaganda that relies on describing the Croatian government as fascist, bent on extermination of the Serb minority in Croatia, loses its appeal once the Army begins to extend its actions beyond Serb-inhabited areas of Croatia. The Army's presence in the Knin 'Krajina' (majority-Serb) can be presented to a Serb public as logical and desirable; its actions in Baranja and Slavonia (minority-Serb) may still find some rationale; but everybody knows that the population of Dalmatian cities are overwhelmingly Croat.

It is important to understand that no Greater Serbia could be achieved without destroying the stability of the whole region, since resistance would be not just strong but permanent. What is more, the fact that the attempt has already led to outright war in Yugoslavia bears witness not just to the Serbian régime's intransigence, but equally to the resilience of the Federal model created under Communist rule. Had this structure not been in place, Serbia's subversion of Yugoslavia would have passed unnoticed. The attack on Slovenia would have been presented – and accepted by the world community – as a simple police exercise. As things are, however, Slovenia was able to organize an effective resistance, and few in the outside world questioned its right to do so. The Croatian government, though operating under different conditions, cannot be denied such legitimacy either. There is no getting round the fact that Yugoslavia's republics and provinces[6] are the legitimate heirs of the disintegrating Yugoslav Federation. The latter's central institutions – Assembly, presidency, government – have long been little more than expressions of a general consensus. It is symptomatic that the attack on Slovenia and the onslaught on Croatia should have been undertaken without any authorization from the Yugoslav presidency: no presidency could have authorized war against a Federal republic. It is the republics that have (already) proved to be sovereign, not Yugoslavia as such. A stable order in the Balkans thus cannot be conceived without recognizing the permanence of the post-1945 international settlement in this fundamental respect.

Although Croatia is being systemically destroyed, it shows no sign of surrender. Key cities of its eastern plain – Vukovar, Osijek and Vinkovci – remain uncaptured. The war has lost its momentum. It is the future of Serbia that today remains most uncertain. With successive republics declining to send recruits to fight the war in Croatia, the burden of the war effort has fallen almost exclusively upon the Serb and Montenegrin population. It is doubtful that they can bear it for any length of time. The fact that the call-up of reservists in these two republics is now being conducted by compulsion; that, in the occupied areas of Croatia and in large parts of Bosnia-Herzegovina, civilian government has been replaced by military administration; and that thugs are increasingly being used to beat up the few brave Serbians who openly resist the war, suggests an ebbing of popular enthusiasm for the war among the Serb population.

Milošević's project of unifying Yugoslavia by force – and failing that, creating a Greater Serbia by means of an outright war – has brought about a regional cataclysm. Offered as a substitute for the necessary economic and democratic reform, this war has turned also into a Serb national catastrophe. It is Bogdan Bogdanović, ex-mayor of Belgrade and internationally renowned architect, who in a recent interview has spelt out perhaps most eloquently the scale of Serbia's current tragedy:

> Serbia has lost this war. When I say 'this war', I am thinking not only of the current one, but of all our modern wars and our entire modern history from the Hatt-i-Sherif[7] to the present day. One hundred and seventy years have passed since the proclamation of the Hatt-i-Sherif, and in the course of all that time a state like Serbia – in Europe – should have made a far greater civilizational, cultural and economic leap. Today we should be at least where Hungary is, or where the Czechs are. A feeling of failure lies at the very heart of Serb nationalism, and with that come all the various justifications for this failure: all the various Cominterns, Vaticans, Freemasonries and their unbelievable plots. There is indeed a sense of having missed out. This history gambled away – this century and a half gambled away – is what can be described as a lost war. But when I speak of the lost war, I am speaking also of the events taking place today. Whether we like it or not, when we look on TV at the various maps showing Serb and non-Serb villages, and how far the 'defenders of Serb villages' have advanced, we see that these 'defenders of Serb villages' are attacking towns! The 'defenders' are surrounding Vukovar; the 'defenders of Serb villages' are attacking Osijek. We see the map of destruction broaden. The irresponsible, indeed disgusting Belgrade press presents these as some kind of victory. They write about advances, liberation, etc. and the ordinary, already deeply indoctrinated, people acquire the feeling that we Serbs are winning the war. This is a terrible misconception. Firstly, from a political–military point of view, they cannot possibly win, since nobody sensible would allow anything to be changed by force at the end of the 20th century. Sooner or later those who are there will be forced to withdraw shamefully – unless they are thrown back by the Croat defence effort itself, which if the war spreads will be aided from outside. Secondly, this war has been lost at another and even more terrible level: it is destroying our Serb feeling that our wars were just wars and that we behave honourably. The war now being waged is not an honourable war.[8]

If Milošević's régime, backed by a free-falling Yugoslav Army Command, was the initiator of this war , there is little doubt that only with Europe's good will can conditions for an honourable, lasting peace be created in what used to be the Socialist Federative Republic of Yugoslavia.

(November 1991)

Notes

1. The suspension of parliamentary democracy ten years after the formation of Yugoslavia was a direct consequence of the unresolved national question, and opened the door, in 1941, to the country's rapid capitulation and the subsequent all-out civil war.
2. See 'The Spectre of Balkanization', Part III, Chapter 2, this volume.
3. The Moslems were given the full status of a nation only in the mid-1960s.
4. *Closing Circle – The Outcome of the 1971–2 Split*, Sarajevo 1991. The author was

secretary of the League of Communist of Serbia in the second half of the 1960s. She was purged – together with other prominent Serbian liberals, and following a similar purge of the Croatian party – in 1972. It could be argued that these purges, authorized by Tito, were a principal cause of Yugoslavia's subsequent troubles. The book, though published only recently, was in fact written immediately after the purge.

5. The term 'Krajina' is used as a shorthand for these entities, which were in fact given more fancy names. For example, the one formed in (predominantly Croat) eastern Slavonia was named the 'Autonomous Region of Slavonia, Baranja and western Srem'. Each Krajina was constituted as a little state, with Prime Ministers, Ministers of Internal and Foreign Affairs, etc.

6. The case of Kosovo is particularly strong in this respect, given the compactness and numerical size of its overwhelmingly Albanian population.

7. The Hatt-i-Sherif (Imperial Decree) of 1829 established Serbia's autonomy within the Ottoman Empire.

8. For my translation of the Bogdanović interview, see *International Viewpoint*, no. 215 (28 October 1991).

Balkanization or Lebanization?

Balkanization denotes the break-up of a larger state into several smaller ones, the word normally used in a derogatory sense implying that smaller states are less viable than large ones. Being a citizen of a country created out of the wreckage of Austria-Hungary – then the second largest state on the European continent – it has always puzzled me why the Habsburg state itself was not perceived as unviable, given that it broke up in the first place. And there is the question of how large is large? Compared to Canada or China, Great Britain is a small country. Compared to Great Britain, Holland is small indeed. Yet if you question this assumption about the privileged link between size and viability in regard to Yugoslavia, you will only hear mutterings about the irrationality of nationalism.

The secret of Austria-Hungary's dissolution, of course, is shrouded in the circumstances of World War One. Its demise being a fact of history, no one feels obliged today to know anything about its internal strains and conflicts. But what if a state breaks up when the rest of the continent is at peace? In the case of Yugoslavia, failure to understand the reasons for its break-up is treated almost as a mark of intellectual respectability. Who, after all, can understand the irrationality of nationalism? 'Ethnic wars', 'the Balkan cauldron', 'centuries of national intolerance', 'the Theodosian division', etc. are some of the stereotypes used to veil not only ignorance but also lack of interest in this first continental war since 1945. Yet this war could turn out to be a major all-European tragedy as well.

In an article published two and a half years ago in *New Left Review*, I wrote about the spectre of Balkanization haunting Yugoslavia. It seemed obvious to me already then that the policy of Milošević's régime towards the two-million-strong Albanian nation in Yugoslavia was leading inexorably towards the country's break-up. Unpalatable as the prospect was, it was necessary to face it. Yugoslavia, after all, could stay together only by respecting, and building upon, the postwar political settlement based on full national equality. Take away Albanian national rights, and the whole thing comes down like a pack of cards.

How many cards? According to my calculation, the number has always been eight: the six republics (Bosnia-Herzegovina, Croatia, Macedonia, Montenegro, Serbia and Slovenia) and two provinces (Kosovo and Vojvodina) that made up the Yugoslav federation. To my mind, there is no doubt that these eight federal units are the only legitimate political subjects (assuming, of course, their own democratic constitution). In the event of Yugoslavia's break-up, they are its only rightful successors.

Since the mid-1980s, though, other counts have been made. Thus in 1985, Vojislav Šešelj – now leader of the Serbian Chetniks and a member of the Serbian parliament – was sent to prison for producing a map of Yugoslavia containing only four units: Croatia, Greater Serbia, Macedonia and Slovenia. Since that time Šešelj has added Macedonia and a large part of Croatia to his Greater Serbia. A few years later, the Slovene youth paper *Mladina* scandalized official Serbia and the Army by dividing Yugoslavia into two parts: western and eastern, the former including Bosnia-Herzegovina, Croatia and Slovenia, the latter being allocated the remainder. There were others. Maps of Greater Croatia and Greater Albania also appeared (albeit in these cases published abroad). Some Slovenes started to throw wistful glances at the Croatian peninsula of Istria. Kosovo's decision to declare itself a republic in its own right (winter 1990) – in response to the Serbian Assembly's unilateral and unconstitutional alteration of the province's status within Serbia and Yugoslavia – did not alter the total number of constituent elements (and the Kosovars explicitly emphasized their continued membership of the Yugoslav federation); but implicit in their decision was the *right* (enjoyed by the republics) of unilateral secession from Yugoslavia.

By the time of the break-up of the League of Communists of Yugoslavia (spring 1990), maps of various kinds were openly circulating throughout the country, the vast majority of them marking the borders of a Greater Serbia incorporating all Yugoslavia bar Slovenia and a much reduced Croatia. In Belgrade, countless volumes and articles have been published arguing the imperative need to unite all 'historic and ethnic Serb lands' into a single state. What was special about the Greater Serbian project was that it was not only backed by the Serbian Academy of Arts and Sciences (in the notorious 1986 Memorandum) but also officially endorsed by the Serbian régime. No other republican government has sought a redrawing of Yugoslavia's internal borders. A tentative suggestion by Croatian president Franjo Tudjman, in July 1991, that Bosnia-Herzegovina might be divided up between Croatia and Serbia was promptly drowned by a chorus of disapproving voices raised both in Croatia and in Bosnia-Herzegovina. Sanctity of the internal borders has remained the official policy of Croatia, Slovenia, Macedonia and Bosnia-Herzegovina.

What about the provinces? In April 1991, Slovenia and Croatia proposed a loose confederation of six units – i.e. of the six republics – thus making clear that the fate of Vojvodina and Kosovo was Serbia's internal affair. Bosnia-Herzegovina and Macedonia concurred in the idea that there were six that counted. But in the event, of course, all these hypothetical tricks were trumped by Milošević's Great Serbian card. And the joker in the pack turned out to be the Yugoslav Army.

As I write these lines, the Great Serbian plan is being implemented by force of arms. Slovenia has been practically expelled from Yugoslavia, after an attempted occupation. A total war is being waged against Croatia, involving mass destruction of its economic infrastructure and civilian habitat; one third of its territory is now under occupation and most of the population driven out. In Vojvodina and Kosovo, the earlier extensive institutions of self-government – which had made the two provinces virtually equal to the republics – have been destroyed, leaving them with fewer powers than are enjoyed by a London borough. In Kosovo, this could be achieved only by military force. Montenegro has been practically annexed by Serbia, producing a state of incipient civil war in the republic. In Bosnia-Herzegovina, central government has disintegrated as a result of the Serbian-dominated army's decision to build up Serb-inhabited areas into bastions of its war effort against Croatia. In the south, Macedonia's fate remains highly uncertain, with threats against Macedonian 'secessionists' filling the pages of Serbia's official press. The Yugoslav house of cards has not only collapsed – the cards themselves have become damaged in the process.

If Yugoslavia survived for a time (1987–91) by treating Kosovo and Vojvodina as Serbia's internal problem, the army's attack on Slovenia signed its death certificate. Since then the Federal institutions, already much undermined, have been disintegrating at an accelerating pace. Symbolic of the current state of affairs is the recent missile attack on the offices of Franjo Tudjman, which almost killed not only the Croatian president, but also Yugoslavia's Federal president, Federal prime minister and Federal foreign secretary – men who, in order to reach Zagreb from Belgrade, had been forced to travel by way of Hungary!

A few days earlier, the latest – and final – in a series of constitutional coups against the Yugoslav state had been carried out, installing an all-Serb body as the 'Yugoslav collective presidency'. To present Greater Serbia as Yugoslavia is an attractive option for the Serbian régime, with obvious economic and political advantages. Yet it turned out to be a major miscalculation so far as the outside world was concerned. Even the most obtuse European government now had to admit that Yugoslavia no longer existed. Why, then, is the deceased being buried so surreptitiously? Is it in order to prevent the sound of the ex-Yugoslav army's remorseless pounding of Croatia's cities and villages reaching the ears of the 'peacemakers' in The Hague?

The war being waged against Croatia is ostensibly to protect the Serb minority there, but in reality it is little more than a war of territorial conquest. Part of the preparations for it was an instrumentalization of the Serb minorities living in neighbouring republics. Since August 1990 Serbia, with the military's support, has carved three so-called Krajinas out of Croatia, in two of which Serbs formed a small minority of the population. Four such 'Krajinas' have also been established in Bosnia-Herzegovina. The plan is clear: to break up these two republics, by forming out of their territories an archipelago of Serb-inhabited islands tied to Mother Serbia. To be sure, the Serbian régime would never allow its own republic's parcelization, despite the fact that it is ethnically the least homogeneous of Yugoslavia's republics. But if the Krajina recipe were to be followed consistently, the number of cards in play would climb vertiginously. Each municipality, town or village could become a 'Krajina'.

The Krajina formula of 'self-determination' for every minority, in other words, leads inexorably to the Lebanization of Yugoslavia. This means the collapse of all central authority and transfer of power into the hands of local warlords. In Croatia, where 80 per cent of the population is Croat and where central government is still very much in control, this danger is at present not very great (though in the areas that form the war zone, Croat volunteers can be found fighting under their own command with only a tenuous link with the Croatian military authorities). On the Serbian side, on the other hand, in the so-called Krajinas, the fragmentation of military and political authority is far greater – and gaining speed. The mass destruction of the civilian habitat, the looting and killings conducted by Serb and Montenegrin irregulars, have dissolved all semblance of an ordered society. What will happen when this kind of war reaches into Bosnia-Herzegovina, given its ethnic configuration and the absence of a functioning central government?

The shape of things to come was revealed in early October, when units of Montenegrin reservists were sent into western Herzegovina to establish a base for subsequent occupation of the part of Croatia's coast around the city of Dubrovnik. Within hours of their arrival, the drunken men got down to looting local villages and shooting at civilian passers-by (killing two). Thousands of men, women and children were forced to flee their homes. Those who stayed behind have thrown up a line of barricades to keep the invaders out. The irregulars, after all, were publicly boasting that Bosnia-Herzegovina was no more and that this part of it was now Montenegro.

There can be no doubt that for Yugoslavia to fall apart along its federal seams is far more desirable than its fragmentation into a myriad of Krajinas. Balkanization of Yugoslavia, in other words, is far preferable to its Lebanization. Any fragmentation of Yugoslavia's republics and provinces into still smaller units would mean war becoming endemic in this part of Europe. In the face of this danger, the tardiness and conservatism of Europe's response to the war in Croatia can only be described as irresponsible. The British government's position, that a comprehensive settlement must be agreed by the warring parties before the international community can recognize the demise of Yugoslavia's borders, verges on the absurd. After all, the Hague Conference was convened precisely because there is no longer a Yugoslav structure capable of negotiating such a settlement. Unless this fact is fully recognized – by freezing Yugoslavia's seat in the United Nations and recognizing its constituent parts as sovereign entities – the Serbian régime and the army will continue to use the shells of former federal institutions at home and abroad to pursue their destructive aims.

Has deceased Yugoslavia really left no last Will and Testament?

Over the past four or five years, the entire constitutional underpinning of the postwar settlement of the national question in Yugoslavia has been destroyed bit by bit, until it would seem that we are left with nothing but a blank sheet upon which any regional tyrant can draw his own borders. Yet Europe would make a terrible mistake by disregarding, for the sake of a quick solution, the fundamental premisses of the postwar settlement. The six republics *are* nation-states; their borders *are* state borders; the provinces *are* political subjects, distinct from Serbia proper. These eight federal units *are* the only rightful heirs of Yugoslavia and must be recognized as such. If, for ethnic or economic reasons, these eight units have an interest in creating a new association, then let it be done freely – for otherwise it will not work at all. Freedom to decide, however, involves removal of the army from the soil of Croatia, Bosnia-Herzegovina, Macedonia and Kosovo. This can be achieved by prompt, consistent and principled political action by the EC and CSCE. If national minorities are seen as a problem during the period of transition, then international monitors can be sent to the relevant areas to observe the governments' compliance with internationally agreed standards. Any other approach will lead to the spread of war within Yugoslavia and beyond its borders.

(November 1991)

8

A War that Serbia Can Only Lose

One of the hardest things to understand about the war in Croatia is what it seems to tell us about the ephemerality of the Yugoslav project as such. Croatia, Kosovo, Macedonia and Slovenia have all declared an independence backed by popular plebiscite. Bosnia-Herzegovina's parliament has proclaimed the republic to be sovereign. Serbia is attempting to extend its frontiers by force of arms. The recasting of the state system in this part of Europe has been as swift as it has been astonishing. Debate as to whether Yugoslavia has always been an artificial state is thus inescapable. Yet it will remain barren unless one goes beyond Yugoslavia's seventy years of existence as a recognized entity to grasp the complex twofold mediation it has always represented: on the one hand, of the relationship between the Yugoslav nations; on the other, of their individual senses of identity and purpose. The second break-up of Yugoslavia is due to Serbia's decision after 1987 to challenge the entire postwar federal order in favour of its own domination, or, failing that, a Greater Serbia. A Greater Serbia, however, could be created only by war against the very Yugoslavia which had since 1918 curbed and contained earlier dreams of such a state. It also required Serbia itself to be recast in an anti-democratic mould – to become *Milošević's* Serbia. For this, it was necessary to impose upon the Serb nation an embattled sense of being surrounded by racial enemies, so that only their gathering within a single Serb state could ensure the biological survival of the nation. Serbia's return to the past was thus more than a simple repossession of an older national project. Only by releasing the demons of the racial enemy upon the Yugoslav house of nationalities could Milošević be sure of its destruction.

For the Serbs (as for other Yugoslav nations), Yugoslavia was the particular form in which its own national unification took place. In the mid-nineteenth century, out of 3.2 million Serbs only a bare third lived in the semi-independent principality of Serbia, the rest being divided almost equally between the Habsburg and Ottoman Empires – intermingled, moreover, with other Slavs and non-Slavs. That the principality would play the role of national centre pressing for unification was inevitable, but what form this unification would take was disputed. Of the many options, two emerged as dominant: the creation of a Greater Serbia, by way of a territorial expansion of the principality (which meant inclusion of a substantial non-Serb population); or a South Slav (perhaps even Balkan) union of equal nations, to be achieved by joint action. If the first fed the imperialist appetites of the Serbian bourgeoisie, the second became part of the heritage of Serbian socialism and later of its communist extension.

Even though in 1918 'Yugoslavia' was formally to prevail, the circumstances of the new state's creation made it into a *de facto* Greater Serbia. After the 1941 débâcle, to forestall any renewal of the Great Serb stranglehold over a reborn Yugoslavia it was not enough to mobilize the non-Serb nationalities in a common Partisan struggle, it was necessary also to win the Serb nation to the alternative programme of a Yugoslav federation. Postwar Yugoslavia was thus born from the ashes of Greater Serbia. To be sure, it required also the defeat of Hitler's New Order in Europe, in which the Ustasha Greater Croatia had played its part. The Yugoslav Communists, however, did not see Croatian expansionism as a lasting problem. Great Serb nationalism, by contrast, remained a permanent threat, because Serbs were the most numerous and dispersed nationality, because of their interwar domination, and because of the objective tendency for the bureaucratic centralism inherent in the Federal party and state organs to ally itself with the strongest nation – a tendency facilitated by the decision to keep Belgrade as the capital city.

When, in the second half of the 1960s, Yugoslavia embarked upon a major recasting of the federal state system, aimed at divesting the central organs of much of their earlier authority, the success of the reform depended crucially on the attitude of the Serbian Communist leaders. A recently published book by Latinka Perović, Serbian party secretary at the time, gives valuable insight into how the battle for the hearts of the Serb nation was fought during the crucial period of 1967–72 when the greatest constitutional overhaul after 1945 was conducted – the last during Tito's lifetime. The book was actually written immediately after the author's dismissal in the 1972 purge of 'liberals' as a kind of private balance-sheet. Some of its arguments are worth reviewing here, not only because they stand in sharp contrast to the dominant political discourse in Milošević's Serbia, but also because the fate of the Serb 'liberals' – their expulsion from the Party, followed by twenty years of political isolation and disgrace – was to prepare the ground for the eventual resurgence of Great Serb nationalism, hence also for the current war. Reading the book today, four years after Milošević's rise to power, one is struck by its prescience.

To begin with, Perović refutes two theses much in vogue in Serbia today: that the constitution of 1974, which transferred the bulk of power from the Federal organs to the republics and provinces, was imposed on Serbia; and that Yugoslavia's internal borders were always seen by Serbian political leaders as merely administrative. On the contrary, reform of the federation was premissed on the notion of sovereignty of the republics and their titular nations. 'Since the republics were not created through administrative division of a single state territory, but as expressions of the nations' right to their own statehood . . . it is impossible to expropriate in the name of a single political system or market the nations' right to decide for themselves how to allocate the surplus created within their own republics.' Dismantling the economic prerogatives of the central state was seen as necessary, because they led to political impotence in all difficult economic situations. Decentralization of the economy, to be sure, held the danger of a reborn nationalism far more potent than the earlier kind based on the peasantry. Yet it was impossible to continue as before: 'to demand of the League of Communists of Yugoslavia that it should maintain a degree of unity greater than the level of objective economic and social integration within Yugoslavia means pushing it into permanent conflict with reality.' That is why those reformers, in Serbia as in other parts of Yugoslavia, placed their hopes in democratization of the political system by way of the institutions of 'socialist self-management'. The Serb national programme, therefore, had to be rewritten in the new language of democracy and economic modernization.

The Communists were faced with a particularly difficult task in Serbia, where identification with a centralized Yugoslavia had deep historic roots. 'The greater part of [Serbian] public opinion saw the changes not only as a weakening of the position of Serbia within Yugoslavia, but also – given the greater autonomy of the provinces – as Serbia's disintegration from within.' Perović's colleague Milentije Popović, addressing the Serbian Party Central Committee, stressed that: 'as Communists of the most numerous nation, we have the greatest responsibility to ensure that the relationship of forces underpinning national equality [in the country as a whole] is not destroyed within the League of Communists of Yugoslavia.'

The Serb reformers believed that Serbia, instead of 'nurturing imperialist aspirations which for objective reasons it has never been able to sustain, should instead turn to itself and to its own development. It was in the democratic development of Yugoslavia', they argued, 'that we saw the precondition for a cultural and spiritual unity of the Serb nation, which history has divided, scattered and inseparably mixed with other nations.' In a major attack on Great Serb nationalism, Perović spelt out its main components – the very components which fifteen years later would provide the ideological basis of Milošević's régime: (1) the claim that 'Serbia and Serbdom are endangered in this Yugoslavia'; (2) strategic calculations for Serbia based on exploiting Serb populations living in the other republics and the two provinces; (3) the propensity to fan anti-Croat sentiment; (4) readiness to question the equal status of the national minorities within Serbia itself, hence also the status of the two provinces. 'These components put together form a broad basis for a counter-revolution, which aims to foster among the Serb nation illusions regarding its leading role as the largest nation in Yugoslavia.' The other main enemy was Federal centralism, 'which always sought support in Serbia: by ruling Serbia it hoped also to dominate others. In order to weaken the supra-national bureaucracy, which was a threat to each Yugoslav nation equally, it was crucial that the process of democratization of Serbia – and its emancipation from Federal centralism – should not be stopped.'

It is only by recalling the Serbia of 1971 that we can gain a true understanding of the scale of reversal represented by Milošević's Serbia – hence, of the root cause and nature of the current war. As Bogdan Bogdanović, former mayor of Belgrade and a courageous opponent of Milošević, noted in a recent interview, this is an old men's war: a fighting of battles lost at the start of the century, as a substitute for creating a modern nation-state. The tragedy of Yugoslavia, displayed in all its ferocity in the systematic destruction of Croatia by the Serbian-dominated Army, is thus also very much a tragedy of the Serb nation and of Serbia.

What the war has done to Croatia and its people is documented well enough.[1] But the shame of this war lies also in its effect on the Serb nation. Officer arrogance induced by superior firepower; mindless use of military hardware; never-ending production of generals; forced recruitment of Serbian reservists; the social bias of the draft; replacement of the once disciplined Army by drunken volunteers; atrocities committed against civilians and captured 'enemies'; looting and burning of occupied cities and villages; destruction of irreplaceable cultural monuments; wanton disregard of soldiers's lives – all these represent one side of this dishonourable war. The other side is made up of a craven parliamentary opposition, which emulates the Great Leader's tough stand on how 'all Serbs must live in the same state'. Never before has Serbia been reduced to such a state of moral prostration.

It is against this background that the courage of the few who, despite physical attacks and constant threat to their lives, continue to oppose the war, through the written word and through public protests, by encouraging desertion and by helping young men avoid the draft, stands out so clearly. Those like Jelka and Pavluško Imširović who helped to create the Anti-War Centre; Ivan Djurić's Reform Party; the Women's Parliament; the brave editors and journalists of *Vreme*; Nenad Čanak's Social Democrats in Vojvodina; the members of the Yugoslav Democratic Initiative; the war deserters and draft-dodgers; the families protesting against mobilization of their menfolk – and, indeed, all the tens of thousands of young Serbs who rallied against Milošević in March of this year and who form the lifeblood of the anti-war movement – are a proof that Serbia's democratic tradition is by no means exhausted. They alone speak a language to which the other peoples of what was once Yugoslavia can respond.

(November 1991)

Note

1. Documented not just in the Croatian and international press, but often most tellingly in the oppositional weeklies *Vreme* in Serbia and *Monitor* in Montenegro.

9

To Be Against the War in Yugoslavia Means Opposing the Aggressor

The fall of the ruined Croatian town of Vukovar (once a town of some 50,000 inhabitants, 43 per cent Croat, 37 per cent Serb, 20 per cent Hungarians and others), two days after its besiegers had solemnly signed yet another ceasefire agreement brokered by Lord Carrington, stands as a stark monument to the inadequacy (or cynical complicity) of the outside world's response to the degradation of the Yugoslav crisis into war and barbarism. It has been depressing, if perhaps predictable, to see much of the European Left trailing behind the Chanceries of the Western powers in its reactions to the unfolding calamity in Yugoslavia, blindly refusing to face reality or look to the future (just as it did on an earlier occasion, faced with the manifest disintegration of the Hapsburg Empire). Although almost everyone now – inside and outside the country – has proclaimed the old Yugoslavia dead and gone, the logical next step of de-recognition has not been taken, leading to confusion and inaction. Policies continue to be framed as though the country still existed, with the result that the eight former Federal units, which alone can provide the basis for a new order in the area, exist in a kind of limbo; and the war of conquest being fought by the Army and the Milošević régime in Serbia continues.

The best antidote to the misconceptions about this war – about who is waging it, against whom, and for what – is some exposure to the views of the anti-war oppposition in Serbia and among Serbs outside that republic. In a situation where their physical safety is daily on the line, these brave people have had no truck with the idea dear to so many in the British media that this is a war between Croats and Serbs. It is indeed they who have most eloquently described the horror and shame of the war being waged by the former Yugoslav Army and the Milošević régime against the historic interests, and increasingly also the physical integrity, of all the peoples of what used to be Yugoslavia, including, of course, the Serb people.

As Bogdan Bogdanović, former mayor of Belgrade, has said: 'We are confronted with a war that has no aim – from the Serb end of it. The Croats are defending themselves, their aim is clear.' Or Vesna Pešić, Belgrade sociologist and anti-war activist: 'This war is being waged on Croatian territory and the conclusion is inescapable, that Croatia in such a situation is waging a defensive war. . . . Precisely because Serbs are so dispersed, their national programme cannot be offensive, but must base itself upon good diplomacy, tolerance, openness. But in Serbia over the past four years, exactly the opposite policy has been followed, hastening the collapse of Yugoslavia.'

Milan Kangrga, veteran (Serb) Professor of Philosophy at Zagreb University and founder member of *Praxis*, has put it as follows:

Even in the most difficult periods of Stalinist repression, we managed to find ways to raise our voices against all tyranny and despotism. I don't believe [Serbian intellectuals] do not know, or do not wish to know, what the Yugoslav Army and the Chetniks are doing in Croatia – war crimes, directed against the civilian population and against the cultural heritage of a nation. One must raise one's voice against that, just as we used to do against the war in Vietnam, or against apartheid in South Africa. Croatia is occupied. It will also to a large extent be destroyed. There will be great loss of life. But there will develop a general war of liberation in Croatia. The war will be won and Croatia will be freed.

Stevan Dedijer, a Serb from Bosnia, pre-war Communist and brother of the late biographer of Tito and friend of Djilas, saw things no differently last September:

Hundreds and thousands of peaceloving Serbs in Croatia are dying and their villages and towns are being destroyed by the Yugo-Miloševićan Army. I watch how planes,tanks, heavy artillery pound Croatia, while against them people are fighting with light arms. I feel like an anti-Nazi German in the war against Hitler: each plane shot down, each tank destroyed is a victory equally for the Croat and for the Serb – and every other – people in Yugoslavia.

Mirko Kovač, one of the best-known Serbian novelists and a founder of the new Association of Independent Writers in Belgrade, had this to say in a recent interview: 'This war bears a dreadful resemblance to its strategists: it is chaotic, vicious and destructive. For an army which devastates villages – whether Croat or Serb, no matter – devastates itself first and foremost. An army that wrecks towns, cultural monuments and communications, wrecks for ever all bonds between our peoples. This is a strange, Ottoman kind of war: laying waste, plundering, terrorizing. It's straight out of the sixteenth century!'

Vreme, the independent Belgrade weekly which provides a lone voice of sanity amid the war fever in that city ('In Belgrade cafés, streets and houses, you can hear constant war cries: invitations to killing and to hatred' – Bogdanović), has provided the best reporting of this war of devastation. On 11 November, it quoted Tanja Ivančević, a fifteen-year-old Serb refugee from western Slavonia who had carried messages for the Army: 'We don't know where to go, nor does it make any sense to think of returning. Back there, there's nothing left to liberate. Everything has been burnt down, destroyed. In fact, I don't know why we fought or why my friends have died.' In the same issue, one of its journalists wrote: 'Vukovar will remain a blot on the collective memory of tens of thousands of men who risked their lives there, not knowing why. It will serve as a warning that wars fought without a national consensus, a clear aim or moral justification cannot easily be won.' And in the previous issue, another of its journalists had written:

> If anybody has gained by it [the war], it is not the populations of the 'Krajina', Slavonia or Konavlje. Those who have gained are various gangsters, looters, thieves and hyenas. The 'volunteers', according to the testimony of reservists, officers and inhabitants, are mainly concerned with pillaging the conquered villages and transporting the loot by truck to Belgrade, which has been flooded with stolen goods. Some 200,000 people have left the war zone, leaving Slavonia to the Army and to the dead. In the case of both Croats and Serbs, they are more than refugees, they are dispossessed people. Their homes have been destroyed, their cattle killed or stolen, their agricultural machinery and all they owned gone. To judge by the Croats' experience in Slavonia and Krajina, their fate in Dubrovnik does not look good – but, if that is any comfort, it does not look good for any 'liberated' people, be they Croat or Serb. Judging by what has been achieved up to now, the 'liberated territories' are living an imitation of life, with security and prosperity replaced by 'freedom' under the boot and the 'dignity' of eating roots.

Perhaps the last word should go to Drs Vojkan Jakšić and Kay Magaard from Toronto, whose letter was published by *Vreme* on 23 September 1991:

> [We are] a Serb and a German, close friends and colleagues, fifteen members of whose immediate families died in two world wars – on opposite sides, of course. [Our letter is] conceived as an answer to all those who, using superficial logic and powerful emotions, are attempting to justify what is now happening in Croatia by a genocide carried out 50 years ago. It is conceived as an answer to all those who so readily attach the labels 'Fourth Reich' and 'neo-fascism' to that part of the civilized world which protests against the aggression upon Croatia. . . . Serbia needs the world's help as Germany did before 1933. Their [the Serbs'] enemy is the democratically elected leadership of Serbia, people for whom war and propaganda are the only means to retain power. We should never forget the past, but we must learn from it, not repeat it.

In the past few weeks, Serbian anti-war activists like Nenad Čanak and Pavluško Imširović have been beaten by régime *squadristi*, Čanak has been arrested and drafted to the front, the Anti-War Centre in Belgrade has been wrecked, and a lynch atmosphere is being whipped up against peace activists in Vojvodina, especially those from the Hungarian and other minority populations. Those responsible are not just uneducated goons or hack journalists, but, as Bogdanović has pointed out, the 'old men' of the Serbian Academy – men like the novelist Dobrica Ćosić or the former *Praxis* editor Ljuba Tadić – who proclaim that 'Pacifism is treason!': 'They have become warmongers, and one day this will rightly be described as a war crime.'

To take sides in this war is not merely to take the side of one republic – Croatia – which is the current victim of aggression, or of Kosovo and Slovenia the past victims and Bosnia-Herzegovina which stands next in line. It is also to take the side of the anti-war opposition in Serbia and of any hope for a future democratic order in the area that has twice now been known as Yugoslavia.

(December 1991)

Index